Studies of the British Industrial Revolution and of the Victorian period of economic and social development have until very recently concentrated on British industries and industrial regions, while commerce and finance, and particularly that of London, have been substantially neglected. This has distorted our view of the process of change because financial services and much trade continued to be centred on the metropolis, and the south-east region never lost its position at the top of the national league of wealth.

This is a pioneer survey of the mercantile sector of the economy from the end of the eighteenth century to World War I. It complements Dr Chapman's *The Rise of Merchant Banking* (1984), concentrating on the various ways in which British merchants responded to the unprecedented opportunities of the Industrial Revolution and the growth of the British Empire.

The main conclusion is that industrial entrepreneurs contributed only briefly to merchant ventures, and that with limited success. Rather did the established merchant community evolve its own new forms of enterprise to meet the changing opportunities: the 'new frontier' merchant networks of the Atlantic economy, the international houses in continental trade, the agency houses in the Far East, and the home trade houses dominating the domestic market. These resilient organisations enabled the British merchant enterprise to survive longer and in greater strength than in other western economies.

MERCHANT ENTERPRISE
IN BRITAIN

MERCHANT ENTERPRISE
IN BRITAIN

From the Industrial Revolution to World War I

STANLEY CHAPMAN

Pasold Reader in Business History,
University of Nottingham

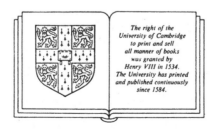

The right of the
University of Cambridge
to print and sell
all manner of books
was granted by
Henry VIII in 1534.
The University has printed
and published continuously
since 1584.

CAMBRIDGE UNIVERSITY PRESS

Cambridge   New York   Port Chester
Melbourne   Sydney

PUBLISHED BY THE PRESS SYNDICATE OF THE UNIVERSITY OF CAMBRIDGE
The Pitt Building, Trumpington Street, Cambridge, United Kingdom

CAMBRIDGE UNIVERSITY PRESS
The Edinburgh Building, Cambridge CB2 2RU, UK
40 West 20th Street, New York NY 10011–4211, USA
477 Williamstown Road, Port Melbourne, VIC 3207, Australia
Ruiz de Alarcón 13, 28014 Madrid, Spain
Dock House, The Waterfront, Cape Town 8001, South Africa

http://www.cambridge.org

First published 1992
First paperback edition 2002

A catalogue record for this book is available from the British Library

Library of Congress Cataloguing in Publication data
Chapman, Stanley David., 1935–
Merchant enterprise in Britain: from the Industrial Revolution to
World War I / Stanley Chapman.
p. oo cm.
Includes index.
ISBN 0 521 35178 2 (hardcover)
1. Great Britain – Commerce – History – 18th century.   2. Great
Britain – Commerce – History – 19th century.   3. Merchants – Great
Britain – History.   I. Title.
HF 3505.C46   1992
380.1′0941–dc20
91-15818   CIP

ISBN 0 521 35178 2 hardback
ISBN 0 521 89362 3 paperback

Contents

List of figures   page viii
List of tables   x
Preface   xiii
Abbreviations used in the footnotes   xvi
Introduction: approaches and concepts   1

PART I   THE SETTING

1 The eighteenth-century structure of merchant
   enterprise   21
2 The consequences of the Industrial Revolution and the
   French Wars   51

PART II   NEW STREAMS OF ENTERPRISE

3 Merchants in the Atlantic trade   81
4 The agency houses: trade to India and the Far East   107
5 The international houses: the foreign contribution to
   British mercantile enterprise   129
6 The home trade houses   167

PART III   RESPONSE TO INSTANT COMMUNICATION

7 Problems of restructuring mercantile enterprise   193
8 British-based investment groups before 1914   231
9 Imperialism and British trade   262

PART IV   CONCLUSIONS

10 Performance of British mercantile enterprise   287
Manuscript sources   319
Index of firms and people   323
Index of places   331
Index of subjects   336

Figures

2.1 The structure of the Philips family businesses in the early nineteenth century   *page* 64
Sources: Philips MSS, Warwick, C.R.O. CR 456/28, 31, 32. A. P. Wadsworth and J. de L. Mann, *The Cotton Trade and Industrial Lancashire* (Manchester 1931) pp. 288–301. *Universal British Directory*, III (1797) pp. 834–5.

3.1 Early members of the Benson and Rathbone families and their marriage connections   94
Sources: S. B. Foster, *The Pedigrees of Birkbeck of Maller-Stang, Braithwaite of Kendal, Benson of Stang End* (1890); information from family records held by Mr J. S. Benson.

3.2 The partnerships and connections of James Finlay & Co. c. 1745–1860   96
Sources: [Colm Brogan] *James Finlay & Co. Ltd.* (Glasgow 1951) pp. 11–12, 15. Bank of England Liverpool letters, 24 Nov. and 31 Dec. 1827, Manchester letters 4 Apr. 1829 (Bartons).

3.3 Partnerships of Fraser, Trenholm & Co., Charleston, USA, 1815–67   97
Sources: Harvard Univ. Baker Lib., Dun & Bradstreet credit registers, Charleston, vols. 1–3. Merseyside County Museums, Fraser Trenholm MSS. E. M. Lander, *The Textile Industry in Antebellum South Carolina* (Baton Rouge 1969) p. 107.

5.1 Alien merchants in Manchester, 1790–1870   139
Source: John Scholes, 'Foreign Merchants in Manchester, 1784–1870', MS, Manchester P.L.

5.2 The Schwabe and Boustead connection   148
Sources: Eric Jennings, 'Bousted History' (unpublished typescript, 1978). Bank of England Liverpool letter books, x (1849) p. 202 (capital), v (1844) p. 378 (Dugdale connection). Manchester P.L., John Graham list of printworks (Rhodes factory, near Manchester).

5.3   The Ralli and Scaramanga partnerships   156
Sources: Nottingham Univ. Archives, Brandt Circulars, 31
Dec. 1856, 30 Dec. 1865, 1 July 1866, 1 Mar. 1833.
Baring Bros. MSS HC 16/2, Report on Business Houses
1850–74. P. Herlihy, *Odessa – A History, 1794–1914*
(Harvard 1986) pp. 93–4, 213.

6.1   The evolution of distributive systems in the textile
industries, sixteenth to twentieth centuries   169

8.1   Structure of the Matheson Investment Group c. 1914   238
Source: see Appendix, Ch. 8.

8.2   Structure of Wogau & Co., Moscow and London, in
1914   244
Source: *Materialy po Istorii SSSR* vi *(Documents on monopoly
Capitalism)* (Moscow 1959) pp. 697–706.

9.1   The Anglo-German financial connection in South
Africa   277
Source: Hans Sauer, *Ex Africa* (1937) esp. pp. 143–4, 179,
214–15.

10.1   Relationships in the structure of the agency house   302

Tables

0.1   Index of English regional income per head based on income tax (1812 to 1879–80A) then on inhabited house duty (1879–80B to 1911–12)   *page* 2

0.2   Occupations of British millionaires and half-millionaires as a percentage of all non-landed wills in the groups   2

0.3   Relative share of six leading European countries' exports in the European total, 1830–1910 (per cent)   5

0.4   Geographical distribution of UK exports and imports 1785–1845 (per cent)   6

0.5   Geographical destination of UK exports and imports 1860–1910 (per cent)   8

1.1   Estimates of mercantile incomes in England in the eighteenth century   22

1.2   Analysis of Mortimer's *Universal Director* (1763)   23

1.3   London's share of English trade in the eighteenth century (per cent)   40

1.4   Shipping owned in some leading English ports (000s tons)   41

1.5   Debts owing to British merchants trading to North America estimated in 1766   42

1.6   Dissent in Bristol in 1717   44

1.7   The increase of trade and merchant bankruptcy in England (1700, 1759) and Great Britain (1800)   47

2.1   Occupations of patentees in England and Wales 1660–1799 (per cent)   58

2.2   Occupations of owners of the largest Lancashire cotton mills c. 1795 (valuation of £5,000+)   60

3.1   Cotton stocks in the ports on 1 Jan. 1812 (bags)   83

3.2   Cotton imports to leading UK ports in 1833 (bags)
                                                                    83
3.3   Number of vessels and amount of tonnage of the
      principal British ports in 1816 and 1850   84
3.4   Major British merchants in the North of England in
      the first half of the nineteenth century (capitals of
      £100,000+)   90
3.5   Some leading German and American merchants in
      the North of England in the first half of the
      nineteenth century   91
3.6   Concentration of mercantile leadership: cotton
      importing   93
3.7   The mid nineteenth-century structure of mercantile
      enterprise   99
4.1   The direction of Indian companies in 1911   122
4.2   Sterling and rupee companies in 1914–15 (£m.)   123
4.3   Shareholdings in Bird & Co., Calcutta, in 1917   126
5.1   Number of German merchant houses in
      manufacturing towns of Britain, 1820–50   138
5.2   Place of origin of visitors to the Leipzig Fairs,
      1748–1840   142
5.3   Leading Greek merchant houses trading in Britain
      1848–50 (top 14)   158
5.4   Location of home offices of British mercantile houses
      established in some foreign countries, 1848–9   162
5.5   Crude estimates of the value of British and foreign
      capital financing British overseas trade, 1836   164
6.1   London connections of Nottingham merchant hosiers,
      1770–5   172
6.2   The City of London textile market in 1817   178
6.3   Capital of leading textile warehousemen c. 1880   183
6.4   Average size of investment in British cotton mills
      (machinery only) c. 1880   184
6.5   Marketing organisation of Rylands and I. & R.
      Morley compared, 1897–1900   184
6.6   Capital of some leading London retailers, 1895–6   186
7.1   Capital of some major US and UK cotton merchants
      in the early twentieth century   197
7.2   Quantity of wheat and wheaten flour imported into
      the UK 1872 and 1903 (qrs.)   203

7.3   Leading importers of grain into Britain from St
      Petersburg, 1878–80   204
7.4   Some major grain merchants of the world in the
      early twentieth century   205
7.5   Some major merchants in new commodities c.
      1910–14   210
8.1   Agencies of Andrew Yule & Co. in India, 1899   236
9.1   The British share of Chinese trade 1870–1891   264
9.2   Geographical distribution of Asia's trade (per cent) 264
9.3   Cotton mill agencies classified by ethnic groups.
      Bombay 1895–1925   268
9.4   Capital of the leading British agency house group,
      Jardine Matheson and Jardine Skinner   270
9.5   Growth of British agency houses in India 1916–39   270
9.6   Growth of British agency houses in Malaysia,
      1913–1940   271
9.7   Professional qualifications of cotton mill directors in
      Bombay in 1925   272
9.8   The share of Indian and British ownership in
      factories in India, 1911   273
9.9   Britain and continental shareholding in the Rand
      mining companies, April 1900   278
10.1 Capital growth of some leading international
      merchants c. 1860–c. 1910   291
10.2 Share of various organisations in financing the
      Indian cotton industry in 1930   307

Preface

During the 1980s the opening and listing of the archives of the Bank of England and a variety of other City of London banks and trading groups made it possible, for the first time, to contemplate filling the major gap in our knowledge of modern British economic history, that of the financial and trading sector. Good materials had been available in Glasgow and Liverpool for some years and recently greatly strengthened with the build-up of Glasgow University's collection of business archives, but London was always the dominant centre of finance and trade. Drawing on some of this rich store I was able to write *The Rise of Merchant Banking* (Allen & Unwin 1984). The present volume was conceived as a complement to this earlier work.

It soon became clear that British merchant enterprise by no means covered all merchants active in Britain. Many of the foremost trading houses from the eighteenth century to World War I were of foreign origin, with cultures and loyalties that were not particularly oriented to English traditions and outlook. The study quickly became one of continental, Ottoman, American and Empire enterprise competing with the 'home grown' firms. Moreover the British group displayed the additional diversity generated by the prominent roles of the Scots, Ulstermen and English Nonconformists in trade, as well as the different approaches of those who came out of northern and midlands industry. Long residence abroad, particularly in British India and South Africa, created the yet different traditions of the nabobs and randlords. The study has therefore become one of diverse origins, cultures, strategies and effectiveness, as British trade not only came to dominate the international economy but attracted a large slice of the world's entrepreneurial talent. The study has resisted the attempts made by some historians and theorists to identify a particular dominant

xiii

characteristic of the mercantile group, preferring to profile the rich diversity of enterprise and show something of its consequences for the unprecedented growth of trade in the period.

Taken as a whole, the century and a half covered by this volume saw as far-reaching changes in the trading as in the industrial sector of the British economy. However, in trade the major watersheds were the French Wars (1793–1815) and the foreshortening of communications culminating in the telegraph, rather than the Industrial Revolution, as industrialists enjoyed little success as merchants. Broadly speaking, the war period saw the concentration of financial control through what later became known as the merchant banks, but it was not until the 1870s and 1880s that the mass of small family merchant enterprises were concentrated into trading groups, or were overwhelmed by competition. The study therefore offers a new perspective on British economic change to that which we have become accustomed, deferring 'revolutionary' change until the later Victorian age and the relative decline of merchant enterprise until after World War I. This harmonises with the recent research on the Industrial Revolution which calculates economic growth was a more gradual and long-term change than the phrase implies.

This book may said to have been written over a period of a dozen years or more as I discovered the numerous scattered sources relating to British merchant enterprise last century. A lot of my earlier research has been published in a variety of academic journals, and the articles form the basis of several chapters. The beginning of my interest can be seen in 'British Marketing Enterprise: the Changing Roles of Merchants, Manufacturers and Financiers 1700–1860', *Business History Review* LIII (1979) (incorporated in Chapter 2) and in 'The International Houses', *Journal of European Economic History* VI (1977) (Chapter 5). Its development can be traced in 'British-based Investment Groups before 1914' and 'Investment Groups in India and South Africa', *Economic History Review* XXXVIII (1985) and XL (1987) (Chapter 8), and further in 'British Agency Houses in the Far East in the Nineteenth Century', *Textile History* XIX (1988) (Chapter 4) and 'The Decline and Rise of Textile Merchanting 1880–1990', *Business History* XXXII (1991) (Chapter 6). Part of Chapter 3 draws on some of the public evidence assembled for my aborted history of merchant bankers Kleinwort Benson. I am grateful to editors, referees and other critics for helping me to sort out my ideas, and to the former for permission to reproduce the substance of the argument in this wider thesis. Chapter 9 owes much to visits to Japan (1987) and South Africa (1985–6), where colleagues not only entertained generously, but were also of inestimable value in comprehending British experience on the other side of the world. More generally, I have drawn freely on the research of colleagues more familiar with the archives relating to the US, Russia, Latin America and Australia; in such a large subject area it is impossible to list them all here, but I hope that the footnotes will indicate my large fund of debts.

Until recently, British business records have not greatly interested the great number of record offices and libraries, and only a handful of major corporations employ an archivist. The researcher who ventures into this area is therefore particularly conscious of the debt he owes to the patient work of the archivists who have saved so much material from salvage and then carefully preserved and catalogued it. My own research has benefited particularly from the large collections at Guildhall Library in the City of London, Liverpool, Cambridge and Glasgow University Libraries, and the Baker Library at Harvard, and from the private collections of Baring Bros. and the Standard Chartered Bank, but, as my footnotes show, I found material in a score of other repositories in Britain and abroad. My final word of acknowledgement and thanks is therefore to those who have built and maintain such collections; without their work studies like mine could scarcely be conceived, let alone sustained.

S. D. CHAPMAN

Abbreviations used in the footnotes

AN   Archives nationales, Paris
B of E Bank of England archives, London EC2
Dun   Dun & Bradstreet credit registers, Baker Library,
        Harvard University, USA
IOL   India Office Library, London SE1
JS   Jardine Skinner MSS, Cambridge University Library
NIRO   Northern Ireland Record Office, Belfast
SBA   Standard Bank Archives, Johannesburg

Introduction: approaches and concepts

During the course of the last few years the period of British history conventionally known as the Industrial Revolution has lost some of its earlier significance as a watershed period. No doubt there is an element of conditioning by later twentieth-century experience in this attitude, for as British economic growth has looked less impressive compared with some of its competitors, so its interpreters have sought for the less spectacular and more evolutionary elements in its development, including the experience of earlier centuries. The 'revolutionary' feature of British economic and social history was taken to be the dramatic growth of the 'great staple' industries of last century – textiles, iron and coal – and their social consequences, and historians showed little interest in what had happened elsewhere in the economy, unless it was related to these major themes. The recent revisions, in suggesting more gradual growth in the old staples, has also served to rekindle interest in some of the continuities of economic and social life that were more taken for granted by contemporaries. Not the least is the traditional British interest in trade and finance.

It must be admitted that econometric measures of the changing structure of the British economy in the Industrial Revolution period, though exhibiting impressive statistical skill, can be no more than 'controlled conjectures'. Moreover, the bulk of the data processed is still drawn from the traditional industries, with little serious attempt to measure change in the service sectors of the economy independently.[1] Certainly the attempts to make independent measures of the service sector, and particularly of commerce and finance, though still in the pioneer stages, have produced more solid results. The most striking is that garnered by Clive Lee from Inland

---

[1] N. F. R. Crafts, *British Economic Growth during the Industrial Revolution* (Oxford 1985). J. Hoppit, 'Counting the Industrial Revolution', *Econ. Hist. Rev.* XLIII (1990).

I

Table 0.1. *Index of English regional income per head based on income tax* (*1812 to 1879–80A*) *then on inhabited house duty* (*1879–80B to 1911–12*)

	1812	1859/60	1879–80A	1879–80B	1911/12
North West	100	100	100	100	100
South East	382	122	147	240	331
West Midlands	102	89	87	80	94

Source: extracted from C. H. Lee, *The British Economy since 1700. A Macroeconomic Perspective* (Cambridge 1986) Table 7.3.

Table 0.2. *Occupations of British millionaires and half-millionaires as a percentage of all non-landed wills in the groups*

	1820–39	1840–59	1860–79	1880–99	1900–19
Millionaires					
in manufacturing	25	40	41	38	17
in commerce and finance	25	60	55	38	54
Half-millionaires					
in manufacturing	21	33	33	36	37
in commerce and finance	63	58	57	44	48

Source: extracted from W. D. Rubenstein, *Men of Property. The Very Wealthy in Britain since the Industrial Revolution* (1981) Tables 3.6, 3.7.

Revenue returns (Table 0.1). The North West region, which comprises Lancashire and the adjacent counties, has been widely regarded as the home of the factory system and hence of British industrialisation, but on this measure it never succeeded in catching up with the South East, essentially London and the Home Counties and the traditional focus of trade and finance, though of course it always supported some industries. The West Midlands, widely thought of as the other centre of British industrial enterprise, evidently fared even worse. W. D. Rubenstein's analysis of British wealth (Table 0.2) shows that more fortunes were won in commerce and finance than in manufacturing industry as the century advanced. Nearly all the millionaires and half-millionaires in trade and finance worked in the London area.

Without entering into further detail at this stage, it is already clear that myopic concentration on this history of British industry in the provinces has produced a distorted economic history. The British economy had (and still has) twin pillars for its support, the wealth accumulated in trade, finance and urban estate in the metropolitan area and Home Counties easily balanced by that generated in the Midlands and North. Though the history of the mercantile side is still relatively unexplored territory, at any rate in the nineteenth century, reconnaissance and surveys have produced a number of very suggestive ideas. Some of the more important of these are briefly reviewed in this Introduction.

THE MERCHANT'S FUNCTIONS

In common parlance a merchant can be almost anyone who buys and sells goods, but such indiscriminate usage is much too wide for manageable research for it must include pedlars, shopkeepers, wholesalers, market stall holders and a host of other traders. Commercial usage was originally much more specific but, because commercial functions changed substantially over the period covered by this book, it is not possible to offer precise definitions to cover the complete time span. Changing functions will be examined as they arise; at this stage it will be sufficient to establish a convention to clear the way for later analysis. In this book merchants are taken to be entrepreneurs engaged in foreign (overseas) commerce as wholesale traders. It is appreciated that Britain had a large and growing domestic seaborne trade in the eighteenth and nineteenth centuries (such as the shipping of coal from Tyneside to London, of copper from Cornwall and Anglesey to the main ports and of grain from Ireland) but this must be left to another volume.[2] Such demarcation of the ground must appear at first sight to conflict with the inclusion of the so-called 'home trade houses' (Chapter 6), but it will be seen that these merchant firms had important overseas business from their earliest years and are an outstanding feature of mercantile development in the period.

Definition of the sphere of merchant activity does not of course prescribe what they did. Apprenticeship saw trainee merchants keeping accounts for their principals, attending to customers, and busy at the quayside keeping tally of incoming and outgoing cargoes. Later they might serve as a supercargo on ships sailing abroad or

---

[2] For a summary see J. H. Clapham, *An Economic History of Modern Britain. The Early Railway Age* (1926) pp. 233–62.

represent their firms in foreign markets. But a successful merchant gave little time to such matters for much of his buying and selling was done through trusted correspondents abroad, while specialist brokers stood ready to serve him in his home port. The one thing he could not delegate was the giving of credit and maintenance of his financial liquidity. The merchant's capital was very largely tied up in stock and credits to customers, and his greatest problem was maintaining cash flow. The pivotal position of the merchant, that is to say, was ultimately based on close financial control.[3] This continued to be true as the general merchant of the eighteenth century gave way to the commission merchant of the nineteenth century, and as manufacturers became merchants and merchants extended to manufacturing.[4] This key point must justify the considerable space devoted to finance and credit in any study of mercantile enterprise.

Some pioneer studies of British trade have devoted a lot of space to examining the differences between the functions of merchants, factors (or commission merchants) and brokers.[5] The functions appear quite distinct and logical: merchants traded on their own account while factors were agents who handled commodities for overseas suppliers and domestic or overseas customers but did not as a rule handle the goods. In practice the functions of all three regularly overlapped and it was often a matter of convention whether a firm would call itself one or the other. The present book concentrates on the actual activities of firms rather than the conventional descriptions they often used to describe themselves.

BRITISH DOMINATION OF WORLD TRADE

Throughout the nineteenth century Britain was much the world's largest trading nation, a remarkable achievement considering the huge (tenfold) increase in trade in the period. The available data show that, although Germany, Russia and Belgium improved their relative positions in Europe (the principal growth area), Britain was still top on the eve of World War I (Table 0.3). American industrial production overtook that of Britain in the 1890s but her share of

---

[3] J. M. Price, 'What did Merchants do? Reflections on British Overseas Trade 1660–1790', *Jnl Econ. Hist.* XLIX (1989).   [4] See below, Ch. 2.
[5] R. B. Westerfield, *Middlemen in English Business 1660–1720* (Yale 1915) p. 349ff. N. S. Buck, *The Development of the Organisation of Anglo-American Trade 1800–1850* (Yale 1925) Ch. 2.

Table 0.3. *Relative share of six leading European countries' exports in the European total, 1830–1910 (per cent)*

	1830	1860	1890	1910
United Kingdom	27·5	29·8	26·6	23·7
France	15·9	19·2	15·3	13·4
Germany	—	18·4	·17·4	20·4
Russia	7·9	5·6	8·3	8·9
Belgium	2·9	4·0	6·1	7·3
Austria–Hungary	4·7	5·8	6·5	5·6

Source: extracted from Paul Bairoch, *Commerce extérieure et développement économique de l'Europe au XIX⁰ siècle* (Paris 1976) p. 77. The data for 1830 is approximate, that for 1860–90 based on three year averages.

world trade remained much smaller down to World War I.[6] In the absence of any overall data for east–west trade in the period, statistics of the traffic through the Suez Canal appear to offer an approximate index of the distribution of trade between various western nations and the Far East. In 1880 British ships made up 80 per cent of the total gross tonnage through the Canal, in 1890 76 per cent and 1910 62 per cent, but these figures dwarfed all rivals. In 1910 the German share had risen to 16 per cent but France and Holland were only 5 per cent each and Austria–Hungary 4 per cent. Much of US imports from the east went through Britain.[7] Moreover the global importance of Britain in trade is understated by these figures inasmuch as the finance of world trade was orchestrated in London and sterling was the main currency of international finance.

British supremacy was not based on the same factors through the period. For the first three-quarters of the eighteenth century it was largely founded on the rapidly developing 'Atlantic economy' (the trade with British colonies in North America); between 1700 and 1773 the trade to America and Africa multiplied 7.75 times while that to continental Europe increased only 1.13 times. The American War of Independence dislocated this trade but when peace was restored the upward trend was quickly resumed. An overlapping phase of development appeared during the early period of the British

---

[6] B. R. Mitchell and P. Deane, *Abstract of British Historical Statistics* (Cambridge 1962) Table xi.3. R. M. Robertson, *History of the American Economy* (third edn, New York 1973) p. 364.

[7] S. Nishimura, *The Decline of Inland Bills of Exchange* (Cambridge 1971) esp. Table 15. M. E. Fletcher, 'The Suez Canal and World Shipping 1867–1914', *Jnl Econ. Hist.* xviii (1958).

Table 0.4. *Geographical distribution of UK exports and imports*
1785–1845 (per cent)
(1785–1815 England, Scotland and Wales only)

	1785	1805	1825	1845
Europe				
exports	46·9	44·2	46·1	44·4
imports	43·8	45·8	40·6	36·8
N. America				
exports	25·8	26·1	18·3	16·5
imports	7·4	10·1	16·0	23·9
Latin America and West Indies				
exports	10·3	19·7	22·3	14·9
imports	22·5	27·0	20·5	13·2
Asia and Near East				
exports	12·8	6·9	11·6	19·8
imports	25·6	16·3	21·4	19·4
Africa and Australia				
exports	4·2	3·1	1·7	4·4
imports	0·7	0·7	1·5	6·6

Source: calculated from Ralph Davis, *The Industrial Revolution and British Overseas Trade* (Leicester 1979) Tables 38–40. The data represent an average of three years i.e. 1784–6, 1804–6, 1824–6. Exports include re-exports. The geographical sectors are assembled to harmonise with those of Paul Bairoch in Table 0.5.

Industrial Revolution when the export of textiles (and especially cottons) increased rapidly, and from the beginning of the nineteenth century to the mid-1840s cottons represented 40 to 50 per cent of all British exports. The greatest impact was initially on the European market, which took around 60 per cent of cotton exports at the end of the Napoleonic War (1815) and 30 per cent in 1855 (Table 0.4).[8]

A third phase began as Europe and the United States responded to British industrialisation by tariffs and adaptation to the new techniques of production. As ocean freight rates and marine insurance rates declined it became economical to draw bulk commodities (basic foodstuffs and raw materials) from distant continents and so generate exchange there. British textiles and other manufactured goods were increasingly directed to markets in the Middle East, Latin America, India, China and the Far East

[8] R. Davis, *The Industrial Revolution and British Overseas Trade* (Leicester 1979) pp. 13–14.

generally; of these destinations India proved much the most important. By 1910 these export markets had become more important than those of Europe and North America (Table 0.5). From 1845 British law placed no restrictions on the export of machinery, and capital goods began to appear a significant component of exports. In the main period of British industrial expansion (1780s–1870s), imports of foreign manufacturers were pretty well eliminated in favour of the cheaper (and often better) home produced goods so that British trade became very largely a business of exporting manufactures in exchange for foodstuffs and raw materials. Inevitably the industrialisation of the United States, Germany and France led to growing imports of manufactured goods from these countries (particularly as Britain was wedded to free trade), but the shift to newer areas of trade served to sustain the opportunities of exporting industrial products in exchange for food and raw materials, with trade deficits with the new manufacturing countries bridged by surpluses in trade with new countries.[9]

This broad outline of British trade is already familiar from several authoritative studies and does not call for addition or refinement here. The aim of the present study is to identify the enterprise and organisation behind these changing patterns, and to examine the motivation and culture of mercantile enterprise from the Industrial Revolution to World War I. This is no easy task for, banks and insurance companies apart, the service industries have left even fewer records than those that produced goods, but patient synthesis of materials from sources in Britain and abroad reveals some interesting patterns suggesting new interpretations of British economic history.

THE INDUSTRIAL REVOLUTION AND MERCHANTS

In the period of British deindustrialisation in the 1980s it became fashionable for historians to contrast the varying fortunes of industry on the one side and commerce and finance on the other, treating the first as if it has been the victim of the prejudices of the second, a group that over a long historical period had represented power, wealth, privilege, metropolitan life and conservatism. The most popular exponent of this view is probably Martin J. Wiener's *English*

[9] R. Davis, *Industrial Revolution*, p. 36. D. C. North, 'Ocean Freight Rates and Economic Development 1750–1913', *Jnl Econ. Hist.* xviii (1958). B. R. Mitchell and P. Deane, *Historical Statistics*, Ch. xi.

Table 0.5. *Geographical destination of UK exports and imports 1860–1910*
(per cent)

	1860	1880	1910
Europe			
exports	34·3	35·6	35·2
imports	31·0	41·4	45·1
N. America			
exports	16·6	15·9	11·6
imports	26·7	30·9	23·8
Latin America and West Indies			
exports	12·0	10·2	12·6
imports	10·1	6·1	9·1
Asia and Near East			
exports	25·7	25·4	25·4
imports	23·2	12·0	10·3
Africa and Australia			
exports	11·4	12·7	16·0
imports	9·0	9·6	11·7

Source: extracted from Paul Bairoch, *Commerce extérieure et développement économique de l'Europe au XIXᵉ siècle* (Paris 1976).

Culture and the Decline of the Industrial Spirit. Wiener has picked on the sporadic infighting between City financiers and provincial manufacturers and exaggerated it until he writes of the industrialist as 'the legatee of an aborted rebellion against the standards of "upper Englishry", standards that refused to take the processes of material production quite seriously'.[10] He makes no distinction between finance and trade. However, the subject has been taken up by two British economic historians, Dr Cain and Professor Hopkins, in a major work of synthesis called 'Gentlemanly Capitalism and British Expansion Overseas', and here the emphasis is very much on the mercantile origins of the economic, social and political divide.[11]

The two authors argue that the period 1688–1945 possesses a fundamental unity in British history in the sense that the growth of the service sector based on the City of London and the South East of England governed the course of the nation's economic policy, Britain's presence overseas (formal and informal empire) and the

[10] M. J. Wiener, *English Culture and the Decline of the Industrial Spirit 1850–1980* (1985) p. 128.
[11] P. J. Cain and A. Hopkins, 'Gentlemanly Capitalism and British Expansion Overseas', *Econ. Hist. Rev.* XXXIX (1986), XL (1987).

course of industrial development. Employment in the service sector enjoyed higher status and rewards than that in industry and it had easier access to political influence. Trade and finance were the basic components of the service sector so this interpretation must be central to the subject matter of this book. The immediate implication is that the traditional British economic history that sees the eighteenth and nineteenth centuries' landscape dominated by the peaks of industrial production, with merchants and traders providing outlets for manufacturing enterprise, must give way to a dualism in which merchants are clearly identified as central figures rather than satellites. The Cain and Hopkins thesis is clearly too wide, and covers too long a period, to be adequately considered in this book. However, it will be possible to assemble evidence on the changing relationship between industrialists and merchants, and between the provinces and City, which is not always the same thing. The culture of 'gentlemanly capitalism', taken in all its subtle dimensions, is also too large a concept to do justice to here, but examination of the extent to which immigrant merchant families retained their own identity and values which challenged the assumptions and conventions of the English 'Establishment' will assess the idea from another angle.

The idea of 'gentlemanly capitalism' is not far from that of an 'aristocratic bourgeoisie' debated by historians of City finance.[12] The starting point is often the passage in Walter Bagehot's *Lombard Street* (1873) where it is suggested that most City merchants 'have a good deal of leisure, for the life of a man of business who employs his own capital, and employs it nearly always in the same way, is by no means fully employed'.[13] Bagehot saw this as the merchant's opportunity to become a director of one or more of the proliferating number of joint-stock companies (banks, insurance and railway companies), but Cain and Hopkins identify leisure as the means of drawing entrepreneurs away from manufacturing industry (which required more continuous and close attention) and providing time to promote political interests, while the 'aristocratic bourgeoisie' group focus on inclinations to an aristocratic life style and amateurishness in business, particularly in the second and subsequent generations.

Bagehot's comment was made almost in parenthesis and, could he

---

[12] S. D. Chapman, 'Aristocracy and Meritocracy in Merchant Banking', *Brit. Jnl Soc.* xxxvii (1986), Y. Casis, 'Merchant Bankers and City Aristocracy', *Brit. Jnl Soc.* (1988) and Chapman's reply.   [13] W. Bagehot, *Lombard Street* (1973) 14th edn, pp. 240–5.

have anticipated the attention it has attracted in the twentieth century, he would surely have taken more care to emphasise that 'leisure' was a product of ample capital and mature experience, and necessary for an international trader who needed time to study the implications of the constant shifts in the trading scene. The idea was better expressed by Samuel Smith, the senior partner in the leading Liverpool cotton brokers Smith, Edwards & Co. and Liverpool partner of James Finlay & Co., one of the most successful of the merchant houses in trade with India. He was a Liberal Member of Parliament from 1882 until his death in 1906 and his words no doubt reflect some of the conventional wisdom of the merchant community at the period:

The head of a great firm dealing with foreign countries needs to be a statesman, an economist, and a financier, as well as a merchant. He must have the power of taking a bird's-eye view of the whole situation; like the general of an army, and like all great commanders, he must be able to discern talent, and promote it to high position. A first-class merchant does not burden his mind with a multitude of details, and *is always seemingly at leisure, while intent upon great issues.* Many such men have I known in the course of my life. The old British merchant as I remember him before the days of syndicates and limited liability, was often a truly great man, honourable, far-sighted, enterprising, yet withal prudent and cautious; simple in his life, and temperate in all things. The great fabric of British trade was built on these foundations.[14] (author's italics)

Smith wrote nostalgically as an old man, fearing that the accepted norms of his best years were under threat, but there was some substance in his interpretation inasmuch as twentieth-century management school studies emphasise the necessity for chief executives to have time to reflect on major policy issues.

The three approaches to understanding mercantile business indicated here – that of 'gentlemanly capitalism', the 'aristocratic bourgeoisie' and what may be called Smith's chief executive – all appear plausible in their different ways and all claim a volume of empirical support. They are not mutually exclusive but their relative importance needs to be assessed as far as the evidence will allow. Each of their exponents offers one approach as a key to understanding mercantile performance in the period so must be carefully considered in the present study.

[14] Samuel Smith, *My Life Work* (1902) p. 36. For a short account of Smith's career see Ch. 7.

COSMOPOLITAN CULTURE

Economists have traditionally taken only limited interest in entrepreneurship on the grounds that their subject is about rational choices in the production and distribution of goods and services rather than about dimensions of personality. However there is now an economic theory of the entrepreneur distinct from mainstream neoclassical economics and this recognises the relevance of culture to the varying performance of firms and of national economies. The contribution of the distinctive cultures of the US and Japan to their successive dominance of world trade this century is apparent to the most casual observer, and a moment's reflection suggests that it could be no less important in the historical context.

In a stimulating essay on 'Entrepreneurial Culture as Competitive Advantage', Mark Casson, one of the foremost exponents of entrepreneurial theory, has proposed the analysis of cultural attitudes to synthesise an entrepreneurial rating for various countries competing in international trade such as the UK, USA, Japan, Germany, France and Italy. The constituents of the different entrepreneurial cultures include factors such as scientific attitude, decision-making process and 'voluntarism' (attitudes to government) that are readily appreciated but practically impossible to measure, at any rate in an historical context. However, some simplified version adapted to our needs may clarify initial understanding.[15]

In the eighteenth and nineteenth centuries the theatre for the various trading cultures was the great cities and ports where merchants competed for trade. An international metropolis, as Fernand Braudel showed in his great work *Civilisation and Capitalism from the Fifteenth to the Eighteenth Centuries*, always attracts cosmopolitan immigrants, and as London succeeded Amsterdam as the dominant capitalist city of Europe, its trading community became a more heterogeneous mix of races than it had ever been.[16] Of course, the origins of the migrants changed; in the eighteenth century it was mainly Huguenots, Dutch and Sephardic Jews, in the nineteenth century Germans (including German Jews), Greeks and Americans, especially those of Protestant Irish origin. Other distinctive merchant

---

[15] Mark Casson, *Enterprise and Competitiveness. A Systems View of International Business* (Oxford 1990) Ch. 4.
[16] F. Braudel, *Civilisation and Capitalism*, III *The Perspective of the World* (1981) pp. 30–1.

cultures were formed within Britain, particularly those of the religious dissenters and the Scots. Together these various ethnic and religious groups play a major part in the study of mercantile enterprise in Britain in the period. Their varying cultural attributes, so far as mercantile success was concerned, can be evaluated under such headings as moral probity, discipline, family and group loyalty, achievement ethic and the degree of inward or outward looking objectivity. (The last idea, which springs from Casson, refers to the extent to which the decision-making members of the firm give their priorities to some 'internal' ideal such as equality of rewards or participatory decision making, or to an aggressive stance towards rival firms and groups.) Sadly, we lack sufficiently detailed evidence to attribute any numerical valuation to these factors, but their importance will be considered from literary evidence.

The foreign merchants who flocked to London and its provincial rivals in the nineteenth century were not of course on the scale of the hordes that crossed the Atlantic to people the New World. Merchant strategy was planned and controlled carefully by men of capital to extend their international trading networks. Typically a trusted son or a clerk earmarked by his talent for early promotion to a partnership was sent to test his metal; not unusually it happened that the fortunate emissary succeeded beyond his father's (or principal's) most sanguine expectations, and before long London or Manchester exchanged places with the home town as centre and satellite of the family's trading activities. Old loyalties and new cultures were fused to create a supra-national outlook.[17] Dr Charles Jones of Warwick University coined the phrase 'cosmopolitan bourgeoisie' for the international trading community that played such an important role in British life last century. He writes of a system 'in which ethnicity and nationality were not the primary determinants of status and where authority over enterprise remained quite decentralised without any apparent sacrifice of the growing economies to be derived from a centralised system of credit and information based upon the London market'.[18] It is easy to accept that this had emerged by the middle of the nineteenth century, but more difficult to share his view, as we shall see, that the outlook of the international merchant houses was subverted by nationalism and imperialism before the end of the century. Much depended on

---

[17] See below, Ch. 5.
[18] Charles A. Jones, *International Business in the Nineteenth Century* (1987) p. 94.

location. Moreover, it must always be borne in mind that the international merchant houses were only part of the British trading scene. As the century advanced, a larger portion of British trade concentrated on India and South Africa where the outlook of most of the firms was never so cosmopolitan as the immigrant firms, but great imperial ports like Hong Kong maintained their cosmopolitan milieu.

Apart from tracing the emergence and contributions of the various trading migrants to London, the cosmopolitan approach must prompt the question of what is a British merchant house in the period. As Dr B. R. Tomlinson, a historian of British economic enterprise in India puts it, 'it is not at all clear that "British" is a meaningful collective adjective to apply to individual firms, or groups of companies, that happened to be owned or run by citizens of the United Kingdom'.[19] Beyond that, there is the problem of centralisation versus local decision making: did the success of mercantile enterprise depend on the former or the latter, or were there strategies to combine the best elements of both? These are topics that will recur through the book and to which we will return in conclusion.

TRADE AND EMPIRE

The interpretation of British economic history just referred to has the further merit of bringing imperialism back into the centre of the picture. The British Empire was not built up simply as a tool of international diplomacy or as the opportunity for off-loading surplus manufactures; it is to be seen rather as a long-term and continuous aspect of the strategy of British mercantile capitalism. The only general thesis on the performance of British merchants compared with foreign competitors is that developed by D. C. M. Platt in his *Latin America and British Trade 1806–1914*. Platt readily acknowledges the ascendancy of German merchants over British firms in Latin America during the course of the century but denies this is evidence of overall decline or failure. He used the extensive series of British consular reports and the experiences of several well-known trading firms to show that as competition intensified British strategy was to concentrate business under the British flag, where there was ample room for growth without the high risks associated with unstable

[19] B. R. Tomlinson, 'British Business in India 1860–1970', in R. P. T. Davenport-Hines and Geoffrey Jones, eds., *British Business in Asia since 1860* (1989) p. 113.

political regimes, erratic consumer demand and perhaps discrimination against foreigners. The British had a greater choice of markets than the Germans and by degrees withdrew from those where conditions were more difficult. Platt concludes that British withdrawal from Latin America was not symptomatic of a general worldwide decline in Britain's competitive power but of a deliberate refining of strategy.[20]

Recent research on British trade with Tsarist Russia has served to lend support to Platt's thesis. British merchants took an early lead in Russian trade and in the eighteenth century they succeeded the Dutch as the premier mercantile community in St Petersburg. However in the next century it became increasingly clear that the Germans had greater advantages in this market, and the British houses that survived there gradually diversified into more secure and profitable markets. The old houses that maintained a foothold concentrated on finance of trade, while the 'British' firms that continued active in the import–export business were characteristically newer enterprises of Anglo-German origin, and maintained close family and business connections in Germany.[21]

There has been as yet no direct challenge to Platt's thesis and, initially at least, some support. The pioneer investigator of the history of British multinational companies, J. M. Stopford, maintained that during the years of the so-called Great Depression (1873–96) the Empire was a market of least resistance to British firms. However, a more recent researcher of this type of business organisation, S. J. Nicholas, using evidence from a slightly larger group of firms, takes a different view, and also links multinational enterprise with the shortcomings of merchant houses. He suggests that direct investment in overseas manufacturing was the consequence of problems in selling through merchants. Such manufacturing enterprise was no more evident in the Empire than in non-imperial territories, he insists, so perhaps the merchant enterprise that preceded it was also impartially distributed? Conceivably the manufacturers who started producing overseas did so where British mercantile enterprise was weaker, or perhaps their activities simply followed the patterns of existing trading activities established by

---

[20] D. C. M. Platt, *Latin America and British Trade 1806–1914* (1972).
[21] S. Thompstone, 'The Organisation and Financing of Anglo-Russian Trade before 1914', Ph.D. thesis, London 1992.

merchant houses. There is certainly a major issue here to be investigated.[22]

There is also a challenge here to examine these developments from the perspective of those merchants that relocated or concentrated their activities on the imperial territories. What advantages were realised, and was their performance superior to foreign merchants trading in independent territories? Did the Empire provide a cocoon that shielded British merchants from the stimulation of competition? Such questions will recur as the different arms of British enterprise are considered in turn.

DISAPPEARANCE OR REGENERATION?

In 1903 a sober periodical, *The Statist*, pronounced that 'the great merchant of former times has become unnecessary, and therefore is rapidly ceasing to exist'. The revolution in communications, it was argued, had effectively cut out the chain of middlemen between the producer and the retailer. The nineteenth century can be seen in retrospect as a long transitional period in which, as it proved less and less necessary to hold large stocks of goods, the initiative shifted to those who could satisfy demand without tying up resources in warehouses and idle inventory capital.[23] The logic of the argument suggests that, by the end of the period considered, mercantile activity must have effectively disappeared except perhaps in a few anachronistic or peripheral areas.

Merchants had been graduating to other occupations for centuries. More than a generation ago, the doyen of economic history of the time, T. S. Ashton, showed that in the eighteenth century the progression of merchants was generally from trading in commodities to dealing in money and shares.[24] More recently economic historians have been tracing some of the paths of merchant migration into finance in the nineteenth century; they were evidently the most important element in the establishment of merchant banks in London and British imperial banks and international banks at home and abroad. They contributed powerfully, as brokers and

---

[22] J. M. Stopford, 'The Origins of British-based Multinational Manufacturing Enterprise', *Bus. Hist. Rev.* XLVIII (1974). S. J. Nicholas, 'Agency Contracts, Institutional Modes and the Transition to Foreign Direct Investment by British Manufacturing Multinationals before 1939', *Jnl Econ. Hist.* XLIII (1983).

[23] S. Nishimura, *Inland Bills of Exchange* pp. 77–9.

[24] T. S. Ashton, *An Economic History of England. The Eighteenth Century* (1959) p. 138.

syndicates, to the development of Lloyds insurance market and to the establishment of country banks and joint-stock banks.[25] But this traditional graduation into 'pure finance' has nothing to do with merchant loss of business into manufacturers' direct sales. Moreover, a distinction has to be made between goods in international trade that were simple and standardised (e.g. grain, cotton, timber) and those that were complex, innovative or perishable, and so required close contact between producer and consumer.[26] Inevitably the growth of the second class in world trade limited the scope of the traditional merchant, but it was not an area in which British manufacturers were conspicuously strong. The rapidly growing world market offered vast scope in bulk products, and in any event there were ways in which merchants and manufacturers could unite.

So while merchants faced direct challenges and were often drawn into financial specialisms, there is also evidence of continuity and of regeneration. The membership of the Manchester Royal Exchange, for instance, which represented the country's cotton piece goods and yarn exporters, maintained its upward trend until 1925.[27] In the course of this book it will be seen that the cotton merchants were only one of diverse forms of specialised trading enterprise that multiplied in Britain through the nineteenth century. Among the most prominent were the 'international houses', the misnamed 'home trade houses' and the so called 'agency houses', each of which covered a plethora of activities.[28]

Nevertheless, there can be no doubt that the later years of the period covered by this book saw British manufacturers directly active overseas and bypassing traditional organisation. Nicholas identifies five stages of development of overseas involvement by British multinationals: (1) exporting through merchant houses on a commission basis with no exclusive agreements, (2) exclusive agency agreements with merchants houses, (3) foreign travellers (representatives) employed by the home firm, (4) selling overseas through sales subsidiaries, and (5) direct investment in foreign production. Twenty-one British multinationals examined developed on something like this pattern, and they included several leaders of the

---

[25] S. D. Chapman, *The Rise of Merchant Banking* (1984). Geoffrey Jones, *History of the British International Banks* (forthcoming). R. Clews, ed., *A Textbook of Insurance Broking* (1980) Ch. 1.

[26] G. Porter and H. C. Livesay, *Merchants and Manufacturers. Studies in the Changing Structure of Nineteenth-Century Marketing.* (Baltimore 1971) Ch. 1.

[27] D. A. Farnie, 'An Index of Commercial Activity: the Membership of the Manchester Royal Exchange 1809–1948', *Bus. Hist.* xxi (1979).   [28] See below, Chs. 4, 5, 6.

various sectors of British industry. Nicholas's model implies that this was in some way a representative experience from the late nineteenth century to 1939, and readers will infer that the period saw multinationals supersede merchants. However, he is the first to recognise the limitation of his 'nonrandom sample' and call for further enquiry.[29] Setting multinational enterprise in the context of the longer period of history of mercantile enterprise, rather than seeing merchants as the prelude to multinationals, will provide another approach to the problem.

Stated more simply, this book has two aims. First it is intended to identify the origins, types and dispersion of merchant enterprise in a century of unprecedented opportunities and challenges. Secondly it aims to evaluate its performance in relation to competition at home and abroad, and from new forms of business organisation active in overseas sourcing and marketing. The record of achievement or failure must be highly relevant to any assessment of British experience yesterday or today, whether in capitalism, industrialism, imperialism, social elites, enterprise cultures or any of a host of other problems that continues to occupy everyone interested in the history of the British economy.

[29] S. J. Nicholas, 'Agency Contracts'.

PART I

The setting

CHAPTER I

The eighteenth-century structure of merchant enterprise

There is a large literature on British merchants and their diverse enterprises in the eighteenth century, and much academic expertise has been invested in calculating and evaluating the growing volume and value of trade in the period.[1] If this scholarship has a limitation, it must be its parochialism, at any rate compared with Fernand Braudel's work *Civilisation and Capitalism*.[2] As the focus of this book is on the changes brought by the Industrial Revolution and the age of the telegraph and rapid communication, it will only be necessary to identify the salient features of merchant activity in the earlier period, especially those that have a particular bearing on subsequent changes. The most important of these are thought to be the early emergence of merchants as an economic and social elite, the major role played by migrants from the Continent and the domination of London in the commerce of Britain, the important role played by Dissenter networks in trade, and the ways in which the high risk of overseas trade made for high turnover of firms and renewal of enterprise. Much of the research on these topics has focused on particular firms, trades, ethnic groups and ports and an attempt will be made, where possible, to evaluate the overall significance of these features. However, the main purpose of this chapter is to provide a backcloth for the changes considered in the rest of the book

---

[1] See especially E. B. Schumpeter, *English Overseas Trade Statistics 1697–1808* (1960); R. Davis, *The Rise of the English Shipping Industry in the Seventeenth and Eighteenth Centuries* (1962); R. B. Westerfield, *Middlemen in English Business 1660–1760* (New Haven 1915); J. M. Price, *Capital and Credit in British Overseas Trade. The View from the Chesapeake 1700–1776* (Cambridge, Mass., 1980).

[2] F. Braudel. *Civilisation and Capitalism from the Fifteenth to the Eighteenth Centuries*. II. *The Wheels of Commerce* (1982).

Table 1.1. *Estimates of mercantile incomes in England in the eighteenth century*

	King 1688		Massie 1759		Colquhoun 1803	
	No. of families	income (£)	No. of families	income (£)	No. of families	income (£)
Merchants (1)	2,000	400	1,000	600	2,000	2,600
Merchants (2)	8,000	200	2,000	400	13,000	800
Merchants (3)			10,000	200		
Totals	10,000		13,000		15,000	

Source: original estimates assembled and examined in P. H. Lindert and J. G. Williamson, 'Revising England's Social Tables 1688–1812', *Explorations in Economic History* XIX (1982) 385–408.

OPEN ELITES

There are unfortunately no truly authoritative estimates of the numbers, wealth or incomes of merchants in eighteenth-century Britain. As trade increased nearly six times during the course of the century we should reasonably expect the numbers and capital to increase significantly, but figures are difficult to obtain.[3] The nearest we can come to specific evidence for the country as a whole are the well-known contemporary estimates of King (1688), Massie (1759) and Colquhoun (1803), the relevant parts of which are assembled in Table 1.1. None of the three defined the classes of merchants which they listed, and Massie evidently had a rather different concept in mind to the other two. Nevertheless, with support from other evidence, some reasonable inferences can be drawn from this very limited data. The number of merchants was rising, but apparently not nearly so fast as the volume and value of overseas trade. Secondly, the number of first class merchants in Massie's list looks similar to that in Mortimer's directory for London in 1763 (Table 1.2) and we may have a shrewd suspicion that his estimate was based on a similar source. Some evidence presented below suggests that trade was being concentrated in fewer hands down to about 1775 (the American Revolution) and increased again with the momentum of the Industrial Revolution so the top line figures are

[3] E. B. Schumpeter, *Trade Statistics*, pp. 15–16. The calculation of 'trade' includes imports, exports and re-exports.

Table 1.2. *Analysis of Mortimer's* Universal Director *(1763)*

	Nos.	%
Total numbers listed		
Merchants	978·5	74·35
Factors	337·5	25·64
	1,316·0	100
International composition		
British surnames	303	23
Foreign surnames	1,013	77
	1,316	100
Sector of international trade		
West Indian	49	11·17
East Indian	$21\frac{1}{2}$	4·90
New England	18	10·15
Virginia, Maryland, Carolina	$26\frac{1}{2}$	
	115	26·22
Italian	$61\frac{1}{2}$	14·03
Dutch and Flemish	$49\frac{1}{2}$	11·29
Hamburg	$38\frac{1}{2}$	8·78
Turkey	$31\frac{1}{2}$	7·18
Russian	$28\frac{1}{2}$	6·50
Scottish and Irish	28	6·38
Portugal	25	5·70
Spanish	24	5·47
Swedish and Danish	14	3·19
South Seas	$13\frac{1}{2}$	3·08
French	8	1·82
Africa	$1\frac{1}{2}$	0·34
General and unspecified	540	55·19
	978·5	100

Notes:
(1) Totals refer to numbers of firms, *not* merchants. Most firms had two, three or sometimes more partners.
(2) Firms often listed their interest in two areas (e.g. West Indies and New England) in which case each was counted a half.

more plausible than they may appear at first glance. Massie's second class seems consistent with merchants for the outports and main centres of trade, while his third class is evidently petty traders. King and Colquhoun are less discriminating but not entirely inconsistent. Of course the most striking feature represented in the table is the dramatic growth of incomes from about 1760. There are no means of testing these figures but they do appear broadly consistent with what is known of merchant capital in the period. The 'common' rate of interest was five per cent, which suggests that incomes of £400 p.a. (1688) were based on average capitals of £8,000, of £600 p.a. (1759) on £12,000 and of £2,600 p.a. on £50,000 or so. The first two figures are consistent with evidence from business records, while it is certain that merchant fortunes did increase dramatically towards the end of the century as trade multiplied.[4] (The total overseas trade of £8·3m. about 1700 reached £10·8m. about 1759 then climbed steeply to £87m. around 1800, see Table 1.7).

It is idle to conjecture any further on the validity of these figures but they do present some broad parameters within which more detailed information can be considered. They offer orders of magnitude and guides to the directions of change. In a population rising from five to eight millions during the course of the century,[5] the merchants were always a small group, and in the first division scarcely increased at all. They were a group that concentrated increasing wealth and income in their hands, in the first part of the century by actual concentration of a gradually increasing trade, in the second half by seizing the marketing opportunities of the country's new manufacturing wealth.

By the second half of the eighteenth century the leading merchants came to constitute something of an elite in British society in London and the other major ports, Liverpool, Glasgow, Newcastle, Bristol, Exeter and Hull, as well as in a few inland centres of trade such as Manchester and Leeds. In earlier years there is some suggestion of the lowly start of numbers of traders in the outports; Liverpool had many merchants that, according to a contemporary, had risen from 'Saylors', while Bristol trade was crowded with 'upstarts and mushrooms', but it is likely that such views sprang as much from preconceptions as from precise knowledge of origins.[6] The only thorough local investigation of the subject, that of Leeds in Dr R. G. Wilson's *Gentleman Merchants*, concludes that the merchant group largely emerged from the class of small land owners, with a minority

---

[4] J. M. Price, *Capital and Credit*, Ch. 3. L. S. Pressnell, 'The Rate of Interest in the Eighteenth Century', in Pressnell, ed., *Studies in the Industrial Revolution* (1960).

[5] E. A. Wrigley, *The Population History of England 1541–1871* (1981).

[6] Quoted in W. E. Minchinton, 'Merchants in England in the Eighteenth Century', in B. E. Supple, ed., *The Entrepreneur. Papers presented at the Annual Conference of the Economic History Society, Cambridge* (Harvard 1957).

rising through the ranks of local traders, but both were well-established before the mid-eighteenth century.[7]

During the course of the century several attempts were made to define the necessary education of the merchant, and all agree that it needed to be extensive and hence (by implication) expensive. The curriculum requirements outlined in R. Campbell's *London Tradesman* (1747) is probably fairly representative:

A Merchant ought to be a Man of an extensive Genius, and his Education genteel; he must understand not only Goods and Merchandize in general, and be a Judge of every particular Commodity he deals in, but must know Mankind and be acquainted with the different Manners and Customs of all the Trading Nations; he must know their different Products, the Properties of their Staple Commodities, their Taste in the several Sorts of Goods they want, their principal Marts and Markets, the Seasons proper for buying and selling, the Character and Humour of their Traders, their Coins, Weights, and Measures, their particular Manner of keeping Accompts, the Course of their Exchange, &c. the Duties chargeable at their several Ports, their Methods of Entry and Clearance; their peculiar Mercantile Customs and Usages, relating either to Payments, or Buying and Selling; the common Arts, Tricks and Frauds, put in practice by the Dealers: In a word, he must be as well acquainted with the Manners and Customs of all the Nations he trades with as his own; all which requires an extensive Genius and great Experience.

As to his Education, he must understand his Mother Tongue perfectly, write it gramatically, and with Judgment; he must learn all the Trading Languages, French, Dutch and Portugueze, and be able to write them ... He must understand Geography and some Navigation, must write a fair legible Hand, and ought to be a compleat Master of Figures and Merchants Accompts.[8]

And indeed, such records as we have rather confirm that the better class of merchants were, by the standards of the age, quite well educated. The *Dictionary of National Biography* includes the names of 361 merchants, 110 of whom were educated at grammar schools, 77 at public schools, 64 at private schools, 62 at home and 44 at dissenting academies, and several went on to the universities.[9] There is no hint of the low born or rags-to-riches in this record.

This is not to suggest that there was never a time when the merchant class was composed of numerous traders with little knowledge, qualifications or capital. In Bristol it was said that 'all

[7] R. G. Wilson, *Gentleman Merchants. The Merchant Community in Leeds 1700–1830* (Manchester 1971) pp. 14–15.   [8] R. Campbell, *The London Tradesman* (1747).
[9] N. Hans, *New Trends in Education in the Eighteenth Century* (1951) pp. 26–7.

men that are dealers even in shop trades launch into adventures by sea chiefly to the West India plantations. A poor shopkeeper that sells candles will have a bale of stockings or a piece of stuff for Nevis or Virginia &c.'[10] This subject has now been investigated by Jacob Price with particular reference to the tobacco trade, where the records are better than in other sectors of transatlantic commerce. He has found that the small shopkeeper adventurer and trading sailors were already being squeezed at the end of the seventeenth century. In 1676 there were 573 firms importing tobacco into London and this was progressively reduced until in 1775 there were only 56 firms, with a dozen taking over 70 per cent of the trade, that is, there were a handful of dominant firms and a long tail of smaller ones.[11] Determined individuals continued to find their way into this and other branches of trade so merchants may be thought of as an *open* elite.

The capital required to become a merchant appears to have declined towards the end of the eighteenth century, as it did in many other occupations. Collyer's *Parents and Guardians Directory* (1761) noted that £3,000 to £4,000 at least was required to engage in foreign trade to any advantage while Mortimer's *General Commercial Directory* (1819) said £2,000 to £10,000, but in the last two decades of the century inflation was high, and as prices as much as doubled the cost of entry at 1761 prices was probably nearer to £1,000 to £5,000. These figures were similar to those required for bankers (£2,000 to £10,000) and practically the highest in both writers' lists, and they find some support in other records. For the period 1660–1730, Peter Earle found that over half the merchants in a sample of London traders had fortunes between £5,000 and £10,000, though in some cases this was after a lifetime of enterprise. In the American trade before 1775 merchants seem to have started with a capital in the range £5,000 to £10,000, though in Glasgow, where partnerships were larger, £1,000 might be adequate to secure a share in a tobacco merchant house. In the European trade it was also possible to begin modestly; the Leeds woollen export trade required a minimum of £1,500 though a few merchants in the town were eventually trading on capitals of £20,000 and more.[12] Entry

[10] Quoted in W. E. Minchinton, 'Merchants', p. 24.
[11] J. M. Price and P. G. E. Clemens, 'British Firms in the Chesapeake Trade', *Jnl Econ. Hist.*, XLVII (1987). D. Ormrod, *English Grain Exports and the Structure of Capitalism* (Hull 1985) pp. 35–40.
[12] Peter Earle, *The Making of the English Middle Class ... London 1660–1730* (1989) esp. pp. 32–5, 107. T. Mortimer, *General Commercial Directory* (1819) p. 1026. J. M. Price, *Capital and*

opportunities evidently varied with the trade sector as well as over time. These details are, however, sufficient to make the point that for most of the eighteenth century overseas trade was an elite activity because of the large capitals required to enter and continue in the occupation. It is therefore not surprising to find that a large part of several trade sectors was commanded by a handful of merchants. Dr Earle says that already in early eighteenth-century London, ten or twenty men dominated the overseas trading world of their day, a few with fortunes topping £100,000. As early as the 1730s the Levant trade was dominated by just five firms. Before 1775 over half of Glasgow's large trade in tobacco was controlled by three groups of firms. On the eve of the American Revolution there were only twenty firms significantly involved in the main colonial port of Philadelphia, mostly from London but a few based in Liverpool, Manchester and other provincial centres. At the end of the century there were still only ten 'American houses' in Liverpool, plus eleven in the trade to the West Indies.[13] A third or more of the trade to Russia passed through the hands of a coterie of ten wealthy merchants. The position seems to be much the same in the provincial centres. Thus in Newcastle, often reckoned the third port after London and Bristol, only seven or eight merchants could be said to have a fairly extensive and varied trade early in the century, and the position does not appear to have changed much as the century advanced.[14] Similarly, in Leeds the European trade was controlled by thirteen wealthy families for most of the eighteenth century, while Exeter's strong connections with the Continent were in the hands of twenty firms.[15] The reasons for this concentration are not far to seek. Capital became cheaper in the eighteenth century and one year's

Credit, p. 38. T. M. Devine, *The Tobacco Lords. A Study of the Tobacco Merchants of Glasgow and their Trading Activities c. 1740–90* (Edinburgh 1975) pp. 10, 76. R. Davis, *Aleppo and Devonshire Square. English Traders in the Levant in the Eighteenth Century* (1967) p. 69. R. G. Wilson, *Gentleman Merchants*, p. 66.

[13] T. M. Devine, *Tobacco Lords*, p. 4. R. Davis, *Aleppo*, p. 60. T. Doerflinger, *A Vigorous Spirit of Enterprise. Merchants and Economic Development in Revolutionary Philadelphia* (Chapel Hill, NC, 1986) pp. 61, 87. Pennsylvania Historical Commission, Harrisburg: Journals of Joshua Gilpin (1765–1840) vol. 4.

[14] A. Kahan, *The Plough, the Hammer and the Knout: an Economic History of Eighteenth-Century Russia* (Chicago 1985) p. 201. Joyce Ellis, 'A Study of the Business Fortunes of William Cotesworth c. 1688–1726', D.Phil. thesis, Oxford 1975, p. 18. L. M. Cullen, *Anglo-Irish Trade* (1968).

[15] S. Thompstone, 'The Organisation and Financing of Anglo-Russia Trade before 1914', Ph.D. thesis, London 1992. R. G. Wilson, *Gentleman Merchants*, p. 20. India Office Library, Charter Series, A/2/11 (24 Mar. 1793).

credit was quite normal in overseas trade. In some branches, such as the Levant, merchants had to wait much longer for their returns.[16] Trade was highly volatile, constantly interrupted by wars, rumours of wars and sudden commercial crises. The bigger firms were more resilient to these forces because they had more resources to carry them through the difficult periods and more access to capital from banks, insurance companies and connections within the elite group. In the outports the most successful merchants were wont to migrate to London, maintaining the capital's leadership despite growing competition from Liverpool and Glasgow.[17] Growing strength also brought increasing control over suppliers. The most lucrative branch of trade in the later eighteenth century was probably that in printed textiles. Such was the power of the two leading London houses (Barclay's and Nash's) before the American Revolution, that they were able to order constantly from practically all the twenty or thirty London printers and must have exercised a powerful influence over their production. In Yorkshire, where the merchant body was served by as many as 5,000 clothiers in the 1760s, such close control was impracticable but they worked to improve the quality of the product.[18]

However, it must be insisted that while merchants were growing richer through the century they were never an exclusive elite or class set apart from lesser traders. It has often been remarked that the most singular feature of eighteenth century English society was its fluidity. There were no formal barriers to upward (or downward) social mobility, and merchants were one of the more dynamic elements. The rapid development of the Atlantic economy through the eighteenth century and the improvements in British manufactures sold in other markets frequently suggested new trading opportunities. At the lower end of the social scale merchants merged into wholesalers and factors, while they in turn merged with the vast and rapidly growing class of shopkeepers. The trade cards of the period, a neglected source which reveal more details about tradesmen than any other single source, often describe them as 'wholesale and retail' while in Bristol, where the port documentation is unusually good, it is clear that such tradesmen continued to send

---

[16] R. Davis, *Aleppo*, p. 69 suggests two to three years.
[17] W. E. Minchinton, 'Merchants', p. 24.
[18] J. M. Price, ed., *Joshua Johnson's Letter Book 1771–4* (1979) p. 38. S. D. Chapman and S. Chassagne, *European Textile Printers in the Eighteenth Century* (1981) p. 8. R. G. Wilson, *Gentleman Merchants*, pp. 55–7.

small quantities of goods to America until late in the century. An interesting case of overlap with wholesale and retail trade is provided by Robert Carr, a highly successful City of London silk mercer who handled every variety of luxury silk fabric. His capital rose from £7,000 (1733) to £30,000 (1764), figures that were well above the range of City merchant fortunes in the early eighteenth century, which Peter Earle has calculated at £5,000 to £15,000. No doubt the City's most successful merchant of the late eighteenth century, Francis Baring, had this structure in mind when he wrote to Prime Minister William Pitt that 'the bulk of the trade of this country is carried on by persons with small capital...such trade is upon the whole more beneficial to the country than that part which is carried on by large capital'. Opportunities for modest enterprise were not to be reduced in the early decades of the nineteenth century.[19]

AN INTERNATIONAL COMMUNITY

Ever since the middle ages there had been merchants of continental birth living in London, but in the eighteenth century their numbers evidently grew apace.[20] The story of the migration of Huguenots and Sephardic Jews to Britain has often been related in terms of religious persecution, but this is not the whole or probably the most important reason for the rise of London and then Leeds, Manchester and other provincial trading towns as major settlements of European merchants. The attractions of British commercial centres long outlived the Inquisition and Revocation of the Edict of Nantes, and were increasingly connected with the rise of London as the premier centre of international finance and payments. Fernand Braudel's *Civilisation and Capitalism* explains that, in any historical period, there must be a single centre and fulcrum of international finance, and that during the eighteenth century London was overtaking Amsterdam to assume that role. Capital is mobile and moves to the international centre where it will earn most, and its owners commonly follow it there.[21]

---

[19] A. Heal, *London Tradesmen's Cards of the Eighteenth Century* (1968). Bristol P. L., Port presentments, 1773 onwards. Peter Earle, *Making of the English Middle Class*, p. 32. N. K. A. Rothstein, 'The Silk Industry in London 1702–6', M.A. thesis, L.S.E. 1961, p. 225. Baring cited in H. C. and L. H. Mui, *Shops and Shopkeeping in Eighteenth-Century England* (1989) p. 189.

[20] T. H. Lloyd, *Alien Merchants in England in the High Middle Ages* (1982). A. Pettegree, *Foreign Protestant Communities in Sixteenth-Century London* (Oxford 1986).

[21] F. Braudel, *Civilisation* II, p. 148ff.

The numbers of foreign-born merchants domiciled in London were already substantial by the middle of the eighteenth century. An address of loyalty to the Crown drawn up in 1744 was signed by some 542 merchants of the City of London, and about one-third of the signatures (180 names) were those of aliens or of men of foreign origin or descent. The largest group, 102 names, were Huguenots, another 40 were Jewish (almost all of them Portuguese) and 37 were Dutch. A larger petition, drawn up on the accession of George III in 1760, carried the names of 810 merchants, at least 250 of which (30 per cent) must have been of foreign origin.[22] But perhaps the most complete list is that contained in Mortimer's *Universal Director* (1763), in which the author claims he had 'endeavoured to form a just barrier between the Merchants and the Warehousemen and Shopkeepers by admitting none into the List... but such as are so in every sense of the word'. Careful analysis with the aid of dictionaries of British surnames leads to the astonishing conclusion that as many as 77 per cent of the firms listed included partners of foreign extraction (Table 1.2). To place this figure in perspective, it may be added that as many as 100,000 British (or their descendants) were said to be settled in Holland about 1720, many of them religious refugees.[23] Of course, some of the London merchants may have been of foreign extraction. Some of these merchants may have been settled in Britain for two, three or more generations, but the strong tendency to Anglicise foreign names must lead us to reject the possibility of significant numbers from distant posterity. At the middle of the eighteenth century London was an international mercantile centre in the sense that as many as three-quarters of its membership was of recent foreign extraction. It was already emerging as the international fulcrum of finance and trade due to the decline of opportunities in the Netherlands, Iberia and Italy and the multiplication of transatlantic trade.

It would be wrong to view the merchants with non-English surnames as sojourners with no plan to settle permanently. It is true that their community lives centred round centres like the French Huguenot Church in Threadneedle Street, the Synagogue in Bevis Marks, and the Dutch Church in Austin Friars, but many of them

[22] C. Wilson, 'The Anglo-Dutch Establishment in Eighteenth Century England', in *The Anglo-Dutch Contribution to the Civilisation of Early Modern Society* (Oxford 1976) p. 11. T. S. Ashton, *An Economic History of England: the Eighteenth Century* (1955) p. 140.

[23] Charles King, *The British Merchant* (1721) I, p. 171. This number represented 4–5 % of the population of Holland.

came to London as established merchants and numbers were readily absorbed into the English 'establishment'. The Huguenot and Dutch families intermarried, while the Jews had mostly come to London from Portugal via Amsterdam. Between 1719 and 1785 at least twenty-five directors of the Bank of England were drawn from the Dutch–Huguenot connection, and twenty-three directors of the London Assurance Company came from the same group.[24]

The immigrants were obviously so numerous that there would be no point in trying to assign the whole group to particular sectors of trade and specialisms, but it is worth mentioning some of the areas in which they were particularly prominent. The British public has for so long been fascinated by the Huguenots that it is strange that their collective contribution to the economy has never been adequately researched. They are often thought to have been closely associated with the silk trade and industry, but this business was never sufficiently large to absorb the greater number of them. In 1765 there were something like over a hundred warehousemen and silk mercers serving the home market but only ten importers of silk.[25] The leading Levant importers included only one Huguenot family (Bosanquet) but French Protestants may have been more prominent as importers from Italy; the names of Aubert, André and Panchaud spring easily to mind.[26]

However, this trade was apparently a small affair compared with what followed. Much of the trade of eighteenth-century Europe was still centred on the great fairs of Leipzig, Frankfurt and other centres at which British-born merchants were scarcely represented (Table 1.3). In the early years of the century a major part of the trade in Silesian linens was conducted by Protestant refugees exporting large quantities to Spain and to Britain via Hamburg and Amsterdam.[27] In the second half of the century this trade evolved into one of exporting linens for printing and, more particularly, trade in *indiennes* or linen and cotton mixtures (fustians) and cottons printed in the oriental styles. Louis Bergeron, in a study of the trade and finance of the period, describes this trade and that in colonial goods

---

[24] C. Wilson, 'Anglo-Dutch Establishment'. S. Minet, 'Huguenot Directors of the London Assurance Co.', *Proc. of Huguenot Soc. of London*, XVIII (1947–52) p. 80.

[25] N. K. A. Rothstein, 'The Silk Industry in London 1702–66', M.A. thesis, London 1961, p. 35.

[26] H. Lüthy, *La banque protestante en France* II 1730–94 (Paris 1961) pp. 93–9.

[27] A.N. 57 AQ 108, Banque Mallet MSS, pp. 33–4.

as *les deux grandes affaires du temps*. In fact, the two branches of trade
overlapped, for much the most lucrative branch of the colonial trade
was that in oriental (particularly Indian) textiles, which for a period
threatened both the traditional silk and linen industries, and so
attracted both Huguenot and English merchants.[28]

Even so, this was not the sector in which the greatest Huguenot
fortunes were made. Apart from their inherited wealth and expertise,
the strength of the group lay in the network of international
connections provided by the dispersed families. The Huguenot
diaspora took them not only to London, but in even larger numbers
to Geneva, Neuchâtel, Basle, Frankfurt and Amsterdam, and,
operating in several major financial centres simultaneously, they
were able to build up what we would now call merchant banking
enterprise. An examination of the source of protested bills of
exchange in English trade in Amsterdam during the first decade of
the century showed that nearly 30 per cent of them emanated from
Huguenot houses, the same as from English houses. (The remainder
were Dutch, Jewish and German.)[29] In a period when communications were still slow and uncertain, family and religious ties offered
the only permanent assurance of mutual understanding, trust and
reliability. The Huguenot diaspora provided the necessary network
ahead of the eighteenth-century expansion of European and world
trade. London bankers had few comparable connections and had to
leave the business of discounting bills of exchange and financing
international trade largely to the immigrant houses. Moreover,
political relations between Britain and France were frequently
troubled or broken during the eighteenth century, which dis-
couraged the establishment of branches in Paris, and the Huguenot
houses also maintained their activities through the American War of
Independence.[30] Herbert Lüthy's extensive study of *La banque
protestante en France* identifies over fifty Huguenot houses with
establishments in London that were more or less regularly involved
in banking activities.[31] Numbers of them shifted from financing
trade to investment in government bonds in the second and third
generations.[32]

[28] L. Bergeron, *Banquiers, négociants et manufacturiers parisiens du directoire à l'empire* (Paris 1975)
p. 189. H. Lüthy, *Banque protestante*, pp. 88ff.
[29] A. C. Carter, 'Financial Activities of the Huguenots in London and Amsterdam in the mid-
Eighteenth Century', *Proc. of Huguenot Soc. of London*, XIX (1957).
[30] H. Furber, *John Company at Work* (Harvard 1948) p. 318.
[31] See especially his index of names.
[32] A. C. Carter, 'Financial Activities', pp. 319–23.

During the 1720s and 1730s the Inquisition renewed its campaign against Portugal's Jewry and those who could escape often fled to Bordeaux, Hamburg, Amsterdam and London. Down to the French Wars, most Jewish merchants in London were of Portuguese (Sephardic) origin and continued to be closely associated with the trade of the Iberian peninsula and with the Portuguese and Spanish colonies in Latin America. They exported great quantities of manufactured woollens and imported gold, silver and diamonds, mostly brought from Brazil. Like the Huguenots, the Sephardic Jews had family connections in strategic places in Europe, particularly in Amsterdam, and so were drawn into dealing in bills of exchange. A Jewish merchant claimed in 1753 that 'The Dutch Jews take such bills for a trifling profit, being by their correspondence more expert in this branch than any other people.' The other area in which Jews were prominent was the import of uncut diamonds from India, and it is said that the first generation of Sephardic Jews in Britain made London the international centre of the diamond trade. The East India Company relinquished the trade to private merchants in the late seventeenth century, the earliest instance of private enterprise in the Far Eastern trade.[33]

Reference to the Jews as being prominent in Britain's premier export trade (woollens) and in the trade in the precious metals may lead to the supposition that they were already the richest ethnic group in the merchant community, but this is not the case. Analysis of shareholding in the Bank of England, East India Company and South Sea Company leaves no doubt that the Huguenot families were not only the most numerous but also the wealthiest, and that only two or three Jews were in the same bracket as the most eminent merchant–financiers of the first half of the eighteenth century.[34] Jewish sources suggest that in 1753 there were only twenty opulent Jewish families in the mercantile community, all belonging to the Bevis Marks Synagogue, where the official language was Portuguese until 1819.[35] In the second half of the eighteenth century a handful of Ashkenazi (German-speaking) Jews came to London from Amsterdam and Frankfurt but they were operating on a more modest scale, very much on the edges of the market. A dozen of

---

[33] G. Yogev, *Diamonds and Coral. Anglo-Dutch Jews in Eighteenth-Century Trade* (Leicester 1978) Chs. 1–4; quotation p. 56.

[34] P. G. M. Dickson, *The Financial Revolution in England* (1967) Ch. 12. L. B. Namier, *Politics at the Accession of George III* (1957) p. 56.

[35] James Picciotto, *Sketches of Anglo-Jewish History* (1875) pp. 93–4. Eighty lesser families were active as brokers.

them, including Levy Barent Cohen, the future father-in-law of N. M. Rothschild, bought damaged fabrics from the East India Company first from Amsterdam then by settling in London.[36] The Sephardim regarded themselves as superior to all other Jews, and their connections with the Ashkenazim were quite peripheral.

The Dutch merchants who settled in Britain were, as we have seen, the smallest of the three ethnic groups mentioned, but undoubtedly they were the most opulent. In the seventeenth century Amsterdam was the premier centre of international trade and finance but as its position was gradually usurped by London and competition intensified, Dutch merchants became increasingly involved in financial dealings rather than trade in commodities. They took an early interest in British investments, and in 1750 Dutch residents owned 78 per cent of the foreign holdings of Bank, East India and South Sea stock. Foreigners who invested or speculated in London funds found it necessary to retain a permanent resident in the City, in practice often a member of their own family. As early as 1724 there were more than fifty London agents of Dutch stockholders. A British government loan issue of 1759 shows that dependence on a clique of Dutch and Huguenot financiers. The Van Necks, the leaders of the Dutch colony, had intimate business and family connections with the Huguenot families who had settled in London.[37]

The international community created by these migrations was sustained by the common practice of sending young entrants to the business for a period of experience with a favoured foreign correspondent. By the early eighteenth century it seems to have been a custom for English youths from the leading houses to serve an apprenticeship in Holland and Dutch ones in England. However, the more important development was the growing practice of sending younger sons to open a branch house in London. The process can be seen most clearly in the history of the Huguenot connection, from which it appears that some of the most eminent families were not represented in London until the middle decades of the century.[38] A similar process, though on a much smaller scale, can

[36] G. Yogev, *Diamonds and Coral*, pp. 259–60, 286. A. Deitz, *Frankfurter Handelsgeschichte* (1925). Amsterdam Municipal Archives, Brant MSS, Nash & Eddowes to Deneufville 17 Jan. 1760. Pierre Pluchon, *Nègres et juifs aux XVIIIᵉs.* (Paris 1984) p. 60.

[37] C. Wilson, *Anglo-Dutch Commerce and Finance in the Eighteenth Century* (Cambridge 1941) pp. 62–6, 97, 111–114. P. G. M. Dickson, *Financial Revolution*, pp. 317, 324.

[38] P. G. M. Dickson, *Financial Revolution*, p. 319. H. Lüthy, *Banque protestante*.

be glimpsed in the cloth trade of Exeter, Bristol and Leeds, where branches of established Huguenot and German Jewish houses were moving into the trade.[39] The migrations were, however, only a trickle compared with the German exodus that took place during and after the French Wars, but that is a subject better left for later chapters.

DIVERSIFICATION

In his celebrated work *Civilisation and Capitalism* Braudel insists that the most outstanding characteristic of the merchant was that he was a general trader rather than a specialist. The seventeenth and eighteenth centuries saw the creation of chains of middlemen in all the important branches of trade (whether wool, cloth, grain, coal or whatever), but the wholesale merchant stood above this system. This was not simply a matter of prudence, of spreading risks across a range of commodities and investments. Rather was it that the mercantile function was, as Braudel writes, 'an indivisibility of interest...standing at the commanding heights of the economy'. He explains that 'as the trading community constantly renewed its structures, there seems to have been one position virtually unassailable, and which by virtue of its very impregnability was strengthened and confirmed as divisions and subdivisions multiplied at lower levels: that of the wholesale merchant with many interests'.[40] The merchant at the apex of the capitalist system is a theme to which we shall turn in various parts of this book; for the moment the priority is to focus on the diversity of interests characteristic of the eighteenth-century merchant.

Probably the earliest and most important mercantile investment was that in ship-owning. The traditional English system of division of the ownership of a vessel into numerous shares evidently originated to spread risks, and was very much older than the practice of insurance in North European ports. Indeed, merchants and ship-owners were not regarded as separate occupations until the nineteenth century. The eighteenth century saw the emergence of a distinct insurance industry which made it less necessary for the shipping entrepreneur to spread his risks, but the old practice of shareholding still continued, sustained by the network of merchant

---

[39] S. D. Chapman *The Devon Cloth Industry in the Eighteenth Century* (Torquay 1978) p. xviii. R. G. Wilson, *Gentleman Merchants*, pp. 20–2. W. E. Minchinton, 'Merchants', p. 24.
[40] F. Braudel, *Civilisation* II, p. 381.

connections that provided assurance as well as insurance in a business in which the individual operator still felt highly vulnerable to unpredictable loss.[41]

It was natural, too, that merchants should be centrally involved in the early development of insurance as a service industry. Insurance brokers and underwriters appear as a distinct specialism about the middle of the eighteenth century, sometimes recruited from the ranks of merchants. Unfortunately there is no adequate history of Lloyds to trace this story in detail. The position with the insurance companies is better documented; in 1780 fifty-three out of the eighty-four directorships of the Sun, Royal Exchange and London Assurance Companies were occupied by merchants of one kind or another. Only the Phoenix, a late eighteenth-century development, was dominated by manufacturers. Investment in insurance company shares was much like that in other company shares such as the Bank of England and East India Company already referred to, and here again the majority of investors were merchants and financiers.[42]

The subject of mercantile investment in landed estate has become a controversial area for historians. In *An Open Elite? England 1540–1880*, Lawrence Stone and his wife insist that only a handful of the very richest merchants sought to buy landed estates and merge into the landed class. Their case is based on an analysis of estate ownership in three very different counties over 340 years. More recently, F. M. L. Thompson has been examining the investments of the very rich in the nineteenth century and found that practically all millionaires bought estates, and a significant percentage of them were merchants.[43]

The 'gentrification' of the most successful merchants has been identified in places as far apart as Leeds, Hull, Glasgow, Whitehaven and Manchester, but it must not be supposed that investment in land and country houses represented a serious haemorrhage of enterprise. An analysis of the economic activities of seventy-four men who served as Aldermen of the City of London between 1738 and 1763 suggests that 'the quest for landed status became less compulsive as

---

[41] R. Davis, *English Shipping*, pp. 87–90.
[42] T. S. Ashton, *Eighteenth Century*, pp. 132–4. R. Clews, *A Textbook of Insurance Broking* (1980) Ch. 1. C. Trebilcock, *Phoenix Assurance* (Cambridge 1985) I, p. 33. P. G. Dickson, *Financial Revolution*, p. 302.
[43] L. and J. C. F. Stone, *An Open Elite? England 1540–1880* (Oxford 1984). F. M. L. Thompson, 'Life after Death: How Successful Nineteenth-Century Business Men Disposed of their Fortunes', *Econ. Hist. Rev.* XLIII (1990).

the century advanced' and 'rarely did it lead to a dramatic exodus from trade'.[44]

Investment in colonial plantations might be thought of as a variant on the theme of landed investment, but here credit entered the equation. By and large merchants and plantation owners were separate groups of people, though every planter was supported by a merchant at one stage or another of his enterprise, and this led in the late eighteenth-century West Indies sugar plantations to such accumulations of debt that most were practically owned by merchants in the home country.[45] But this was ownership by default of payment and merchants resident in England preferred more liquid and less troublesome assets than plantations. The general situation may perhaps be best illustrated by an anonymous pamphlet written about 1805, most likely by Alexander Baring or one of his mercantile associates in the USA. 'The astonishingly low prices of lands in America have hitherto been occasioned by the want of capital to invest in them', he opined. 'Only a few European capitalists have lately understood the subject', and he, being one of the few, invested a fortune in Maine, but the whole speculation proved to be a fiasco.[46]

The notion of merchants being active in eighteenth-century industry is familiar to most students of economic and social history, for the origins of the factory system are often traced back to the Lombe brothers (Sir Thomas and John), London merchants who built the Derby silk mill in 1719–21. But after this date the standard works may appear confusing. Dr R. G. Wilson insists that 'Manufacturing and merchanting were never combined in the Leeds area', though he recognises the two operations had long been united in Halifax and Huddersfield because the industrial units in the kersey and worsted industry were much larger than those in the broad woollen cloth manufacture. Perhaps it was a question of scale; merchants became manufacturers when the initial capital requirements of the factory age were too much for the traditional artisan leadership of the industry they served. This proposition finds positive

[44] R. G. Wilson, *Gentleman Merchants*, pp. 230–6. J. V. Beckett, *Coal and Tobacco. The Lowthers and the Economic Development of West Cumberland 1660–1760* (Cambridge 1981) p. 114. Wadsworth and Mann, *Cotton Trade*, p. 242. N. Rogers, 'Money, Land and Lineage', *Social History* IV (1979).
[45] R. Pares, *Merchants and Planters* (Cambridge 1960) pp. 5, 41, 44.
[46] (Anon.), *Facts and Calculations respecting the Population and Territory of the U.S.A.* (1805), copy in Bank Mees & Hope MSS PA 735. T. Doerflinger, *Revolutionary Philadelphia*, pp. 320–1.

support in Leeds at the end of the century to the extent that several woollen merchants there, no doubt appreciating the challenge to their industry presented by the rise of cotton, invested substantial sums in building and equipping large cotton mills in the town. The Lombe brothers, building their pioneer silk mill in the new hosiery manufacturing region, fit easily into this thesis.[47] This is an important topic to which we will revert in Chapter 2 for closer examination.

Somewhat earlier in the century similar developments can be discerned in London. The country's principal port was the nursery for a number of new industries based on foreign imports or foreign technology, and it is not surprising that the capital and enterprise were often provided by the merchants who brought home the materials that were processed or imitated. The oriental technique of calico printing offers a good illustration of the point. The early factories were all built around London, in several instances with partners who were active importing continental linens which were being displaced by printed Indian calicoes and muslins. Local imitations, often sold in America, offered an alternative outlet for enterprise and capital.

When the industry began to shift its location to Lancashire, the necessary credits were provided by London merchants. The actual migration of industry to the provinces and creation of a national economy was the consequence of the building of a transport system for bulk commodities, which in the eighteenth century context meant a canal network. Research has shown that the larger part of the capital required for the canal system was subscribed by merchants.[48]

The evidence assembled so far provides ample illustration of the diversification of merchants' interests from two apparent motives, the spreading of risks and the extension into adjacent areas to increase or guarantee their existing business when other enterprise was in some way inadequate. The evidence from Glasgow and South Wales presents merchants in an even bolder role, particularly in the first half of the eighteenth century, that of prime generators of the region's industrial economy. T. M. Devine's *The Tobacco Lords*

---

[47] R. G. Wilson, *Gentleman Merchants*, pp. 59–60. Pat Hudson, *The Genesis of Industrial Capital. A Study of the West Riding Wool Textile Industry c. 1750–1850* (Cambridge 1986) p. 261. S. D. Chapman, 'Fixed Capital Formation in the British Cotton Industry', *Econ. Hist. Rev.* XXIII (1970) pp. 259–60.

[48] S. D. Chapman and S. Chassagne, *European Textile Printers*, pp. 28–9. J. R. Ward, 'Investment in Canals in England 1760–1815', D.Phil. thesis, Oxford 1970, p. 97.

investigates the origins of a whole range of manufacturing enterprise in the Scottish Lowlands and concludes that 'there would appear to be a fairly close correlation between the rise of tobacco commerce and the foundation of manufactories'. The system developed by the Scottish merchants involved the exchange of European consumer goods for the primary produce (especially tobacco) of Virginia and Maryland, and once financial resources allowed there was an obvious advantage in having some of the sources of supply in the immediate neighbourhood of Glasgow and under their control. Hence merchant investment in textile factories, ironworks, tanneries, soapworks, bottleworks and sugar houses.[49]

The South Wales iron industry was inaugurated and financed primarily by merchants from London and Bristol, with a small injection of enterprise from the Midlands. There was no indigenous industry or enterprise to speak of before the middle of the eighteenth century, while there was an upsurge in demand for iron during the Seven Years War (1756–63) and the American War of Independence. In much the same way, the Derbyshire iron industry was largely generated and capitalised by mercantile resources because local resources proved quite inadequate. As late as the middle of the nineteenth century, the largest works in Derbyshire (that at Staveley, near Chesterfield) was built up on a fortune made in London in the China trade.[50]

Dr Devine's ultimate explanation of this striking enterprise brings us back to Braudel. He reminds us that our division of economic activity into 'commerce' and 'industry' would have seemed artificial in the eighteenth century for the period was not one of functional specialisation. Standing at the apex of the economic period, the merchant directed his capital and other resources where the pressures and opportunities of the times suggested they would earn most and preferably where he could retain a high degree of liquidity of his assets.[51]

[49] T. M. Devine, *Tobacco Lords*, pp. 34–5, 46–7.
[50] A. H. John, *The Industrial Development of South Wales* (Cardiff 1950) pp. 24–5. S. D. Chapman, *Stanton & Staveley. A History* (1981) p. 41.
[51] T. M. Devine, *Tobacco Lords*, p. 34.

Table 1.3. *London's share of English trade in the eighteenth century (per cent)*

	Imports	Exports of English produce & manufactures	Re-exports
1700	80	69	86
1750	71	62	70
1780	63	52	56
1800	66	62	

Source: E. B. Schumpeter, *English Overseas Trade Statistics 1697–1808* (Oxford 1960) pp. 9–10.

THE DOMINATION OF LONDON

All the available sources confirm the major role played by London in English trade in the eighteenth century. The most complete statistical series are those for imports, exports and re-exports, which show the degree to which trade was concentrated in the metropolis (Table 1.3).

The most obvious explanation lies in traditional trading ties with the Continent, in which London had a clear geographical advantage over the northern and western ports, and the capital's monopoly of the East India trade. However there also appears to have been some cumulative advantages in the country's most important traditional trade, the export of woollens. Though the woollens exported were manufactured in the West Country (Glos., Wilts. and Devon), East Anglia and the West Riding, and each region had its exporting port, 78 per cent of the exports were shipped from London in the period 1715–40. It was the rise of direct exports from Exeter, Bristol, Hull, Yarmouth and other centres that first began to reduce London's share of the trade.[52]

The most comprehensive information on the relative importance of the various ports is drawn from records of shipping registered there (Table 1.4). London easily maintained its lead but grew less rapidly than several of its provincial rivals. However, this information is of only limited value in a study of merchants and overseas trade, for several of the major growth points, especially

[52] House of Commons returns cited in N.I.R.O. T2812/11/1/4. R. Davis, *English Shipping*, Ch. 2.

Table 1.4. *Shipping owned in some leading English ports (000s tons)*

	1702	1788	multiplier
London	140	315	2·25
Newcastle	11	106	9·65
Liverpool	9	76	8·85
Sunderland	4	54	13·74
Whitehaven	7	52	7·26
Hull	8	52	6·85
Whitby	8	48	5·77
Bristol	17	38	2·18
Yarmouth	10	36	3·67
Exeter	7	12	1·62

Source: Ralph Davis, *The Rise of the English Shipping Industry* (1962), p. 35. The ports listed are the largest nine in 1788, plus Exeter.

Newcastle and Sunderland, were more geared to the expansion of the domestic coal trade. Ports with a long-standing interest in the old woollen export business (Bristol, Exeter and Yarmouth) do not seem to have grown so fast as London.

To obtain a clearer view of the rise of new centres of trade it will be necessary to draw on another set of figures. Information compiled by Jacob Price has the merit of focusing on the importance of the rising transatlantic trade in various centres, including Glasgow, which is of course not included in English calculations. The interest of Liverpool and Manchester appears small at this period but was evidently rising rapidly (Table 1.5); during the next twenty years Liverpool leaped ahead of Bristol and by the end of the American War its trade was twice the size of its old rival.[53]

There is ample evidence of the vigour of the enterprise in the provincial centres of trade through the eighteenth century. Glasgow interest in the tobacco trade outstripped that of London by 1750. Leeds, Halifax and Wakefield merchants captured much of the trade of the Blackwell Hall factors (London cloth merchants), first of the markets to southern Europe, then to the Americas. Their enterprise led to the exporting of some two-thirds of Yorkshire's output in the third quarter of the century. In Philadelphia such was the

[53] *Universal British Directory* III (1791) Liverpool section, gives the following customs returns for 1784: London £5·19m., Liverpool £0·64m., Bristol £0·33m.

Table 1.5. *Debts owing to British merchants trading to North America*
estimated in 1766

	£m.	index
To London	2·9	100·0
To Glasgow	0·9	31·0
To Bristol	0·8	27·6
To Liverpool	0·15	5·2
To Manchester	0·1	3·4
To all other centres	0·25	8·6
	5·1	

Source: based on Jacob M. Price, *Capital and Credit in British Overseas Trade*
(Harvard 1980), pp. 10–11.

competition that it was remarked in 1789 that 'The Manchester
folks have made all the retail *shopkeepers* and merchants' *apprentices*
importers!' Liverpool was known to be the fastest-growing port.[54]

Nevertheless, a good deal of this provincial enterprise was financed
by London capital. At mid-century, as has often been noticed, there
was not more than a score of banks outside London, and they were
not spread very evenly. Provincial banks were a relatively late
arrival because the economy of Britain revolved round London, and
the bill of exchange of a London merchant, factor or warehouseman
provided both the credit and the currency for wholesale buying and
selling operations.[55] Henry Thornton, a London merchant in the
Russian trade, wrote in 1802 that London had become, 'especially
of late, the trading metropolis of Europe and, indeed, of the whole
world; the foreign drafts (i.e. bills of exchange) on account of
merchants living in our outports and other trading towns, and
carrying on business there, being made, with scarcely any exceptions,
payable in London'. Thornton wrote from personal experience, for
twenty years earlier his firm had discounted bills in Amsterdam but
were now themselves acting as guarantors for the payment of
Russian bills of exchange.[56] The clearest documentation in the
provinces refers to the textile industries of Lancashire, Yorkshire and

---

[54] Jacob Price, *France and the Chesapeake* (1973) I, p. 590. Pat Hudson, *Genesis*, p. 156. J. Aikin,
   The Country from 30 to 40 miles round manchester (1795) p. 564. T. Doerflinger, *Revolutionary
   Philadelphia*, p. 53. See also below, Chapter 4.
[55] L. S. Pressnell, *Country Banking in the Industrial Revolution* (Oxford 1956) Ch. 1.
[56] H. Thornton, *An Inquiry into Paper Credit* (1802) p. 59. Bank Mees & Hope MSS, accounts.

the West Country. By the 1780s every Manchester merchant and manufacturer found it necessary to employ a London merchant as banker as other bills were likely to be declined for payment. The working relation between the two parties was sometimes so close that they formed partnerships.[57] With industrial growth, the system was changing rapidly in the late eighteenth century, as the next chapter will show.

THE ROLE OF DISSENTERS

Ever since Weber wrote his *Protestant Ethic and the Spirit of Capitalism*, British historians have been fascinated by the role of Dissenters in economic life, but the relation, if there is one, between religious ideology and entrepreneurship has proved unusually elusive. It has for long been widely believed that Dissenters were particularly prominent in the mercantile and industrial enterprise of the country, but there were so many varieties of dissent, with such a bewildering array of theologies, that it seems practically impossible to find a common element of ideology and practice beyond distaste for the Church of England and Roman Catholic Church.[58] The most recent research concludes from a close analysis of church and chapel followings that Dissenters held about as many professional, mercantile and retail positions as Anglicans, but with significant variations between particular places of worship, denominations and towns. It appears that Bristol, Liverpool and Hull had a somewhat higher percentage of merchants in their chapels than churches, while in Newcastle the Church of England was still the major force.[59] London is the great unknown in this matter. The position of Bristol, the most prominent centre of dissent among the provincial ports, is summarised in Table 1.6 for a date at which religious nonconformity was at a pinnacle of popularity. The Evans census of 1717 tabulated here contains the comment that the Quakers included some who were 'large traders and very rich', while the Presbyterian congregations contained numbers of merchants including several who were 'great promotors of the woollen manufacture' in the West of

---

[57] Wadsworth & Mann, *Cotton Trade*, pp. 92–6. Pat Hudson, *Genesis*, pp. 119, 135. J. de L. Mann, *The Cloth Industry in the West of England 1640–1880* (Oxford 1971) pp. 80–3. P.R.O. E112/1535/411, Lingard *v.* Main (1806). E112/1758/5286, Harrison *v.* Harrison (1794).
[58] T. S. Ashton, *Eighteenth Century* (1955) p. 20.
[59] J. E. Bradley, *Religion, Revolution and English Radicalism* (Cambridge 1990) pp. 61–9.

Table 1.6. *Dissent in Bristol in 1717*

Sect	Chapels	Members	Incomes	Average	per cent of town population
Presbyterians	5	c. 4,300	£770,000	c. £200	22
Quakers	?	2,000+	£500,000	c. £250	10
Totals		c. 6,300	£1,270,000		32

Source: John Evans' list of Dissenting Congregations, 1717, p. 147 (Dr Williams' library, London WC1). The original report refers to 'wealth' but this evidently means incomes rather than capital (see Table 1.1).

England. The calculation of *average* incomes produces a remarkably high figure, but is broadly consistent with the historian's impression that at this period the wealth of Bristol and its hinterland were second only to that of London.[60]

More specific information on the occupational distribution of one branch of dissent is given in the minute books of the Bristol Quakers. Of 330 men listed between 1682 and 1704, nearly a third were wholesalers of one kind or another and approaching 10 per cent general merchants.[61] It was during this period that Defoe toured the area and reported that 'it was no extraordinary thing to have clothiers in that country worth from £10,000 to £40,000 [capital] a man, and many of the great families who now pass for gentry in those counties have been originally raised from and built up by this truly noble (woollen) manufacture'.[62] He might have added that many of the great families were also members of the dissenting chapels, and in this respect at least were significantly different from the old land-owning class. Interest in dissent appears to have declined in the middle decades of the eighteenth century but in Manchester an American visitor noticed in 1777 that 'The Dissenters are some of the most wealthy merchants and manufacturers here.' Nonconformist religion was an expression of middle class emancipation from the traditional structure of society with its 'vertical' loyalties to the

---

[60] C. G. A. Clay, *Economic Expansion and Social Change: England 1500–1700* (Cambridge 1984) I, p. 201.
[61] R. T. Vann, 'Quakerism: Made in America?' in R. S. and M. M. Dunn, eds., *The World of William Penn* (Philadelphia 1986) p. 161.
[62] D. Defoe, *A Tour through the Whole Island of Great Britain* (1724–6) 1927 edn, I, p. 282.

squire and parson, so it is not altogether surprising to find support for the belief that many, if not most merchants were Dissenters.[63] Less detailed or specific information is available for London but it seems most probable that a majority of merchants were non-Anglicans simply because such a large part of them were of foreign extraction. Huguenot, Jewish, Dutch and German settlers all built their own places of worship, especially in the districts where they were most numerous. However, these churches were no more familiar landmarks of urban life than the chapels of English Dissenters. Merchants are known to have been prominent in some branches of the 'Old Dissent', especially the Presbyterians, Independents (Congregationalists) and Quakers. The first of these declined during the century, to be superseded at the end by the Unitarians.

So far as eighteenth-century mercantile enterprise is concerned, dissent seems to be important in three ways, connections, doctrine and credit. In the eighteenth century communications were still slow and difficult, and the ultimate problem of the overseas merchant was maintaining understanding, policy and trust with correspondents that he might meet or speak to only at intervals of several years. The easiest way of bridging the trading centres was by the spontaneous harmony of thought processes and values within a family, but, as no family was large enough to include correspondents in all its supply ports and market, merchants had to seek correspondents with whom there was a significant degree of empathy. Membership of a dissenting chapel and sect introduced the merchant to an international community which shared and sometimes enforced similar values and outlook, including those of commercial ethics. Integrity was a *sine qua non* of long-term survival in trade and its precepts were preached in chapel and synagogue.[64]

If this point seems little more than common sense, religious bigotry made it less obvious to eighteenth-century minds. Despite the relative toleration of liberalism of the age, some sects were still actively disliked and there was much hostility to Jews, who were widely regarded as dishonest. The truth was perceived by Bethmann, Frankfurt's leading Christian banker, in 1805. 'As for the morality of the Jews, as for the Christians, our century can make no boast, it is in the prime interest of every man who wants to succeed to be

[63] H. Perkin, *The Origins of Modern English Society* (1969) pp. 196ff. J. Seed, 'Gentleman Dissenters', *Historical Journal* xxviii (1985).
[64] P. H. Emden, *Quakers in Commerce* (1940). G. Yogev, *Diamonds and Coral*.

upright and faithful in his transactions...'[65] Some of the Dissenters set new standards of commercial morality, and Jacob Price, the leading American authority on eighteenth-century trade, ascribes the long life of Quaker businesses to this factor.[66]

In the later eighteenth century some significant differences in the economic ideology of different sects appeared, particularly in the matter of use of wealth. The best-documented contrasting cases are the Unitarians and Quakers. The Unitarian churches attracted some of the wealthiest merchants of Liverpool, Manchester, Leeds, Hull, Newcastle and other commercial towns but required little commitment nor an ascetic life style. 'Owing their situation...neither to blind fate nor to divine will but, they believed, to their own hard work, calculation and planning, they found rational dissent legitimating both the accumulation of capital and the enjoyment of its fruits.'[67] Quaker merchants were prominent in the trade of London, Bristol and Liverpool, having strong transatlantic ties with Philadelphia and other Puritan towns of the USA. Quaker letters and diaries are full of forebodings about the consequences of wealth, while discipline and teaching required members to devote a part of their time to charitable and public work. Refusing to benefit from war, they sometimes lost major trading opportunities, as during the American War of Independence.

The whole of the increasingly complex structure of trade depended on the provision of credit, in which merchants played a pivotal role. Credit required trust, and trust could only be accorded to customers whose means and probity were assured. Merchants regularly exchanged confidential information on actual and potential customers, but there was no substitute for personal knowledge. The intimate family and religious ties of some dissenting sects (especially Huguenots and Quakers) and some other minorities (notably Jews) provided the vehicles for the transmission of credit and trading reports, spanning the major trading centres. As communications steadily improved, such connections became rather less essential, but in the course of this book it will be seen that they retained a place for most of the nineteenth century.

[65] Amsterdam Municipal Archives, Hope MSS, PA 753/24, information books III, no. 235.
[66] J. M. Price, 'The Great Quaker Business Families of Eighteenth-Century London', in R. S. and M. M. Dunn, eds., *William Penn*.
[67] John Seed, 'The Role of Unitarianism in the Formation of Liberal Culture 1775–1851: A Social History', Ph.D. thesis (Hull 1981) p. 108.

Table 1.7. *The increase of trade and merchant bankruptcy in England*
(1700, 1759) and Great Britain (1800)

Period	Nos. of merchants	Overseas trade	Average capital per merchant
c. 1700	10.000	£8·3m.	£8,000
c. 1759	13,000	£10·8m.	£12,000
c. 1800	15,000	£87·0m.	£50,000
		average bankrupt	*bankruptcy rate*
c. 1700	10,000	325	1 in 308
c. 1759	13,000	294	1 in 386
c. 1800	15,000	644	1 in 233

Source: Overseas trade data (net imports + domestic exports) calculated from R. Davis, 'English Foreign Trade 1700–1774' *Econ. Hist. Rev.* xv (1962–3) and his *Industrial Revolution and Trade* (1979) p. 86. The periods chosen to correspond with the available figures on numbers of merchants (Table 1.1) are 1697–1701, 1752–1754 and 1804–1806. Bankruptcy data in Julian Hoppit, *Risk and Failure in English Business 1700–1800* (Cambridge 1987), p. 97. The periods chosen are 1701–10, 1755–64 and 1791–1800. For merchant capital, see p. 26 above.

THE GROWTH OF TRADE AND OF MERCANTILE
BANKRUPTCY

The eighteenth century was unquestionably a period that saw a considerable growth in British overseas trade; no doubt that there were considerable fluctuations in both imports, exports and re-exports but the overall trend was undoubted (Table 1.7). Allowing for inflation, average capital per merchant doubled in the last forty years of the century. This was a climate in which merchants should have prospered and contemporaries were in no doubt that merchant incomes – and particularly those of the top class of merchants – were rising, and indeed rising fast towards the end of the century (Table 1.1). However, it is also true that the bankruptcy rate among merchants was rising in the later decades of the century (Table 1.7) and this complicating factor needs some explanation as the high mortality of enterprises will be a recurrent theme throughout this book.

Julian Hoppit identifies merchants as the most vulnerable group of his study because they, more than any other class of entrepreneurs, shouldered the burden of the major risks in the running of the economy. As communications gradually improved and experience grew, it seems that the risk of failure diminished somewhat, but that trend was reversed in the acceleration of economic growth that took place soon after mid-century, despite the great increase in merchant capital. Hoppit thinks that increasing opportunities prompted a growth in risk taking and attracted new entrants to trade, but simultaneously there was an increase in the less predictable elements in the merchants' calculations as more traditional industries and manufacturing regions (e.g. serge making in Devon) gave way to new ones (e.g. worsteds in the West Riding). Many merchants were also driven into bankruptcy as a result of the American War of Independence (1775–83) and the Revolutionary War (1793–1801).

We may accept his point but with two riders. The restructuring of the economy in the Industrial Revolution period is increasingly seen as more gradual than was once supposed. Significant industrial growth was already taking place in the first half of the century which had profound implications for merchants. In this period two mercantile tendencies are discernible which, in a very modest way, foreshadow the more momentous developments associated with the Industrial Revolution and the nineteenth century. British manufacturers, sometimes aided by preferential customs, were beginning to make the country more self-sufficient in several products and so lessened the need of various imports and consequently of the old-style general merchants. There was also a concomitant tendency for merchants in the sectors of overseas trade closest to home, notably Ireland and Holland, to lose business to direct connections between manufacturers, who were growing stronger, and overseas customers. The overall growth in trade and continued increase in the number of merchant houses swamped this counter tendency, but it is worth consideration at the conclusion of this chapter as a harbinger of future changes.

Self-sufficiency is a key development that can be illustrated from the experience of linen, one of the more important manufactured products in pre-industrial England. At the end of the seventeenth century most of the imported linen came from Holland, but Dutch merchants brought it from Westphalia, Silesia, Juliers, Flanders and Brabant, bleaching it in Haarlem. During the course of the first half of the eighteenth century, Irish and Scottish linen superseded continental supplies. Though customs protection offered material help, advancing technology, particularly at the bleaching and printing stages, helped British manufacturers to rely less and less on overseas supplies. 'The Irish...have been getting ground of you for some years, and as this further duty is laid upon Hollands, the sale of Irish linens must necessarily increase', a London merchant wrote to his correspondent in Amsterdam in 1747. Meanwhile, London, Dublin and (somewhat later) Glasgow rose as centres of fine textile printing and Leeds and Barnsley of linen production, while Amsterdam declined. In 1751 another London merchant house wrote to Amsterdam that 'your printers cannot possibly execute those fine patterns like ours', and in 1765 the British Consul in Rotterdam reported that 'All the shops of the country [Holland] are filled with English printed linens, which is the common summer wear in all the towns.' By this date printed textiles were reckoned to be the largest single item of European trade along with colonial goods (tobacco, sugar etc.) so the loss to Holland was no small matter.[68]

Some similar developments are discernible in other branches of industry. The migration of Huguenots at the end of the seventeenth century gave London a firm foothold in the silk industry and so diminished dependence on French exports. The rise of the English framework knitting (hosiery) industry in the first half of the eighteenth century was so strong that Amsterdam manufacturers gave up and their frames were sold in Mansfield (Notts.). Small metal goods enjoyed a comparable measure of success.[69]

The proximity of Holland and Ireland, and the large British trading communities in both countries, made it easy for London wholesalers to import direct from those countries, bypassing the general merchant. There is quite a lot of contemporary comment on this development. As early as 1714, an Exeter merchant was complaining that 'the shopkeepers of London sell German linens here...cheaper than is done by the merchants here', and this practice increased through the first half of the century until, in 1755, it was said that 'the trade is now entirely in the drapers' hands'. From the 1760s bankruptcy rates among linen drapers was unusually high. In much the same way, but at a slightly later date, Irish manufacturers and bleachers learned to bypass the merchants of Dublin. A similar development evidently took place in the silk trade, where Robert Carr & Co., the most successful London mercer from

[68] L. Bergeron, *Banquiers, négociants et manufacturiers parisiens*, p. 189.
[69] N. K. A. Rothstein, 'Silk Industry', p. 225. D. J. Ormrod, 'Anglo-Dutch Commerce', p. 17. H. Hamilton, *The English Brass and Copper Industries* (1926) p. 300.

the 1730s to the 1760s, imported silk on his own account. Merchants also lost ground in the export trade when continental buyers ordered direct from West Country and Yorkshire clothiers. No doubt such discouraging changes encouraged enterprising merchants to look farther afield for more profitable ventures.[70]

In this first half of the century we have seen that there are some interesting examples of merchants who moved into manufacturing (usually, it seems, to procure supplies that were not otherwise available) but this line of development was still relatively unusual. In the second half of the century the opportunities were so much greater and the incomes and capitals of successful merchants rising so rapidly that more found the chance of profit difficult to resist. This is probably the important dimension of increased risk that Hoppit misses, for merchants who had diversified into manufacturing continued to describe themselves only by their former occupation.[71] At any rate, the subject is so important both for understanding the subject and for the subsequent evolution of the structure of mercantile enterprise that it must be reserved for the next chapter.

[70] N. B. Harte, 'Linen', pp. 87–91. L. M. Cullen, *Anglo-Irish Trade* (1968) p. 108. N. K. A. Rothstein, 'Silk Industry', p. 225. D. J. Ormrod, 'Anglo-Dutch Commerce', pp. 194–5. A. N. 57 AQ 108, information book of Massieu of Caen 1758–80.
[71] J. Hoppit, *Risk and Failure in English Business 1700–1800* (Cambridge 1987) Ch. 9.

CHAPTER 2

The consequences of the Industrial Revolution and the French Wars

One of the features of the Industrial Revolution that has often been remarked on is the multiplication of the functions of entrepreneurs as merchants became manufacturers and financiers and manufacturers extended to importing, exporting, finance, landholding and other activities. This development increased the number of people engaged in trade and further blurred the traditional boundaries of mercantile enterprise. The increase of economic activity broadly coincided with long and difficult periods of war, notably those with the American colonists (1776–83) and with the French (1793–1815), which enervated or destroyed much hereditary enterprise and introduced some unprecedented opportunities for new firms. From this ferment there emerged an entirely new structure of mercantile enterprise and finance which lasted until the final quarter of the century. The process of restructuring forms the main subject matter of this chapter.

WAR, TRADE AND ENTERPRISE

The American War of Independence and the French Wars coincided with the periods of major technical innovation and restructuring of the textile and iron industries of Britain. There was major interaction between the political and economic developments of the period and clearly one cannot be adequately understood without the other, but for the purposes of exposition it is convenient to consider them separately at this initial stage. Broadly speaking, war changed the composition of the merchant body by placing a premium on bold entrepreneurship and by the arrival of a new wave of refugees, while new industrial development changed the traditional functions of both merchant and manufacturer. In this section we concentrate on the effects of war.

In the literature of economic and social history war has been recognised as a source of considerable commercial and industrial profit for most of the eighteenth century from the increase in demand for ships, ordnance and victualling contracts. Some of the most successful merchants of the century moved from their provincial homes to London to obtain the government patronage necessary to secure such contracts. Other merchants added to their fortunes by investing in the government loans that invariably accompanied the progress of war.[1] However, such opportunities were only open to those at the pinnacle of wealth, and it is best to start with the more general situation. More generally, war should be recognised as increasing the risks involved in trading in the affected areas, so that a few bold, clever or lucky firms were able to take advantage of the situation and multiply their profits while others languished from dislocation of trade, or were destroyed or enervated by government policies that left them helpless.

In the American War of Independence it is certainly true that a handful of American merchants made unprecedented fortunes but for the great majority the benefits scarcely matched the losses. The numbers of active merchants in Philadelphia fell from about 320 before the War to about 200 towards the end. Before the Revolution few Philadelphia merchants had more than £20,000 capital but by 1790 capitals of more than £20,000 were commonplace.[2] Of course, American experience in this period was not the same as the British, and the record on this side speaks mainly of the losses of those merchants that had extended credit to Americans and failed to have their debts settled. In 1784 Lord Sheffield claimed that the liberal credit system had bankrupted three-quarters of the London merchants trading to the USA, and though this was evidently a partisan account, it is certainly true that eighty London merchants went bankrupt in 1781, 1782 and 1783, while some others never regained their former prosperity.[3] However, it does look as if the North of England, that was riding the crest of the first wave of expansion of the cotton industry, suffered little loss; this is the period in which Arkwright, Peel, Livesey Hargreaves & Co. and other

---

[1] F. Crouzet, 'Wars, Blockade and Economic Change in Europe', *Jnl Econ. Hist.*, XXIV (1964). L. B. Namier, *The Structure of Politics at the Accession of George III* (1928) pp. 45–58. P. G. M. Dickson, *The Financial Revolution in England* (1967).

[2] T. Doerflinger, *A Vigorous Spirit of Enterprise. Merchants and Economic Development in Revolutionary Philadelphia* (Chapel Hill, N.C., 1986) pp. 133–4, 213–15.

[3] J. L. Neel, *Phineas Bond: A Study in Anglo-American Relations* (Pennsylvania 1968) pp. 23–9.

leading manufacturer–merchants made fortunes. Their rise was not unconnected with the misfortunes of the Londoners in various ways. The London merchants were important dealers in linen and printed calicoes, and their stock had traditionally been drawn from the East India Co., the London printers and the Continent. The northern manufacturers now enjoyed the benefit of London credits to produce imitations; at Livesey Hargreaves' bankruptcy in 1788 it was revealed that they had credit from nine London merchants and three bankers, and Peels evidently benefited from similar sources.[4] However, it must not be supposed that the London merchants all lost money during the American War; indeed there are some indications of substantial gains. Thus a Philadelphia firm wrote in 1794 that Harrison, Ansley & Co. of London 'have been by far the greatest shippers here since the war, as well as in a considerable degree a few years previous to it...'; this notwithstanding the fact that the firm were in the textile trade, were still carrying a quantity of pre-war debts in the early 1790s and still providing 'the usual credit of 12 months'.[5] Similarly David Barclay & Sons, the linen merchants already identified as one of the leading houses in Anglo-American trade before the War, not only survived the long interruption of trade but shortly emerged as City bankers, and founders of the company that still bears their name.[6]

Econometric work has demonstrated that the French Wars slowed British economic growth by diverting savings to military expenditure and depressing living standards, but, aided by the flight of continental merchant capital, such problems did not discourage the bolder entrepreneurs.[7] The most successful British merchant of the age left a clear record of his experience in a letter to his Amsterdam friend Henry Hope at the end of 1802:

Commerce... in my opinion... not only increases but produces more profit and furnishes the means of a more beneficial employ for capital, nay I will go a step further to a point that the risk has diminished in proportion as the profits have increased. I am justified in this opinion by my experience for

[4] S. D. Chapman and S. Chassagne, *European Textile Printers in the Eighteenth Century* (1981), Ch. 1. See also *Circular to Bankers* 15 Aug. 1828.
[5] Library of Congress (USA), Stephens Collins MSS, vol. 64 A (14 June 1794 quoted); see also vol. 25 (esp. 20 Oct 1783) and vol. 41.
[6] Friends Meeting House Library, London, *Directory of Quaker Biography* (typescript) for Barclay.
[7] Larry Neal, *Rise of Financial Capitalism* (Cambridge 1990) Ch. 9. J. G. Williamson, 'Why was British Economic Growth so slow during the Industrial Revolution?' *Jnl Econ. Hist.* XLIV (1984).

I think we have lost less during the whole of the War than we lost in liquidating our peace concerns in the commencement of the War [1793]. The reason is obvious – credits *à découvert* are much curtailed and seldom expected, whilst commercial profits being larger, our correspondents gain by their Adventures [i.e. trading ventures] have of course [become] much safer.

Baring's capital rose steeply from £72,000 in 1790 to peak at £450,000 in 1806. The curtailment of unsecured credits is not surprising, given the hazards of trade in wartime, but it evidently did not put a brake on established houses. Evidence from the West Riding suggests that with increasing competition credit terms *lengthened* during the war years, encouraging smaller firms.[8]

From this time to the end of the War (1815) it was said that mercantile activity became even more bold and speculative. The main reason was the short periods in which Napoleon's embargoes on British trade with Europe were effective (1808 and 1812) and the short war with the US (1812–14). Industry was growing rapidly and there was a desperate search for alternative markets. In the cotton industry numerous merchants were ruined in prospecting new markets, particularly in Buenos Aires in 1806, Rio in the winter of 1808–9, and the Continent at the conclusion of war in 1815–16. Stocks increased rapidly. Much of this activity, according to the contemporary view, was financed by profits made in the Lancashire cotton industry, with manufacturers moving into trade themselves (see next section) or financing Liverpool merchants. At this period it was commonly remarked that Liverpool was mortgaged to Manchester – i.e. that the profits of the spinners, manufacturers and printers furnished the means for the mercantile enterprise of Liverpool.[9] It was said that as many as 90 per cent of the continental merchant houses of London were eliminated during the French Wars, and in Manchester a third were lost, but again these figures no doubt exaggerate the change. While many small firms fell away, there were unquestionably merchants who strengthened their position during these years; among the well-documented cases are James Finlay of Glasgow in the continental trade, Samuel Greg and the Philips family of Manchester in the American trade, and

---

[8] Rijksarchif Amsterdam, Mees & Hope MSS, Diversen Documenten 1802–8, p. 211. Baring Bros. Archives, London, annual accounts. Pat Hudson, *The Genesis of Industrial Capital. A Study of the West Riding Wool Textile Industry* (Cambridge 1986) p. 263. P.R.O. C12/227/2 (1796) shows Baring credit was two years.

[9] F. Crouzet, *L'Economie britannique et le blocus continental* (Paris 1958) II, pp. 238, 617, 695. *Circular to Bankers* 28 Nov. 1828.

Horrocks Miller & Co. of Preston in the Far East trade.[10] Perhaps the more important point is that the period saw a shift in the centre of enterprise from London to the northern centres. As in the earlier period, while many were destroyed or enervated by the chaotic trading conditions of the period, a few emerged with greater wealth and status. The implications of this development will be explored later in the present chapter; for the moment it is necessary to concentrate on another dimension of the northern challenge, that which emanated from the settlement of a new wave of refugees.

The importance of the role played by the Huguenots, Sephardic Jews and Dutch in London commerce and finance was noticed in the last chapter. The French Wars saw the arrival of yet another group, German Jews from Frankfurt and Hamburg. Here again the motives were an unquantifiable mixture of repulsion (arising from war and hostility to religious and ethnic minorities) and the attraction of new trading opportunities. Eighteenth-century Frankfurt saw recurrent struggles between the municipal authority (controlled largely by Lutheran artisans), the colony of foreign merchants (who were mainly Calvinists from France and Switzerland) and the Jewish ghetto. Frankfurt was an international entrepôt and a centre of finance and exchange, rather than a manufacturing city, and numerous Jewish families made a living by money-lending and petty trade in textiles. In the early eighteenth century, a few of them turned to the English trade, which meant importing woollens both from London and from the rising provincial centres such as Leeds, Exeter, Norwich and Halifax, and then cotton goods from London and Lancashire, competing with the richer Huguenot merchants of their city. Eventually a dozen Jewish firms and half-a-dozen Christian ones became dominant in the trade. A trickle of scions of both settled England in the eighteenth century, but the main movement was delayed until the period when Manchester cottons conquered all competition.[11]

Another reason for the settlement of Jewish merchants at this period is connected with the credit structure in Britain. Through the eighteenth century the Bank of England stood at the apex of commercial credit in England and world trade, and the Bank's directors were known to be anti-semitic. There was no secret about

---

[10] M. Lévy-Leboyer, *Les banques européennes* (Paris 1964) p. 513. [C. Brogan], *James Finlay & Co. Ltd.* (Glasgow 1951). M. B. Rose, *The Gregs of Quarry Bank Mill* (Cambridge 1986). Lancs. R.O., Horrocks ledgers DDHs 1. For Philips see below, Ch. 3.

[11] A. Deitz, *Frankfurter Handelsgeschichte* (Frankfurt 1925), iv p. 331 f.

this; it was a recognised feature of their policy. Alexander Baring (son of Sir Francis) wrote in 1836 about a family of Dutch–Jewish financiers of the Napoleonic era: 'In my days of Bank direction [1810–20] we never let the new money jobbers discount there. The Goldsmids who were the Rothschilds of their day and conducted an immense circulation [of bills of exchange] during the week never had an account of discount. I apprehend this is all changed...' In 1815 a well-known firm of London merchants wrote to their Amsterdam correspondents 'Notwithstanding the preference given here to Christian houses, the Jew house you enquire after, B. A. Goldsmid & Co., enjoys excellent credit.' The anomaly of being ostracised by the Bank of England but enjoying 'excellent credit' was carefully explained by Sir Francis Baring:

Before the Revolution our Bank [of England] was the centre upon which all credit and circulation depended, and it was at that time in the power of the Bank to affect the credit of individuals in a very great degree by refusing their paper. The Bank is still the pivot for circulation but no longer for credit and discount. In the distress of 1793, they committed a fatal error by deciding that all merchants and traders were entitled to their proportion of accommodation as the Bank was a public body and ought not to discriminate between individuals... they determined that merchants of the first class should never exceed £50,000 by them and £50,000 more *upon* them...

Following this decision, twenty or more 'inferior houses' found support. Since that time, as a consequence, 'The opinion of the Bank is therefore in a considerable degree a matter of indifference, so long as the credit is good in private discount. Their opinion upon the general solidity of parties may produce an influence upon the credits of individuals but which can never effect you or me.' In other words, at the end of the eighteenth century the favour of the Bank of England became less relevant to status in the City, enabling Jewish houses and other affluent newcomers to take advantage of the opportunities of the period to outpace firms that relied on the Bank's rationed credit. The Rothschilds were the best-known beneficiaries of this fortuitous development, but other continental houses were not slow to follow. The ways in which the new arrivals helped to change the pace and direction of trade forms an important part of the story of mercantile enterprise in this period of change, and will be particularly considered in Chapter 5 of this book.[12]

[12] Various sources cited in S. D. Chapman, *The Raphael Bicentenary 1787–1987* [merchants, bankers and stockbrokers] (privately published, 1987) pp. 7–9.

THE INDUSTRIAL REVOLUTION

In a much-quoted essay called 'The Entrepreneur in the Industrial Revolution', Professor Charles Wilson developed a view that the period saw the extension of the traditional role of the entrepreneur. The distinctive characteristic of the great figures of the period, he wrote, ·'was that they fulfilled in one person the functions of capitalist, financier, works manager, merchant and salesman'. There was a powerful but not ubiquitous tendency, he believes, 'for the entrepreneur's intervention in certain important fields of industry to widen into an all-embracing function'. To illustrate his point, he chose the West Riding of Yorkshire, where rapid growth in the late eighteenth century saw many merchants gaining absolute control over production by becoming manufacturers themselves. The contrast with the decadent cloth industry of Devon, where no such expansion of function took place, seems to make the point.[13]

The problem is that the only historian to make a close study of merchants in a provincial centre denies that merchants were expanding into manufacturing in any significant numbers. Dr Richard Wilson (no relation to the Professor) in a scholarly study of eighteenth-century Leeds insists that 'The long-established merchants of Leeds and Wakefield … showed no inclination towards manufacturing.' Only three Leeds merchants of the early 1780s appear among fifty-four 'Principal Woollen Manufacturers of Leeds and the neighbourhood' a generation later. The main development in the West Riding, so far as entrepreneurship is concerned, was the expansion of the roles of the clothiers (i.e. manufacturers) in the Halifax and Huddersfield area, who brought all the processes into the factory and then expanded into marketing their popular cloth.

If Dr Wilson's interpretation of West Riding history is equally true in other industrial regions of Britain, it would presumably mean that the traditional mercantile role was hemmed in, if not indeed invaded by the expansion of manufacturing activity. To test this hypothesis we must turn to other evidence and other expanding industrial regions. Since the question is evidently related to industrial innovation, it is sensible to focus on the role of merchants in that activity. In the eighteenth century merchants often appeared as patrons or partners in the development of patents, but their relative role compared with industrial producers was a shrinking one

---

[13] C. Wilson, 'The Entrepreneur in the Industrial Revolution', *History* XLII (1957).

Table 2.1. *Occupations of patentees in England and Wales 1660–1799*
(per cent)

	1660–99	1700–49	1750–99
professional	13·5	16·4	11.5
merchants/wholesalers	57·7	18·9	10·0
industrial producers	28·8	61·0	76·1

Source: C. MacLeod, *Inventing the Industrial Revolution. The English Patent System 1660–1800* (Cambridge 1988) p. 135.

according to a recent analysis by Christine MaCleod (Table 2.1). This research appears to lend credence to Dr Wilson's view that 'The aim of a wealthy merchant in life was to lead the life of a solid country gentleman, not to spend 15 hours a day running the largest factory in town.'[14]

However, the acid test of mercantile activity must surely be the Lancashire cotton industry, which witnessed the most dramatic expansion of industry and trade in the Industrial Revolution period. The most comprehensive guide appears to be the Manchester section of the *Universal British Directory*, which was published in 1794 and lists over 700 manufacturers (of fustians, cottons, muslins, checks, calicoes and other fabrics) and 135 merchants. Some sixty leading firms combined mercantile and manufacturing activities according to their entries, but a check back to Bailey's *Northern Directory* (1784) suggests that all but five of them were originally manufacturers. More than half of the merchant–manufacturers were new firms, or at any rate, firms that were not accorded an entry in Bailey. However, one is slightly uneasy about this simple analysis in so far as Bailey's typical entry for these firms, 'fustian manufacturer', is known, in a few cases, to have covered mercantile activity. Thus Peter Drinkwater, the leading Manchester merchant who was ignorant of factory techniques according to Robert Owen's autobiography, was described as a fustian manufacturer in Bailey. Rather similarly Henry and James Barton & Co., called fustian manufacturers in 1784, were said in 1829 to have been a family of general merchants established for three generations. The solution is that, just as Benjamin Gott in Leeds was able to employ skilled

[14] R. G. Wilson, *Gentleman Merchants. The Merchant Community in Leeds 1700–1830* (Manchester 1971) esp. pp. 105–7. Pat Hudson, *Genesis* p. 262 concurs with this view for the West Riding woollen industry.

mechanics and engineers, so Drinkwater recruited the talented Robert Owen and the Bartons were able to command technical expertise for their big textile printing works at Strines Hall. In Manchester the model was probably Barlow & Whittenbury, who offered Arkwright a partnership when he built his first mill in the town.[15]

The main limitation of using local trade directories is that they have no account of the relative importance or durability of the firms listed, and sometimes overlook firms manufacturing in the region that maintained their head offices (warehouses) in their home district. For such purposes the insurance registers are much more informative. They reveal that around 1795 while only six Leeds merchants owned woollen mills, a further eight merchant houses built big cotton mills and three more mills were built by investors with mercantile connections. In 1797 there were about 130 firms in the woollen trade in Leeds, so the proportion of mercantile origin was clearly significant, and the more so when it is acknowledged that the investments of leaders like Benjamin Gott in wool and Markland, Cookson & Fawcett in cotton were several times those of the typical clothier. However, it is in the fastest growing industry that the major initiative can be seen.

In the cotton industry, the relative importance of the investment of merchants and manufacturers can be gauged from an analysis of the forty-three biggest investors in cotton mills (Table 2.2). The merchants identified included Joseph Haigh, Wells, Heathfield & Co. and J. & J. Parker & Co., all of whom had made substantial fortunes in trade in London. The firms that transferred capital included two in the silk trade (Daintry, Ryle & Co. of Macclesfield and Bott & Co. of Tutbury) and one from the woollen trade, Edmund Lodge & Sons of Halifax.[16] The Manchester fustian merchants in the list include some important firms that had also been engaged directly in overseas trade. Perhaps the earliest and most interesting is Samuel Greg, who succeeded his uncles R. & N. Hyde, Manchester check and fustian manufacturers who were exporting direct to Philadelphia before the American Revolution. Greg expanded this trade after the Revolution and also built the now-famous cotton mill at Styal, eight miles south-west of

---

[15] W. H. Chaloner, 'Robert Owen, Peter Drinkwater and the early Factory System in Manchester', *Bull. of the John Rylands Lib.* xxxvii (1954). Bank of England Manc. ltrs 4 Apr. 1829. Guildhall Lib., Sun Fire Office Registers.

[16] Full bibliography of all these firms in S. D. Chapman, 'Fixed Capital Formation in the British Cotton Industry', *Econ. Hist. Rev.* xxiii (1970) pp. 257-8.

Table 2.2. *Occupations of owners of the largest Lancashire cotton mills*
c. 1795 (valuation of £5,000 +)

	number of firms	insured capital	percentage of total capital
Manchester fustian merchants	12	£255,960	33
Country manufacturers	10	88,000	12
Calico printers and merchants	4	234,590	31
Former mechanics and managers	3	65,050	8
Migrants from other industries & regions	14	122,100	16
	43	765,700	100

Source: S. D. Chapman, 'Fixed Capital Formation in the British Cotton Industry
1770–1815', *Econ. Hist. Rev.* XXIII (1970) pp. 249, 257–8.

Manchester.[17] The most successful of the country manufacturers (i.e.
those operating outside Manchester) that built mills included
Robert Peel & Sons whose printed calicoes were being exported
direct to Boston, Massachusetts, before the Revolution, and the
Philips family of Tean (Staffs.) who sold smallwares in America in
the 1780s.[18] Not all the country manufacturers that ventured into
overseas trade had large capitals and long-established positions; a
study of a fustian manufacturer at Little Longstone, a hamlet in the
Peak District, shows him sending one of his family to St Petersburg
in 1784 and then building his first cotton mill in 1785–6. The
autobiography of William Radcliffe of Mellor (Stockport), who
began his working life as a handloom weaver and was employing a
thousand looms in the country districts around his home before the
end of the eighteenth century, shows a country manufacturer selling
direct to the great trade fairs at Frankfurt and Leipzig.[19]

In some other eighteenth-century manufacturing regions, the
extension of the functions of leading entrepreneurs is also evident. In
the West Country cloth industry merchants like Barings, Milfords
and Kennaways were simultaneously operating as serge 'manufacturers', export merchants and bankers. In Glasgow half the

[17] Winterthur Museum, Del., USA: Wister papers, order book 1784–9. Lib. of Congress,
Stephen Collins letter books 1758–96.
[18] S. D. Chapman and S. Chassagne, *European Textile Printers*, p. 86.
[19] S. D. Chapman, 'James Longsdon, Farmer and Fustian Manufacturer', *Textile History* 1
(1970). W. Radcliffe, *Origins of Power Loom Weaving* (Stockport 1828) pp. 10, 16, 24.

merchants involved in the American trades (85 out of 163) had a share in at least one partnership engaged in manufacturing and extractive industry. In Birmingham and Wolverhampton the manufacturers shook off their dependence on London export merchants in the second half of the eighteenth century as a first generation of local merchants began to supply the American market direct for five per cent commission; there were already 34 of them when the first local directory appeared in 1767. The only eighteenth-century records to survive show a local partnership, Ketland, Cotterill & Son, 'designed for the collection of hardwares, buckles, buttons and all other articles which are manufactured in this and neighbouring towns and exported to the United States of America and elsewhere'.[20]

The emergence of this new breed of merchant–manufacturer in the provincial industrial regions was facilitated by the increase in size, wealth and expertise of the merchants of Liverpool. Already in the 1790s there was specialisation by export destination and by commodities in a similar way to that listed by Mortimer in 1763 for London; Joshua Gilpin listed ten American merchant houses, eleven West Indian merchants, a dozen corn merchants and a number of American shippers. Liverpool shippers provided a service for manufacturers with customers abroad, while the merchants assumed the role of their London antecedents by purchasing on their own account from inland manufacturers or from the various trade warehouses that stocked goods for export. Thus Sparling & Bolden, who exported woollen goods, printed cottons, carpets, hosiery, linens and a variety of other manufactured goods to Virginia, drew their supplies from a circle of firms in Manchester, Halifax, Colne, Rochdale, Leeds, Wakefield, Kendal, Keswick and Mansfield. They followed the trade practice of paying in bills on London at two or three months' date. London merchant houses, acting generally as bankers, accepted bills for consignments to America and other markets from all parts of the world, and paid the drafts of foreign merchants to the order of British manufacturers. Bills on London

---

[20] Pennsylvania Historical Commission, Harrisburg: Journals of Joshua Gilpin (1765–1840) vols. 28, 49. W. G. Hoskins, *Industry, Trade and People in Exeter 1688–1800* (Manchester 1935) pp. 45–9. T. Devine, 'The Colonial Trades and Industrial Investment in Scotland', *Econ. Hist. Rev.* XXIX (1976). Sketchley's *Birmingham Directory* (1767). B'ham Univ. Lib., Scholefield, Goodman & Sons records. Further references to Birmingham exporters in the 1790s appear in P.R.O. C12/246/25 and C12/251/240.

houses also financed the purchase of cotton and other Liverpool imports, so the port was financially dependent on its southern rival.[21]

The extension of the role of the manufacturers to overseas marketing, and of merchants into manufacturing, was evidently familiar in all major manufacturing regions of Britain in the last quarter of the eighteenth century. No contemporary seems to have provided a precise explanation of it but the reasons are sufficiently clear. For more than a century, dynasties of provincial organisers of domestic industry had been growing in experience, capital and connections, gradually freeing themselves from dependence on London merchants and factors by opening their own offices in the capital and selling direct to overseas importers. The great spurt in British textile manufacturing that took place after about 1770 found the existing marketing structure inadequate to meet the aspirations of the more ambitious northern industrialists. Moreover, much greater fixed capital formation (factories, warehouses, etc.) compelled them to try to maintain their investment more fully employed all the year round, rather than following the traditional seasonal cycles. The vanguard of entrepreneurs in this energetic period, following the lead of Drinkwater, Dale, Greg, Gott and other celebrated leaders of industry, built up complex integrated concerns, not only in manufacturing and marketing but also, characteristically, in importing supplies, factory building, transport, banking, mining and estate development. This forward and backward integration, that is to say, was characteristic of the dramatic period of growth on the 'new frontier' regions. In later chapters it will be seen that as the ancillary transport, financial and marketing services reasserted the economies of specialisation, the empires built by the Industrial Revolution pioneers proved difficult to maintain. Meanwhile, it must be recorded that merchant enterprise played a very significant role in the energetic expansion of entrepreneurial functions observed by Professor Wilson in this period.

SOME MAJOR MANUFACTURER–MERCHANTS

It is probably true that most manufacturers who extended their activities to merchanting did so with very little experience of overseas markets and an inadequate appreciation of the risks

[21] Joshua Gilpin's Journals vol. 4. B. H. Tolley, 'The American Trade of Liverpool in the early Nineteenth-Century', M.A. thesis, Liverpool pp. 67–8, 72–3. M. M. Schofield, 'The Virginia Trade of Sparling & Bolden of Liverpool 1788–99', *Trans. Hist. Soc. of Lancs. & Chesh.* CXVI (1964). B. A. Heywood, *Observations…on the Banking System* (1812) pp. 36–7.

involved and capital needed. The earliest export sales were characteristically spillovers from their domestic selling, though this was not necessarily unrealistic in a period when new fashions took months or even years to reach remote regions of settlement. Before rushing to castigate the naïveté of such apparently haphazard marketing operations, several factors should be called to mind. There is evidence to show that already by the end of the eighteenth century manufacturers were specialists in particular overseas markets, and this continued through much of the nineteenth century. Thus in calico printing we are told that Claytons of Bamber Bridge targeted the Russian market, Wood & Wright of Bank Bridge (Manchester) specialised in turbans and dresses for the Turkey market, James Hardcastle & Co. of Bradshaw Hall (Bolton) produced large quantities of prints for the German market, Matley & Sons of Hodge Mill (Mottram) concentrated on the Greek market, John Bradbury of Ardwick 'had a very good East India trade entirely to himself for some years in dresses and handkerchiefs', while Heywood & Palfreyman of Wildboarclough (Macclesfield) were more committed to the US market than any other printers early in the century. Similarly in cotton spinning, Arkwright's former partners in the Holywell Co. (Chester) went for the Russian market while Finlays of Glasgow concentrated on their German connection. Comparable market specialism was reported for the Staffordshire potteries as early as 1796. In textiles, selling was made easier by the ubiquitous practice of selling by small samples pasted on to printed cards. Until after the French Wars, much European trade was conducted through the great fairs, and it seems to have been relatively easy for a beginner like William Radcliffe of Mellor (Stockport) to sell there.[22]

However, it must be emphasised that a few leading manufacturers built up much more sophisticated marketing organisations than that required by simple opportunism. Two or three of these firms are well documented and their experience repays close study. The enterprise of the first generation of the Philips family of Tean (Staffs.) is featured in Wadsworth and Mann's classic study of *The Cotton Trade and Industrial Lancashire* but the next generation built a much more impressive organisation. At the turn of the century the structure

---

[22] Manchester P.L., John Graham, 'History of Printworks in the Manchester District from 1760 to 1846' (MS, c. 1846). *Minutes of Evidence ... on Orders in Council*, Parl. Papers, 1812, III, p. 297, ev. of G. Palfreyman. Gilpin's Journals vol. 25 (1796). J. Butterworth, *The Antiquities ... and ... History of the Trade of Manchester* (1822) p. 66.

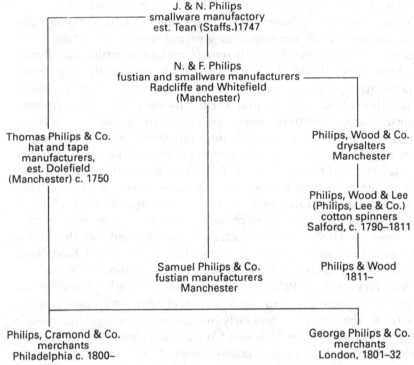

Figure 2.1. The structure of the Philips family businesses in the early nineteenth century.

encompassed four main centres (Tean, Manchester, Philadelphia and London) as shown in Figure 2.1.

In Manchester the Philips family became part of the Non-conformist commercial network that included the Gregs, the Heywoods and the Hibberts. Thomas Greg, father of the better-documented Samuel Greg (leading cotton spinner), was probably the most successful of this group, at any rate in American trade, where he presently assumed the business of the eminent house R. & N. Hyde.[23] In the early 1790s we see Philips developing their trans-atlantic trade though Greg, who had now moved to London. In 1793, George Philips already had his eye on a prospective American partner, a young Philadelphia merchant, and was only frustrated by the war situation. He wrote to Thomas Greg:

[23] Sir George Philips, *Memoirs* (c. 1845), microfilm at Warwicks. R.O.
M. B. Rose, *The Gregs*, p. 16.

Cramond's business is going on very prosperously and all his schemes have lately been successful. His commission business is also very much increased and the number of his correspondents is daily augmenting. If a peace should take place, or our government should desist in acting so offensively towards the Americans, I have no doubt that his most sanguine expectations will be realised and that his house will become one of the most considerable and respectable in that part of the world.[24]

A partnership, Philips, Cramond & Co., was formed at the end of the decade, but this was only the preliminary to more important developments.

The London merchant house was opened in 1801 by the future Sir George Philips and his two brothers to exploit the connections already developed by the family on the Continent (mainly Hamburg and Amsterdam) and the USA. The new partnership also started out with abundant capital and good information from America provided by Philips, Cramond & Co. of Philadelphia. The partners' initial circular maintained that they were to undertake general commission and insurance business on terms that 'are of course the same as other houses'. More specifically, these services and charges were as follows:

Commissions on invoices and sales 2.5 %
Del credere   1.0 %
Acceptances [i.e. endorsing bills] 1.0 %
Remittances   0.5 %
Insurances (underwriting)   0.5 %

Advances against consignments were allowed from 50 % to 66 % of the amount of the invoice. After a little experience they insisted that they would not be under acceptance for more than £5,000 at a time for any single firm. They assured potential clients that 'as our business will be confined entirely to the commission line, our friends can apprehend no interference from speculations of our own'.[25]

Inevitably most of the business came from the various Philips' businesses in Manchester and Tean. As the London partners acknowledged, 'the generality of good houses here have some connection or other in your town' and so were not particularly looking for others. Despite the linking partnership in Philadelphia, the London house soon burned its fingers on an American deal. George Philips wrote angrily:

[24] Staffs. R.O., J. & N. Philips MSS D 644/1/16, letters of 5 Oct. and 20 Dec. 1793.
[25] Warwicks. R.O., Philips MSS CR 456/28, letter of 2 Nov. 1801.

It is almost unnecessary to say that we have a very bad opinion of
Americans and their business in general but are at the same time assured
that there must be some good solid connections which it would be worth
our while to get hold of... Commercial houses (particularly those who trade
beyond their credit which is the case with all Americans) adopt different
modes to establish their credit,

and they wondered how to identify 'a respectable solid set of
correspondents'.[26] Not surprisingly, experience proved to be mixed.
In 1808 one of the partners of Thomas Philips & Co. in Manchester
gave evidence to a government inquiry that his firm now had an
'extensive trade to America'. About a third of the business was done
on six months' credit, the remainder on a nominal credit of twelve
months which in practice extended to eighteen months on the
average, he said. Their books carried some 'good' (as distinct to
'doubtful') debts of two to five years.[27] Clearly a large capital was
needed to maintain such uncertain credits, and the risks were high
during the war period, but the profits were as well and the family
fortune seems to have been founded on this period of trade.

At any rate, production at Cheadle and Tean reached a plateau
about the end of the French Wars despite the rebuilding of the mills
in 1822.[28] However, the London and Manchester mercantile
operations continued through the nineteenth century, from 1832 in
partnership with James Chadwick & Brother, who also came of a
manufacturing background. The significance of the Philips' commercial success was more than that of making a fortune and living
expensively. Sir George Philips was an MP in the reform cause,
effectively representing Manchester from 1830 to 1852, his brother
Mark sat for Manchester from 1832 to 1847, and Robert Needham
Philips was an MP for periods from 1857 to 1885. This public
eminence served as an advertisement of the rewards of commercial
enterprise.[29]

The Fielden family offer a case study which differs from that of the
Philips in two striking ways. They belong to the Lancashire 'self-
help' tradition, at any rate in the sense that they did not emerge
from any socio-religious network or elite, and they were not a

---

[26] Warwicks. R.O. CR 456/31, 4 Nov. 1801.
[27] *Minutes of Evidence... Orders in Council*, Parl. Papers, 1808, x, pp. 1–13, ev. of G. W. Wood
and S. Philips.
[28] Staffs. R.O. D 644/1/4: the data in this sales record suggest that the enterprise produced
120 m. yds of tapes in 1821 and 128 m. yds in 1841.
[29] *J. & N. Philips & Co.* (brochure, 1914); copy in Staffs. R.O. D 644/9/7. See also B. of E.
Manc. ltrs 5 Nov. 1836.

leading textile family in the eighteenth century. Joshua Fielden abandoned hill farming and domestic industry to give his full time to jenny spinning in two cottages in Todmorden in 1782 and left five small mills when he retired in 1803. But it was his sons (and especially John) that created the largest textile concern of their day when they took an early lead in power loom weaving in the 1820s.[30] Fieldens' capital rose from £10,000 or £15,000 at the time of the founder's death (1811) to £470,000 in 1836 and nearly £700,000 in 1845. In the next generation, John Fielden's sons lifted it to over £1.0m. in the early 1860s.[31]

In a frequently quoted remark, Benjamin Gott, the Leeds merchant who became a pioneer of factory production in the woollen industry, admitted that he extended his interests from having abundant capital rather than technical know-how, and he was able to employ the expertise of others in the different branches of manufacturing. The record of the Fielden brothers is equally explicit that they moved from manufacturing into merchanting from having surplus capital rather than any specific experience or preparation for overseas trade. Father built five spinning mills and the four sons added six more, plus two vast power loom sheds and extensive warehouses, but the problem soon became one of disposing of the huge output rather than of production, so there was both opportunity and motive for forward integration. As the Bank of England's agent (branch manager) in Liverpool reported in 1839, 'having had a large surplus capital they became...partners in the firm of Wildes, Pickersgill & Co. of Liverpool [and New York] who receive and dispose of all their produce which is imported on account of [textile] shipments made by the manufacturing firm to all parts of the world'. He meant that the marketing of the Fieldens' cheap mass-produced fabrics in poor countries involved the acceptance, sometimes by barter, of return cargoes which then had to be sold in Liverpool. Large sales and slow returns in Buenos Aires, to take just one instance, involved importing and selling large quantities of hides. In the 1840s Fieldens appear as much the biggest importers of

---

[30] (Anon.) *Fortunes made in Business* (1884) 1, pp. 413–56. S. A. Weaver, *John Fielden and the Politics of Popular Radicalism 1832–47* (Oxford 1987) Ch. 1.

[31] Estimate based on Bolton Civic Museum, Crompton 1811 Survey of Mule Spinners; spindles are valued at the conventional 17s. 6d. (£0.875) for buildings, power and machinery. Records of Mrs Anne Stevens (née Fielden), Longden Manor, Shrewsbury: Fielden Bros. private ledger 1832–65. Rylands Lib., Fielden MSS, correspondence 1814–50.

US cotton, no doubt to try to balance their sales of manufactured textiles to North America.[32]

All the evidence shows that such multilateral trade to distant parts of the globe was a high-risk activity. In the depression of 1837–42 several large manufacturers who had ventured into this kind of trade went bankrupt, often because of foreclosure by inexperienced and insecure Lancashire banks.[33] Nevertheless Fielden Bros. continued to concentrate on the foreign market: 'they sell little or nothing for home consumption but ship out to various parts of the globe nearly the whole of what they manufacture', the Bank of England's Liverpool agent told his London office in 1840. When Wildes, Pickersgill & Co. collapsed the next year, Fieldens had to take over the remnants of the business and only survived with the aid of a substantial loan from the Bank.[34] The banks were generally reluctant to tie up capital in supporting manufacturer–merchants, and the Bank of England only supported Fieldens because the brothers had made large investments in good securities, more especially railway stocks, which they could offer as collateral.

These case studies, and others that can be cited,[35] make it abundantly clear that even the wealthiest and most enterprising manufacturer–merchants found overseas trading a great financial burden and nearly all were forced to abandon it sooner or later. The theme is one to which we shall revert in later chapters, for new and old manufacturers never failed to covet the merchant's profit margin. For the present it is sufficient to make the important point that new trading and financial organisation had to be devised to replace both the eighteenth-century type of independent trading merchant and the manufacturer–merchant. The system that emerged in the later years of the French Wars and the early post-war years is the subject of the next section.

COMMISSION AGENTS AND ACCEPTING HOUSES

In the closing years of the French Wars difficult trading conditions led to the bankruptcy or retirement of many of the old merchants of London, Liverpool and Bristol, and the simultaneous withdrawal of a large number of manufacturers who had ventured into overseas

---

[32] B. of E. Manc. ltrs 10 Dec. 1839, L'pool ltr bks IV p. 381.
[33] S. D. Chapman, 'Financial Restraints on Firms in the Cotton Industry 1790–1850', *Econ. Hist. Rev.* XXXII (1979) esp. pp. 62–4.   [34] B. of E. L'pool ltr bks I (1840) p. 55.
[35] S. D. Chapman, 'Financial Restraints'.

marketing. In their place there emerged a new generation of specialists, commission agents resident in foreign commercial centres (but usually having a partner or agent in Britain), and a handful of wealthy merchants who had graduated to pure finance and provided the credits for manufacturers to send their goods to agents abroad. These merchants later became known as merchant banks or 'accepting houses' as much of their business came from 'accepting' (or endorsing) the bills of exchange signed by the less creditworthy enterprises who were their clients. The commission agents were characteristically young men of modest capital who went to seek their fortunes abroad. At the end of the French Wars most of those selling British goods appear to have been British born, but during the next twenty years, and particularly after 1825, the European and North American markets were increasingly served by the junior partners of United States, German, Greek and other foreign merchant houses who came to British industrial towns to select goods.[36] Meanwhile British commission agents moved out into the less developed but more distant markets, particularly Latin America and the Orient, no doubt hoping for less competition and more profit. In 1834 Lord Liverpool (Prime Minister from 1812 to 1827) believed that two-thirds of the entire trade of Britain was conducted by commission merchants, and it was particularly important in the export business of Lancashire and Yorkshire. At the same period, the *Circular to Bankers* estimated that the merchant bankers were providing as much as 80 per cent of the finance required for exporting to Britain's biggest customer, the United States. This influential periodical maintained that these bankers had brought greater stability to the transatlantic trade by their discretion in regulating the traffic in bills of exchange. Major American and German merchant houses bought directly from the warehouses of British manufacturers in London or Manchester, very often financed by London merchant banks. The manufacturers benefited because they were less exposed to the risk of selling in overseas markets.[37]

The early retirement of old-style merchants and merchant-manufacturers was accelerated by changes in trading habits. The tempo of trade was quickening in the second half of the eighteenth century. During the Napoleonic War, sudden scarcities and gluts

---

[36] See below, Ch. 5.
[37] N. S. Buck, *The Development of the Organisation of Anglo-American Trade 1800–1850* (Yale 1925) p. 17. *Circular to Bankers* 23 June 1837.

encouraged stockpiling and speculation, practices that regularly led the less cautious to bankruptcy and the more prudent to withdraw in despair. In the post-war years, increasing competition among exporters slimmed profit margins, but growing trade rapidly increased the turnover of the more capable entrepreneurs, further increasing the lead of the pacemakers over the 'old guard' and the struggling newcomers. This situation was responsible for the precipitate post-war decline of such old centres of trade as Wakefield, Norwich and Exeter, for many established merchants preferred to retire to their country estates than to change their lifestyle. Dr Wilson's *Gentleman Merchants* shows how the eighteenth-century merchant elite of Leeds melted away at the intensification of competition after 1805.[38]

The accepting houses specialised in the finance of particular branches of trade. The leading firms in the early nineteenth century were Barings, Brown, Shipley & Co., and (until 1836) the 'three W's' (Wiggins, Wilsons and Wildes) all specialising in transatlantic finance, and some firms of European origin, notably Rothschilds, Huths and Souchays. The distinguishing feature of the accepting houses was a large capital linked with intimate knowledge of some foreign markets, acquired by one or more of the partners having spent part of his (or their) careers abroad. A number of the best-known accepting houses were founded on fortunes made in textile trade, Barings in Exeter and the East India Co., Browns in the Philadelphia linen trade, Rothschild and Wiggin in Manchester, Morrison and Wilson in Liverpool, Souchay and Du Fay in the continental trade in printed cottons. Most based themselves in London but had offices or partners in Liverpool but Browns retained its headquarters in the northern centre of trade until late in the century. The accepting houses were prepared to advance up to two-thirds of the invoice to recognised clients for limited periods, three to four months for sales in North America, and up to twelve months for oriental markets.[39] In the boom trading conditions of the middle 1830s, accepting houses competed with each other and with discount houses like Overend, Gurney & Co. for business. 'I learn that one of the partners in Overend's house is now in Birmingham offering round at the houses of foreign merchants [with] money at $3\frac{1}{2}$ per cent on first rate acceptances', the Bank of England agent there

---

[38] *Sel. Comm. on Manufacturers*, Parl. Papers, 1833, VI, p. 23, ev. of L. Lloyd, banker. R. G. Wilson, *Gentleman Merchants* Ch. 6.

[39] S. D. Chapman, *The Rise of Merchant Banking* (1984) esp. Chs. 1, 7.

reported to his directors. At the same time, Rothschilds of London were trying to secure a bigger share of the French trade with British India by charging one per cent less than other houses, while Lizardis were investing heavily in their newly opened New Orleans office. The collapse of the 'three W's' (three of the leading transatlantic accepting houses) in 1836 checked rather than reversed the rise of the remaining accepting houses.[40]

Most of the commission merchants of the early decades of the nineteenth century were evidently in a very small way of business. An account of them in John Mortimer's *Mercantile Manchester Past and Present* (1896) offers a good picture:

The business of many of these merchants was carried on within very narrow limits, the warehouse staff in most cases consisting of the principal, a book keeper, a salesman, and a packer, with a traveller or travellers outside. Though a house might deal in prints, flannels, fustians, greys and dyed goods, very little stock would be kept. The orders were taken from patterns or sample pieces, and the goods obtained afterwards from the respective manufacturers of them. This was usually the morning occupation of the principal – who was often both buyer and salesman – the delivery of the goods being made in the afternoon... Sometimes the merchant would be, to a certain extent, a manufacturer also, having his winders and warpers... located in the upper storey of his warehouse, and to him came handloom weavers.

Scores of these little enterprises were crowded into the courts and alleys off Market Street, Shude Hill, Hanging Ditch and the other narrow streets of old Manchester, where they could consort easily with the country manufacturers who collected at the inns in the area or rented adjacent properties. Towards the middle of the century a few of the 'shipping houses' (exporters) began to build in a palatial style, but so late as the 1880s there were still numerous little home trade houses in the town.[41]

The problems of commission agents selling in the more distant foreign markets are vividly illustrated in the letter books of Hodgson & Robinson, who started in Buenos Aires in 1817 importing 'Manchester goods' and sending hides, tallow, bullion and other South American products to Britain. James Hodgson canvassed for commissions by assuring manufacturers that in general they could expect returns within a year, but in practice trade proved to be

---

[40] B. of E. B'ham ltrs 29 Jan. 1835. Guildhall Lib., Morrison Cryder MSS, letter from C. J. Weber, 15 May 1836. B. Gille, *La Maison Rothschild* (Geneva 1965) I, p. 403.
[41] J. Mortimer, *Mercantile Manchester* (1896) p. 69. R. Spencer, *Home Trade of Manchester* (1890) pp. 45–7.

much slower as the Spanish–American dealers were reluctant to
meet their debts. Moreover, the market suffered from recurrent gluts
and shortages because communications with Britain were irregular
so that the foreign agents' connections at home all received
information about profitable lines at the same time. These difficulties
were exacerbated by spasms of civil war and subsequent falling
exchange rates that could drastically reduce the value of remittances
or compel British manufacturers to accept payment in kind. Local
fashions could be as erratic as politics, and indeed at times the two
were not unconnected. Hodgson wrote to a manufacturer in 1840:
'there are some pieces [of printed cottons] which have the colours of
Light Blue & Green very prominent & which would be unsaleable
under the present regime here...' Hodgson & Robinson's best
connections were Fielden Brothers, the Todmorden spinners and
weavers, and Owen Owen, Manchester merchant and father of the
better-known John Owen. These and other principals suggest that
Hodgson & Robinson were amongst the best-connected commission
houses serving the textile trade. It is no wonder that turnover of firms
was high in this type of business.[42] In much the same way, Antony
Gibbs & Sons, who were commission agents with offices in Lima
(1822) and Santiago (1826), found that remittances for cloth sold
were so long delayed that some of their most valued clients suffered
financial embarrassments.[43]

   Post-war developments in the textile trade were followed, at
varying intervals of time, by similar changes in other branches of
overseas commerce. In Birmingham, the commission agent had
eclipsed the old-style general merchant by 1827 according to the
Bank of England's agent there. His description of the new system
shows the precise relationship of agent, customer and financier:

There are persons in Birmingham who are designated as merchants but
who act rather as agents having in fact few or no mercantile transactions
of their own. Many of these agents are highly respectable in their character
and conduct, although generally speaking not possessed of much property.
They are paid by a commission on the transactions which they effect and
for the most part, when they receive orders from abroad, particularly from
America, they are furnished with bills on London and Liverpool [merchant]
houses, with which they pay for goods purchased for their correspondents.

[42] Rylands Lib. Manchester, Hodgson & Robinson letter books (unlisted); quotation 30 Oct.
      1840.
[43] J. A. Biggs, *The History of Antony and Dorothea Gibbs* (1922) esp. pp. 384–451. Guildhall Lib.
      Gibbs MSS 11,053/3a, ledger of 1823–5.

These bills are frequently drawn by the Bank of the U.S. and generally on the most eminent houses in this country, such as Baring Brothers & Co., Thomas Wilson & Co., Finlay, Hodgson & Co., Thomas Dickinson & Co. and others, and in Liverpool on Cropper, Benson & Co., Sands, Hodgson & Co., W. & G. Maxwell, Maury, Latham & Co., W. & J. Brown & Co., and others. The paper which these mercantile agents negotiate is held in high estimation by the banks here [in Birmingham] and is perhaps on the whole considered the best in the market.[44]

In other words, Birmingham commission agents depended on London and Liverpool acceptance houses for their export finance. The agents operated on a modest scale because the industry they served was a conglomerate of small workshops; according to information collected for the Bank of England the average annual returns of the Birmingham manufacturers did not exceed £3,000 each at this time.[45]

Case histories of commission merchants illustrate their characteristic evolution. William Chance established himself as a merchant in Birmingham about 1770, exporting to America. Sixty years later his son (William II) was still in the same trade, but confined himself to executing orders from abroad, employing a modest capital of some £14,000. Brother Edward opened a warehouse in London in 1835, exporting Birmingham and Sheffield hardware, guns, lamps, glass ware, paper and other products of the 'Black Country', generally ordered from samples and trade lists.[46] Smith, Walker & Co. were founded in 1777 and were the principal merchants in the Birmingham area until 1819, when they went bankrupt. The son, John Walker, entered the American trade as a commission agent in 1820 and seven years later was selling goods to the value of £30,000 a year on a capital of £1,500, with W. & J. Brown of Liverpool providing the necessary acceptances.[47] Chance and Walker appear to have been typical of their home town, but a few merchant–manufacturers survived the vicissitudes of wartime trade and post-war depression, trading on capitals more comparable to those in Lancashire and the West Riding textile regions. Thus Joseph Tarratt & Son and William Briscoe & Son, both founded in Wolverhampton in the late 1780s, were trading on capitals of more than £50,000 half a century later, while Birmingham merchant–manufacturers Charles & James Shaw traded with Dublin and

[44] B. of E. B'ham ltrs 22 Jan. 1827.   [45] B. of E. B'ham ltrs 29 Jan. 1827.
[46] B. of E. B'ham ltrs 7 Feb. 1827. Brandt Circulars, 1835.
[47] B. of E. B'ham ltrs 19 Feb., 18 Mar. 1827.

Buenos Aires with £60,000 capital.[48] The organisation of the Sheffield export trade was evidently much like that of Birmingham, with most of the exporters operating on small capitals and consequently dependent on a small number of accepting houses. In 1832 it was explained that it was 'the custom of many Sheffield houses to draw upon W. & J. Brown & Co., Bolton Ogden & Co., Rathbone & Co., and others of Liverpool, which drafts are generally good for goods shipped on American account'.[49]

In the iron smelting industry, even the firms with the biggest investment of capital gradually declined marketing operations and by the 1830s there was little direct contact between the consumer abroad and the home producer. Sales were conducted through a corps of specialised agents established at the ports (especially London, Liverpool and Bristol) who charged one per cent for their services. Foreign buyers were expected to lodge a credit with one of the accepting houses, and Crawshay recommended Rothschilds, Browns and Barings. The system developed, according to one producer, because of the buyers' preference for dealing with one agent, and it was so popular that in the course of the first half of the nineteenth century the agents took control of the domestic as well as the foreign market. The producers' marketing organisation was atrophied by the preferences of the consumers.[50]

CONTINUITIES IN ORGANISATION: FACTORS, BROKERS AND MARKETS

The dramatic growth in manufacturing activity in several provincial industrial regions from the 1770s to 1815 must suggest the possibility that the dominant position that London held for much of the eighteenth century was challenged and perhaps even led to relative decline. Certainly the first half of the nineteenth century saw the South East of England nearly surrender its overall superiority in wealth; the index of regional income per head (see Introduction) based on the North West with a 100 in both 1812 and 1859–60 shows the South East with 382 in the former and only 122 in the latter year. To judge from the experience of cotton, the change probably came

[48] B. of E. B'ham ltrs 1 Jan., 30 Mar., 1 Oct. 1827.
[49] B. of E. Leeds ltrs 28 Mar. 1832.
[50] J. P. Addis, *The Crawshay Dynasty* (Cardiff 1957) pp. 98–9. M. Elsas, ed., *Iron in the Making: Dowlais Iron Co. Letters* (Glamorgan 1960) pp. 120–8. A. H. John, *The Industrial Development of South Wales* (Cardiff 1950) p. 125.

about in the two decades following the conclusion of the Napoleonic War (1815). Michael Edwards' *Growth of the British Cotton Trade 1780–15* observes that for much of the period the London commission agents and wholesalers took the lead in the marketing of cotton materials. They no doubt possessed greater capital resources and more ready access to the financial markets of the City of London.[51] The more successful provincial manufacturers opened warehouses there and were thus drawn into the metropolitan trading system. However, in 1833 Joshua Bates, a partner in the leading merchant bank Baring Bros., gave evidence to a government inquiry to the effect that manufacturers' agents in London had been closed because of the greater accessibility of Manchester. By this date several London merchants banks had opened branches in Liverpool while others had been born out of the trade of the northern cities.[52]

Bates's remarks were a significant overstatement of the changes, for in 1833 he had just persuaded his conservative partners to open the firm's Liverpool branch. It will be seen in Chapter 6 that London was already fighting back by establishing the cheap warehousing system of which Bates, as a recently arrived American, had evidently no knowledge, though it was given a lot of attention in the *Circular to Bankers* at the time.[53] However, the intention of this section is to confine attention to the continuities in the mercantile activities of the City of London rather than the innovations, which belong to later chapters of the book.

The chains of middlemen characteristic of British trade in the seventeenth and eighteenth centuries did not coalesce until the age of the telegraph, and the brokers, in particular, continued to be an important and growing group. With the great increase in overseas trade, brokers were an established group who advanced credit to both farmers and merchants. Brokers were a familiar feature of medieval trade, their essential function being to act as intermediaries between merchants and inland buyers or purchasers at auctions. In the eighteenth century there were still many general brokers but in the course of the internationalisation of trade they became specialists in colonial produce, sugar, grain, coal, cotton, wool and other commodities of world trade.[54]

[51] C. H. Lee, *The British Economy since 1700* (1986) p. 131. M. M. Edwards, *British Cotton Trade*, pp. 177–8.
[52] N. S. Buck, *Anglo-American Trade*, p. 103. S. D. Chapman, *Merchant Banking*, Ch. 1.
[53] See below, Ch. 6.
[54] G. L. Rees, *Britain's Commodity Markets* (1972) pp. 46–9, 61.

As is well known, the specialised trading activities of London first clustered around the coffee houses, but already in the eighteenth century commodity exchanges were being built. The most famous was the Corn Exchange which was opened in Mark Lane in 1749, originally as a domestic market. The corn merchants of Liverpool built themselves a corn exchange in 1808 and other provincial centres such as Glasgow and Leeds followed at intervals of time. The first market specifically for imports was the London Commercial Sale Room in Mincing Lane, London, opened in 1811. The provincial centres quickly adopted the broker and factor system but leaped ahead in organisation. It was the cotton trade that gave the great impetus to the development of specialised commodity markets and associations, institutionalising a system of trading that had existed for centuries.[55]

In eighteenth-century Liverpool the brokers were initially in a general way of trade, rather than being specialists, and met in the open air to transact business. Cotton rapidly multiplied their turnover and this trade already overtook that of London in the 1790s. An exchange was built in 1808 followed by a newsroom the next year. At the beginning of the nineteenth century brokers took to buying by sample instead of by inspection of all the cotton bags. Monthly reports were started by one of the leading brokers (Ewart & Rutson) as early as 1787, and this became weekly in 1805. The first exclusive weekly cotton circular was started the same year. Several of the brokers came together to produce a 'General Circular' in 1832, and this led to the establishment of the Liverpool Cotton Brokers' Association in 1841, with an initial membership of ninety firms. By small degrees the Association assumed the function of regulating the trade.[56]

While Liverpool quickly emerged as the centre for dealing in raw cotton, a large and increasing part of which was imported from the United States, Manchester came to concentrate on cotton fabrics. The Manchester exchange was inaugurated in the 1720s as a public market but in 1809 the merchants joined together to erect their own building where they could meet the country manufacturers. Like that at Liverpool, the essential features of the building were the newsroom and trading floor, but Manchester never published the general circular familiar to all in the Liverpool trade; everything

[55] H. Barty-King, *Food for Man and Beast* (1978) pp. 15–16.
[56] T. Ellison, *Cotton Trade of Great Britain* (1886) pp. 166–86.

was left to the individual firms, numbers of which circulated their own commentaries on the market. The initial membership exceeded 1,500 and grew until it topped 4,000 in 1860 and 10,000 in 1913. The building had to be enlarged in 1841 and rebuilt in 1867–74. The new exchange rapidly developed as a market for exports, particularly after Manchester merchants were able to sell directly to India without the mediation of the East India Company (1814). The termination of other trading monopolies saw them enter the Levant market (from 1826) and China (from 1834). It was Manchester and Liverpool exchanges that provided the local setting for the enterprise of many of the merchants whose activities are described in the next three chapters of this book. The response of the rival centre in London forms a substantial part of Chapter 6.[57]

There has been a lot of confusion about the roles of brokers and merchants, mainly caused by the verbose attempts of lawyers to make fine distinctions where they seldom existed and the entrepreneurs' silent determination to pursue profit wherever it beckoned. Eighteenth-century merchants were still primarily concerned in handling the commodities of the import–export trade, while the nineteenth century saw a shift to the provision of services, exemplified by the growing specialisation of commission merchants, produce and bill brokers, but in practice distinctions were blurred.[58] At the beginning of the century Nicholas Waterhouse, an eminent Liverpool cotton broker of the first generation, was charging 10s. (£0.50) commission to both importing merchants (the sellers) and country manufacturers (the buyers) on every £100 worth of cotton that passed through his books, but he also earned an increasing income from extending credit to both parties and was not averse to doing a little direct trade of his own on the side. When he died in 1823 he had a capital of well over £100,000, as much as any substantial merchant of the period.[59] In the later years of the century, Caesar Czarnikow, the leading London sugar broker, also had a range of functions and a large capital. He earned large

[57] D. A. Farnie, 'The Membership of the Manchester Royal Exchange 1809–1948', *Bus. Hist.* XXI (1979). For members circulars see e.g. Rothschild Archives London.
[58] N. S. Buck, *Anglo-American Trade*, pp. 17–25. P. Chalmin, 'The Rise of International Commodity Trading Companies in Europe in the Nineteenth Century', in S. Yonekawa and H. Yoshihara, eds., *Business History of General Trading Companies* (Tokyo 1984) pp. 273–91. Cf. T. S. Ashton, *Economic History of England. The Eighteenth Century* (1955) p. 135; J. H. Clapham, *Economic History of Modern Britain* I (1926) pp. 260–2.
[59] F. Hyde, S. Marriner and B. B. Parkinson, 'The Cotton Broker and the Rise of the Liverpool Cotton Market', *Econ. Hist. Rev.* VIII (1955–6).

commissions from sugar shipped from the West Indies for transhipment to agents in Central Europe and granted credit with the financial support of Anglo-German merchant bankers like Schröders, Kleinworts and Rothschilds. But he also made direct investments, for instance in the establishment of the London Produce Clearing House (1888) which dealt in colonial produce of all kinds. On the eve of World War I he had a capital approaching £1.om., which exceeded most of the merchant banks.[60] Both of these entrepreneurs will be encountered again; for the moment they simply serve to illustrate the point that the nomenclature of the period offers no infallible guide to real functions, and in this book we shall try to concentrate on actual activities and relations.

[60] Hurford James and H. J. Sayers, *The Story of Czarnikow* (1963). Baring Bros. MSS CRD 3/3 p. 107.

PART II

New streams of enterprise

CHAPTER 3

Merchants in the Atlantic trade

The most dynamic sector of overseas trade in the eighteenth century was undoubtedly that conducted across the Atlantic. Trade with the rest of Europe was buoyant, and that with India and the Far East showed real promise, but the great multiplication of activity was with the rapidly growing North American seaboard (Table 0.4). The major British ports for this trade were originally London, Glasgow and Bristol (Table 1.5), but as the northern industrial regions accelerated their growth, Liverpool and Manchester became the fastest growing centres of trade. In the nineteenth century the two centres advanced by leaps and bounds until, at mid-century, Liverpool's shipping tonnage exceeded that of London. This development is clearly one of the most outstanding in the growth of British trade to its dominant position, not only in the Atlantic economy but also at a later stage in the trade to the Far East. The enterprise of the northern ports will be examined in this chapter to identify their main characteristics.

Subsequent chapters will deal with other sectors of British trading enterprise and the specialised types of mercantile organisations that served them: Europe (the international houses), South and South-East Asia (the agency houses) and the home market (the home trade houses). In each case, the culture and British approach to the particular trade sector stimulated the evolution of particular types of enterprise. In practice, there were of course overlaps as some merchants shifted from one sector to another (for instance the international houses into India and home trade houses into the 'white colonies') but these variants can be coped with within the relevant chapters and then brought together in the final section of this book.

THE RISE OF LIVERPOOL

The most outstanding feature of British mercantile enterprise in the first half of the nineteenth century was the rise of Liverpool from being a small provincial port to a very close competitor with London. Other provincial ports, notably Hull, Glasgow and Newcastle also saw rapid growth in the period, but none on the scale of Liverpool.

In the first chapter of this book it was noticed that London dominated all other ports through the eighteenth century; in 1800, despite some decline in overall share of British trade, it still took two-thirds of imports and nearly the same proportion of exports (Table 1.3). However, there were already omens of Liverpool's rise before the end of the eighteenth century. The *Universal British Directory*'s long section on Liverpool recorded in 1791 that 'The merchants trade here to all parts of the world except Turkey and the East Indies [i.e. India], but the most beneficial trade is to Guinea and the West Indies, by which many of them have acquired very large fortunes. Liverpool, during the last War, carried on more foreign trade than any town in England.'[1] The Guinea trade was the slave trade, and that to the West Indies was in cotton as well as sugar and tobacco. But the most striking suggestion here is that Liverpool already overtook London for a brief period during the American War of Independence (1774–83), when metropolitan merchants were hamstrung by their inability to realise their assets in the North American colonies. An American visitor to Liverpool in 1800 recorded the names of ten prominent American houses and eleven prominent in the trade to the West Indies; clearly the trade with the mainland had risen fast in the 1790s. The 'American' houses included several – Rathbones, Bensons and Browns, for instance – who were to be prominent in Liverpool for two or more generations; the West Indies included such well-known dynasties as Gladstone and Brocklebanks.[2]

The French Wars (1793–1815) and the dramatic rise of the Lancashire cotton industry accelerated Liverpool's position rapidly. Towards the end of the war period, in 1812, Liverpool was importing about half as much cotton as London, though most of it came from one growing area, the USA (Table 3.1). In the early post-

---

[1] *Universal British Directory* III (1791) p. 646.
[2] Pennsylvania Historical Commission, Harrisburg: Journals of Joshua Gilpin (1765–1840), IV (1795).

Table 3.1. *Cotton stocks in UK ports on 1 Jan 1812 (bags)*

	India	Brazil	W. Indies	USA	Smyrna	totals
London	80,000	110,000	9,000	3,000	2,000	204,000
Liverpool	2,500	3,200	18,000	300,000	500	101,000
Glasgow	—	2,443	6,082	4,558	—	16,383

Source: Liverpool Mercury 5 Feb. 1813. The total stock of cotton at the ports, 332,900 bales, is approximately equal to the imports for the year, which were 326,231 bales, T. Ellison, *The Cotton Trade of G.B.* (1886), chart inside back cover.

Table 3.2. *Cotton imports to leading UK ports in 1833 (bags)*

Liverpool	840,953	90·4%
London	40,350	4·3%
Glasgow	48,913	5·3%
	930,216	100·0%

Source: E. Baines, *History of the Cotton Manufacture in Great Britain* (1835) p. 318. Seventy per cent of the imported cotton came from the USA at this date.

war years Liverpool quickly overtook and then ousted London from the cotton import trade completely; by 1833 it had over 90 per cent of the rapidly growing new business (Table 3.2). By mid-century, Liverpool had overtaken London in total tonnage and had vastly outpaced Hull, Glasgow and Newcastle (Table 3.3).

About a quarter of the shipping of Liverpool was engaged in the slave trade according to an estimate made while the abolition was being debated.[3] It was a tribute to Liverpool enterprise that it was able to replace this notorious trade with an entirely new development, the trade to India. William Rathbone IV joined the campaign for the termination of the East India Company's monopoly in 1792, and although this was a failure the interest of the younger men in his firm was aroused. The campaign was renewed in 1812–13, when the Company's charter was due for renewal, as a result of which the trade to India was opened to licensed private traders shipping to Bombay, Madras, Calcutta and Penang. Ships had to be at least 350 tons burthen (the typical Liverpool ships of the

[3] H. Smithers, *Liverpool, its Commerce, Statistics and Institutions* (L'pool 1825) p. 105.

Table 3.3. *Number of vessels and amount of tonnage of the principal
British ports in 1816 and 1850*

| | 1816 | | 1850 | |
	ships	million tons	ships	million tons
London	6,198	1·25	16,437	3·29
Liverpool	2,946	0·64	9,338	3·62
Hull	1,185	0·18	4,249	0·84
Newcastle	1,127	0·16	7,206	1·16
Glasgow	89	0·01	1,470	0·30

Source: T. Baines, *History of the Commerce and Town of Liverpool* (Liverpool 1852) p. 825.

period were around 200 tons), and were not allowed to carry Indian goods direct to the ports of continental Europe. Despite these restrictions, Liverpool merchants decided to take the initiative. The first ship to leave the port for the East was John and Robert Gladstone's *Kingsmill* in May 1814, and the second the *Bengal*, owned jointly by Cropper, Benson & Co. and Rathbone, Hodgson & Co., which sailed a year later. The aim of Lancashire merchants and manufacturers at this period was to build up a cotton trade with India comparable with that to the United States. An early attempt by the Peels to sell printed cottons in India had lost money, but the continued fall in prices gave rise to new hopes. Cropper Bensons also admitted in 1823 that attempts to foster the extension of the India cotton crop also proved disappointing initially, and the firm were consequently involved in the import of a wide variety of oriental products, notably spices, silk, sugar, dyestuffs, hemp, rice and coffee.[4]

The sale of Lancashire prints in India obviously required a local agent and in 1816 Cropper Bensons sent out Matthew Gisborne who had been trained in their counting house. Though he went out to Calcutta as an agent without capital, he pretty soon picked up some trade of his own and shortly began business for himself. Nevertheless, the Liverpool house continued to entrust him with the whole of their eastern trade, 'having every reason to be well satisfied with his

[4] K. Charlton, 'Liverpool and the East India Trade', *Northern History* VII (1972). S. D. Chapman and S. Chassagne, *European Textile Printers in the Eighteenth Century* (1981) pp. 92–3.

conduct and management'. In 1826 Gisborne & Co. was sufficiently flourishing for the young entrepreneur to recruit two partners from Alexandre & Co., then one of the five great 'agency houses' engaged in a multitude of economic activities in India, including banking. Gisborne returned to England in 1829, 'having acquired a pretty handsome capital for one who went out with nothing', but Cropper, Benson & Co. continued to deal exclusively with his firm. The financial basis of the connection was explained by a Glasgow correspondent of Baring brothers in 1830:

> Messrs Gisborne & Co. have a large share of the consignment of British manufactures from this [area] and Lancashire and their constituents have been so well pleased with their management that they have urged the formation of a similar establishment in Bombay, which is now being formed...You are aware that shipments to so distant a market as India cannot be obtained, to any extent at least, and especially from Scotland, without the aid of advances, this accommodation Messrs Cropper, Benson & Co. have given, and continue to give freely on shipments to Messrs Gisborne & Co., Calcutta, and have also agreed to do the same on shipments to Messrs Gisborne, Menzies & Co., Bombay.

This letter is quoted at length because it shows quite clearly that already in the 1820s Cropper Benson & Co. were fully committed to the financing of international trade as much as to the work of commission merchants.[5]

Meanwhile an important innovation had taken place in the transatlantic trade from which Liverpool was the major beneficiary. At the end of 1817 a consortium of New York merchants introduced the principle of 'line' or 'berth' service, with ships sailing on regular schedule between two ports. The celebrated 'Black Ball Line' inaugurated a schedule of monthly sailing between New York and Liverpool, with four square riggers of about 400 tons each, at the time about twice the size of the largest ships being built on the Mersey. The essential innovation was that the ships would sail 'full or not full' and being 'all remarkably fast sailers' would complete the voyage in an average of twenty-eight days, summer and winter. The owners were Isaac Wright & Sons, Francis and Jeremiah Thompson and Benjamin Marshall, an intermarried group of Quakers who were correspondents of Cropper, Benson & Co. in New York, forwarding bales of raw cotton and importing British textiles. Not surprisingly, the firm became the principal agents of the new line, shipping all their cargo in its ships and persuading their

---

[5] Guildhall Lib., Baring MSS HC 6.3.1, Gisborne letters, 5 Jan. 1831.

Liverpool friends to avail themselves of its regular services. In Liverpool, the major problem of prompt sailing was waiting for an east wind to carry ships down the Mersey, but now new technology came to the rescue with the use of steam tugs. The Black Ball Line was a most successful enterprise almost from the first, and must have contributed strongly to Liverpool's reputation and volume of business. Moreover, it enabled its merchants to reduce the proportion of their capital invested in ships.[6]

THE STRUCTURE OF MERCANTILE ENTERPRISE

Unfortunately there has been very little systematic research on the structure of British mercantile enterprise in this period so that it is not possible to offer generalisations for several ports or for long periods of time. However, there is one published analysis, that of Liverpool merchants in the cotton trade in the period 1820 to 1850, and its conclusions are all the more acceptable because they harmonise with those on the eighteenth-century tobacco trade summarised in Chapter 1. Bills of Entry show that in the first half of the century cotton importing was increasingly concentrated into the hands of a small group of thirty or so operators who generally undertook a much narrower range of functions than the 'generalists' of the eighteenth century had done. They tended to specialise in the import of the one commodity (cotton), and in the export of cotton yarns and piece goods.[7]

The letters of the Bank of England's agent (manager) in Liverpool offer more striking commentary on the firms in this concentration. In 1829 the five biggest merchant houses imported 18 per cent of total British imports of cotton; in 1842–3 the leading six importers took 27 per cent of total imports. The leading importer in the late 1820s was W. & J. Brown & Co., a firm of Irish–American origin with bases in Philadelphia and New York. They were followed by Alston, Finlay & Co., who were a branch of an old-established Glasgow house (James Finlay & Co.), and then by Cropper, Benson & Co., the English Quaker firm with close family ties with the Rathbones and with the American Quaker cousinhood already referred to in connection with the Black Ball Line. These diverse

[6] R. G. Albion, *The Rise of New York Port 1815–60* (N.Y. 1939) pp. 38–43. R. G. Albion, 'Planning the Black Ball Line', *Bus. Hist. Rev.* xli (1967) pp. 104–7.

[7] D. M. Williams, 'Liverpool Merchants and the Cotton Trade 1820–50', in J. R. Harris, ed., *Liverpool and Merseyside* (1969).

origins reflected those in the port at large; among twenty-nine leading firms identified by the Bank at the end of the 1820s, at least six were of US origin and three were Scottish. This variety of background, which was maintained in the society and culture of Liverpool in these years, accords with knowledge of the boom ports of earlier centuries, Amsterdam in the seventeenth and London in the eighteenth centuries. At the end of the 1820s some leading London merchants like Barings, Schröders, Kleinworts and Huths opened important branches in Liverpool, and in the 1830s they were joined by a number of smaller firms that were offshoots of continental houses.[8]

Sometimes the elements of Liverpool's rich ethnic and religious groups appeared in competition with each other, sometimes they joined in coalitions to try to secure some particular trading or financial advantage. The famous cotton speculation of 1825 provides an interesting illustration of the rich mix of enterprise and intense competition in the port.

According to Vincent Nolte, a German-born merchant who acted as New Orleans agent for a number of English houses, James Cropper was responsible for a widely circulated idea that the natural (i.e. climatic) limits of cotton growing and the supply of slaves following the British abolition of the slave trade was producing a situation in which consumption was overtaking production, and this would inevitably drive up the price of cotton. The early 1820s were a period of buoyant trade and rising prices so the idea had immediate appeal and evidently won support among Cropper's circle of friends. So in 1823 Cropper formed what Nolte called 'the Quaker Confederation' to speculate on the rising price of cotton. The members of this loose group, apart from Cropper Bensons, were Rathbone Bros. and Isaac Cooke of Cooke & Comer, an American-based Quaker firm of cotton brokers that had succeeded Waterhouse as the first in Liverpool. They drew in Daniel Willink, the son of an Amsterdam merchant and himself Dutch Consul in Liverpool, and Hottinguer of Le Havre, a member of the Parisian banking family who had been trained for a period with Cropper, Benson & Co. Willink was supported by Barings of London, the leading merchant bankers of the day, and Hopes of Amsterdam, partners of Barings in numerous ventures and probably the best-known bank in that city.

---

[8] See Appendix, pp. 104–6. For London migrants, S. D. Chapman, The *Rise of Merchant Banking* (1984).

Hopes were so taken with Cropper's ideas that they also speculated extensively on their own account. The other people involved were Cropper Bensons' and Rathbones' New York agents, the Quakers Jeremiah and Francis Thompson, already noticed as joint founders of the Black Ball Line.[9]

Jeremiah Thompson was said to have been 'by far the largest shipper of cotton' from America to Europe, employing agents in all the southern ports (New Orleans, Savannah, Charleston etc.) to buy for him, and 'also the heaviest importer of British cloths, having special agents in New York and Philadelphia to effect sales for him'. The Thompsons' Black Ball Line of packet ships had built their fleet up from four to fifteen ships by 1825. Jeremiah Thompson had made his fortune quickly by 'buying cotton on time here [New York] and in the southern markets, and by selling bills for cash, drawn on houses he consigned the cotton to, for nearly the current price of cotton'. Many of these bills of exchange evidently originated with Cropper, Benson & Co., and (the writer is effectively saying) could be discounted in New York at the highest rates because of the high standing of this and other Liverpool houses. Thompson's turnover of bills was higher than that of any other American house except Brown Brothers & Co. (W. & J. Brown in Liverpool) and Prime, Ward & Sands (later King & Gracie of Liverpool), 'the first large genuine private bankers in...New York'.[10] The speculation reached a frenzy in 1825, when the bubble was burst by James Dennistoun of Dennistoun Mackie & Co., one of the small group of Scottish merchants in Liverpool, importing some 5,000 bales below the market price. The subsequent collapse of prices led in the course of the next two years to the bankruptcy of Nolte, Willink, Jeremiah Thompson and several smaller Liverpool houses. Isaac Cooke was reported to have sustained heavy losses, and as Cropper, Benson & Co. were major creditors to Nolte, they inevitably suffered along with the rest.[11]

The long tail of smaller firms persisted for much of the century because it continued to be possible for anyone who could secure an

---

[9] V. Nolte, *Fifty Years in Both Hemispheres* (1854) pp. 288–320.

[10] W. Barrett, *The Old Merchants of New York* (N.Y. 1870) I, pp. 10, 186, IV, pp. 214–7, V, p. 122. For the Thompsons see also H. Heaton, 'Yorks. Cloth Traders in the U.S. 1770–1840', *Thoresby Society Miscellany* XI (1945).

[11] V. Nolte, *Fifty Years*. *Liverpool Mercury* 22 Apr. and 5 Aug. 1825. Brit. Lib. Add MSS 38,746–7, John Gladstone to W. Huskison 31 Dec. 1825. Liverpool Ref. Lib., W. & E. Corrie Trade Circulars. B. of E. Liverpool agent's letters 30 Nov. 1827, 17 Jan. 1829, 11 Apr. 1829, 21 Sept. 1829 record the losses.

agency for a manufacturer to enter trade. A few telling examples must serve to explain the situation further. In 1832 Moore, Hardwick & Co. were a Leeds firm of commission merchants with branches in Rio de Janeiro and Bahia Blanca. The Bank of England agent thought their capital of £25,000 quite adequate because the business was confined to agency work for other establishments, never purchasing for their own account 'but taking charge of the shipments of various manufacturers consigned to their foreign establishments, and receiving and appropriating to each their returns'.[12] Similarly, Thornton, Atterbury & Co. of Leeds and Manchester, who were one of the leading Anglo-American houses in the 1840s, had a capital of £40,000 (£25,000 in Leeds), and there was a linking partnership in Glasgow with a capital of £30,000. Again according to the Bank's agent in Leeds, 'they may not possess much money but they have the best correspondents [i.e. customers] in the United States who send them funds or credit upon London or Liverpool' firms.[13] Again, George Fraser, Son & Co. were commission agents in Manchester with a capital of £16,000 in 1846. The Bank agent thought this was sufficient to work the business 'without giving them the power (they being purely *agents*) to grant facilities to their correspondents'.[14] Owen Owen & Son, who began as commission merchants in Manchester in 1792 and had accumulated something over £100,000 by the early 1840s were believed by the Bank agent to be 'very wealthy people'.[15] They were, however, on the bottom rung of the league of major merchants in the North of England (Tables 3.4 and 3.5).

The capital of the major Liverpool merchants was still quite modest, Gladstones apart, around 1830. James Finlay & Co. and W. & J. Brown, probably the second and third largest houses, were estimated at £125,000 while Cropper Benson had £60,000 or so (Table 3.4).[16] Apart from Gladstones, who appear to have been in a class of their own, practically all the big merchants in the North of England in the first half of the nineteenth century were in reality merchant–manufacturers, i.e. they were successful manufacturers who were exporting their output direct to overseas agents and

[12] B. of E. Leeds ltrs 15 Dec. 1832.
[13] B. of E. Leeds ltr books IV (1847) pp. 179, 195.
[14] B. of E. Manc. ltr books V (1846) p. 47.
[15] B. of E. Manc. ltr books III (1842) p. 81. B. W. Clapp, *John Owens* (Manchester 1965) p. 162.
[16] Table 3.4. For Cropper Benson see the records of James Cropper Esq., Tolson Hall, Kendall, esp. Edward Cropper to his father, 26 Nov. 1824.

Table 3.4. *Major British merchants in the North of England in the first half of the nineteenth century (capitals of £100,000+)*

	Firm	Home base/s	Sectors	Capital (£)	
M	Gladstone	Liverpool	West Indies India	500,000	(1830)
M–M	Fielden Bros.	Todmorden Manchester Liverpool	cotton mills and trade	277,000 694,000	(1832) (1845)
M–M	Barton	Manchester	calico printing	470,000	
M–M	R. Gardner	Manchester	cotton mills	344,000	(1847)
M–M	Butterworth & Brooks	Manchester	calico printing India	300,000 200,000	(1834) (1828)
M	Dennistoun	Glasgow Liverpool	USA Australia	300,000	(1846)
M–M	Horrocks, Miller & Co.	Preston	Far East America	290,000 350,000	(1836) (1842)
M–M	Birley & Hornby	Liverpool	Russia	270,000 160,000+	(1827) (1846)
M–M	H. Bannerman & Sons	Manchester	cotton mills home trade	160,000	(1846)
M–M	Jas. Finlay	Glasgow Liverpool	cotton mills India	125,000+ 200,000	(1827) (1861)
M–M	John Rylands	Manchester	cotton mills home trade	100,000+	(1850)
M–M	John Leech	Stayley Bridge Manchester	cotton mills	500,000	(1850)
M	Owen Owens & Son	Manchester	S. America	100,000+	(1845)

Note: M–M = merchant–manufacturer, M = merchant.
Sources: Longden Manor MSS, Fielden Bros. private ledger 1832–65. [C. Brogan] *James Finlay & Co. 1750–1950* (Glasgow 1951) p. 37. B. W. Clapp, *John Owen* (Manchester 1965) p. 162. All other data from Bank of England Liverpool and Manchester agents' letters (later letter books) for years given.

sometimes trading in overseas ports through agents. Thus Fieldens had made their fortune in cotton mills in Todmorden, Horrocks in mills at Preston, Finlays in mills around Glasgow, Rylands in a mill at Wigan and so forth; the sole exception, Owen Owen, had had a sleeping partnership in a cotton mill for several years. Other firms like Bartons and Butterworth & Brooks owned major calico printing

Table 3.5. *Some leading German and American merchants in the North of England in the first half of the nineteenth century*

Firm		Base(s)	Trading sector(s)	Capital (£)
American				
M–M	Schunk, Souchay & Co.	Frankfurt Manchester London etc.	Continent	330,000 (1835)
M	Du Fay, Colin & Co.	Frankfurt Manchester	Continent Latin America	200,000 (1829–33)
M	Liepmann, Lindon & Co.	Berlin Manchester	Germany Russia E. Indies	200,000 (1836)
M	Reiss Bros.	Frankfurt Manchester	Continent	80,000 (1836) 100,000 (1848)
MB	F. Schwann	Huddersfield Manchester	Continent	100,000 (1844)
American				
MB	W. & J. Brown	Liverpool	USA	150,000 (1827) 1·22m. (1836)
M	Charles Tayleur & Sons	Liverpool	New Orleans Mexico S. America	300,000 (1847)

Note: M–M = merchant–manufacturer, MB = merchant banker, M = merchant.
Sources: Bank of England Manchester, Leeds and Liverpool agents' letters and letter books, 1827–50. Lancs. R.O., Horrocks Crewdson MSS DDHs/76. E. J. Perkins, *Financing Anglo-American Trade* (Harvard 1975) p. 37. J. E. Darnton, *The von Schunk Family* (1933) p. 172.

works. The slight qualification that needs to be made to this point is that some of these merchant–manufacturers could trace their trading origins back into the eighteenth century, when their forebears had been merchants; such for instance were Bartons, Dennistouns, Birley & Hornby and Finlays (Table 3.4). What little we know of leading German and American merchants settling in England at this period suggests they were operating on a comparable range of capitals (Table 3.5). In the published literature the path of development that led in the eighteenth century from merchant to manufacturer is most familiar in the career of Benjamin Gott of Leeds.[17] He was by no means typical of his generation and post-war conditions scarcely

[17] H. Heaton, 'Benjamin Gott and the Industrial Revolution', *Econ. Hist. Rev.* III (1931).

encouraged manufacturers to become merchants (Chapter 2), but a few outstanding entrepreneurs continued to venture their capital overseas.

Developments in commercial organisation in the 1830s increased the financial demands on merchant houses. As background it will be recalled that in the most rapid period of industrialisation of the textile districts of the North of England (1780–1815), many manufacturers integrated forward into merchanting, partly because the profits in this pioneer period offered a strong incentive, but more particularly because the existing mercantile community did not have the knowledge and capacity to cope with new (or improved) products and rapidly extending markets. At the same period, a number of merchants in various manufacturing centres integrated backwards into manufacturing, seeking the high profits enjoyed in these years. But after the French Wars, and more particularly after the boom of 1825 subsided, increasing competition among manufacturers steadily reduced the interest of the group as a whole in overseas trade and finance (Chapter 2). The development was more fully explained by Henry Menzies, partner in Gisborne, Menzies & Co., Cropper Benson's Bombay operation, in 1835:

The small percentage to which competition has reduced profits in Manchester and Yorkshire has given such an advantage to the Merchant over the manufacturer in shipping abroad that the foreign export trade of this country is returning more and more every year to the 'purchase system'. A [merchant] buyer can ensure a good and comprehensive assortment. He ships at the best seasons, watching the terms of prices at home, and the quantities of goods going forward to the place of consumption, while with a few exceptions the manufacturer's plan is to *sell* where he can and ship only his surplus...[18]

In other words, the eighteenth-century overseas merchant who, in the course of industrial expansion, had become a commission merchant, was now reverting to his earlier more independent role. But in the forty or fifty years that separated these two changes, British overseas trade had increased dramatically in volume and moved towards more distant markets, so that it was no longer possible to conduct and finance a diversified overseas trade on a small capital.[19]

The big merchants tended to increase their lead during this period

[18] Baring MSS HC6.3.1, H. Menzies to Gisbornes 10 Aug. 1833.
[19] S. D. Chapman, 'British Marketing Enterprise: the Changing Roles of Merchants, Manufacturers and Financiers 1700–1860', *Bus. Hist. Rev.* LIII (1979).

Table 3.6. *Concentration of mercantile leadership: cotton importing*

	1820	1826–7	1830	1832	1839
Percentage of cotton imported by					
top 3 importers	9	23	13	15	17
top 6 importers	16	32	23	24	28
top 10 importers	24	39	35	32	38

Source: extracted from J. R. Killick, 'The Cotton Operations of Alexander Brown & Sons in the Deep South 1820–1860', *Jnl. of Southern History* XLIII (1977) Table 1.

because during the recurrent trade crises they were generally more cautious and consequently emerged largely unscathed while more bold but less prudent concerns were ruined. This process is fairly well documented in the histories of firms of the stature of Barings and Brown Bros. that were emerging as merchant bankers in the first half of the nineteenth century. The tendency is nicely illustrated in data collected by John Killick (Table 3.6) from which it can be seen that the leading firms in the cotton trade increased their share of an increasing market in the periods following the crises of 1825 and 1836–7, slipping back a little in the periods of crowded enterprise between. The London merchants that opened offices in the North of England often had more capital at their disposal. Thus Schröders put £50,000 into their Liverpool enterprise when it opened in 1840 and declared themselves willing to contribute another £150,000, an investment that was instantly ahead of all but the most wealthy local enterprises and threatened to push local merchants into the background.

COUSINHOODS AND NETWORKS

So long as communication between trading centres continued to be slow and uncertain, the only way in which merchants could repose confidence in their correspondents' discretionary decision making was to employ members of their own families, or, failing that, the 'extended family' of co-religionists. Consequently we find that every port was a focus of networks of family connections by means of which goods and credit moved with a degree of assurance. Mercantile records are pretty scarce in Britain, but there are sufficient available to illustrate this process in some depth.

It is easiest to begin with the Quaker connection already

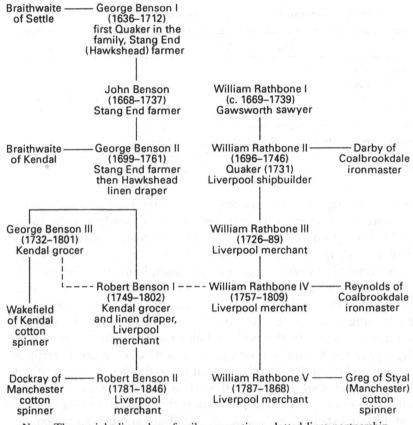

Note: The straight lines show family connections, dotted lines partnership connections.

Figure 3.1. Early members of the Benson and Rathbone families and their marriage connections.

mentioned several times in this chapter, and in particular the Rathbone and Benson families. The pedigree in Figure 3.1 depicts the emergence of the two families from modest origins, the Bensons originating as farmers and small tradesmen in Cumbria, the Rathbones as sawyers and shipbuilders in the vicinity of Liverpool. William Rathbone III was, as we have seen, one of the pioneer generation of Liverpool merchants trading with America, and in 1789 his son invited Robert Benson I from Kendal to be his partner. By this time the families were already linked to various Quakers prominent in manufacturing round the country, notably with such ironmasters as the Darbys and Richard Reynolds of Coalbrookdale and Lloyds of Birmingham, the Wakefields of Kendal who had a cotton mill, woollen mill and powder mill in the locality, and Joseph Foster of Bromley Hall, Bow (East London), owner of the famous calico printing works. The next generation saw further marriage connections with leaders of the early cotton industry as Figure 3.1 shows. It was probably because the Rathbones and Bensons (later Cropper, Benson & Co.) reposed so much confidence in Jeremiah Thompson and other Quaker merchants in New York and Philadelphia that they did not establish branches in North America.[20]

The Finlay family of Glasgow built up a more representative structure. James Finlay, the founder, began in a small way, probably as a pedlar or 'packman' in textiles, gradually extending his clientèle from Scotland and England to the Continent. When he died in 1790 the assets of his partnership added up to £11,785. It was therefore his son, Kirkman Finlay, who was the real creator of the Finlay enterprises. He bought three Scottish cotton mills on the Arkwright system and exported yarns to the Continent, mainly through the German partners shown in Figure 3.2. Then he opened branches in Liverpool, Charleston, New York and New Orleans and became one of the leading British importers of American cotton. However, the development that secured the long-term future of Finlays was the opening of trade with India. In 1812, when he was Lord Provost of Glasgow, Kirkman Finlay led the campaign against the East India Company's monopoly and continued it unrelentingly as a Member of Parliament.[21] It was probably because of his eminence in public life as well as his established position as a cotton manufacturer that he was able to secure the partnership of Henry & James Barton for his initiative in Far Eastern trade. Bartons were a much richer firm with capital nearly four times that of Finlays (Table 3.4). They were the third generation of a family firm that had begun as fustian merchants and now owned a large calico printing works at Strines Hall, Disley (Derbyshire). Ritchie, Steuart & Co. of Bombay evidently built up a successful business in printed cottons, most probably made with yarns from Finlays' mills and shipped

---

[20] W. Rathbone, *A Sketch* p. 23. Letter book of James Cropper (1773–1841) owned by James Cropper Esq. of Tolson Hall; see esp. letters of 3 Feb., 16 Feb. and 2 June 1795.

[21] [C. Brogan], *James Finlay & Co. Ltd.* (Glasgow 1951) Chs. 1–6. Mitchell Lib., Glasgow: Minute Book of Glasgow E. India Assoc. 1812–13. The extensive Finlay MSS (Glasgow Univ. Lib.) are thin for this period.

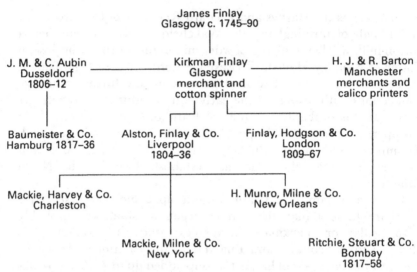

Figure 3.2. The partnerships and connections of James Finlay & Co.
c. 1745–c. 1860.

from their Liverpool warehouse. The later history of the business will be picked up in subsequent chapters.[22]

It has already been noticed that the transatlantic trade was conducted to a considerable extent by families and partnerships with bases in both Britain and America. Some were founded or sustained by Americans whose partners became British in the course of long settlement, others by Scottish and English emigrés who by degrees acknowledged themselves as Americans. The former group included Brown Bros. of Liverpool, A. & S. Henry and Thornton, Atterbury & Co. already mentioned. The latter can be exemplified in the history of Fraser, Trenholm & Co. of Charleston.

John Fraser seems to have been a typical Scots migrant who began in a small way in Charleston at the close of the Napoleonic War. Like many of his countrymen he may have been a pedlar at the start; certainly merchants who won much bigger fortunes began in this way. (Stuart Bros. and Seligmans, who rose to New York bankers from what Americans call the 'dry goods' trade, both began as pedlars.) Thirty years after his settlement in Charleston, Fraser was reckoned worth $100,000 (£20,000). The firm prospered in the

[22] B. of E. Manc. ltrs 4 Apr. 1829. W. Bailey, *Western and Midland Directory* (1784). *U.B.D.* III (1791) p. 794. Manchester P.L. MSS, John Graham, 'History of Printworks from 1768 to 1846'.

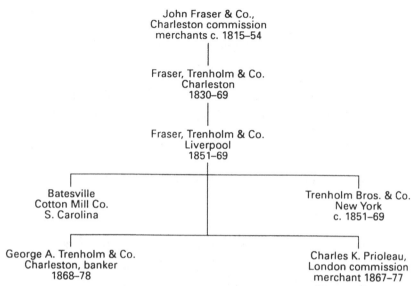

Figure 3.3. Partnerships of Fraser, Trenholm & Co., Charleston, USA, 1815–67.

1850s with the planting of branches and local partners in Liverpool and New York. In 1855–6 the sober Dun & Bradstreet credit register was reporting that Trenholm was 'one of the first merchants in the country' and that he was said 'almost to govern the City' (of Charleston). By the end of the decade the firm maintained that it had a 'solid capital' of a million dollars (£200,000), with investments in real estate, shipping and slaves, as well as trading stock.

Bankruptcy continued to be common among practically all classes of mercantile houses through this period, but dramatic rises and falls appear to have been particularly characteristic of American-based firms. The meteoric Fraser Trenholm suddenly suspended payment in 1859 following a sudden fall in the price of cotton, but their 'large and bold operations' no doubt contributed to a rapidly changing reputation in Liverpool and the USA. During the American Civil War (1861–5) the Liverpool house became the British agents of the Confederate Government and the senior partner (C. K. Prioleau) became a naturalised British citizen. Meanwhile Trenholm became banker to the Confederate States Treasury. No doubt benefiting from cotton speculations, the firm's capital reached $3.0m. by the end of the war (£600,000), a figure that put it ahead of any comparable British merchant enterprise at the time. But prosperity did not survive long. After the war the firm was pursued with relentless zeal by the US Government until their commercial credit was affected, and it failed with debts of $2.5m. in 1867. The firm was finally wound up in 1869, but not before Trenholm had established himself as a banker in Charleston. A credit report of 1870 observed that he had 'more influence than any man in the City; [the bank] controls through his influence several corporations and has a large proportion of our wharf property...their credit is high and our banks take their exchange freely'.[23] It was this kind of dazzling but unpredictable career that both contributed to the hazardous nature of trade and credit on the new frontier, and brought large turnovers in the mercantile community of Liverpool, Glasgow and other ports trading with North America.

THE MID-NINETEENTH-CENTURY STRUCTURE OF MERCANTILE ENTERPRISE

It has been shown that as a result of the convulsions of trade during the French Wars, the characteristic type of eighteenth-century general merchant gave way to a new structure. Many merchants were ruined or enervated, but a few survived with enhanced fortunes, and some of them presently emerged as accepting houses (merchant banks), financing lesser houses in the various sectors of world trade. The numerous new or impecunious enterprises became commission merchants in domestic centres or foreign ports. In practice, commission agents were characteristically young men of modest capital and few connections who went to seek their fortunes abroad, often in the less developed and more geographically remote markets, particularly Latin America and the Orient (Chapter 2).

A neglected census of commercial representation in foreign territories ordered by Lord Palmerston in 1842 and 1848 offers some notion of the spread of British, American and French overseas enterprise at the period. Evidently German enterprise was not considered sufficiently important to be worth counting at this period (Table 3.7) though a few British consuls' reports referred to growing competition from this source. The picture of US enterprise is unfair as most American merchants trading to Europe had their bases in Liverpool or Manchester, and so of course were not included in the survey. Palmerston's survey has other blemishes, notably

---

[23] Harvard Univ. Baker Lib., Dun & Brandstreet credit registers, Charleston, I pp. 183, 231, II pp. 379, 409, 418, 658. Merseyside Museums Dept., Fraser Trenholm MSS. J. D. Bullock, *The Secret Service of the Confederate States in Europe* (1883) II, pp. 416–17.

Table 3.7. *The mid nineteenth-century structure of mercantile enterprise*

		Numbers of firms		
Geographical sector	Ports	UK	USA	French
Europe (except UK)	42	501	33	68
North America	10	142	—	41
Mediterranean and the Middle East	41	281	3	215
Latin America	38	460	93	181
India and China	3	111	n.d.	n.d.
	134	1,495		

Source: P.R.O. FO 83/111, 115.

inconsistencies and incomplete returns, but it is adequate to make two basic points. At mid-century there can be little doubt that British mercantile enterprise was much the most extensive in the world, and it was not obviously concentrated on the colonial or former colonial territories. In the Mediterranean, Middle East and Latin America, it met the competition on more or less equal terms and, so far as numbers can tell, was generally more successful.

Palmerston's consuls offered little evidence of the financial resources of British commercial houses in their regions, but the indications are that the great majority continued to be in a very modest way of business. In 1878 it was estimated that a hundred British merchants resident in Latin America were worth on average only £15,000 each.[24] There has been a lot of research on American wealth around the mid nineteenth century, and numbers of the merchants whose capital was estimated were British or of immediate British descent. The subject is a large one, and it will be sufficient to note here that fortunes of above $50,000 (£10,000) were rare in the east coast ports at the period.[25] It will be expected that the capital of British houses trading in India was more considerable, but nearly all the old agency houses were swept away in a spate of bankruptcies in 1830–5, and the most prosperous survivor, Jardine Skinner, found a liquid capital of £100,000 sufficient to run their business in 1845–8.[26] As a comparative point, it is interesting to note that a large

[24] M. G. Mulhall, *The English in South America* (Buenos Aires 1878) p. 529.
[25] Edward Pessen, 'The Wealthiest New Yorkers of the Jacksonian Era', *N.Y. Hist. Soc. Quarterly* LIV (1970).
[26] Cambridge Univ. Lib., Jardine Skinner MSS, File 5/5 (1848).

part of British trade to Europe was conducted by German families with branches resident in Manchester, Bradford, Liverpool and other centres, and that the largest of these had a capital of over £300,000 at mid-century though there was a long tail of much smaller concerns (Table 3.5).

Perhaps the most interesting feature of the Palmerston survey is that it drew attention to some interesting deficiencies in British mercantile enterprise. From Boston (USA) the British consul reported that with two exceptions British trade was conducted by US citizens, while at Mobile it was said that there were several mercantile houses conducting a large English business whose partners were all Americans. In Philadelphia most of the British 'merchants' appear to have been agents for Sheffield and Birmingham manufacturers. An American of the period offered a candid explanation of the absence of 'dry goods' (textile) merchants: 'With respect to foreign dry goods, the [US] importing houses of Philadelphia... enjoy unusually favourable connections in Europe... The stocks are generally selected by resident partners who know the wants and consult the interests of purchasers, and therefore they consist, less than some others, of the unsaleable refuse of London warehouses.' Evidently the long use of the North American market as overspill had spoilt the trade. In the Middle East ports the trade was often largely in the hands of Greek firms – such at any rate was the case in Cairo, Beirut, Adrianople (Turkey) and Cyprus, while those of the southern Russian ports of Odessa and Taganrog were occupied by Greeks and German Jews. German competition was also reported from Latin America: in Mexico the principal houses in British trade were said to be German and Spanish, while in Haiti it was said that many English goods were consigned to German merchants in eastern Europe, and in 1865 Germany superseded Britain as Russia's premier trading partners.[27]

PROBLEMS OF MERCHANT–MANUFACTURERS
AND RAILWAY INVESTORS

It may seem surprising that manufacturers continued to expose themselves to the high risks of exporting, but there are two important explanations. The connection between economies of scale and

[27] M. W. Shoemaker, 'Russo-German Economic Relations', Ph.D. thesis, Syracuse 1979, p. 22. E. T. Freedley, *Philadelphia and its Manufacturers* (Phil. 1859) p. 96. P. Herlihy, *Odessa. A History 1794–1914* (Cambridge, Mass., 1986) pp. 88–95.

overseas marketing was explained in 1833 by Gabriel Shaw, a partner in a London firm of commission merchants:

The savings arising from operations upon a very large scale are considerable; for instance a difference of three to four per cent between operating with £20,000 and operating with £40,000, and these savings I believe may be greatly increased. Some of our manufacturers employ £100,000 or £200,000 or £300,000 capital. Suppose I make 100,000 pieces of goods, and I made ten per cent [profit] upon 75,000 pieces, there is a positive gain [in manufacturing on this scale]; then I export the residue and incur a small loss; I am fully compensated for that loss by the profits I realized upon the three-fourths...[and] I produce the whole cheaper.

In spinning and weaving, economies were available on the use of steam power and in factory building from at least 1800, and in practice it was only the biggest firms who obtained the benefits of the most up-to-date labour-saving machines. Alexander Andelle, a French government agent, concluded his report on the Lancashire cotton industry in 1819: 'It is clear that it is their vast establishments and large quantities that they produce by the skill of a single man that accounts for the low price at which their mills manufacture.' Andelle was thinking particularly of Horrocks, whose enormous production was maintained by large exports.

The other explanation is that Lancashire production of textile goods outpaced the capacity of domestic and overseas markets to absorb them, especially in the second quarter of the century. The underlying problem was that the rising trend in the supply of ever cheaper raw cotton, and of investment and productive capacity, was not so readily matched by the growth of overseas markets. The consequent frustration is seen in the politics of the period: the 'monopoly' of the Bank of England or the East India Company was blamed for every crisis, and free trade was proclaimed as the panacea, at any rate by the voluble group of leading merchants and manufacturers.

As American and European merchants or their agents came to Britain to buy the cottons in demand in their markets, so British mercantile enterprise was forced into the more distant oriental and South American markets, where returns were much slower. The restraints that this situation placed on the growth of firms can be illustrated from the experience of two or three in different branches of the cotton industry. Ainsworth & Co. of Preston were a firm of spinners and manufacturers with a capital, in 1847, of some

£100,000, largely invested in mills and machinery; that is, they were in the top league of established concerns. Nevertheless, Ainsworth sought discounting facilities from the Bank of England because 'having shipped largely [he] may be pinched for want of his returns'. Robert Gardner was probably the most successful of Manchester's self-made men of the post-war generation. Entering business about 1810, he bought a large spinning mill in 1824, and by 1835 had 4,500 handloom weavers on his payroll, mostly in the peripheral Preston area; but his main investment was in selling overseas. When he became bankrupt in the crisis of 1847, it was revealed that his debts, mostly for bills payable, were only a little over £100,000, while his assets were valued at nearly £350,000, almost £200,000 of which was in goods shipped to Brazil, the USA and other parts of the world. Freehold property – warehouses, spinning and weaving mills – were worth £92,000. Gardner's evidence to parliamentary inquiries shows a man with a liberal mind and a sound grasp of the problems of the cotton trade and industry. But the Bank of England took a poor view of him; he had 'risen from nothing', and was 'a wild speculative man, dogmatical in all his opinions and views, and not easily guided...he is always borrowing money and he conceives the only use of a Banker is to lend money'. Such views no doubt contributed to Gardner's fall.

Even firms with partners who were bankers were not immune from problems. Butterworth & Brooks were one of half a dozen big calico printers with such advantageous connections; the works were founded about 1798 by Henry Butterworth, who took John Brooks of the Blackburn bankers Cunliffe, Brooks & Co. as a partner. In 1834, Brooks had a personal fortune of over £300,000, including £214,000 invested in the print works. He embarked on a programme of exporting to various countries, particularly Latin America, India and China, selling through leading commission houses like Antony Gibbs & Sons (S. America), Kelsalls (Calcutta) and John Macvicar (agent for Jardine Mathieson & Co. of Canton). In 1836 it was reported that he was 'short of cash to carry on his current operations while the market is unfavourable for selling' and that he had £50,000 worth of unsold stock in South America. The next year, Cunliffe, Brooks & Co. attempted to restrain Brooks's operations by withholding facilities and in May he had debts on his books of £259,000, all due from export houses and agents abroad. By 1846 Brooks had had enough, and determined to retire from business 'while he has yet a considerable surplus' – in fact £150,000 to £200,000, little more than half his capital of ten years earlier.

Perhaps the most striking case of problems of liquidity in exporting comes from the experience of Fielden Brothers, the well-known spinners, manufacturers and merchants of Todmorden and Manchester noticed in the last chapter. The four brothers had a combined fortune of half a million pounds, much of it invested in their mills and in foreign securities. In 1840 it was reported that 'they sell little or nothing for home consumption, but ship out to various parts of the globe nearly the whole of what they manufacture, so that at times when returns are not made so quickly ... they may be pressed for money'. They were particularly pressed that year, for Wildes, Pickersgill & Co., the Liverpool merchant house in which Fieldens were partners and which disposed of all the produce bartered for textiles, was refused an advance of £100,000 by their local bankers. The problem, that is to say, did not end with the sale of the Lancashire manufactures, but often extended to the acquisition and disposal of barter cargoes. The records of some other Lancashire firms, notably Cardwell, Birley & Hornby, Horrocks, Miller & Co., Thomas Ashton of Hyde and Butterworth & Brooks show that at one time or another they were also involved in barter trade in order to dispose of their cotton goods in South America or the Orient.[28]

The problems just described were further exacerbated by the attraction of merchant capital into railway finance. The 'Liverpool party' and their Manchester friends, as is well known, were responsible for raising the capital for much early railway development, and mercantile families like the Gladstones, Fieldens, Hornbys, Rathbones, Schusters and Jacksons were heavily involved.[29] According to the Bank's agent in Liverpool, writing on the eve of the 1847–8 commercial crisis, bankers all agreed that 'the resources of our commercial community have, to an enormous extent, been diverted from their legitimate objects to speculations in railways', and that this had 'perhaps in some degree' adversely affected their ability to cash their long-dated bills of exchange. The crisis itself was particularly attributed to the 'railway mania', and

[28] S. D. Chapman, 'Financial Restraints on the Growth of Firms in the Cotton Industry 1790–1850', *Econ. Hist. Rev.* xxxii (1979).

[29] M. C. Reed, *Investment in Railways in Britain* (Oxford 1975) pp. 206, 237. S. D. Chapman, *The Clay Cross Co. 1837–1987* (1987) p. 25. W. Rathbone, *A Sketch*, p. 134.

though there were several other factors in the equation, North of England merchants were prominent in the long list of mercantile failures, which included three Liverpool banks. Watson Bros. & Co. of Liverpool, who were in the Mexico trade and had conducted 'an excellent business' with a capital of over £100,000, were said to have lost it all in railway speculations. However, this was probably not representative; certainly other houses like Littledales, the Liverpool brokers, and Gardner, the Manchester merchant who suspended payment, presently paid all their debts and recovered much of their earlier business.[30]

APPENDIX

List of the principal Liverpool importers of cotton ('American Houses'), 1827–9

From the literature the same firms can be identified as leading exporters of 'Manchester goods'. The list is in approximate order of size. Source: Bank of England Archives, Liverpool Agent's Correspondence, letters of 24 Nov. 1827, 20 Oct. 1829. Additional references from the Bank of England archives and from published sources have been added to aid identification and analysis.

(1) W. & J. BROWN & CO. were 'interested' (i.e. financially committed) in a 'great part' of their imports. Established in Liverpool in 1810 as a branch of an Irish Protestant firm at Baltimore, E. J. Perkins, *Financing Anglo-American Trade: the house of Brown 1800–1880* (Harvard 1975); capital £15,000 in 1827.

(2) CROPPER, BENSON & CO. were 'interested to a considerable extent but probably not so heavily as Browns'. A Liverpool Quaker firm; see K. Charlton, 'James Cropper and Liverpool's Contribution to Anti-Slavery Movement', *Trans. Hist. Soc. Lancs. & Chesh.* CXXIII (1973).

(3) RATHBONE BROTHERS & CO. mainly imported on account of a fellow Quaker, Jeremiah Thompson of New York, a Yorkshire emigré. Established in Liverpool in 1746 and intermarried with the Bensons; see *D..N.B.* (William Rathbone) and H. Heaton, 'Yorkshire Cloth Traders in the U.S.', *Thoresby Society Miscellany*, XI (1945).

(4) BOLTON, OGDEN & CO. New York firm of English extraction; see J. Killick, 'Bolton, Ogden & Co.: A Case Study in Anglo-American Trade', *Bus. Hist. Rev.*, XLVIII (1974).

[30] B. of E. Manc. ltr books VI (1847) p. 72, Liverpool ltr books IX (1848) p. 2. D. M. Evans, *The Commercial Crisis 1847–8* (1849) pp. 92–4, 103–4.

(5) ALSTON, FINLAY & CO. and

(6) FINLAY, HODGSON & CO., two of the partnerships formed by Kirkman Finlay of Glasgow, the former in Liverpool in 1804, the latter in London in 1809, with branches in New York, Charleston and New Orleans. See B. of E. L'pool ltrs, 31 Dec. 1827, and [C. Brogan], *James Finlay & Co. Ltd.*, (Glasgow 1951), pp. 12, 15. Capital £125,000 in 1827.

(7) WRIGHT, TAYLOR & CO. a branch of a 'very respectable' house in the US, but almost bankrupt and broken up in 1829; see B. of E. L'pool ltrs, 20 Oct. 1829.

(8) MAURY, LATHAM & CO. were mainly 'consignees' of cotton. James Maury was the American Consul in Liverpool; see B. H. Tolley, 'The American Trade of Liverpool in the early Nineteenth Century', M.A. thesis (Liverpool 1967), p. lxi.

(9) BEN BUCHANAN, branch of a Glasgow house who 'regulated' imports into Liverpool and were 'deeply interested [financially] on their own account'.

(10) CRARY, CRAIG & CO., a firm of Scots origin with a house in New York called Fish & Grennill; imported for the most part on their own account or in shares. Having 'Found their concerns too heavy for them', they transferred a large part to Browns; B. of E. L'pool ltrs, 3 Oct. 1831.

(11) PECK & PHELPS of New York were importers of ironware and tin plate, sending cotton to Liverpool as return cargoes. See also Phelps, Dodge & Co. MSS, New York Hist. Soc. MSS.

(12) ALEX MACGREGOR & CO. received much cotton on consignment from 'many valuable friends in America', but also imported on their own account. Small capital (£15,000); see B. of E. L'pool ltrs, 10 Mar. 1829.

(13) T. & J. D. THORNELEY imported mainly on consignment.

(14) TAYLEUR, SON & CO. Liverpool house with offices in New Orleans, Mexico and S. America; 'their funds are frequently remitted in silver from Mexico to New Orleans and invested in cotton on their own account'. Capital £300,000 in 1845.

(15) MARTINEAU, SMITH & CO. Liverpool house with a branch in Orleans through which their imports were received, 'mainly on their own account or by advances and shares'.

(16) SANDS, HODGSON & CO. Sands was an American by birth, Hodgson a relative of Pares & Co., the Leicester merchant hosiers, cotton spinners and bankers. They had a house in New York (Sands, Spooner & Co.) and another at Vera Cruz (B. of E. Leeds ltrs, 13 Jan. 1829). They were principally commission merchants.

(17) HENRY DIXON & CO. received cotton mainly from a US house (unknown) on consignment.

The following names appear in the 1829 list, but not in that for 1827:

(18) WAINWRIGHT & SHIELS failed in 1825, but were still trading in 1831.

(19) ISAAC COOKE & CO., a Quaker firm of cotton brokers, formerly belonged to the well-documented firm of Nicholas Waterhouse & Co. Sustained heavy losses in 1825, but still 'in the highest degree of credit' in 1829. B. of E. L'pool ltrs, 11 Apr. 1829.

(20) HAGARTY & JARDINE failed in 1825 but were still trading in 1831.

(21) RAINSDON & BOOTH failed in 1825. (For continued trading, see B. of E. L'pool ltrs, 22 Aug. 1831.)

Analysis of the Twenty Leading Firms (no. 21 not included).

SOCIAL ORIGINS: 6 out of 20 firms US, 3 + out of 20 Scots, no Europeans.

COMMISSION AGENTS: 5 out of 20 firms.

BANKRUPT OR NEARLY SO IN 1825: 5 out of 21 firms; others (Rathbone, Crary, Craig & Co.) must have suffered strain during this crisis.

STRUCTURE OF TRADE: In 1829 the five biggest firms (Browns, Wright, Taylor & Co., Wainwright & Shiels, Alston, Finlay & Co. and Cropper, Benson & Co.) imported a total of 133,000 bags or 18 per cent of total imports. In 1842–3 the 'big six' cotton importers took 269,227 bags, or 27 per cent total imports. The leaders now included two European firms, Victor Pontz and Collman & Stellefeht, B. of E. L'pool ltrs, IV (1843), p. 381.

CHAPTER 4

The agency houses : trade to India and the Far East

The most far-reaching change in the pattern of British overseas trade in the nineteenth century was the shift from the 'old' markets of Europe and North America to the newer markets of Africa, Australia and (above all) the Far East (Tables o.4, o.5). Liverpool and Manchester merchants helped to break the East India Company's monopoly of trade to the East but the northern enterprise described in the last chapter was by no means the only or most significant commercial initiative in the subcontinent. The most important development was the evolution of the type of organisation known as the 'agency houses', later the 'managing agency system'. As there has been a good deal of confusion about these organisations, it will clear the path if we define the species at the outset of this chapter.

The name 'agency house' originally implied nothing more than an establishment where business was done for another, so it was more or less synonymous with the more common name of 'commission house', and most firms in British India started as representatives of domestic merchants or manufacturers. However, the opportunities for making (and losing) fortunes were much greater in the Far East, turnover of firms and partners was high, and from the earliest years a core of strong firms, encouraged by the opportunities opened up by British imperial expansion, used their large capitals to secure a stronger base by local investment. 'Agency houses' came to imply this kind of mercantile organisation. Strictly speaking the managing agency implies something rather different. One of the house histories defined it as an individual or firm that contracts 'to organise the activities of a company, to appoint managers and other key personnel, and to conduct its day-to-day affairs, always subject to the overriding control of the company's board ... In many instances the managing agent has taken the initiative in starting a company and holds a proportion of its shares.'[1] This last sentence brings the two ideas together because, in order to gain control of local property and business with minimal risk, the agency houses floated and managed companies, but seldom owned all the equity of them. The evolution of the system was more or less continuous from commission house to 'agency house' (as commonly understood) to managing agency.[2] It is the function of this chapter to trace this evolution, and to link it with the British investment group into which it often merged towards the end of the century.

The geographical distribution of the system also needs to be clear. An Indian historian wrote over forty years ago that the managing agency system 'has no counterpart in any other part of the world', and this superficial comment has been widely adopted. From the perspective of the present exercise this cannot be right, for the record of agency houses being active in several parts of the world apart from India is perfectly clear – Mathesons and Swires in China, Wallace Bros. and Steel Bros. in Burma, Hendersons in Borneo, Siam and Java, Mackinnon Mackenzie in East Africa, Finlay Muir in South Africa, Guthries, Bousteads and Symes in Malaya, Lloyd Scott and other houses in Persia and so on. Moreover Kling's ideas that the managing agency system originated with Carr, Tagore & Co. of Calcutta between 1836 and 1846 and was therefore Indian cannot hold water. Tripathi and other scholars have traced the system to the five great agency houses that were founded towards the end of the eighteenth century and became insolvent in 1830–5, and recurrent crises in oriental trade showed again and again that the system was indispensable.[3]

More generally, it must be said that the agency houses have been badly represented in serious and more popular writing. A sequence of Indian historians, identifying them as agents of British imperialism, have been almost uniformly disparaging and have made no serious attempt to understand their nature. The recent *Cambridge Economic History of India* has inherited the same bias.[4] A string of centenary histories, mostly published by surviving houses in the

---

[1] G. Harrison, *Bird & Co. of Calcutta 1864–1964* (Calcutta 1964) p. 24.
[2] Cf. Blair B. Kling, 'The Origin of the Managing Agency System in India', *Journal of Asian Studies* XXVI (1966–7) argues that the system began with an Indian-owned firm, Carr Tagore & Co., but misses the context represented in several more general studies, eg. A. Tripathi, *Trade and Finance in the Bengal Presidency 1793–1833* (Calcutta 1956) pp. 230ff. M. Greenberg, *British Trade and the Opening of China 1800–1842* (Cambridge 1951) Chs. 2, 6.
[3] S. D. Chapman, 'Investment Groups in India and South Africa', *Econ. Hist. Rev.* XL (1987).
[4] D. Kumar, ed., *Cambridge Economic History of India* II 1757–1970 (1983) pp. 575ff.

1950s and 1960s, are all more or less amateur. Business records are still patchy in their coverage, but it is possible to synthesise a more balanced account of the changing characteristics of the system for most of its history.

EARLY CHARACTERISTICS OF THE AGENCY HOUSES

There are two characteristics of the agency houses that clearly distinguish them from other nineteenth-century mercantile houses. The term 'agency houses' implies that, like most other British merchant enterprises of the period, they worked on commission, acting as agents for domestic manufacturers or merchants. This was indeed the way that most of them began, but by the middle 1830s increasing numbers were trading on their own account, sending buyers round the North of England and Scottish factories to buy textiles.

Lancashire and Glaswegian manufacturers were originally quite ignorant of the requirements of the Far Eastern market, and their early consignments were 'hit-and-miss' affairs. Peels, the leading northern calico printers, are supposed to have been the first to send a cargo of their goods to India, but the venture was a failure.[5] Gradual success began a dozen years later, in 1811, when Donald McIntyre of Duncan, McLachlan & Co. began studying the native shopkeepers' interests in particular patterns. 'The first [such] experiments were all on our own account, without any orders', he said. 'After that I received orders from the native merchants, and when I saw that a certain pattern suited their fancy, I ordered it from this country [i.e. from British manufacturers] ... trade increased in everything in which we could do.'[6] In other words, the original initiative in the oriental textile trade, the principal British export, came from the agency houses.

When the trade to India was freed from the control of the East India Company in 1815 numbers of northern and Scottish manufacturers responded by exporting goods on consignment, and sent out agents to manage their sales, but this often proved an expensive speculation. George Larpent, a partner in Cockerell & Co., maintained in 1835 that 'the bulk of the export trade has been in the hands of these parties', and the same year the *Circular to*

---

[5] S. D. Chapman and S. Chassagne, *European Textile Printers in the Eighteenth Century* (1981) pp. 92–3. This was in 1798–9.
[6] *Sel. Comm. on Foreign Trade, Third Report, East Indies and China*, Parl. Papers, 1821, p. 295.

Bankers declared that four-fifths of the British exports to China were sent by the manufacturers. However, it seems that this information was already dated, or the situation changing rapidly. John Innis, another witness to the government inquiry to which Larpent gave evidence, said that 'The capital embarked in the India trade is chiefly furnished by the [merchant] houses there. Some of the [British] manufacturers...send out goods upon their own account, but not to a great extent, for they depend principally upon the orders and advances they receive from the merchants in this country [Britain], acting as agents for their correspondents in India.'[7]

This division of experience between the partners of two leading houses can only be interpreted by reference to the experience of those in the vanguard of changes that were taking place. Gisborne & Co. of Calcutta wrote to Barings in the same year, 1835, that 'Our consignments from England have almost ceased...impressions from visiting the manufacturing districts were decidedly in favour of purchasing on our own account under the management of an experienced and active agent...people here generally are growing tired of the advance systems. Some houses have pursued the plan of purchasing on their own account for some time, and have found it much the most profitable of the two.' Barings' initiative was directed by their commercial partner, Joshua Bates, who was described by the *Edinburgh Review* in 1834 as 'perhaps the most extensive and certainly one of the best informed merchants in the country'. Questioned by a government commission, he agreed that the system by which manufacturers consigned goods direct to commission agents overseas was widespread but his simple affirmative concealed the growing control of firms like his own. American-born Bates had already seen the ruin of many British manufacturers in the US in the 1820s. Barings and other rich houses not only supplied the credits to commission agents like Gisbornes they also provided the ships. Bates confided his real motive to his diary: 'By reason of the many failures we cannot fail to become receivers of a large proportion of the goods from that country [the Far East], the return cargoes of the agency houses.' The unspoken implication of these records is that profit margins were more substantial in trade than in manufacturing, and capitals appreciated rapidly, giving the leading agency houses

---

[7] *Circular to Bankers* No. 363, 3 July 1835. *Sel. Comm. on Manufacturers*, Parl. Papers, 1833, pp. 141, 191.

all the purchasing power they need to conduct trade on their own account.[8]

The first characteristic of the agency houses that marks them off from other mercantile enterprises, at any rate for most of the nineteenth century, is that of heavy fixed capital investment in the locality of the overseas station. This development began with indigo estates. Until about 1790 the production of indigo was entirely in Indian hands but the quality was thought inferior by Europeans and the trade inconsiderable. Then the British became indigo planters and the standard so improved and the acreage so extended that by 1830 India became the world's principal supplier. The merchants apparently became directly involved in the plantations as creditors to the planters, who often fell seriously into debt. The bankruptcy of Palmers, once the biggest agency house, has been traced to the steep decline in the price of indigo in the late 1820s.[9]

The other characteristic of the agency house that distinguished them from other mercantile partnerships was that of heavy public deposits of savings. It became the practice of larger houses to receive deposits from their many friends and acquaintances in the service of the East India Company, and this increased in 1822 when interest on the Company's debts was reduced from 8 to 4 or 5 per cent. There were no European banks in the Far East at this time so expatriates were glad of the privilege of leaving large sums on deposit at 4 or 5 per cent which the houses could lend at 12 per cent. The six great agency houses of the period – Palmers, Alexanders, Mackintoshs, Fergussons, Colvins and Cruttendens – invested these deposits in indigo factories, sugar plantations, ships, building speculations, docks, loans to people in and out of the services, and to mercantile firms in Singapore, Java, Manila and other developing centres of trade in the Far East. They issued their own notes as security for their debts to depositors. The conspicuous wealth of the early partners who returned home with fortunes persuaded people that the agency houses were solid as the Company itself, but heavy withdrawals by retired partners compelled them to function on borrowed capital. They controlled some of the newspapers published

---

[8] Guildhall Lib., Baring Bros. MSS, Gisborne & Co. to Barings 14 Feb. 1835, H. Menzies (Liverpool) to Gisbornes 10 Aug. 1835. Joshua Bates's journals 8–15 Sept. 1833 (private ownership).

[9] Canadian Public Archives (Ottawa), Baring MSS 80,061, *The East India and China Trade* (1829). M. Greenberg, *British Trade*, p. 166.

in India, and two or three of the earliest banks, so that it was difficult to escape their grip on the commercial life of the subcontinent.

The opening up of trade to India led to the establishment of 'small commission houses', often as agents of merchants and manufacturers in Glasgow, Liverpool and Manchester. The new houses competed vigorously with the older concerns, who tried to protect their position by making large advances to the indigo planters, £1·2m.–2·0m. a year according to one source. More than a third of these advances proved to be uncalled for or unproductive, but the companies' depositors still collected their interest. This development was the origin of the collapse of the 'big six' agency houses, which began with Palmers in 1830.[10]

The huge losses suffered by the agency houses' depositors in 1830–5 made their very names the abomination of commerce and finance, but it could not destroy the system they had created. Details are sparse because information suggesting any association with the discredited system was kept secret, but the planters still needed credit and a few of the successors of the 'big six' made large fortunes. In any event, the indigo factories, sugar estates and other fixed capital investments could not be sold, and the liquidation of the old firms dragged on for years. The agency houses do not appear to have lost the respect of the Indian communities, and indeed the native merchants subscribed £200,000 for the reinstatement of Palmers. The European settlers were the main losers in 1830–5, while the Indians appear to have emerged unscathed, and in course of time the latter became depositors in a new generation of agency houses.[11]

It is instructive to notice that the new generation houses were investing even before the 1830–5 crisis was over. In 1835 Cockerell Laing & Co. and Carr Tagore & Co. were making overtures to buy the East India Company's filatures, while Gisborne & Co. were trying to secure Baring Bros.' financial support for the same venture. Investment continued despite the well-founded anxieties of bankers at home; in 1844 the Bank of England's confidential files rated only four out of twenty Liverpool 'East India houses' as in first class credit.[12] There was a second round of bankruptcies of firms in the

---

[10] J. W. MacLellan, 'Banking in India and China', *Bankers Mag.*, LV (1893) pp. 50–5.
[11] M. Greenberg, *British Trade* pp. 165–7. A. Tripathi, *Bengal Presidency*, pp. 230–50. J. W. MacLellan 'Banking in India', p. 53. Bodleian Lib., Palmer MSS D105, private letter books p. 14B, letter to Barings 21 Jan. 1833.
[12] Guildhall Lib. Baring MSS, Gisborne & Co. to J. Bates 14 Feb. 1835. B. of E. Liverpool ltr bks V (1844) p. 2.

East India trade in 1847–8, when Cockerell, Larpent & Co. were found to have £200,000 of their £900,000 assets locked up in Mauritius sugar estates and extensive interests in indigo and sugar plantations and a teak forest in India. Similarly, Reid, Irving & Co., another old house bankrupted in the same crisis, owned extensive estates in Mauritius, and Lawrence Phillips & Sons had a coffee plantation in Ceylon. Between 1836 and 1846 Carr Tagore & Co. promoted and managed six joint-stock companies, including the Steam Tug Association, the Bengal Coal Co., the Bengal Docking Co., the Bengal Tea Association and Bengal Salt Co. One suspects that these disclosures were the tip of the iceberg, but even so the scale of investment was modest compared with what followed from the 1860s.[13]

There are two further characteristics of the agency houses which, though not unique in the mercantile world, were particularly strongly developed. One was that there were close connections with the City of London, or with the wealthiest families of Glasgow and Liverpool from the earliest years. Profits could only be assured by employing a large capital because of the risks associated with distance, war and commercial crises. Such connections had a long and interesting future. The other characteristic was that the expansion of Britain's Far Eastern trade was largely the work of family and clan groups among whom the Scots were particularly prominent. Greenberg ventures to explain this in terms of superior education but this is not very convincing. The more plausible interpretation is that in the pioneer years of the export of British textiles, most of the goods were manufactured in Glasgow rather than Manchester, where the agency houses had their home base. Moreover several of the leading East India houses in Liverpool were Scots migrants, among them Gladstone & Co., Arbuthnot Ewart & Co., Matheson & Scott and Ogilvy, Gillanders & Co. It is not a coincidence that most of the few surviving records refer to firms of Scots origin.[14]

[13] D. Morier Evans, *The Commercial Crisis of 1847–8* (1849) Appendix pp. v–xvi, xxi–xxiii, xxxvii. *Sel. Comm. on Manufacturers*, Parl. Papers, 1833, pp. 126–46 (Cockerells). Blair B. Kling, 'Agency System'.

[14] M. Greenberg, *British Trade*, pp. 35–40. *Sel. Comm. on Manufacturers*, pp. 138–9. Bank of England Liverpool ltr bks v (1844) p. 2, VIII (1847) p. 7, for lists and rating of East India houses. Stephanie Jones, *Two Centuries of Overseas Trading ... the Inchcape Group* (1986) p. 7.

AGENCY AND FIXED CAPITAL INVESTMENT

The records of Jardine, Skinner & Co. are the most complete of any Indian agency house. Fortunately they appear to be a fairly representative firm, at any rate in their origins, trading activities and attitudes to investment. The correspondence frequently refers to the experience of various competitors in Calcutta and elsewhere so that, taken along with other records and some published material, it is possible to allow them to bear the major burden of illustrating the trade experience at large, or at any rate that of the Scottish houses, in the middle period of development (1835–c. 1885).[15]

Jardine, Skinner & Co. was originally founded in Bombay in 1825 by two young Scots, then re-formed in 1844 in Calcutta by their successors David Jardine and C. B. Skinner. The records effectively begin with this reconstitution and from this period the correspondence files are fairly continuous down to the First World War. When they open, the firm, typical of agency houses of the period, was established in the textile trade, importing cotton piece goods from Glasgow and Manchester agents, and exporting indigo for Mincing Lane brokers, together with some silk and (later) jute. For some years the Glasgow agents were James Ewing & Co., who were well known for their 'Turkey red' prints, and Matheson & Scott in Manchester, a branch of Matheson & Co. of London and Jardine Matheson & Co. of Hong Kong. A letter of 1847 speaks of Ewings' plans to send £100,000 goods a year from which Jardine Skinner hoped to earn £5,000 to £7,000 p.a., but only after making a £25,000 cash advance to enable the agents to procure the necessary consignments.[16] It was more difficult for a Scottish house to draw consignments from Manchester for, as Hugh Matheson of Jardine Matheson explained, 'Lancashire manufacturers prefer Lancashire houses and consign to half a dozen in Calcutta and are ready to break off with any of them on the smallest pretence'. The trade was evidently highly competitive and, at times, precarious, so that Jardine Skinner & Co. were pleased to augment their commission income sending opium to their 'friends' Jardine Matheson in China. In 1846 Jardine believed that 'the palmy days of the trade in that article are past, although probably even now it

---

[15] Cambridge Univ. Lib., Jardine Skinner MSS, subsequently referred to as J S. The letters to Calcutta for 1843–51 are typed transcripts in five files, those for 1852–61 are missing.
[16] J S blue file 1, 18 Jan. 1845, green file 1, 9 Aug. 1847.

pays better in proportion to what anything else is doing...'[17] By 1860 they were also in the tea trade in a big way and later into timber and petroleum.

No account books have survived for Jardine Skinner but the letters contain several allusions to capital and profits from which it is possible to reconstruct the basic pattern of growth in the Victorian age. Soon after the reconstitution of the firm the capital was very close to £100,000, and it rose erratically to £1·3m. in 1890. Interpolation with the guidance of profits earned by Jardine Matheson suggest that capital reached £660,000 by 1860, £760,000 by 1870 and £990,000 by 1880.[18] These figures place Jardine Skinner among the richer agency houses, particularly as recurrent crises weeded out the less prudent houses. Jardine Skinner were fortunate that their credit was supported by Matheson & Co. of London; in the crisis of 1848 David Jardine wrote to his partner 'I cannot for a moment believe you will experience the slightest difficulty in drawing upon Matheson & Co.... at as good if not better rates than Baring's credits command', and in the crisis of 1866 Mathesons again stood behind the connection.[19] In 1890, when Mathesons were in deep water, it was Jardine Skinner that took some of the strain. The Scots, like other ethnic and religious groups in trade, commonly supported each other.[20]

The tensions in the firm come out well in the partners' letters. Broadly these were in two categories. Living in India in a closed society, there was inevitably tension between aggressive entrepreneurship and the easy 'live and let live' of the club house. When David Jardine first went out in 1840 he was advised that 'You will at all events find plenty of work and the very existence of our business depends upon everyone sticking closely to it and thinking of nothing else.' Four years later at the foundation of Jardine Skinner we find the hardworking Jardine writing that:

no one shall ever by my partner until he is capable of taking a certain lead in some department of the office, and until he has had some experience in his acts being in that correct and well judged nature as will give me

---

[17] J S blue 1, 6 Dec. 1844, 4 Apr. 1842; green 1, 22 Nov. 1846.
[18] Interpolated from two figures for capital: £100,000 in 1845–8 (J S blue file 1, 1 Oct. 1845) and £1·3m. in 1890. Jardine Matheson profit figures kindly given by Lord Blake who has been commissioned to write a history of the firm.
[19] J S blue 1, 4 Sept. 1848; in-letters LXXVIII, 10 July 1866, Jardine Matheson's capital was said to be about £1·0m. in 1848 and £1·72m. in 1891, M. Keswick, ed., *The Thistle and the Jade* (1982) p. 191.   [20] J S blue 1, 16 July 1891ff.

confidence as to what he does being correct. Money and connections are entitled to a certain weight in every house of business, but if they alone are looked to and no notice taken of talent, efficiency, industry, zeal and ability, what a pretty firm JS & Co. or any other would be.[21]

But by 1860, when a new partner had to be appointed to replace Jardine, Skinner was writing of a possible successor as:

An honourable and conscientious man of business, painstaking and plodding, but *not* clever or apt in initiating measures. This certainly when he comes to be head of a house is a disqualification, but not in our case sufficient to weigh against the positive advantages of being a *gentleman*, respectable and respected, of honourable principles, well known to most of us, and already thoroughly acquainted with Calcutta and its trade and acclimatised to India.

The plodder was duly appointed though, perhaps fortunately for Jardine Skinner, he never became senior partner.[22]

The other recurrent conflict in the firm, which was certainly familiar to other houses, was that between the extension of enterprise through integration back into factory and plantation ownership, and the need to retain a high degree of financial liquidity. Not surprisingly, letters on the problem proliferate in the crisis periods, while more 'liberal' views are taken in the periods of boom. Thus we find David Jardine, who in 1846 agreed to advance over £40,000 to various indigo factories insisting in 1848 that 'We must avoid blocks [illiquid investments]. We cannot afford even the most trifling amount of capital from our business for the purpose of carrying our indigo factories or anything else, and as for M[agniac] J[ardine] & Co., they have a horror of such business...' Nevertheless, in 1853 Jardine Skinner could not resist the opportunity to buy shares in one of the larger factory enterprises so as to secure control of the management. Like Ogilvy Gillanders, and most probably other houses, they were frequently to lose money on these commitments.[23]

The experience of Gillanders, Arbuthnot & Co., the Gladstone family's operation in India, was particularly poignant. According to the firm's early historian, who evidently had had to sort out some of the losses, the firm was slow to learn the lessons:

[21] J S blue 1, 4 Apr. 1840, blue 2, 10 June 1844.
[22] J S green 4, 3 Mar. 1860. The partner referred to, Deffell, died in 1863 before he could succeed as senior partner.
[23] J S blue 1, 6 Apr. 1846, 19 Jan. 1848; blue 3, 8 Nov. 1853. J. S. Gladstone, *History of Gillanders, Arbuthnot & Co.* (1910) p. 93.

Although the firm had from time to time lost heavily over indigo concerns, nevertheless the business had a great attraction and agencies were taken up freely despite the risk of losses...Numerous instances occurred where Gillanders, Arbuthnot & Co. lent money to enable the purchase of a factory to be made in the hope of securing commissions on the sale of indigo, but in almost every case this proved fatal and ended in heavy loss to G.A. & Co. Frequently G.A. & Co. were forced to take over shares in factories in satisfaction of debts, and in instances...they were forced to become sole proprietors.

At one time or another they were agents for forty-three indigo factories. When the synthetic dye was introduced they decided to terminate their investment, but it was not until 1906 that the last account was closed.[24]

The quite exceptional profits earned by merchant houses in cotton and piece goods trade during the American Civil War was the principal cause of a shift in policy during the early 1860s.[25] C. B. Skinner's letters to Calcutta allow us to monitor the change of emphasis in the direction of the agency houses at this period:

If piece goods are to remain so dear in this country I fear there will be little chance of our employing any money profitably...I have a great objection to buying and locking up money in blocks, but if there are any *good* concerns such as you might *safely* carry on at a fair rate of interest, getting the produce consigned for sale, you might earn both a com.[n] and interest on money to help P & L A/c (9 Sept. 1862).

I am glad that you are turning your attention to *tea*. If the Co.[y] you refer to is limited [i.e. joint-stock] and offers a fair prospect of a remunerative return, and is moreover under JS & Co. management, I can see no objection to your investing a portion of the firm's capital in it. I don't think I would go beyond a lac of rupees [£10,000]...(24 Jan. 1863).

There can be no harm I should think in getting as many tea companies into your hands as you can, provided they don't involve us in a larger outlay than is pleasant, and we are sufficiently secured...I suppose there is no house now in Calcutta who have not more or less engagements of this kind (17 Sept. 1863).[26]

This was the period at which the other Scots agency houses also invested heavily in new lines. James Finlay & Co., one-time owners

---

[24] J. S. Gladstone, *History*, p. 93.
[25] R. H. Macaulay, *History of the Bombay Burmah Trading Corporation Ltd 1864–1910* (1934) p. 4.
[26] J S green 5, for the dates cited in the text.

of three huge cotton mills in Scotland, also moved into tea, to be
followed by Gillanders, Arbuthnot & Co. Meanwhile Hendersons,
well known as agents to the Borneo Company, a firm that like
Jardine Skinners now had a 'huge amount of idle capital on their
hands', moved into jute milling. Parrys of Madras had already
shifted their main interest from the indigo trade into distilling, while
Wallace Bros. moved strongly into the teak trade in Burma following
an 1863 incorporation.[27]

Clearly both problems of the agency houses could be solved by
recruiting better quality management. Such evidence as we have
suggests that David Jardine's insistence on basic competence in the
central management was general but it took longer to build up a
reliable hierarchy in the plantations and industrial enterprises. The
problem was most clearly exposed at the time of the 'tea manias',
when the managers of tea gardens were 'a strange medley of retired
or cashiered Army or Navy Officers, medical men, engineers,
veterinary surgeons, steamer captains, chemists, shop keepers of all
kinds, stable keepers, used-up policemen, clerks, and goodness
knows who besides,' many of whom were complete failures in their
new-found occupation. It was easier to obtain competent mill
managers and overlookers as experienced men could be drawn from
Lancashire and Dundee, but here the problem was that the central
management of the agency houses, being trained as merchants, were
often ignorant of the machinery and processes of manufacture.[28]
Until after the turn of the century there was no regular system for
recruitment and training.[29]

FINANCE CAPITAL C. 1870–1920

Inevitably the opening of the Suez Canal (1869) and the extension
of the telegraph to India changed the old style of trade. Business
become faster and more competitive, and margins tighter. However,
this did not lead to any sudden restructuring as many of the agency
houses were already embarked on plantation and industrial
investment. On a fairly general and superficial level, all that

[27] [C. Brogan], James Finlay & Co., pp. 45–8. D. R. Wallace, The Romance of Jute (1928) p. 15.
Hilton Brown, The Parrys of Madras (Madras 1954) pp. 82–5. A. C. Pointon, Wallace Bros.
(Oxford 1974) p. 16. J. S. Gladstone, History, p. 93.
[28] H. A. Antrobus, History of the Assam Co. (1957) pp. 144–5. Sir P. Griffiths, History of the
Indian Tea Industry (1967) pp. 105–6. R. S. Rungta, Rise of Business Corporations in India
(1970) p. 232.   [29] R. H. Macaulay, History, pp. 23–4.

happened was that these houses developed and extended their already existing investments, often becoming specialists in one industry or another. In this way, Birds and Shaw Wallace & Co. shortly emerged as the leading specialists in coal mining, Parrys in distilling, Finlays, Duncans and other houses in tea, Yules in jute, Greaves, Cotton & Co. and Binnys in cotton mills, Mackinnon Mackenzie & Co. in shipping, MacNeills in inland waterway transport, Killick Nixon & Co. in branch line railways that served the plantations, and so forth. A few houses continued to specialise in commodity trade, notably Ralli Bros. in wheat and cotton, Steel Bros. in rice, Forbes & Co. in hides and Wallace Bros. in teak, all commodities stimulated by the opening of the Suez Canal. However, nearly all had some fixed-capital investments, for instance Ralli Bros. in press houses for jute, Steel Bros. in rice mills and Wallaces in saw mills.[30]

Moreover, most houses preferred to maintain an interest in *diverse* investments. This was partly because few firms seemed to be able to resist the latest investment passion (whether it was indigo, tea, jute, oil, gold or whatever) but mainly because experience had taught them not to put all their eggs in one basket. Indian historians have often generalised from the cotton mills which were seldom managed by European agency houses. In fact the agency house system did much to create an industrial sector that was entrepreneurial, diversified and efficient. The numerous houses competed strongly for agencies and outstanding entrepreneurs collected companies quickly, while incompetent or lazy managing agencies that failed to satisfy the shareholders were liable to lose control at an early date. Strong agency houses sometimes took over weaker ones. It is noticeable that several of the late nineteenth-century leaders of the agency houses were relative newcomers who had won a reputation for 'turning round' languishing enterprises. Birds are the best documented case, but Shaw Wallace, Yules, Martins, the Duncan Group and Mackinnon Mackenzie also fall into this category.[31]

These successes were won by houses that had the best managers. By 1917 Yules were at the head of the list of agency houses,

---

[30] A. K. Bagchi, *Private Investment in India 1900–39* (Cambridge 1972) pp. 177–9. List of house histories in the Appendix. 'The British in India' oral archives (1975–6) at India Office Lib.

[31] House historians listed in the Appendix. *Indian Industrial Commission*, confidential inspection notes 1916–18, p. 18 (I. O. L.). S. M. Rutnagur, *Bombay Industries: The Cotton Mills* (Bombay 1927) for abuses of the system.

managing over sixty companies, with a specialism in jute mills.[32] By contrast, the old-established firm of Jardine Skinner could make only 2 or 3 per cent on its capital in the boom years of the 1880s, and as the senior partner wrote, the reasons became clear enough in London:

> There is an impression which, however exaggerated, is none the less widely spread on this side, and has, I am told, been the subject of a good deal of comment at the Oriental Club, your juniors have not been giving the attention to the business which might have been expected of them – Watson's [ruinous] finances, the Banian trouble and Gregsons racing [losses] have all helped to pile up the indictment against us... It is not to be wondered at that... looking to the continuously unprofitable character of Watson's [silk] business... the Board should have been anxious to satisfy themselves as to the reliability of the management in India.[33]

Even the best firms had their rotten apples. Finlay's, who by 1898 had £4·4m. in the tea trade, suffered from at least one bad manager and J. S. Skinner wrote that 'It shows how the best of concerns – tea or other – will go wrong from bad management.' Similarly, Ralli Bros., who prided themselves on their disciplined and dedicated staff, suffered from the mismanagement of their colliery interests, while Wallace Bros. had sporadic problems with the management of their Burmese teak forests. But persistent problems could be remedied by strong houses. Jardine Skinner's perennial problem was their managing agency for J. & R. Watson's indigo plantations. In 1902 Yules took over the 2,400 square miles of plantations and brought them to profitability by changing to new crops.[34] *The Times* obituary of Sir David Yule (1858–1928) draws attention to a very different kind of entrepreneur to that of the languishing expatriate of popular novels. His life

was one of complete absorption in business and of an almost hermit-like retirement. There were few, if any, of his European compatriots in Calcutta, with the exception, in later years, of his partner, Sir Thomas Catto, who could speak of him as a personal friend. They never met him at the Bengal club, on the racecourse or the golf links, or even at meetings of the Calcutta Chamber of Commerce and other mercantile bodies. For

[32] *Andrew Yule & Co. Ltd., 1863–1963* (1963). Morgan Grenfell & Co., London, retain the accounts of Yules and some other records from 1917.
[33] J S blue 1, 17 May 1894, 15 Feb. 1895.
[34] [C. Brogan], *James Finlay & Co.* p. 47. J S. Senior partner's letters to Calcutta 5 Apr. 1906 (re Rallis). R. H. Macaulay, *History*, p. 24. *Andrew Yule & Co.*, p. 11.

many years before his marriage [in 1900] he lived a bachelor life over his business premises and there were many prominent business men and officials in Calcutta who had never seen him and he was never seen at Government House. His absorption in business had its reward in the remarkable success of almost everything in merchandise and Indian industrial enterprise to which he put his hand.[35]

A comparable calibre of entrepreneurship can be discerned in the careers of the heads of several other houses, particularly Sir Ernest Cable of Birds. A member of the firm mantained in 1915 that

The managing agency system has been, and is, to my mind a considerable factor in many successful ventures, in this part of India [Calcutta] at any rate. Powerful firms, by reason of their large stake in enterprises, often protect a languishing or difficult scheme from premature liquidation by providing that second string of security which a board of directors alone could not provide.[36]

New sectors of the economy were no less interesting to the agency houses; thus in 1895–1915 Martins brought the giant Bombay Iron & Steel Co. from loss to profit.[37]

Entrepreneurship and management were the principal but not the only ingredients of the growth of the agency houses. The other was the flow of capital from London. In the earlier periods investment was embarked on, sometimes reluctantly, as a means of securing the trade of the house; it was ancillary to mercantile interests. With much improved communications it was easier for British manu-facturers and wholesalers to undertake their own marketing in India, and trading margins became tighter.[38] At the same time, capital became more abundant and easier to control at a distance, so the leading agency houses gradually shifted the emphasis of their business from trade to investment management.

Some of these changes are reflected in data in Tables 4.1 and 4.2. Total investment in companies in India increased from £349m. in 1905–6 to £528m. in 1914–15 but it is not until the end of the period that it is possible to obtain any kind of breakdown of the source of this financing. The 'sterling companies' were those floated in

---

[35] Obituary in *The Times* 4 July 1928. *Thomas Sivewright Catto. A Personal Memoir and a Biographical Note* (1962) pp. 62–5.

[36] W. A. Ironside in evidence to *Indian Industrial Cmn.* 1916–18, xviii, p. 869.

[37] I. O. L. *Indian Industrial Cmn* confidential notes pp. 24–6. The capital of this Company was £575,000 and the payroll 10,000.

[38] S. J. Nicholas, 'The Overseas Marketing Performance of British Industry 1870–1914', *Econ. Hist. Rev.*, xxxvii (1984).

Table 4.1. *The direction of Indian companies in 1911*

| | No. of companies | Company directors | | | Private firms | |
		European	Indian	both	European	Indian
Tea plantations	927	681	32	0	116	98
Cotton mills	168	14	98	25	0	30
Jute mills	50	49	0	0	1	0
Collieries	331	133	17	26	13	142
Cotton presses	681	18	180	14	0	418
Jute presses	109	50	16	0	7	36

Source: Industrial Census of India, 1911; 'European' includes Anglo-Indians.

Table 4.2. *Sterling and rupee companies in 1914–15 (£m.)*

	Sterling	Rupee	Totals
Tea companies	19·7	2·9	22.6
Cotton companies	0·4	13·0	13·9
Jute companies	2·7	7·8	10·5
Coal companies	1·1	3·8	4·9
Gold companies	2·3	0·3	2·6
Cotton and jute presses	1·2	1·2	2·4
	27·4	29·0	56·9

Source: Indian Industrial Commission, II, p. 854.

London and the capital was overwhelmingly British. The 'rupee companies' were floated in India, often both British and Indian capital combined. Sterling companies were for the most part a relatively later (post-1890) development, but not always limited to those companies in which the agency houses characteristically invested.

These investments were dwarfed by those in Indian railways (£346m.). Beyond that, the main British interest was evidently in tea plantations, while most of the cotton mills and up-country cotton presses were Indian owned, the consequences of fortunes made during the cotton famine (1861–5). The British controlled practically all the jute mills and most of the collieries, which were generally the more capital-intensive forms of enterprise.

The agency houses were well placed as company promoters. Their name and reputation attracted both British and Indian capital. Oriental investments generally had only limited and intermittent appeal in the London and provincial stock exchanges but the names of the leading houses easily attracted private capital. Indeed, in the 1880s and 1890s the problem of the older houses was not finding the means to invest in India so much as finding investment opportunities for their abundant capital. John Stewart, the senior partner of Jardine Skinner, explained in 1890 that

under present conditions of mercantile business so few opportunities now occur for the profitable employment of capital in trading operations. In fact, outside of the employment we now find in the various producing industries in which we are employed, there is practically no direction in which...we may obtain, even with all the advantages of our position, safe,

strong and remunerative occupation except in that enlargement of our
Agency business, and that is not always to be had for the wishing...[39]

This comment is particularly striking when it is realised that Jardine
Skinner controlled six out of the twenty-one jute mill companies in
existence at this time in India. In much the same vein, a partner in
Wallace Bros. recalled that 'about the year 1895 money in London
was almost unemployable', so Wallaces had few distractions from
financing the extraction of tropical timber, even when prices were
low. One of Bird's partners remarked in 1915 that 'From my
personal experience the finance of industrial enterprise [in India]
has presented little difficulty... I consider the average bank manager
in this country [India] in advance of the British banker in providing
financial assistance.'[40] Nevertheless, company promotion was a
relatively late development, largely, it seems, because of the
traditional mercantile preference for liquidity described above.

It was not until 1890 that Jardine Skinner seriously considered the
idea of floating companies with shares that could be sold on the
London Stock Exchange. The senior partner in Calcutta proposed a
project to raise £5m. to build a new jute mill, cotton mill, paper mill
and jute press, but this scheme never came to fruition due to the
trauma following the Baring crisis. Matheson & Co. advised that it
would be better to issue all the shares in Calcutta, 'where from their
local knowledge of the capital and business, investors may be content
with less stringent terms, and where probably there might be a
market for them... which they cannot have in England owing to the
smallness of the issue'. In London Jardine Skinner's senior partner
mused that 'it would have been better for us, on the whole, if we had
begun earlier to practice the habit now so common (and adopted
long before us by our China friends) of financing outside and using
our own capital largely as margin'.[41]

In the context of the history of the agency houses as promoters,
Jardine Skinner were not particularly late arrivals. It is true that
there were earlier precedents – Hendersons promoting the Borneo
Company as early as 1856, Wallace Bros. the Bombay-Burma
Trading Co. in 1864, and Mackinnon Mackenzie the India Jute

---

[39] J S In letters, IC, 11 Sept. 1890.
[40] D. R. Wallace, *Jute*, p. 63–4. R. H. Macaulay, *History*, pp. 26, 130. Stephanie Jones,
    Inchcape Group, p. 184. *Indian Industrial Cmn* 1916–18, xviii, p. 869; see also p. 747.
[41] J S in letters, IC, 11 Sept. 1890; out letters 19 Aug. 1890. J S Guard Books 6, 16 Nov. 1894.
    J S blue 1, 28 June 1894. 'China friends' refers to Jardine Matheson & Co.

Mills at Serampore in 1866, for instance – but those were *ad hoc* initiatives, and developments of the 1870s and 1880s generally made little impact on the London Stock Exchange after the 'tea mania' of the early 1860s.[42] There were only twenty-one jute mill companies down to 1885 and collieries do not seem to have become a major investment area until the 1890s. Rubber of course did not attract investors until after the turn of the century, while the cotton mills remained predominantly in Indian hands.[43] The major growth of the agency houses as investment management groups dates, that is to say, only from the 1890s.

The numerous agencies maintained by the leading house on the eve of World War I give an impression of great size and concentration of capital, but financial data are incredibly difficult to come by. Yules' sixty companies (including nine jute mills, sixteen coal companies and sixteen tea plantations) provided employment for about 200,000 people, but further details are lacking.[44]

However, in 1917 W. A. Ironside of Bird's disclosed the structure of his firm's shareholding to the Indian Industrial Commission, expressing the view that in this respect it was fairly typical of agency houses at the period (Table 4.3). The data did not include the firm's interest in a new engineering works, a fireclay and silica works, a coke manufacturing plant and an electric supply company, so presumably the total shareholding was in excess of £2·0m. The same year, Birds were merged with an old rival, F. W. Heilgers & Co., an energetic former German firm that managed seven coal companies, two jute mills and two paper mills. The combined organisation, which was second only to that of Andrew Yule & Co. in India, had a capital investment valued at £20m., an annual profit of £3m., and employed directly or indirectly over 100,000 people.[45] Much the most interesting feature is that from a dispersed shareholding of perhaps £2–3m., Birds and Heilgers were able to direct an investment of £20m. Yules' capital was only £1·2m. and it looks as if the firm controlled an even larger capital investment than Birds. Bagchi supposes five to eight other Indian agency houses in the same bracket as Birds and Yules in 1911, including Jardine Skinner. There

[42] Sir P. Griffiths, *History of the Inchcape Group* (1977) p. 130. R. H. Macaulay, *History*, p. 4. D. R. Wallace, *Jute*, p. 25.
[43] D. R. Wallace, *Jute*, pp. 63–4. D. Kumar, ed., *Cambridge Economic History of India* II, p. 537f. Harrisons Crossfield, *One Hundred Years as East India Merchants* (1943) Ch. 3.
[44] *Andrew Yule & Co.*, p. 11. Yules' accounts at Morgan Grenfell. See also p. 236 below.
[45] G. Harrison, *Bird & Co.*, pp. 115–18.

Table 4.3. *Shareholdings in Bird & Co., Calcutta, in 1917*

	Numbers	Value (lacs)	Value (£)
10 coal companies:			
Europeans	1,551	97	
Indians	405	8	
Americans	59	n.d.[1]	
		105	£699,300
8 jute companies:			
Europeans	2,471	148	
Indians	423	25	
		173	£1,152,180
			1,851,480

[1] Assumed to be very small and treated here as negligible for the purposes of calculation. Calculation of exchange rates: 1 lac (lakh) = 100,00 rupees. One rupee = 1s. 4d = £0.06.
Sources: Report of the Indian Industrial Commission 1916–18, Parl. Papers, 1919, XVIII, ev. of W. A. Ironside for financial data, p. 881. The numbers of Bird's jute companies are given in G. Harrison, *Bird & Co. of Calcutta 1864–1964* (Calcutta 1964), p. 144.

appears to have been a comparable development in Singapore and Malaya in the first decade of the century. The six leading houses there (Boustead, Guthrie, Paterson, Simon, Gilfillan Wood, the Borneo Co. and Behn Meyer & Co.) held 365 agencies in 1911, an average of over 60 each. Burma was dominated by two agency houses, Wallace Bros. and Steel Bros., plus the Burma Oil Co. Jardine Mathesons took an early grip on British trade to China, and only Swires and Dodwells could offer any serious rivalry to them. There is a frustrating lack of hard evidence, but it looks as if British trade in the Far East was concentrated in the hands of little more than twenty firms by 1914.[46]

TRADING RISKS

Indian historians have been highly critical of British agency houses, Rungta frankly accuses most of them of inefficiency. 'It would be wrong...to tar all the managing agents with the same brush...Yet,

[46] A. K. Bagchi, *Private Investment*, pp. 176–8. J. H. Drabble and P. J. Drake, 'British Agency Houses in Malaysia', *Journal of S. E. Asian Studies* XII (1981). General impressions from bibliography of agency house histories (see Appendix).

when all is said, one is still left wondering whether the mis-management was not the rule rather than the exception', he wrote. Bagchi, in a rather more studied approach, suggests they formed an oligopoly that dominated the Indian economy. Ray believes they lacked enterprise as they 'prospered only too well along conservative and stereotyped lines'. These appear damning indictments, none of them are based on business records, nor is any critic able to offer any substantial evidence of lack of competition.[47] The source material remains inadequate but with more sensitive use of firms' records and privately published memoirs it is possible to explain most of the problems. Anti-colonial zealotry must be laid aside in the interest of historical objectivity.

Trade to the Far East continued to be a high-risk business despite constantly improving communications. Calamitous losses did not end with the collapse of the five great houses in the early 1830s; so late as 1906 two of the most prestigious names (Binnys and Arbuthnots) disappeared in the bankruptcy court. Merchant credit, notwithstanding the ever present menace of illiquidity and lock-ups of capital, continued to be essential in colonial trade as elsewhere. This highly vulnerable system functioned through an hierarchy of managers and clerks that were all too often less than equal to their task, for the London office characteristically lacked policies to recruit good men, and training facilities beyond learning on the job did not exist. Binny's collapse was directly attributed to mismanagement and lack of judgement in every branch of the business, which included cotton mills, coffee estates, coal mines and sugar plant-ations.[48]

A few accounts reveal just how vulnerable the system was, and these come from the more successful houses. Wallace Bros.' Burmese operation, the Bombay-Burmah Trading Co., was the leading firm in the teak trade. From 1864 to 1890 it was mainly confined to financing the extraction of timber by advancing money to foresters and receiving logs at delivery points on the rivers, but there was no serious consideration of how to recruit, let alone train suitable men, and lamentable deficiencies in local organisation were admitted in the 1890s. Steel Bros., who emerged as the leading house in the rice trade, originally bought from local traders who bargained with the

---

[47] R. S. Rungta, *Business Corporations*, p. 252. A. K. Bagchi *Private Investment*, pp. 176—8. Rajat K. Ray, *Industrialisation in India...the Private Corporate Sector 1914–47* (Delhi 1979) p. 30.   [48] P. Griffiths, *Inchcape Group*, p. 46.

peasants for cash payment. When the firm took to jungle buying, it was with the aid of Burmese assistants who went out armed with sacks of cash whose value was hundreds of times their annual salaries. In the Indian rice trade, Ralli Bros., as they recorded in 1888, 'used to buy from Mussulman dealers, but as their means are small it was difficult in advancing markets to obtain delivery of our purchases, and it often happened that we were unable to complete our shipping arrangements owing to the unsatisfactory way they delivered to us and to the bad stuff they tendered'. The solution found was to 'buy only from a rich native merchant, who makes advances in the interior, and can secure large quantities at a time', but this evidently introduced a dependency on one supplier and hence another type of vulnerability. These examples are at any rate sufficient to make the point that, even at the end of the century, colonial trade was not the easy ride perceived by some critics of the system.[49]

However, the main criticism is reserved for the transport, plantation and (more especially) industrial investments of the agency houses. These really belong to the period in which the trading houses were evolving into investment groups, and are therefore better reserved for Chapter 8, where fixed capital investment is examined, and Chapter 9, where comparison with German and Japanese competitors is made in the imperial context.

[49] R. H. Macaulay, *History*, pp. 23–4, 130. H. W. E. Braund, *Calling to Mind... the first 100 Years of Steel Bros.* (1975) pp. 37–8. Cambridge South Asian Archive, Ralli Bros. *Calcutta Handbook* (1888) II, Ch. 5, p. 9.

CHAPTER 5

The international houses: the foreign contribution to British mercantile enterprise

In the Introduction and first two chapters of this book it was recognised that the migration of foreign merchant families to London and provincial centres was a salient feature of British mercantile development in the eighteenth and nineteenth centuries. The policies, development and contribution of these families must now be given closer attention. They had a distinct character for which 'international houses' seems the best epithet. Their characteristic form can be traced back to the Florentine banks of the middle ages, which consisted of a parent partnership, characteristically located in Florence, with a controlling interest in several subsidiary partnerships, one for each branch abroad.[1] For later centuries an international house may be defined more generally as a merchant enterprise simultaneously functioning in two or more countries. The organisation persisted from the middle ages, but did not receive a major fillip until economic expansion coincided with persecution and dispersion of religious minorities in the late seventeenth and eighteenth centuries.

The outlook and practice of the international houses is best identified in relation to more familiar European and American mercantile habits and conventions. Postlethwayt explained in 1774 that 'The most capital houses of mercantile trade throughout Europe being generally composed of several partners, it is customary for one or the other to travel into foreign countries to make better judgement of the credit and fortune of their correspondents, cement ties of commercial friendship, and extend their traffic in general. As foreign merchants resort to England with this intent, so the English

---

[1] R. de Roover, 'New Interpretations of the History of Banking', *Cahiers d'Histoire Mondiale*, II (1954) pp. 47–8. D. S. Landes, *Bankers and Pashas* (1958) pp. 16–28, for a lively survey of international financial houses.

frequently take the tour into foreign countries.'[2] But such commercial exploration was typically for periods of up to two or three years, seldom longer, except in the case of Russia, and in no sense implied permanent residence.[3] A growing number of young men went to North America, the West Indies, India and (later) South America to make their fortunes, but they too travelled in the hope of a successful return within a measurable period of time. The second component of the international house, that is to say, is that its international representation was permanent; it was not a temporary situation that arose when sons or partners were abroad.

Several historians have drawn attention to the considerable number of foreign-born merchants permanently resident in London by the middle of the eighteenth century.[4] This group of alien residents included the Dutch Jews who came over as London succeeded Amsterdam as a centre for international exchanges and played such a major role in London banking and insurance and as investors in government stocks.[5] From French historians we are also familiar with the activities of the 'international Huguenots', whose family dynasties linked Geneva, Berne, Paris, Frankfurt and other European centres with London, and who (in the words of Lüthy) 'practically monopolised the financial relations between England and France' in the eighteenth century.[6] It was these wealthy eighteenth-century families, characteristically operating in two, three or four mercantile centres simultaneously, that represented the successful revival of the practice of the international house. The aim of this chapter is to trace their continuing importance from London into the provinces, and into support of the 'new frontier' industries of Britain, in the late eighteenth and early nineteenth centuries.

It might easily be supposed that as Britain emerged as the premier world trading nation, and the United States as the country par excellence for migrants, the mercantile families of these two countries would generate more international houses than any other country. Certainly it can be shown that in 1850 (and probably much earlier)

[2] M. Postlethwayt, *Universal Dictionary of Trade and Commerce* (1774) article on 'Mercantile College'. R. Campbell, *The London Tradesman* (1747) pp. 293–4.

[3] Russia was an exception to this generalisation for alien merchants who did not become naturalised were greatly disadvantaged, P.R.O. FO 83/111.

[4] T. S. Ashton, *An Economic History of England: the Eighteenth Century* (1955) p. 140.

[5] C. Wilson, *Anglo-Dutch Commerce and Finance in the Eighteenth Century* (Cambridge 1941) pp. 42, 54, 94, 106–7, etc. A. C. Carter, 'Financial Activities of the Huguenots in London and Amsterdam in the mid-Eighteenth Century', *Proc. of Huguenot Soc. of London*, XIX (1959).

[6] H. Lüthy, *La Banque protestante en France*, II, *1730–1794* (Paris 1961) p. 318.

there were more British firms resident abroad than those of any other single country.[7]

But these firms were invariably commission agents, men of little capital out to seek their fortunes and return home, much as the eighteenth-century adventurers had done. The growing trade areas of the first half of the nineteenth century, India, the Far East and South America, offered little incentive to Europeans to permanent settlement. What was characteristic of Britain was even more true of the United States. Merchant houses sent partners or agents abroad for two or three years, so the number of American firms established abroad was small in relation to the country's trade. Until at least the middle of the nineteenth century, US firms preferred the 'adventure' kind of enterprise, with the ship's captain fulfilling the main entrepreneurial role.[8]

During the French Wars (1793–1815), the French and Dutch emigrés were overtaken by a new wave of international trading families, many of them, like the Huguenots and Amsterdam Jews, deriving from religious or ethnic minorities. The Jews and other German families from Hamburg, Frankfurt, Berlin and Leipzig were settling in London and northern industrial towns at the same time as some notable Irish Presbyterian families with US trading connections. They were followed, in the 1830s and 1840s, by large numbers of Ottomans, mostly from the Greek Orthodox religious minority. These groups shared common characteristics with the Dutch Jews and Huguenots. They had a similar international commercial outlook that often survived into the third and fourth generations, and an un-British reluctance to desert trade for the security of landed estate, the Church or the professions. They had sufficient capital, credit or connections, and adequate commercial experience, to keep one step ahead of the vagaries of fashion, war, revolution and royal folly. And they shared a sectarian outlook that interlocked families in chains of partnerships and marriages and loyalties that spanned the dispersed partnerships.

Inevitably some families were more successful than others, but the very process of separation of the strong from the weak seemed to make the outstanding firms seem even more powerful. As in

---

[7] Table 3.7, above.

[8] B. of E. Archives, Manc. ltrs, 17 Jan. 1837: 'Very few of the parties who represent the American houses in our market can be looked upon as permanent residents as they are constantly changing...' V. B. Reber, 'British Mercantile Houses in Buenos Aires, 1810–80', Ph.D. thesis, Wisconsin 1972, pp. 123–5. The point is developed more fully below, pp. 149–153.

biological evolution, the strong chose the strong as partners, so that out of a crowd of small and middling firms, a core of dynastic houses persisted, with partnership changes, for much of the nineteenth century. But the continuity of the house was never left to the forces of hereditary and marriage alone. The new generation was carefully tested by experience in two or three countries, and shifted where need and opportunity offered; mediocre sons were dropped in favour of more talented nephews, sons-in-law, second cousins or talented outsiders.[9] Promising family connections were sponsored or encouraged in new outposts of the dynasty's trade, all of course sheltered by the assurance of the Pax Britannica and, very often, of British nationality in the relevant branches of the family.[10] The international house was, as we shall see, an organisation well suited to the uncertainties and vicissitudes of nineteenth-century trade, flexible enough to respond to the opportunities of developing industry, yet sufficiently stable to draw on the credit of traditional channels of trade. Its smooth competence kept it out of the news and hence of historical annals, so that its contribution to British commerce has been largely overlooked.[11]

There is not space in this chapter to describe the long process of urban and mercantile evolution that had shaped these migrant families, but two important factors must be underlined. The cities from which they were drawn – principally Frankfurt, Hamburg and Constantinople – were not only imperial cities, but also international entrepôts. Their prosperity was derived from their location at the focus of a mosaic of small states and at the meeting point of different ethnic and religious traditions, so that over the centuries each evolved an elite of mercantile families drawn from various races and creeds. Their situation, that is to say, had been broadly favourable to the development of what Bergeron calls 'an aristocracy that knew no national frontiers', and had limited local loyalties.[12] The other important point is that the course of trade development in the eighteenth century generated a strong interest in 'colonial goods' –

[9] The 'black sheep' of the family is seldom mentioned in business histories or biographies, but for a telling case see the MS diaries of George A. Brown (1803–61) of Brown, Shipley & Co., Liverpool merchant bankers (L'pool P.L.).

[10] British nationality was often required to open accounts with English banks.

[11] The main exceptions to this generalisation are B. Gille, La Maison Rothschild, 2 vols. (Geneva 1965–7) and E. J. Perkins, Financing Anglo-American Trade: the House of Brown 1800–80 (Harvard 1975). Both are thin on Britain.

[12] L. Bergeron, 'Les banquiers rhenans, fin du xviiie siècle au debut du xixe siècle', Bulletin du Centre d'Histoire economique et sociale de la région lyonnaise, 1975.

sugar, tobacco, cotton, 'drugs' (mordants and dyestuffs), printed textiles etc. – a trade which increasingly centred on London but circulated through Europe, often through the channels provided by the Huguenots and Dutch Jews.[13] Inevitably, the most enterprising of these international families sought a direct interest in Britain's growing colonial and transatlantic commerce. The extension of their family interests to Britain, and the organisation and results of their trade here, form the main subject matter of this chapter.

GERMAN MERCHANT HOUSES IN BRITAIN

The first settlement of German international houses came as the immediate consequence of two late eighteenth-century developments, the triumph of the British cotton industry and the curtailment of the normal channels of trade caused by the prolonged period of European war. In London, the Germans joined an established community of some forty Hamburg merchants, many of them of German origin, but in the North of England the settlement of foreigners was a novel experience. At the turn of the century, the traditional commerce of the great German fairs of Frankfurt-on-the-Main, Leipzig, Brunswick and Nuremberg, was being bypassed by direct consignments to particular mercantile houses,[14] a process as much encouraged by German importers visiting Manchester and Glasgow as the merchants of those towns touring their correspondents in Europe. The first German settler of whom we have any considerable knowledge, N. M. Rothschild of Frankfurt, one of the sons of a Jewish house specialising in the English textile trade, at first conducted most of his trade with visitors from his own country.[15] In a typical letter, he explained how residence in Manchester could be more profitable to him and his buyers:

The Manufacturers of Muslin Goods having generally at the close of the Year a great Necessity for money in order to settle their accounts are obliged to sell their goods 10 and 12 p. ct. cheaper than they would at any other time and sometimes at prime cost, so that I can send you goods of good quality in the month of November ... 10 p. ct. cheaper than what you

[13] For French interests, see H. Lüthy, *La Banque protestante*, For German, A. Dietz, *Frankfurter Handelsgeschichte*, IV (1925). In 1810 there were ninety merchant houses in Frankfurt trading in 'colonial goods', see list in [Anon.], *Geschichte der Handelskammer zu Frankfurt a.M., 1707–1908* (Frankfurt 1908) pp. 188–9.
[14] A. Redford, *Manchester Merchants and Foreign Trade* (Manchester 1934) p. 95.
[15] Letter books of N. M. Rothschild (& Sons), 17 Oct. 1802. He charged his customers five per cent commission.

would get for them in the Spring at the fair in Frankfurt. The goods...will arrive at Liège 4 or 5 weeks before the Fair at Frankfurt.[16]

Such a profitable business, buying when prices were low and bypassing the traditional intermediaries, soon attracted the younger sons of other established houses. Souchay and Du Fay, two Huguenot families well established in Frankfurt, sent members of their families soon after the turn of the century, and other merchants of the town in the English trade followed. Oppenheimer & Liepmann of Berlin settled in Manchester in 1801, and H. J. Merck of Hamburg in 1806, each to be followed by a larger contingent from his trading community.[17] Young Rothschild brought his own train of relatives and connections, notably the Reiss brothers of Frankfurt and Amsterdam, one of whom took up residence in Glasgow in 1803, his distant cousin, N. M. Rindskopf, who settled in London in 1805, and his brother-in-law Benedikt Worms, who opened his London bank in 1815.[18] Clusters of family enterprises, already a familiar feature of the Huguenot and Jewish merchants of London, were to become characteristic of the newcomers as each successful entrepreneur attracted his relatives to join him.

Hamburg and Frankfurt were occupied by Napoleon's army between 1806 and 1812 and their trade suffered from the blockade. London became the principal centre for trade with Russia and the newly opening markets of Latin America, as well as with the colonial territories of the West Indies and India, and the USA. So several Hamburg houses tried to keep in business by moving to London, or more likely following the traditional practice of sending one or more of their sons.[19] Among the best known firms that were founded in this way, Hambros came in 1800, Schröders in 1802, E. H. Brandt in 1805, Frederick Huth in 1809 and Fruhling & Goschen in 1814. The early history of some of these firms is not easy to discern, but it seems that the first three were engaged in the Baltic trade and the last two in Spanish–American business.[20] Rothschild moved from

---

[16] Rothschild ltr bks., 17 July and 31 Oct. 1802.
[17] See List of Early German Houses in Manchester, 1797–1815, in John Scholes MS, Manchester P.L.
[18] Rothschild ltr bks, 8 Oct. 1805 et seq., A. Dietz, *Frankfurter Handelsgeschichte*, p. 331. Other emigrants included M. A. Rothschild's son-in-law, B. J. Sichel, and brother-in-law, N. L. Hanau.
[19] H. Kanter, *Die Entwicklung des Handels...zu Frankfurt a.M.* (Tübingen 1902). A. Dietz, *Frankfurter Handelsgeschichte*, p. 333.
[20] Records of J. H. Schröder, Wagg & Co., London and Hamburg. E. Amburger, 'William Brandt and the Story of his Enterprises' (trans. of German typescript, 1937) and Brandt

Manchester to London in 1805, leaving his chief clerk in charge in the north, and Souchay opened an office in London in 1806. The new arrivals built on existing continental firms in London, Brandt on Rougement & Behrens, the leading Huguenot house, Huth on Firmin de Tastet, a well-known Spanish house, and Rothschild initially on Soloman Solomans and Goldsmid & Eliason, two Dutch–Jewish merchant houses with whom his father had close connections in Frankfurt.[21] J. F. Schröder seems to have functioned as an accepting house from his arrival in London, no doubt drawing on his father's £200,000 fortune, while Souchay's simultaneous opening of offices in London and Manchester hints at similar enterprise, though he did not formally identify himself as a merchant banker until 1825.[22] In Manchester, the position is not so well documented, but there is some evidence of a comparable network of credit between old and new continental houses. For instance, Oppenheimer & Liepmann acted as Manchester agents for Barrick & Simon of Berlin, and were granted credits by London merchants Donaldson, Glenny & May under the guarantee of Conrad Donner of Altona.[23]

The London merchants who functioned as accepting houses preferred to allow credit to agents permanently resident in Britain, and commonly insisted on such residence because experience had taught them that the legal process of recovering debts abroad was impossibly expensive. Thus Firmin de Tastet advised Boulton & Watt it would be rash to rely on foreign guarantees when selling their steam engines abroad. 'Were we in your place', his firm wrote in 1794, 'we would...not be satisfied with a guarantee abroad but we should require one in England, and if you cannot do foreign business on these terms you will in our opinion do better not to undertake it.'[24] Such a policy evidently favoured the new German arrivals and ensured the continuity of their trade when the war was over. Moreover, the 'old style' merchants expected a net profit of fifteen to twenty per cent on their sales, while Rothschild and his

MSS, Nottingham Univ. Lib. J. R. Freedman, 'A London Merchant Bank in Anglo-American Trade', Ph.D. thesis, London 1967, pp. 11–13. T. J. Spinner, *G. J. Goschen: the Transformation of a Victorian Liberal* (Cambridge 1973) p. 2.

[21] Brandt letters, 1818 bundle (Nottingham Univ. Lib.) Olver–Huth letters, 1812 (Devon R.O., Plymouth). Rothschild ltr bks, 1800–5.

[22] Rothschild ltr bks, 3 Nov. 1802. A. Dietz, *Frankfurter Handelsgeschichte*, p. 331.

[23] P.R.O. E112/1792/6456 (1804).

[24] Boulton & Watt MSS, Box 36 (Birmingham Ref. Lib.). Reference kindly sent by Dr Jennifer Tann.

successors hoped to obtain a much bigger turnover with a commission of five to ten per cent, a rate which he insisted (no doubt with justice) was 'much less than what most Houses in Manchester would do business for'.[25] There can be little doubt that the evolution of commercial practice in the first half of the nineteenth century was on the trend of rising turnover and thinner profit margins, a trend which harmonised with, if it was not led by the practices of the Napoleonic generation of German immigrants.[26]

A combination of circumstances after the French Wars, more especially the high rate of turnover of firms, falling profit margins, unstable banking conditions and increasing cost of overseas selling, led to the ruin or enervation of many of the northern merchant–manufacturers and old London merchants.[27] Chapter 2 showed that in their place there emerged a sequence of specialists in London and the northern industrial towns, accepting houses (or merchant bankers), 'foreign houses' (i.e. exporters on commission) and commission agents resident abroad, typically specialising in a sector of overseas markets such as North America, Europe, India and China, or Latin America. The merchant–manufacturer so far declined that by the middle of the nineteenth century it could be said that 'at least seven-eighths or three-fourths' of the entire export business of Lancashire and Yorkshire was conducted by them, and a parallel change took place in Birmingham and Glasgow.[28] As the export trade of other leading industrial centres was financed by the same bankers, it is clear that the development was a national one. In 1836 it was explained that 'Trade has...undergone a great change during the last ten years; weak and struggling manufacturers no longer consign goods to commission houses at New York, Philadelphia, Hamburg, Frankfurt and St Petersburgh, but those who supply the consumers in the countries where the great commercial cities are situated come to our markets to select and purchase their own goods, and they pay for them by the aid of the wealthy and powerful firms connected with their respective localities.

---

[25] P.R.O. E112/1773/5722 (1798), Love v. Hepburn, for profit rates. Rothschild ltr bks, 17 Oct. 1802, 29 Aug. 1804.

[26] See eg. *Sel. Comm. Manufactures*, Parl. Papers, 1833, VI, pp. 86, 254, 317 etc.

[27] See eg. M. M. Edwards, *Growth of the British Cotton Trade, 1780–1815* (Manchester 1967) pp. 22–3 (Lancs. merchant–manufacturers). *Sel. Comm. on Handloom Weavers*, Parl. Papers, 1834, p. 164 (Glasgow merchants), 1835, p. 168 (Leeds merchants).

[28] *Royal Cmn on Depression in Trade*, Third Report, 1886, pp. 15, 21 (ev. of Sir J. C. Lee). For Birmingham see B. of E. B'ham ltrs, 22 Jan. 1827; for Glasgow *Sel. Comm. on Handloom Weavers*, 1834, pp. 51, 100; for Liverpool *Sel. Comm. on Manufactures*, 1835, pp. 251–2.

The agents who are called into operation to effect mercantile transactions are changed from commission merchants to commission bankers ... [as] all their pecuniary affairs are of the nature of banking commissions ...'[29]

Contemporaries believed that these changes amounted to 'quite a revolution in trade',[30] and it was supposed that foreign traders had largely occupied the gaps left by British failures. 'The convulsions of [the commercial crisis] of 1825–6 extended all over the commercial world and greatly affected the operation of the [British] continental merchants', the *Circular to Bankers* noted in 1828. 'The vocation, as exporters of manufactures and produce, of that class of London merchants from which most of our Bank Directors were selected, is taken up by men of inferior station. The Jewish merchants of Prussia, Russia, and Germany (*sic*), who were formerly content with the trade of supplying the countries situated near to the Eastern boundary of Europe with British commodities, which they purchased from London merchants, are now as familiarly known as purchasers in the markets of Manchester, Bradford, Leeds, Paisley and Glasgow, as the London warehouseman.'[31] In Manchester, the success of the 'foreign houses' attracted local entrepreneurs to try to adopt the same technique; so early as 1817 Swan & Buckley launched their partnership on the precise principles followed by N. M. Rothschild in his early years in the town (1799–1805), and they did not attempt to conceal their debt. The most important of the objects of their 'General Agency Business for the purchasing of Cotton Twist and Manufactured Goods' were said to be:

(1) To purchase all goods from the manufacturer, either in the grey or finished state, without the intervention of a second party between the merchant and manufacturer
(2) To finish all goods, whether for dyeing, printing or bleaching, upon the most reasonable terms that can be obtained, the best arrangements having already been made with the most respectable houses in the various departments.

'Since the return of peace,' they explained, 'our relations with the rest of Europe have become almost general, and so directly is this

---

[29] *Circular to Bankers*, 1 July 1836, p. 404; 2 Sept. 1836, p. 51; 15 Jan. 1836, p. 201.
[30] *Sel. Comm. on Manufactures*, 1833, p. 95, ev. of G. Shaw, whose firm traded with Germany, Italy and the USA [Harry Behrens], *Sir Jacob Behrens, 1806–89* (1925) p. 32.
[31] *Circular to Bankers*, 7 Mar. 1828.

Table 5.1. *Number of German merchant houses in manufacturing towns of Britain, 1820–50*

	c. 1820	c. 1830	c. 1840	c. 1850
Manchester	28	61	84	97
Bradford	0	3	25	38
Leeds	0	2	10	?6
Nottingham	0	1	4	7
Birmingham	3	6	7	c. 12

Note: A few houses operated in more than one town, and so may be counted more than once.
Sources: Manchester: John Scholes, *Foreign Merchants in Manchester 1784–1870*, MS, Manchester Ref. Lib. Bradford and Leeds: E. M. Sigsworth, *Black Dyke Mills* (Liverpool 1958), p. 65, quoting local directories. Nottingham: White's *Directory* (1832); Pigot's *Directory* (1841); Lascelles' *Directory* (1848); A. Dietz, *Stammbuch der Frankfurter Juden* IV pp. 377–9; Birmingham: local directories.

market connected with the principal ones on the Continent, that from that period several foreign establishments have been formed here who are enjoying all the benefits we propose to you...'[32]

The number of German houses in the provinces grew particularly rapidly in the 1820s and 1830s (Table 5.1, Figure 5.1). More young adventurers came over, but these were often members of, or connected with, existing families. Existing houses strengthened their position by increasing the number of branches in Britain and abroad and (less often) by partnership linkages with British manufacturers. Repeated use of the patronymic forenames, intermarriage of the same families over two or three generations, and interlocking partnerships make it difficult to untangle the various enterprises and networks, even where pedigrees are available.

There were other reasons for the migration of young Germans to Britain. It was customary for Hamburg merchants to send their sons abroad for some years, and as the main trade of this great port was with London, numbers of them came to the British capital.[33] In 1822, a young friend from Nantes wrote to Daniel Meinertzhagen of Bremen that 'for learning commerce, London is without exception the best school. You are here in the centre of universal business, and you can know [at first hand] what goods come from each country

[32] Trade circular in Brandt letters, 1818 bundle.
[33] *Reports from H. M. Diplomatic and Consular Offices*, Parl. Papers, 1860, LVXI, p. 104.

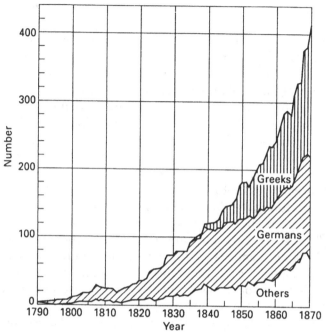

Figure 5.1. Alien merchants in Manchester, 1790–1870.

and what goods they want in return.' Shortly afterwards, Daniel came to London and was taken into the house of Frederik Huth & Co., a leading firm in the Latin American trade.[34]

Many of the German merchants who settled in other countries were Jews, and there can be no doubt that they were seeking social acceptance as well as economic gain. It is impossible to say how many Jewish merchants left Germany and where they went, but some details assembled in Alexander Dietz's *Stammbuch der Frankfurter Juden* give a useful impression of the dispersion of trading and professional families. Of 356 men who left the town in the early nineteenth century, 113 went to France (nearly all to Paris), 89 to Britain (London 66, Manchester 14), 52 to the USA (of which New York 31), 47 to the Low Countries, 41 to Vienna, and 14 to various Italian cities. A dozen Jewish families trading in English textiles sent one or more of their sons to follow N. M. Rothschild to Manchester.[35] The dispersion not only created a web of trading connections, but

[34] G. Meinertzhagen, *A Bremen Family* (1912) p. 251.
[35] A. Dietz, *Stammbuch..* .(1907) pp. 371, 377–9; *Geschichte*, IV, p. 333.

generated a flow of information on the degrees of toleration afforded
to Jews.

It is difficult to assess the strength of feeling on such matters
because there is little biographical evidence and attitudes changed
after 1848 with the rise of German national feeling, but some
guidance may be found in the general history of Jewish emancipation
in Germany. The policies of the various states varied considerably,
but there is a common theme in the legal emancipation of the Jews
in states occupied by the French and the retraction of civic rights in
the conservative reaction of the post-war years. At the Congress of
Vienna (1815) it was the premier trading cities of Hamburg,
Frankfurt, Bremen and Lübeck that pressed for the revocation of the
rights granted during the French era. Sporadic progress was made in
the next fifty years, but it was 1871 before full emancipation was
achieved.[36] In Manchester and Nottingham, a number of the emigré
Germans became members of the Unitarian Church, a religious
denomination noted for its liberal theology, intellectual culture and
progressive philanthropy, and attractive to those seeking cultural
assimilation. Later, German Lutheran churches were built in
Manchester and Bradford, attracting Jews as well as Christians into
membership, but orthodox Jews were equally anxious for social
acceptance.[37] In Bradford, the German colony met at the
Schillerverein, a club endowed with the principles of liberalism and
democracy, and the local population believed that 'Many of these
merchants were men of liberal opinions who knew they could be
happier outside Germany.'[38] In Manchester the Schiller Anstalt,
which had a large Jewish membership, had a similar outlook.[39]

Not all the German houses established in Britain were branches of
established concerns in Hamburg, Frankfurt, Leipzig and other
commercial centres. The rapid growth of British export trade
brought a large increase in employment opportunities for literate
continentals to work for British merchants and manufacturers as
clerks and 'outriders' – i.e. commercial travellers. The earliest
example on record concerns William Uhde, who came to Manchester
in 1788 as a clerk in the employ of Taylor & Maxwell, a well-known

---

[36] R. Rurup, 'Jewish Emancipation and Bourgeois Society [in Germany]', *Leo Baeck Institute Yearbook*, 1974.
[37] B. Williams, *The Making of Manchester Jewry* (Manchester 1976) pp. 82–3, 334. The 'German Church' in Bradford was formed in 1875, B. Williams, p. 13.
[38] J. B. Priestley, *English Journey* (1934) pp. 158, 160.
[39] B. Williams, *Manchester Jewry*, p. 260.

firm of cotton manufacturers, dyers and printers, whose main interest was in foreign markets. Uhde was soon being employed as an outrider, selling textiles and collecting debts both in England and Germany, and took the opportunity to earn some commissions from other Lancashire firms, notably Peels, the premier textile printers and merchants. In 1794, Uhde opened his own warehouse in Manchester, taking into partnership another of Taylors' clerks called Justamond, a name that suggests German origins.[40] The practice of employing German travellers continued well into the nineteenth century; indeed it was regarded as an important innovation when a young Bradfordian learned German to serve his firm abroad.[41] The ubiquitous presence of German clerks and travellers is probably explained by superior education as much as opportunities in Britain; certainly German merchants were to supersede their British rivals in Russia because of their much better commercial education. And in Britain, many foreign-born clerks rose to be partners in the firms they served.[42] Rothschilds, Huths and other merchant banks were generous to their senior clerks, so that some were able to become merchants.[43]

The final and most important impetus to migration was the decline of the great international fairs at Frankfurt and Leipzig as centres of commerce in British manufactured goods. The only available statistics for Leipzig (Table 5.2) leave much to be desired, but they show that while the fair continued to grow in size over the period 1748–1840, West European, as distinct from Prussian and Saxon interest, declined from the 1820s. Unfortunately, British and French attendance is not registered separately after 1790, but the interest of these countries is clearly expressed in the figures for Hamburg and Frankfurt. According to the *Circular to Bankers*, the decisive changes came about as a consequence of the commercial crisis of 1825–6. The convulsions of the crisis extended all over the commercial world, leading to the bankruptcy of some merchants trading to the Continent and a reduction of the scale of operations of others. But commerce abhors a vacuum, and despite the thinner

---

[40] P.R.O. E112/1541/589, C12.1739/6. Another case, E112/1530/224, suggests that it was not unusual for an outrider to be retained by several firms.
[41] William Rothenstein, *Men and Memories* (1931–2) I, p. 7. G. L. Anderson, *Victorian Clerks* (Manchester 1976) pp. 61–5.
[42] D. Mackenzie Wallace, *Russia* (1877) I, p. 277. W. F. M. Weston-Webb, *Autobiography of a British Yarn Merchant* (1929) pp. 111, 129–30.
[43] [David M. Evans], *The City, or the Physiology of London Business* (1845) p. 174.

Table 5.2. *Place of origin of visitors to the Leipzig Fairs, 1748–1840*

	1748	1780	1790	1820	1834	1840
England	6	12	60 ⎫			
France	7	64	60 ⎪			
Holland	45	50	34 ⎬	not stated separately		
Italy	0	33	52 ⎪			
Poland	67	368	569 ⎭			
Greece & Turkey	22	125	117	87	108	86
Hamburg	331	206	185	514	334	214
Frankfurt (aM)	48	119	165	605	247	170
Berlin	149	309	344	711	867	975
Saxony	1,494	3,904	3,934	5,540	8,168	8,070
All visitors	5,263	8,952	8,994	21,656	26,444	21,458

Source: E. Hasse, *Geschichte der Leipziger Messen* (Leipzig 1885) pp. 304–8.

profit margins of the later 1820s and 1830s, new enterprise moved in to fill the place of the old. Following the long tradition of German commerce, Jewish traders moved in to fill the gaps left in the system.[44]

Some further explanation of developments was furnished by the British Consul in Leipzig in 1837. By this time, most of British goods sold at the Leipzig Fairs were printed calicoes, and the dealers there preferred to give their orders direct to their agents in England, so that 'with one or two exceptions the English frequenters of the Leipzig Fairs are now restricted to the woollen manufacturers who visit Germany for purpose of purchasing wool and who (in some cases only) avail themselves of the opportunity to obtain orders for their manufactured goods'. The Consul, no doubt reflecting the prejudices of the times, insisted that the whole trade had fallen into the hands of one sect. 'These are the Hamburg Jews established here, whose connections in Manchester and other manufacturing towns take advantage of every favourable opportunity of purchasing parcels of goods which the necessities of our manufacturers compel them to part with on low and but too often losing terms. These are then brought over to the fairs of Leipzig and other towns of Germany, where they are disposed of on terms which defy all competition on the parts of the more regular traders. The... Hamburg houses force off their goods, especially among the Poles

[44] W. E. Mosse, *Jews in the German Economy* (Oxford 1987) Ch. 1.

and the Jews and the Greeks from the [Danubian] Principalities by the temptation of long credits...'[45]

PARTICULAR FIRMS

From the reasons for the establishment of the large German merchant community in Britain, we may turn to individual firms to seek some guidelines on capital, credit and markets. The evidence leaves no doubt that both young Rothschild and the Schröder brothers came to Britain to invest part of their fathers' fortunes, and it seems probable that the other early firms brought capital with them. A dozen Frankfurt Jewish houses that sent sons to Britain had family connections with bankers.[46] The more numerous smaller firms who settled in the 1830s and 1840s were more dependent on the credit of others, and had to draw on the established merchant houses of their own cities, thus maintaining a flow of capital from the German states to Britain. This was the period of massive peasant redemption payments, which the landlords deposited with the Fürstenbank, Rothschilds and other banks, and which may have been channelled into British commerce. Moreover, several German merchants resident in Britain married into eminent continental banking families, unions that hint strongly at earlier commercial connections. Thus Jacob Behrens (Bradford) married a daughter of Hohenemser, the Mannheim banker, Emil Springmann (Liverpool) married a Wichelhaus daughter, from a well-known Cologne banking house, and Moritz Rothenstein (Bradford) won the hand of a Dux lady, of the Hildesheim bank.[47]

However, by the 1830s, capital had become plentiful and cheap in Britain, with the accepting houses competing with each other for business, so that London merchant banks began to provide credits for exports from Hamburg and other German towns.[48] Consequently, it is difficult to decide whether Britain was a net importer of capital from Germany or not. The only clue available is J. B. Smith's

---

[45] P.R.O. FO 68/42, 13 Nov. 1837.
[46] S. D. Chapman, 'The Foundation of the English Rothschilds', *Textile History* VIII (1977) Appendix.
[47] H. Winkel, *Die Ablosungskapitalien aus der Bauernbefreiung in West- und Suddeutschland* (Stuttgart 1968). [Harry Behrens], *Sir Jacob Behrens. Jewish Telegraph*, 5 Dec. 1969 (Rothenstein article). Information from Robin Brackenbury whose mother was a Springmann.
[48] *Sel. Comm. on Manufactures*, 1833, pp. 119 (ev. of T. Wiggin), and 196 (ev. of John Innis, in the Indian trade). Letters to Morrison, Cryder & Co., eg. from Louis Bene (Hamburg), 14 June 1836.

'guesstimate' of the proportion of capital provided by Britain for various sectors of world trade in 1836 (Table 5.5). Smith supposed that Britain provided 33 per cent of the capital for British–European trade, and as the only other major contributor of capital was the German states, it may well be that 50 or 60 per cent of the 'outside' capital came from that country. Quite possibly London increased her proportion up to about 1860, but this is an impression, not a fact.[49]

Although many of the emigré merchants came with limited capital, the available evidence shows they had little difficulty in building on their commercial experience and connections with established international houses on the Continent or in Britain. The experience of Jacob and Louis Behrens from Hesse-Cassel, who were among the first German merchants to settle in Bradford, is instructive. They had little capital, but their experience as commercial travellers in their father's business stood them in good stead. 'Commissions to buy...came at once from the chief textile houses of Hamburg – Horwitz & Meyer, Oppenheims, and Saalfelds – and these gave them [the Behrens] such good standing on the market that any opponents were easily overcome.'[50] Philip Henry Muntz, who settled in Birmingham in 1834, said in 1848 that he frequently discounted bills in Hamburg in preference to discounting in England as the ordinary rate was 'generally rather lower on the Continent than it is here'.[51] Frederic Schwann was the German traveller for a Huddersfield firm that went bankrupt in 1825. He had very little capital to being with, but cultivated the connections he had made in Germany and Italy. He bought goods in the Huddersfield and Bradford markets on commission, generally for ready money by drawing on Schunk, Souchay & Co. (of Frankfurt, London and Manchester) and other houses in London with whom credits had been lodged by foreign correspondents.[52] These examples, and others that are available, show how young German merchants were able to benefit from the established continental merchants and Anglo-German houses in London.[53]

By the 1830s it is clear that the leading German houses were

[49] *Reports from H. M. Diplomatic and Consular Offices*, Parl. Papers, 1857–8, LV, p. 85.
[50] [Harry Behrens], *Sir Jacob Behrens*, p. 34.
[51] *Sel. Comm. on Commercial Distress*, Parl. Papers 1848, pp. 106–7. This is consistent with Professor E. Schremmer's calculation that Baden-Wurtenburg was a net exporter of capital at the period.   [52] B. of E. Leeds ltrs, 13 Mar. 1828, 16 Oct. 1833.
[53] See also De Jersey, Fericks & Co., B. of E. Manc. ltrs, 10 Nov. 1831; H. Reddelieu (Hamburg), B. of E. Manc. ltr bks, v (1845), p. 281.

among the most enterprising in Britain. There is only space here to illustrate these developments with a few examples. The most successful firm was probably Schunk, Souchay & Co., originally a family of Frankfurt Calvinists. Various members opened branches in Manchester (1805), London (1806), Leeds, Leipzig and Berlin.[54] In 1825 they built a calico printing works near Manchester, said to be worth £100,000, and later had two cotton spinning mills and their own fleet of ships. Schunk retired in 1835 but the partnership capital was still £365,000. In the 1830s the firm extended their operations by sending young men whom they had trained in their business to other markets, to St Petersburg, Alexandria, Milan, Rome, Lille and other cities. The new firms were conducted under the names of the respective men sent out, but Schunk, Souchay & Co. supplied the necessary capital and they were effectively branches of the parent house.[55] Reiss Brothers, also Frankfurt Protestants, were no less enterprising. Two of the four brothers came to Manchester in 1818 with a small capital. Thirty years later they were trading with a capital of £100,000 and had a partner in China, still a difficult market for British goods.[56] Other international houses established in Manchester at the opening of the century, Du Fay and Liepmann, Lindon & Co. (formerly Oppenheim & Liepmann of Berlin), were said to be trading on a capital of £200,000 each by the middle 1830s, the former in six centres, the latter in three.[57] Among the self-made men who linked themselves with international houses, we may instance Frederik Schwann of Manchester and Huddersfield, who in 1844 was thought to be worth more than £100,000 and was considered the 'Rothschild of Huddersfield'.[58] Oppenheim & Co., of Hamburg and Manchester, who failed in the crisis of 1842, had assets of £100,000 and liabilities of 90,000.[59] The wealth of some of the German–Jewish families was not always regarded dispassionately by British observers; thus a Lancashire bank wrote of L. R. Bischoffsheim of London: 'First rate credit, some very weak parties draw on him from abroad … but I am assured that L.R.B. is worth nearly £100,000; [he] is a Jew & a great screw.'[60]

[54] A. Dietz, *Frankfurter Handelsgeschichte*, pp. 331–2.
[55] J. E. Darnton, *The Von Schunk Family. A History of the Hanau Branch and Connections* (privately published, 1933) pp. 171–2. B. of E. Manc. ltrs 4 Oct. 1837.
[56] B. of E. Manc. ltr bks, VII (1848) p. 21. Brandt Circulars 1852 p. 355.
[57] B. of E. Manc. ltrs, 14 Mar. 1829, 12 Dec. 1836.
[58] B. of E. Manc. ltr bks, IV (1844), p. 259.
[59] B. of E. Manc. ltr bks, III (1842), pp. 139, 144.
[60] Preston Bank 'Character Book', p. 106. Lancs. R.O.

The financial standing of such firms has been compared with some of their leading English and Scottish contemporaries in Tables 3.4 and 3.5. The best-known German international houses were evidently not far behind the leading indigenous firms if one excepts the most eminent, notably Fieldens and Gladstones. In the early years migrants from the Continent generally fulfilled a complementary role in established houses, concentrating on supplying their parent firms, but diversification soon appeared. Again the leader was N. M. Rothschild, this time breaking into merchant banking.[61] The Rothschilds' capital was, as might be expected, in a class of its own. Starting in Manchester with £20,000, Nathan is said to have tripled his capital within a short period, probably by the time he moved to London in 1805. At the close of the Napoleonic War he was worth £90,000. But it was the post-war government loans that brought him the really colossal increases, for he had half a million in 1818 and was a millionaire by 1825. At this date he was substantially wealthier than the leading Anglo-American banks, Brown Brothers (£350,000) and Barings, who had accumulated £490,000 by 1830. The Rothschild family capital was much larger, passing £4m. in 1825, but by this time most of this was employed in state loans rather than in commerce and industry.[62]

At the end of the French Wars, the German market was the most important destination for Manchester printed cottons, followed by the Low Countries (subsequently Holland and Belgium) and Italy. However, as the relative importance of the Continent as a market for piece goods began to decline, and as the experience and capital of the vanguard firms increased, they began to diversify their markets and trade. Thus Leo Schuster, who first came to Manchester in 1816, said in 1840 that he was exporting more than 100,000 pieces a year 'to almost every part of the world'.[63]

In addition, numbers of Manchester 'foreign houses' developed an interest in the worsted trade, opening branches at Bradford to import Saxon wool and export piece goods. Leo Schuster, Engels (father of Marx's famous partner), Soloman Flersheim of Frankfurt

---

[61] S. D. Chapman, 'The Establishment of the Rothschilds as Bankers', *Trans. Jewish Hist. Soc.* xxix (1986).
[62] B. Gille, *Rothschild*, I, p. 458. E. J. Perkins, *Financing Anglo-American Trade*, p. 19.
[63] *Sel. Comm. on Copyright of Designs*, Parl. Papers, 1840, p. 61. T. Ellison, *Cotton Trade of G.B.* (1886) p. 64, calculates that the export of cotton piece goods to Europe fell from 51 percent of the British total in 1820 to 16 per cent in 1850. 'Europe' here excludes Turkey.

and other successful Manchester houses were early in this trade.[64] Other firms, like Schwabe & Sons of Hamburg and Manchester, opened branches in Glasgow,[65] while Alexander Brothers of Hamburg and A. J. Saalfeld & Co. extended from Manchester into the Nottingham lace trade, to be followed by several other German houses. Other firms again specialised in the export of 'cotton twist' to Eastern Europe.[66]

Firms with more capital moved out of Europe into the more rapidly growing textile markets of the Orient and the Americas. Du Fay, the Frankfurt Huguenot house established at Manchester in 1800, had established in Mexico, Buenos Aires, Messina and Genoa by the spring of 1829, the latter presumably to import Italian silk, a growing Manchester industry in the 1820s and 1830s.[67] Reiss Brothers, also from Frankfurt, opened a branch in Philadelphia and moved into the trade in India, China and South America, while Liepmann, Lindon & Co. of Berlin were active in the trade to India, China and the Cape.[68] Troosts of Hamburg and Lieberts of Berlin also had interests in India, while Sykes, Schwabe & Co. of Liverpool, in partnership with an agency house (Bousteads), were 'doing a very respectable business' in Manila and Singapore in the 1830s and 1840s[69] (Figure 5.2). The following decade, A. S. Sichel of Frankfurt was building up a connection in Australia, and J. P. Kessler (Frankfurt, Manchester and Bradford) in New York.[70]

Other successful London-based international houses turned to pure finance, providing accepting house facilities for the younger houses, and competing for the United States business. J. H. Schröder opened in Liverpool in 1839 with an initial investment of £50,000, taking as partners a corn merchant's son and young Mahs from Hamburg.[71] Frederick Huth & Co. started a Liverpool branch the

---

[64] See list of members in *First Annual Report of the Bradford Chamber of Commerce*, Jan. 1852. For Engels see B. of E. Leeds ltrs 28 Sept. 1831, 10 May 1833; for Schuster B. of E. Manc. ltrs 18 Jan. 1837; for Flersheim, ltr bks, v (1846), p. 102. Other firms that functioned in both towns were Reiss Bros. and J. P. Kessler.
[65] B. of E. Manc. ltr bks, vi (1848) p. 33.
[66] B. of E. Manc. ltrs 8 Feb. 1834, 12 Mar. 1836, 17 July and 8 Dec. 1838; Leeds ltr bks, i (1840) p. 75.   [67] B. of E. Manc. ltrs, 14 Mar. 1829.
[68] P.R.O. FO 83/111. B. of E. Leeds ltrs 22 Oct. 1836, Manc. ltr bks vii (1849) p. 21. B. of E. Manc. ltrs, 12 Mar. 1836.
[69] B. of E. Manc. ltr bks, v (1845) p. 143. B. of E. L'pool ltr bks, v (1844) p. 378, x (1849) p. 39.
[70] B. of E. Manc. ltr bks, ix (1854) p. 31. A. Dietz, *Handelsgeschichte*, iv, p. 332.
[71] B. of E. L'pool ltr bks, i (1840), p. 137.

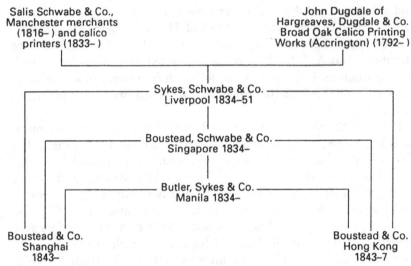

Figure 5.2. The Schwabe and Boustead connection.

same year, bringing in the managing partner of their South American establishments as local partner.[72] Very likely both were trying to fill the gaps left by the collapse of three Anglo-American finance houses in 1837. Meanwhile, N. M. Rothschild & Co. had moved competitively into continental and North American accepting house business.[73] From 1825, Souchays were helping to finance such cotton spinners as Milnes & Travis of Oldham and Samuel Marsland & Co. of Stockport.[74] Ambitious Manchester and Bradford German houses like Reiss Brothers, Abraham Baver & Co. and A. J. Saalfeld & Co. tried to establish themselves in London as merchant bankers.[75]

In a few instances, notably in calico printing and fashion goods, the market expertise of the international houses led them into manufacturing, with further beneficial consequences for British exports. Salis Schwabe, originally a calico printer from Oldenburg, came to Manchester by way of Glasgow, and was so successful that in 1840 his firm was the second largest printers in the industry.[76]

---

[72] Brandt Circulars, 1839; Huths had branches in Lima and Valparaiso.
[73] Morrison Cryder letter from C. J. Weber, 15 May 1836. B. Gille, *Rothschild*, I, pp. 402ff.
[74] B. of E. Manc. ltr bks, v (1845) p. 81, v (1846) p. 106.
[75] B. of E. Manc. ltr bks v (1845) p. 160, vii (1849) p. 109. Brandt Circulars, 1852.
[76] N. J. Laski, 'The History of Manchester Jewry', *Manchester Review*, 1956, p. 374. G. Turnbull, *History of the Calico Printing Industry of G.B.* (1951) p. 423.

Schunk, Souchay & Co. built a 'very extensive' printworks near Manchester in 1837, said to have cost £100,000, an enormous figure for a factory at the time.[77] Behrens had another printworks at Garstang. Lewis Heymann came to Nottingham about 1834 as junior partner in A. J. Saalfeld & Co. (Hamburg, Manchester and Leeds). According to a Nottingham local historian, Heymann 'had no money, but he had what is better – character joined with energy, good taste, and agreeable manners...He had designers in his warehouse where he could supervise them several times a day...not only did he extend the trade in Nottingham goods [i.e. lace] by his knowledge of languages and of houses abroad, but he developed taste and skill to such an extent that the *Arts Journal Illustrated Catalogue of the International Exhibition of 1862* declared that "the productions of Nottingham now surpasse those of French".'[78] Heymann's status in Nottingham was so high that in 1857 he was invited to become Mayor, the first former German Jew to hold the office in a British industrial city.[79]

AMERICAN MERCHANTS IN BRITAIN

N. S. Buck's *Development of the Organisation of the Anglo-American Trade, 1800–1850* shows that British merchants and manufacturers dominated the trade with the United States until at least 1830. He maintains that up to the end of the French Wars British export merchants, often supported by one of the Anglo-American banking houses in London or Liverpool, conducted most of the trade across the North Atlantic, though a few American importers had branches or agents in Britain, and a few major manufacturers were prepared to assume mercantile functions.[80] In the next fifteen years, as we have already seen, the export merchant gave way to the manufacturer and commission agent, with the accepting houses competing strongly for their business, so it was not until after about 1830 that the American importer became an important figure in North Atlantic commerce.

---

[77] B. of E. Leeds ltr bks, II (1842) p. 24.
[78] R. Mellors, *Men of Nottingham and Notts* (1924) p. 221.
[79] *High Pavement Chapel, Nottingham. Biographical Catalogue of Portraits*... (1932) p. 28. Other manufacturers included Abraham Baver (fringe works), see B. of E. Manc. ltr bks II (1841) p. 29, and Louis Schwabe (embroidery factory), see B. of E. Manc. ltrs 17 Dec. 1839. Three other German firms invested in cotton mills.
[80] (Yale 1925); Chs. V–VII.

Buck's description of the trade can be given more precise support from evidence that has become available more recently. In Liverpool, the main British centre for United States commerce at this period, there were said to be seventeen principal importers of cotton in 1827 and nineteen in 1829. Only three of these, W. & J. Brown & Co., Peck & Phelps and Wright, Taylor & Co., were American and the last of them went into liquidation soon after the second count.[81] All the rest were English and Scots. At mid-century there were eighteen American houses in London, but most of them were small and only four in first-rate credit. Only two of the four, George Peabody and A. S. Henry, were American born, and we shall see that the latter was in fact a Manchester house that considered itself Irish.[82] There were a few other international houses of American origin in the 1830s and 1840s, but they are not easy to find. The five volumes of Barrett's *Old Merchants of New York City* describe the work of Lewis Rogers & Co. of New York, Richmond, New Orleans, London and Le Havre and Goodlive & Co., who opened commercial houses in London, St Petersburgh, Canton, Calcutta and other centres, but the kind of international organisation we have been discussing does not appear to have been a prominent feature of American trade at this time.[83]

The typical position of the American importer was summed up by the Bank of England agents in Manchester. 'Very few of the parties who represent the American houses in our market can be looked upon as permanent residents as they are constantly changing…'[84] Moreover, the partners or agents who came to Britain on two and three year tours did not open an office, but merely had the use of a desk in the counting house of W. & J. Brown, A. & S. Henry, Thornton, Atterbury & Co. of Leeds, or one of the few other American houses who kept large establishments in Britain.[85] United States' traders in other world markets, notably South America, are known to have followed similar practices, operating abroad in the

---

[81] B. of E. L'pool ltrs, 24 Nov. 1827, 20 Oct. 1829. See above pp. 104–6.
[82] B. of E. Leeds ltr bks, v (1850), p. 15. The other two 'first class' houses were Wm. Chance & Sons (Birmingham and London) and Matheson & Son (Glasgow and London).
[83] W. Barrett, *Old Merchants of New York City* (New York 1885) I, pp. 23, 45. The Morrison Cryder letters reveal only one further American-based international house, J. & F. Dorr (New York, Paris and Manchester, 15 Dec. 1835). Moira Wilkins, *The Emergence of Multinational Enterprise* (Harvard 1970) found little evidence of US interest in other countries before 1865.
[84] B. of E. Manc. ltrs. 17 Jan. 1837.
[85] B. of E. Manc. ltr bks, IX (1853) p. 122.

name of two or three established concerns.[86] There was no need for any more elaborate arrangement because there were already ample facilities to buy from both large and small British manufacturers. From before 1815, manufacturers kept representatives of warehouses in Liverpool for such specialisms as Manchester goods, Nottingham hosiery and lace, London carpets, Staffordshire earthenware and so on, often advertised as suitable for the American market.[87] After the French Wars these warehouses took the American trade from London and Liverpool export merchants, and from manufacturers who had been in the habit of exporting on their own account. By 1835, the London export of textiles was largely controlled by a dozen of these emporia under the leadership of Todd, Morrison & Co. 'The magnitude of the traffic and the punctuality of payment of such houses', according to the *Circular to Bankers*, 'have rendered their acceptances current among bankers', and millionaire James Morrison was ready to grant easy credits to exporters.[88] Commission agents acting for American merchants also made their own purchases at the cloth halls in the North of England.[89]

The only really strong international houses in the American trade in Britain were, therefore, W. J. Brown & Co. (later Brown, Shipley & Co.) and A. & S. Henry. Alexander Henry arrived in Manchester from Philadelphia in 1804, and William Brown in Liverpool from Baltimore in 1810. Both came of first generation Irish Presbyterian (i.e. Ulster Scots) families that had not had time to become Americanised. Each managed to combine rigorous individualism and Nonconformist devotion to business with family loyalties strong enough to bridge the Atlantic. Shrewd anticipation of markets at the close of the American War (1812–14) raised Browns' capital from £100,000 to over £500,000, and new branches were opened in

---

[86] The difference in mercantile practice between the USA and European countries can be measured by comparing the number of vessels of each country entering a port (e.g. Buenos Aires) in a particular year (eg. 1850) with the number of foreign import houses of that country in the port at the time:

	vessels	houses	ratio
Britain	107	52	2:1
France	52	21	2·5:1
USA	53	5	10:1

See P.R.O. FO 83/111 and V. B. Reber, 'British Mercantile Houses in Buenos Aires', pp. 123, 297, 319.

[87] B. H. Tolley, 'The American Trade of Liverpool', M.A. thesis, Liverpool 1967, pp. 72–3.

[88] *Circular to Bankers*, 10 Oct. 1834, p. 90, 18 Jan. 1836, p. 201. In 1836 Morrison formed the London merchant bank, Morrison Cryder & Co.

[89] B. of E. Leeds ltrs, 16 Sept. 1832.

Philadelphia (1818) and New York (1825) under the direction of William's brothers. Surviving the crisis of 1825–6 without any apparent difficulty, Browns emerged as the leading North of England firm providing credit for American agents touring Britain to order goods from manufacturers at Manchester, Birmingham, Sheffield and other industrial places. Meanwhile, Alexander Henry established himself in Manchester by shipping goods to his partners (Thomas & William Henry) in Philadelphia. His brothers also imported goods through New York commission agents like Bolton, Ogden & Co., which was perhaps why young Henry decided to establish his independence, taking his younger brother Samuel as travelling partner. By 1826 he was trading on a capital of £50,000 and emerging as the leading commission agent for the purchase of Manchester goods. From cottons they moved to woollen and worsted goods, then linen, silk and other manufactures, opening branches in Leeds (c. 1836), Huddersfield, Bradford (1848), Belfast and Glasgow, and also became manufacturers, owning Thomas Jowett & Co. of Bingley.[90]

A. & S. Henry's papers appear to have perished, but it is not difficult to recognise the reason for their growing popularity from other sources. Hagues, Cooke & Wormald of Dewsbury mills, who were to become the leading West Riding blanket manufacturers, at first exported to the US through Thomas Dixon & Co., a New York agent with a Yorkshire family background. However, in the commercial crisis of 1825–6, when widespread losses were suffered as a consequence of the bankruptcy of the leading London accepting house specialising in North American trade, Hagues & Co. solicited a connection with A. & S. Henry to reduce their marketing risks in the US. The link lasted into the 1860s, and it seems quite likely that it was the key to the extension of the Henrys' clientèle into the West Riding woollen and worsted trade.[91] The advice given by Firmin de Tastet to Boulton & Watt in 1794[92] was evidently no less relevant a generation later, but it was Browns and Barings (an Anglo-American partnership from 1828, when Joshua Bates of Boston

---

[90] E. J. Perkins, *Financing Anglo-American Trade*, esp. pp. 20–5. [Anon.], *Fortunes made in Business*, III (1887) Ch. 4. B. of E. Leeds ltrs, 28 Mar. 1832, 1 Mar. 1837, L'pool ltrs 8 Sept. 1827, Birmingham ltrs 22 Jan. 1827, Manc. ltrs 1 Jan. 1827, 7 Sept. 1827. See also letters of T. & W. Henry in Bolton Ogden MSS, boxes for 1816, 1818 and 1820s. (New York Historical Soc. References kindly supplied by John Killick, Leeds Univ.)

[91] F. J. Glover, 'Thomas Cook and the American Blanket Trade', *Bus. Hist. Rev.*, xxxv (1961).   [92] See above, p. 135.

joined them[93]) that took the lion's share of the finance of this trade, rather than the old London merchant houses.

Both Henrys and Browns were evidently much closer to Scots practice than American. The most impressive international houses founded in Britain were developed for the trade to the Far East. 'The whole trade was largely developed by family and clan groups, largely Scots, with family connections in every port east of the Cape,' the historian of Jardine Matheson writes.[94] The prototype may have been James Finlay & Co. of Glasgow, who had branches in Liverpool, London, Calcutta, New York, Charleston and New Orleans by the middle 1820s, and Scots traders were strong in both Liverpool and Manchester.[95] It is clear that both families identified themselves with this interesting minority group. Seventeen years after the Brown brothers settled in Liverpool, the Bank of England agent wrote that the 'partners are not men of much education and mix very little in the best society...'[96] When William Brown and Alex Henry were elected to Parliament, Brown described himself as one of Lancashire's two *Irish* MPs, and the second generation Mitchell Henry, MP, identified himself completely with Irish development and political problems at Westminster.[97] At mid-century, when the second generation retired from active business, administrative rationalisation was undertaken by a scion of one of the German–Russian international houses, apparently reinforcing that cosmopolitan outlook characteristic of the international houses.[98]

GREEK MERCHANTS IN BRITAIN

The migration of large numbers of Ottoman merchants to Britain had similar causes to those that prompted German migration, but followed at an interval of ten or twenty years. British manufactured goods had reached Eastern Europe through the Leipzig Fairs, where until the 1850s the traders of the Ottoman Empire – Greeks, Armenians, Arabs and Turks, but in Britain collectively referred to

---

[93] H. R. Fox Bourne, *English Merchants*, II (1866) p. 248.
[94] M. Greenberg, *British Trade and the Opening of China 1800–1842* (Cambridge 1951) p. 38.
[95] B. of E. L'pool ltrs, 31 Dec. 1827.
[96] B. of E. L'pool ltrs, 8 Sept. 1827. In fact, the Brown boys were educated at an English school! A. Ellis, *Heir of Adventure* (1960) p. 89.
[97] Information from John Killick, Leeds. [Anon.] *Fortunes made in Business*, Ch. 4.
[98] This was (Sir) Mark Willis Collet. See Collet MSS, Kent R.O. for his background and letters.

as Greeks – assembled twice a year to buy from the German–Jewish merchants who kept large warehouses there and provided long credits for their customers. Two-thirds of the British cottons that were sold to Leipzig in an average year were re-exported to the Danubian principalities and to Russia. After the French Wars, the shipping trade of the eastern Mediterranean, and especially that from the Levant to Italy, fell increasingly into the hands of Greek merchants because their freights were cheaper. As the British textile industry continued to grow, the Greeks ventured further afield to make direct purchases in London and Liverpool, and by the close of the 1850s only buyers who needed long credits were attending the Leipzig Fairs. Migration received additional impetus from the growing Turkish persecution of the Greek Orthodox minority. The earliest important arrivals were John and Constantine Ionides, who first visited London in 1815. John Ralli came from Chios, a Greek island off the coast of Anatolia, where the population was massacred by the Turks in 1822. Ionides had traded in English textiles in Constantinople until the Turks robbed him of his inheritance.[99]

Chios, the home of most of the migrant families was said to have been the most autonomous of the Ottoman territories, and in the eighteenth century became the most commercial of all the Greek communities. Consequently, its history was one of dispersion of mercantile families both within and beyond the Ottoman Empire, in a manner reminiscent of the Germans and Scots. Commercial education was highly developed, as that among the Jews and Scots was, boys learning the French and Turkish as well as Greek language. Moreover, like the Jews, there was 'no serious occupation open to the Chians for the employment of their energies other than the furtherance of business, [so] they naturally gave the whole of their attention to the god of Commerce, and he, in return for their devotion, rewarded them quickly and generously'. As in Scotland, the mountainous terrain offered scant reward to agrarian enterprise except for a handful of farmers, and the sea beckoned to prizes over its horizon. Already, in the eighteenth century, the Chians had established branches of their enterprise in Amsterdam, Leghorn, Marseilles, Trieste, Malta, Alexandria, Moscow, Taganrog (on the Sea of Azov), Odessa, Vienna, Constantinople, Smyrna, Thrace, Syria and other parts of Asia. In the French Wars, 'enormous gains'

[99] *Reports from H. M. Diplomatic and Consular Offices*, Parl. Papers, 1859, xxx, p. 338. *Sel. Comm. on Foreign Trade*, Parl. Papers, 1820, pp. 32–3. A. C. Ionides, *Iōn. A Grandfather's Tale* (1927) p. 1.

were made from a hazardous trade delivering corn and other provisions into blockaded ports. The Chians also had a traditional trade in home-manufactured cottons and silks; this declined about 1810, most probably from competition with British goods. Even without a massacre, the Chians would certainly have moved into West European trade.[100]

In their migration westward the more successful Greek houses spawned new branches, and tracing these reveals the pattern of extension of their interests. Ralli Brothers, the Chian family in the vanguard of the migration, opened branches at Odessa, Marseilles, London and Manchester (1828), and were soon exporting cotton twist to Germany as well as the Levant.[101] In 1865, at the summit of their mercantile achievement, the Rallis were operating through interlocked partnerships in fifteen centres, spread across Europe, India and the Middle East (Figure 5.3). An American cotton importing operation was run as a separate business. Their relatives Rodocanachi, Sons & Co., starting at the same place (Odessa), had establishments at Marseilles, Leghorn, London, Manchester (1842) and St Petersburg (1851). By 1854, they were acting for Ralli Bros. and on their own behalf, buying cotton in New Orleans.[102] Rocca Brothers evidently concentrated more on the Mediterranean trade, with branches at Odessa, Berdyansk (Ukraine), Naples, Genoa, Marseilles and finally (1856) London.[103] Cassavetti Brothers & Co. (otherwise Cassavetti, Cavafy & Co.) had establishments at Cairo, Alexandria, London, Liverpool and Manchester, buying considerable quantities of Manchester goods for sale in Egypt. The resident partners there, the Cavafy brothers, toured the country with their camel caravans, exchanging textiles for bullion.[104] Paul and Peter Cababé, who started in Manchester in 1840, 'for many years had almost a monopoly of the Syrian trade with Aleppo', while Guistiniani & Nepoti had their bases in Damascus, Aleppo, Leghorn, London and Manchester.[105] Other firms, operating on a more

[100] A. M. Vlasto, *A History of the Island of Chios* (1913) Chs. 13, 18. P. P. Argenti, *Libro d'oro de la Noblesse de Chio* (1955) for family pedigrees.
[101] Figure 5.3 footnotes. B. of E. Manc. ltrs, 18 Nov. 1839.
[102] Brandt Circulars, 1851, 1860. John Scholes, 'Foreign Merchants in Manchester 1784–1870' (MS, Manchester P.L.). Dun & Bradstreet Credit Registers (Harvard Lib.), New York, vol. 330 p. 1120, vol. 344 p. 423.
[103] Brandt Circulars, 1856. P. Léris, 'La colonie grecque de Marseille', *Rev. des Français*, XVII (1913).
[104] B. of E. L'pool ltr bks, XI (1850) p. 42. S. Fairlie, 'The Anglo-Russian Grain Trade, 1815–61', Ph.D. thesis (London 1959) p. 275.
[105] L. M. Hayes, *Reminiscences of Manchester*... (1905) pp. 306–7. P.R.O. FO 88/111 (Damascus list).

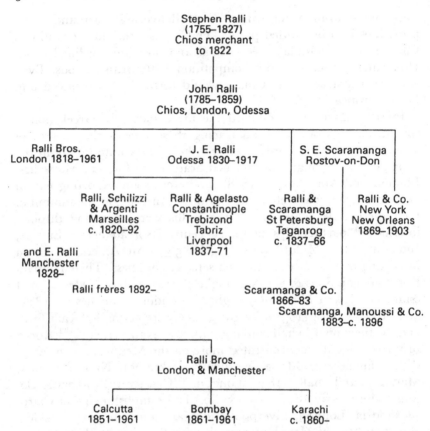

Note: Successive leaders of Ralli Bros. married Scaramangas. This family opened in London and Manchester c. 1848 and took over Ralli's Russian business on the death of Pandias Ralli in 1866.

Figure 5.3. The Ralli and Scaramanga partnerships.

modest scale, simply provided a direct connection between Constantinople, Alexandria, Cairo or Jassy and London or Manchester. The Greek houses retained their hold on shipping into the 1860s, and there are indications that they were prepared to be more speculative than their British competitiors.[106]

---

[106] Eg. Boglios, Beshiktaslian and Gallipoliti & Co. from Constantinople, Lafuente and Emetrio & Co. from Alexandria and Benjanowitz from Jassy. B. of E. Mac. ltr bks, VIII (1852) pp. 42, 73; X (1857) p. 145; VI (1848) p. 107; VII (1850) p. 64; X (1857) p. 93. P.R.O. FO 83/111 (Cairo list). S. T. Xenos, *Depredations* (1869) for Greek shipping interests.

The number of Greek firms settled in Manchester rose dramatically in the late 1840s and 1850s, and in the middle 1860s they exceeded the number of German houses in the town. In 1850 there were 55 of them (97 Germans), in 1860 there were 87 (114 Germans) and in 1870 the total reached 167 (153 Germans).[107] In London there were at least 86 established Greek houses at around the peak in 1860 and they appear to have been larger and more stable than their northern counterparts.[108] There are several reasons for this spectacular success. The most important is that they succeeded in finding new markets for cotton piece goods in a part of the world where British representation was weak, or at any rate thin on the ground.[109] Export of these fabrics to Turkey, Egypt and Africa (substantially the Ottoman Empire) increased from 9·5m. yards in 1820 to 194m. yards in 1850 and 670m. yards in 1870, a fifth of total export sales.[110] The Greek merchants appear to have acted as the terminal and starting point for larger numbers of Greek middlemen and native dealers trading through the particular port; for instance, at Beirut twenty-nine local merchants served four Greek houses: Spartali & Co. (Marseilles, London, Liverpool, Manchester), N. S. Frangopulo & Co. (London and Manchester), P. Mana & Co. (London) and Paul Cababé (Manchester). At mid-century there were apparently no merchants of British birth resident in the port.[111]

Another reason for the success of the Greek houses is that they developed a new form of reciprocal trade between Britain and the Middle East, exporting textiles and importing grain from the Black Sea ports and (to a much smaller extent) from the Baltic. Peel's celebrated repeal of the Corn Laws (1846) was the signal for the rapid growth of this trade. The trade was financed by a system started, or strongly developed, by the Ralli Brothers. The merchant loading the cargo in Odessa dispatched the bill of lading and sample to his partner in England, who sold it in anticipation of its arrival. The cash paid might then be used for purchase of textiles, coal or other return cargoes.[112]

The innovations in trade had won substantial fortunes for the

[107] J. Scholes, 'Foreign Merchants in Manchester'. Scholes's list omits a few names.
[108] B. of E. MSS 3394, Greek Firms' Accounts 1848–52. Baring MSS Customer Reference Books, 1 (insert.)
[109] M. Lévy-Leboyer, *Les banques européennes*... (Paris 1964) p. 511 n6, p. 516 n32 P.R.O. FO 83/111 (Odessa, Tehran, Tabriz).
[110] T. Ellison, *Cotton Trade of Great Britain* (1886) pp. 63–4.
[111] P.R.O. FO 83/111 (Beirut). A. Kitroeff, *The Greeks in Egypt* (1989) p. 86.
[112] The system is described at length in S. Fairlie, 'Grain Trade' Ch. VI.

Table 5.3. *Leading Greek merchant houses trading in Britain 1848–50* (*top 14*)

	Bank of England discount limit (£)	Estimated capital (£)
Ralli Bros.	30,000	500,000 (1848–50)
Spartali & Lascardi	30,000	100,000+ (1857)
Micrulachi & Co.	20,000	
Ralli & Co.	15,000	
Rodocanachi, Sons & Co.	15,000	200,000+ (1860)
Argenti, Sechiari & Co.	10,000	500,000+ (1850)
Abet Bros.	10,000	
Cassavetti, Cavafy & Co.	10,000	20–30,000 (1850)
Rossetto, Carati & Co.	10,000	
Schilizzi & Co.	10,000	
Ralli & Maviojani	10,000	
Ionides Bros. & Co.	7,000	30,000 (1860)
Ionides Sgouta & Co.	7,000	
P. T. Ralli	5,000	90,000 (1860)

Sources: discount limits: Bank of England MS 3394; capital: Bank of England Liverpool and Manchester Agents' letter books. Baring Bros. MS 16/2, Reports on Business Houses (P. T. Ralli) and Customer Reference Books, Europe 1. Guildhall Lib. MS 23,830, private ledger of Ralli Bros. 1827–50.

leading Greek houses by mid-century. Both Ralli Bros. and Argenti, Sechiari & Co. had already reached half a million sterling having been connected with Constantine Ionides, the first Greek merchant to trade in Britain (Table 5.3). Rodocanachis already had a capital of at least £200,000 by 1860. A Greek source maintains that Rallis employed as many as 4,000 clerks and 15,000 workmen (warehousemen, porters etc.) in the 1850s.[113] This seems scarcely credible until it is recognised that during this period Rallis were building up a massive mercantile operation in India – soon to be the largest in the country – as well as maintaining an extensive business with numerous agents all over the grain areas of the Ukraine and southern Russia. The most recent historian of Odessa shows that Rallis were overall the largest traders in the port by mid-century, while Rodocanachis were the biggest importers, with seventeen branches in different parts of the world.[114] At mid-century, or soon after, the two leading Greek merchant houses most probably had the

[113] Dunn, New York, vol. 330 p. 1120., vol. 344 p. 423. T. Catsiyannis, *Pandias Stephen Ralli* (1986) p. 118.
[114] P. Herlihy, *Odessa. A History 1794–1914* (Harvard 1986) pp. 93–330.

largest organisations and capitals of any merchants operating in London. Only Rothschilds were substantially richer, and they were now financiers rather than merchants; moreover their total staff did not exceed a hundred before World War I.

But the great number of Greek merchant houses active in Britain in the 1850s were trading on capitals of less than £10,000, and needed extensive credit for their purchases.[115] Perhaps because the new system was not generally understood, or because it was difficult for bankers to identify tangible securities, the Greek merchants nevertheless remained an object of some suspicion to conventional financiers. The Bank of England recorded in 1850 that 'it is most difficult to define the actual [financial] position of the Greek houses, there are but one or two of the whole number that may be ranked as "first class", the others being so mixed up together that it is impossible to ascertain the amount of capital employed and how it is distributed'.[116] The outcome was that most of the credit granted to these firms came from the manufacturers most directly concerned in their trade, the calico printers, and from James Cunliffe (of Cunliffe, Brooks & Co.) whose banking house had close connections with the calico printing industry.[117] A rather jaundiced account of a Greek who became bankrupt in 1853 called attention to a list of his creditors which showed 'the extent to which a person of his class, a foreigner and a stranger, may creep into credit... the list is composed of almost every respectable [calico] printer in the trade'.[118] In other words, where the banks failed to provide credit, the manufacturers were persuaded to support those who could find markets for them. And the close financial connections between the calico printers and the Greeks hint strongly at close working relations between the two parties, for sales depended above all on the right choices of colours and patterns, and the best results were attained in personal connections.

One final feature of the Greek merchants is worth noticing. The members were undoubtedly the closest of the foreign groups prominent in London and Manchester last century. In an anonymous but damaging work of fiction called *The Bubbles of Finance* (1866), M. R. L. Meason devoted three long chapters to the Levant trade and maintained that the Greeks were the only people

---

[115] B. of E. Manc. ltr bks, VIII (1852) pp. 4–6.
[116] B. of E. London to Leicester letter, 7 Aug. 1850.
[117] B. of E. Manc. ltr bks, VIII (1852) pp. 4–6.
[118] B. of E. Manc. ltr bks, IX (1853) p. 54.

in the world whose members had implicit confidence in one another. 'Whatever a Greek may be to a foreigner, he is always true to his countrymen.' Meason believed that the numerous small Greek houses were able to survive in the risky Levantine trade because the better-known Greek firms discounted the bills of exchange of the smaller ones at extortionate rates, 'often as much as nine or ten per cent for three months, being at the rate of 30 to 40 per cent per annum'. It might be inferred that it was in this way that Rallis, Rodocanachis, Ionides and other leading houses became rich, particularly when it is remembered that in the 1860s some of them formally moved into banking.[119]

However, this seems unduly hard on the Greeks. It has already been noticed that much credit came from the northern textile manufacturers. The Ralli partnerships later claimed to be built entirely on cash trading and it is difficult to suppose that their relatives the Rodocanachis were willing to risk their credit standing with upstart competitors. A more likely explanation of Greek mutual support is that, unlike most Germans, German Jews, Dutch and other migrants, they arrived in a period of nationalist passion and so were slow to anglicise. The Greeks collected together in the Finsbury Circus area of the City of London, piously supported the Greek Church on London Wall, and were loyal to successive Greek Consuls, in particular to Pandias Ralli (Consul 1835–53) and Alexander Ionides (1853–66). Stephen Ralli, who was the leader of the Ralli Brothers from 1865 to 1902 'may be said to have been the president, Nestor and father of the Greek community in London', according to his biographer.[120] In any event, Greek solidarity did not insulate the community from financial difficulties. Ionides' Bank of London failed in 1866, the leading Anglo-Greek shipping line went down in the Overend Gurney crisis of 1867, and Rallis' partners and successors in Russian trade, the Scaramangas, became insolvent in London in 1888. Franghiadi & Rodocanachi had to suspend payments for a period in 1869 then Rodocanachis' Imperial Bank was sold to the Midland. Numerous small Greek houses disappeared in the Constantinople chain of bankruptcies in 1860, and in this decade others were ousted from the Odessa grain trade by German–Jewish competition. Rallis survived and prospered by

---

[119] Anon. [M. R. L. Meason], *The Bubbles of Finance* (1866) pp. 163–4, 187. T. Catsiyannis, *The Rodocanachi of London* (1987) p. 70 and the same author's *Constantine Ionides* (1988) p. 44.
[120] J. Gennadius, *Stephen A. Ralli* (1902) pp. 24, 29. Obituary of S. A. Ralli in *The Times* 30 Apr. 1902. T. Catsiyannis, *Ralli* pp. 62–3, 102, *Ionides* p. 44.

concentrating on India while Rodocanachis presently invested in Ukrainian industry.[121] These later developments will be examined below in Chapter 8.

CONTRIBUTION OF THE FOREIGN HOUSES

At first glance, the settlement of so many German, Greek and Irish–American houses in Britain in the nineteenth century might seem evidence of entrepreneurial failure on the part of British merchants, but any such notion is dispelled by the figures in Table 3.7. The 1,500 British merchant houses abroad in 1848–50 greatly outnumbered the foreign houses settled in Britain, and their distribution in Europe was not obviously weak. Unfortunately, Palmerston's inquiry into merchant houses abroad did not cover German firms, but occasional figures that are available again point to the dominance of the British at this period. For instance, a count of the number of foreign houses in Buenos Aires in 1836 showed forty-one British houses, seven German, six French and four American; Britain had more than the other countries put together.[122] Other scattered evidence supports the conclusion from this source.

The major influx of foreign mercantile enterprise came to the manufacturing districts of the North of England, so it might seem reasonable to argue that the German immigration was a response to lack of mercantile experience in the 'new frontier' industrial growth areas, and there is certainly evidence for this in the case of Bradford. However, there was also a major growth of indigenous mercantile enterprise in Manchester, Liverpool and Glasgow, and this may be illustrated in several ways. The returns from Palmerston's inquiry only rarely give the home town of British houses abroad, but those that do show more connections with provincial towns than London, Liverpool and Manchester being particularly strong (Table 5.4). In addition, we know that a growing number of agency houses for the Indian and Far Eastern trade were based on these two centres and on Glasgow.[123] Two of the leading Anglo-American merchant banks of the 1830s, Morrison Cryder & Co. and Timothy Wiggin, traded on fortunes made in Manchester, while a third, Brown Brothers, was

---

[121] T. Catsiyannis, *Ionides* p. 44. S. T. Xenos, *Depredations* (1869) passim. Baring MSS CRD 24, Bankrupts' estates 1861–1915. P. Herlihy, *Odessa*, pp. 212–15. R. Seyd, *Record of Failures and Liquidations ... 1865 to 1876* (1876).
[122] Morrison Cryder letters, Marrell Wright & Co. to John Cryder, 14 Jan. 1836.
[123] *East India Register*, 1803 onwards, M. Greenberg, *British Trade*, p. 38.

Table 5.4. *Location of home offices of British mercantile houses established in some foreign countries, 1848–9*

U base	Rio de Janeiro	Montevideo	Buenos Aires	Chile	Pernambuco	Rio Grande	Philadelphia	New Orleans
London	5	6	5	4	4	0	2	0
Liverpool	12	13	19	11	8	6	0	5
Manchester	7	2	4	2	3	1	5	0
Glasgow	3	2	3	3	0	0	0	2
Birmingham	1	2	1	0	0	1	4	0
Sheffield	0	0	0	0	0	0	11	0
Nottingham	0	1	0	0	0	0	2	0
Belfast	0	0	0	0	0	0	0	0
Totals	28	26	33	20	15	8	24	7
British houses in these ports	47	34	55	29	30	17	35	23

Source: most informative returns in P.R.O. FO 83/111, 115. Houses with more than one home office (e.g. in London and Liverpool) were counted in each heading. The other British houses (e.g. 47−28 = 19 at Rio) had no recorded base or partners in the home country.

essentially Liverpool based.[124] Barings, Huths, Schröders, Lizardis and other London merchant banks found it worth while to open offices in Liverpool.[125]

Down to the end of the French Wars there are indications of a shortage of capital in the rapidly growing manufacturing regions, and Rothschild, Schröder , Souchay and other German accepting houses were able to insert themselves in the money market without any apparent difficulty. After the Wars, and more especially after 1825, there appears to have been an overall surplus of capital in Britain, and it may be supposed that foreign merchants were no longer important as transmitters of continental capital. However, the numerous small firms of Birmingham, Sheffield and the growing textile regions suffered intermittent shortages of ready cash and easy credit, and were evidently ready to deal with any merchant or agent who could offer them immediate relief.[126] To support this point, it is useful to add that German and Swiss merchants largely controlled the Lyons silk trade, acting as middlemen between the manufacturers and the continental markets. The Germans were already masters of Lyons in 1811, an élite of merchants who profited from the competition of some 300 manufacturers.[127] Moreover, Greek merchants played an important role in the trade of Marseilles. Clearly the international financial families were ready to enter the trade wherever low prices and inexperience of foreign markets offered the prospect of profits. The evidence collected in this chapter suggests that they did not so much displace British merchants as fill their depleted ranks at the recurrent financial crises. A contemporary estimate shows that the contribution of the foreign exporters to the capital invested in exporting to Europe was already substantial in 1836 (Table 5.5), perhaps as much as two-thirds.

A further important contribution of the international houses is connected with the nature of marketing in foreign countries before the days of the marine telegraph and rapid communications. Selling abroad was essentially a speculative business, not only because anticipation of consumer taste was often a groping hit-or-miss

---

[124] *Sel. Comm. on Manufactures*, Parl. Papers, 1833, p. 119. *Circular to Bankers*, 10 Oct. 1834. E. J. Perkins, *Financing Anglo-American Trade*.

[125] Liverpool directories, 1835–40.

[126] S. D. Chapman, 'Financial Restraints on the Growth of the Firms', *Econ. Hist. Rev.* xxxii (1979).

[127] M. Lévy-Leboyer, *Les banques européennes*, p. 513. For Greeks in Marseilles, see Ralli, Rodocanachi and other dispersed trading families.

Table 5.5. *Crude estimates of the value of British and foreign capital financing British overseas trade, 1836*

Sector	British contribution	
India and China	'nearly the whole' – say	95%
South America	'at least seven-eighths' – say	90%
North America		80%
Continental Europe		33%
'Colonial trade'[1]	'the whole'	100%

Note: [1] West Indies, Africa, Australasia.
Sources: J. B. Smith, *Report... on the Effects of the Administration of the Bank of England* (1839), p. 15, for all proportions except North America, which is from *Circular to Bankers*, 23 June 1836, pp. 401–2. Estimate of the total capital employed in trade at £30–40 m. is in *Sel. Comm. on Banks of Issue*, Parl. Papers, 1840, VI, p. 3, evidence of J. B. Smith.

process, but also because foreign markets could be glutted or starved by the chance circumstances of epidemic, war, peace and competitors' guesses about these matters, and foreign debts were practically impossible to recover.[128] A large merchant–manufacturer from Glasgow who had offices abroad probably represented the general view when he said that 'sometimes our foreign markets give us very large profits, and at other times we get less than the goods cost us; but at present [1836]... we should be glad to contract to deliver our goods upon a profit of 3 to 5 per cent upon our capital, over and above interest... '[129] Robert Gardner, a leading Manchester merchant–manufacturer, felt much the same. 'Ever since I have been in business [1815–35]', he said, 'I have known no period in which some of the foreign markets have not been overstocked... we send [abroad] ten different articles, and one will sell at 50 per cent profit and another at 20 to 30 loss because the one particular market is overstocked and the other understocked... We sometimes have goods sell at an extravagant profit and other goods in the same shipment which, in consequence of the goods being out of fashion or the market overstocked, have sold at a loss... '[130]

British merchants pioneered the trade in manufactured goods in India, South America and China, and, with the exception of a few

[128] E. M. Sigsworth, 'Fosters of Queensbury and Geyer of Lodz, 1848–62', *Yorkshire Bulletin*, III (1951) for a case-study of the problems of recovery of foreign debts.
[129] *Sel. Comm. on Manufactures*, Parl. Papers, 1833, p. 329, ev. of Wm. Graham.
[130] *Sel. Comm. on Handloom Weavers' Petitions*, Parl. Papers, 1835, p. 159.

locations, dominated international trade in these sectors for most of the nineteenth century. The characteristic British overseas operator was the commission agent trading on the capital of the acceptance houses and the manufacturers, but the most successful of these concerns, like Antony Gibbs & Sons in South America, James Finlay & Co. in India and Jardine, Matheson & Co. in China, built chains of partnerships similar to some of those examined in this chapter.[131] However, these Germans and Greeks possessed superior expertise in Eastern Europe and the Middle East, and the Ulster Scots had more enduring family connections with North America. Backed by British financial organisations, these minorities assumed (or resumed) trade leadership in these sectors. The Greeks, in particular, sought out new markets in 'distant and semi-barbaric regions where Manchester fabrics were before as unknown as the very name itself in England'.[132] There were few attempts to link British and German or Greek houses in partnership, and the exceptions did not succeed for long.[133]

The supra-nationalist outlook of religious and ethnic minorities gave them distinct advantages. Intimate local knowledge was the best defence against commercial and political threats, and the family network transmitted intelligence most readily and was quickest to respond to it. And while each family maintained a rivalry with others in the 'tribe', there was sufficient understanding between them for members to insulate each other against crises, and to act collectively to improve or maintain their national image.[134] The importance of such tribal solidarity is best understood by reference to the activities of other foreigners trading in Britain. Despite their early involvement in British finance, the Dutch failed in their endeavour to find a footing in northern commerce. Daniel Willink,

---

[131] [C. Brogan], *James Finlay & Co. Ltd., 1750–1950* (Glasgow 1951) Ch. II. J. A. Gibbs, *The History of Antony and Dorothea Gibbs* (1922), p. 451. M. Greenberg, *British Trade*, p. 38.

[132] Quoted in S. Fairlie, 'Grain Trade', p. 290.

[133] For Anglo-German connections see eg. Finlays and Baumeisters (C. Brogan, *James Finlay*, p. 12) and James Holford of Manchester and Holfords, Sauer & Co. of Hamburg and St Petersburg. (Brandt Circulars, 1837, 1840. B. of E. Manc. ltrs, 11 Feb. 1832.)

[134] Eg. (1) J. H. Schröder & Co.'s absorption of debts of six Schröder partnerships that went bankrupt, two in 1848, three in 1857 and one in 1869. ('Private ledger of J. H. S. & Co., London. Bad Debts since 1848' in the Company's archives.) (2) The Bank of England's Manchester Agent reported in 1851 that bankruptcies among Greek firms were 'generally kept very quiet by the parties involved in order that they may get out of their difficulty the more favourably...' (B. of E. Manc. ltr bks, VIII (1852) p. 5). On protection of the national image see J. James, *History of the Worsted Manufacture* (1857) p. 411, and B. Williams, *Manchester Jewry*, passim.

the Dutch Consul in Liverpool, speculated in cotton backed by his Amsterdam and New York family, Labouchère (late of Hope & Co.), Barings and others, but failed for some £70,000 in 1829.[135] Da Costa, the Portuguese Consul at Liverpool, failed twice.[136] The international Huguenot families maintained a commanding position in Frankfurt well into the nineteenth century, but in Britain they faded out during, or soon after, the French Wars, except in a few cases where they had united themselves with German trading families.[137] Their only distinguished successor was Franciso de Lizardi & Co., who had offices in Paris, London, Liverpool and New Orleans, and was heavily involved in financing the transatlantic cotton trade, but he was not French by birth.[138] A handful of French, Italian and Spanish commission agents settled in Manchester and Liverpool, but they do not appear to have achieved any eminence.[139]

We may conclude, therefore, that the international houses played an important part in the development of the British economy, not only because of their enterprise and commercial expertise, but also because of their family-centred loyalties. They increased industrial prosperity by stimulating the local manufacturers to make fabrics, hardware and other goods most suited to their own home areas and the markets where they were familiar with the local terrain. Their judicious buying helped to smooth the momentum of industrial advance because they made their purchases when prices were low and the rest of the market slack.[140] And finally, their migration brought valuable reserves of entrepreneurial experience to Britain at a period when resources of enterprise were extended and bankruptcy was regularly depleting the ranks of the mercantile class. The industrialisation of Britain was a genuinely international process, in which Germans, Greeks, American Irish and a smattering of other races (Dutch, French, Italians and others) contributed their expertise, much as British enterprise was contributing to the development of commerce and industry on the Continent and in the newly developing regions of the world.

---

[135] B. of E. L'pool ltrs, 21 Sept., 1 Oct. 1829. J. A. Willink letter books, 1817–19, 1826–8, New York, Historical Society, for further details of the family.
[136] B. of E. L'pool ltrs, 24 Jan. 1829.
[137] [Anon.], *Geschichte der Handelskammer zu Frankfurt a.M.*, esp. pp. 103–11. English Huguenots in H. Lüthy, *La Banque protestante*, II, checked in London directories.
[138] B. Gille, *Rothschild*, I, p. 403, B. of E. L'pool ltr bks, x (1849), p. 159.
[139] Their names are listed in J. Scholes, 'Foreign Merchants in Manchester'.
[140] Rothschild letter books, 1800–5; J. James, *Worsted Manufacture*, p. 411.

CHAPTER 6

The home trade houses

One of the apparent anomalies of economic history is the continued development of London as a major centre of the textile trade through the eighteenth and nineteenth centuries. Textile manufacturing largely deserted the metropolis during the Industrial Revolution period, slipping away to a variety of regional settings. The northern regions soon raised their own trading centres – Manchester, Leeds, Glasgow, Nottingham and others, but London was never entirely eclipsed. Of course, the sheer size of London's population and the concentration of wealth, fashion and conspicuous consumption in the capital inevitably sustained an entrepôt trade, but there was more to London's role than this. The textile sector of the City of London, the narrow streets between Wood Street and St Paul's churchyard, evidently retained a momentum of its own, both in its particular forms of enterprise and its relations with the provinces. Strangely enough, no one has ever attempted to piece together the story of this enterprise, at any rate not beyond the period of Defoe's classic account. Perhaps this is mainly for want of material, for most of the evidence was lost in the blitz, but it is possible to discern some of the salient features of change in the textile market in the two centuries after Defoe.

PHASES OF CHANGE

The records are unusually thin, but it does seem possible to identify five distinct organisational patterns that succeeded each other as London struggled to accommodate itself to changes in the manufacturing centre and the rise of new rivals in the north. This framework is admittedly tentative, but it will at least aid understanding of the details assembled in this chapter. The sequence of systems is as follows:

(1) *The Blackwell Hall period*

The rise of the domestic system in the later middle ages saw provincial organisers (*verlegers*) focussing on the various London markets. These markets served not only the population of the capital but, increasingly, shopkeepers and dealers who came to London to buy their stocks. This is the system so strikingly portrayed, at a mature period of its development, by Defoe, and in our own century by R. B. Westerfield.[1] So far as we are aware, there was no particular dominant party in the distributive chain; indeed the system recalls that of the constitutional system of checks and balances in which the eighteenth century rejoiced. However, London was undoubtedly the fulcrum of the system and London merchants much the richest and most numerous in the land.

(2) *The Lancashire period*

The second half of the eighteenth century saw not only the dramatic rise of the factory system in cotton, but with it the rapid emergence of a class of successful mill owners who became merchants. For more than half a century (c. 1760–1815), the northern manufacturer–merchants set the pace, though Liverpool and Manchester did not supersede the capital much before the end of the century.[2]

(3) *The Morrison period, c. 1820–65*

The commercial tribulations of the Napoleonic War and post-war depression ruined or enervated much of the first generation of northern producers, and the post-war depression saw calamitous overproduction and tumbling prices.[3] In this climate, a group of opportunist London drapers led by James Morrison seized the initiative, establishing a new style of high turnover warehouse. The northern manufacturers never regained the marketing initiative, but a handful of Manchester warehousemen imitated the London system.

(4) *The wholesalers (Rylands and Morley) period c. 1865–1940*

Ultimately the most successful of the great warehousing concerns were Cookes and I. & R. Morley in London and John

---

[1] D. Defoe, *A Tour through the Whole Island of Great Britain* (1724–6). R. B. Westerfield, *Middlemen in English Business 1660–1760* (New Haven 1915) Ch. 5.
[2] M. M. Edwards, *The Growth of the British Cotton Trade 1780–1815* (Manchester 1967) esp. pp. 107–11, 147ff.
[3] S. D. Chapman, 'British Marketing Enterprise; the Changing Roles of Merchants, Manufacturers and Financiers 1700–1860', *Bus. Hist. Rev.*, LIII (1979).

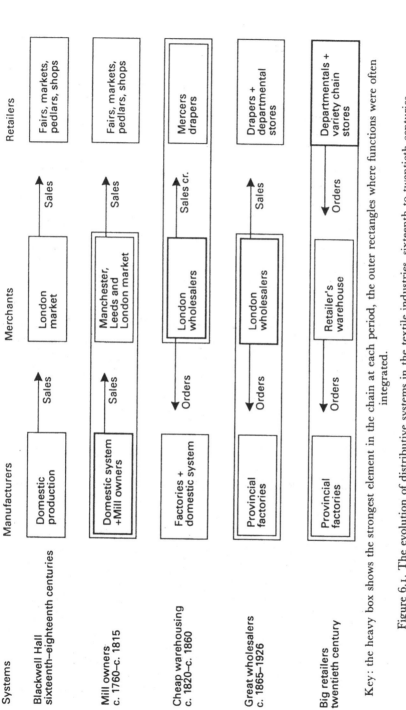

Figure 6.1. The evolution of distributive systems in the textile industries, sixteenth to twentieth centuries.

Key: the heavy box shows the strongest element in the chain at each period, the outer rectangles where functions were often integrated.

Rylands & Co. in Manchester. In the second half of the nineteenth century these and other successful firms increased their grip on the trade by integrating backward into manufacturing, buying up factories during periods of depression in trade. They generally succeeded in keeping the manufacturers and retailers well apart, despite a few challenges from 'up-market' producers.

(5) *The variety chain store (Marks and Spencer) period, 1926 to date*

Growth in the scale of retailing, and much improving communications, evidently offered the possibility of direct links between manufacturers and the great stores from at least the end of last century. Grocers, chemists and other variety chain stores are known to have dealt directly with their respective producers,[4] but it was not until Marks & Spencer took the initiative in the 1920s that the warehousemen's control was challenged and then their control superseded.

If this model is even approximately right, the London system not only survived through the nineteenth century but was probably most dominant then. The reasons for this remarkable situation must now be probed at greater depth, initially returning to our point of departure in the eighteenth century.

PROVINCIAL INDUSTRIALISTS IN THE MARKET

One of the most familiar themes of English economic history in the seventeenth and eighteenth century is that of the development of regional specialisation of manufacturing to serve the London market.[5] The textile industries evidently played a major role in this development, and there is a large bibliography on the growth of provincial manufacturing industry at this period, but the role of *verlegers* in marketing their goods in London has never been fully worked out. Are we to understand that the model was Samuel Oldknow, simply receiving and discharging orders from a London wholesale merchant?[6] Or did provincial manufacturers take any direct initiatives in marketing in their principal domestic market?

[4] Eg. P. Mathias, *Retailing Revolution* (1967), S. D. Chapman, *Jesse Boot of Boots the Chemists* (1974) pp. 91, 103.
[5] F. J. Fisher, 'The Development of London as a Centre of Conspicuous Consumption', *Trans. Royal Hist. Soc.*, xxx (1948).
[6] G. Unwin, *Samuel Oldknow and the Arkwrights* (Manchester 1924) Ch. 4. See also M. M. Edwards, *British Cotton Trade* p. 150.

Possibly the most complete information on the eighteenth century available at present is for the East Midlands hosiery industry. The fire insurance records make it possible to analyse the London connections of the seventy firms who controlled the Nottingham hosiery industry in 1770–5, showing that at least forty of them had some kind of permanent base in the City of London, mostly in rooms at the inns that formed the termini of the regular coach services. From mid-century there were at least ten coaches a week from London to both Nottingham and Leicester.[7]

It seems that the subsequent growth of the London market led more and more Midlands firms to seek permanent bases in the Wood Street area. These crowded streets were shared with a variety of other textile specialists, including warehousemen specialising in 'Manchester goods', in silks and ribbons, woollen goods and gloves. Others again dealt in variety and were content to be called general merchants and warehousemen. Their concentration in a small area comes out very well in the earliest complete street list, Johnstone's *London Commercial Guide* (1817), the details of which are set out in Table 6.1. Other premises were occupied by carriers, insurance brokers and others offering specialised services to the textile tradesmen.

It is interesting to note that 20 of the hosiers can be connected with Nottingham, evidence of a continuing strong connection, but comparison with the 36 of 1770–5 in a period in which the provincial industry at least doubled in size indicates growing concentration of the trade in fewer hands.[8] The trade in 'Manchester goods' in London looks much smaller than that in hosiery and lace and silk goods; Michael Edwards notes that only the big Lancashire firms had their own warehouses in London, and most of the firms in Johnstone's lists were probably just agents for northern manufacturers.[9] In part, the preponderance of hosiery, lace and silk may be interpreted as the continuance of a traditional connection between the East Midlands, Spitalfields and London, but it may also have something to do with the prominent role of such goods in the fashion trade, of which London continued to be the centre.

There is no direct or very clear evidence of the size of these concerns, but such evidence as we have suggests that at the turn of the century they were still on a very small scale. The largest and most

---

[7] R. Baldwin, *A Complete Guide to ... the City of London* (1752, 1755, 1760, 1763 etc.).
[8] *Nottingham Directory*, 1818.   [9] M. M. Edwards, *British Cotton Trade*, p. 148.

Table 6.1. *London connections of Nottingham merchant hosiers*
1770–5

Permanent stock at London inns:		
Cross Keys, Wood St	13	
Blossom, Laurence Lane	8	
Swan, Lad Lane	1	
Castle, Wood St	1	
Angel	1	24
City warehouse or dwelling house		12
City agent		4
		—
		40
		—
Main market in Leeds, Glasgow		2
No information (may have lodged at		
other inns)		28
		—
		70

Source: S. D. Chapman, 'Enterprise and Innovation in the British Hosiery Industry 1750–1850', *Textile History* v (1974) pp. 33–5.

enterprising of the Nottingham firms represented in the City at this time was that of the Hayne brothers, who specialised in lace net. One of the brothers kept a house in Wood Street, and large quantities of net were exported to France, but the domestic selling operation was apparently limited to two young men who went round the London drapers once a week, and to a single traveller in the provinces.[10] It seems probable that Haynes' organisation was no larger than those of the leading City retail drapers. At this time, and for a generation or more, the City houses rather than the West End ones occupied the highest position in public estimation, and were not averse to doing some wholesale trade with lesser firms in the provinces.[11]

The Manchester warehouse region grew up in much the same way as that in London, in the yards of inns in the narrow streets of the old commercial centre. When the *Universal British Directory* was drawn up for Manchester about 1795, as many as 51 country manufacturers gave their address as New Boar's Head in Hyde's

[10] Nottingham Univ. Lib. Archives, Kirk White MSS, C123, C166. For Hayne Bros. see G. Henson, *History of the Framework Knitters* (1835) pp. 304–17.
[11] W. H. Ablett, ed., *Reminiscences of an Old Draper* (1876) esp. pp. 58, 76. A. Adburgham, *Shops and Shopping 1800–1914* (1964) pp. 8–9.

Cross, while there were 16 at the George and Dragon in Withy Grove, 15 at the Lower Ship in Salford and 13 each at the Griffin in Long Mill Gate and Higher Swan in Market Street Lane. Thirty other inns were the town home of from one to ten *verlegers*. At this date only the foremost country manufacturers had their own warehouse.[12] The largest of them was quite possibly Arkwright's in Cromford Court, a four-storey building with weavers' windows, standing at the bottom of the court surrounded by the premises of satellite manufacturers.[13] The yarn warehouses were probably little more than distribution depots for the benefit of the country manufacturers, and if we are interested in the diffusion of new innovation and fashion, the warehouses of the calico printers are no doubt more important. At any rate, it was Peels who initially set the standard in building purpose-built and prestigious warehouses as a means of attracting customers.[14] This development put Manchester well in advance of London, but the typical merchant's enterprise evidently remained small. This view is supported by nineteenth-century reminiscences of the small scale on which many Manchester merchant houses were operating at this period, which were quoted in Chapter 2.

Selling by pattern was linked to 'the tally trade' and was evidently the reason for the continuance of the large number of small merchant houses at the period, both in Manchester and London.[15] An explanation of the large number of small sales rooms – already more than 1,500 in 1815[16] – is also offered by the growing practice of Scots and Irish manufacturers, as well as the 'distant English manufacturers', of keeping a warehouse in Manchester. John and Peter Duncan, Dundee linen manufacturers, offer a striking illustration of the early pull of Manchester. Their father had a house in London in the same trade from 1811–15 but in 1824 the sons preferred to make Manchester their main outlet despite the easier access (by sea) to the metropolis. The Duncans' linens were sent to Manchester to be 'disposed of amongst an extensive country connexion, some of whom are waited upon by their travellers and

---

[12] *Universal British Directory*, III (1795).
[13] J. Loudon, *Manchester Memoirs* (1916) p. 130.
[14] J. Ashton, *A Picture of Manchester* (1816) pp. 221–2.
[15] J. Mortimer, *Mercantile Manchester, Past and Present* (1896) p. 69. 'The Tally Trade', in J. R. McCulloch, *Dictionary of Commerce*, II, p. 110.
[16] R. Lloyd Jones and M. J. Lewis, 'The Economic Structure of "Cottopolis" in 1815', *Textile History*, XVII (1986).

others are in the habit of making their purchases in person... thus giving them an opportunity... of seeing the buyers in their line who are continually visiting this great emporium'.[17]

The dispatches of the Bank of England branch managers in Manchester and Leeds support the general impression that home trade houses were rather late in developing; no doubt it was the railway network that really made Manchester's commercial sector. The earliest firm to obtain significant mention was Henry Bannerman & Sons, said to have been started by a wealthy Perthshire farmer and his three sons in the first decade of the century. In 1846, when the third generation had taken control, the firm was reported to have a capital, excluding its warehouses, of £160,000, perhaps £200,000 in all.[18] Four years later, in 1850, John Rylands, the future doyen of the trade, was reported to employ £100,000 capital, half of it at his Gorton Mills, and to serve about 2,000 customers in the general and country trade.[19] Rylands was evidently an important man in the industry and trade, but his capital, fifty years after his family firm had been established, does not look anything extraordinary alongside some of Manchester's leading export merchants of the day. As early as 1829 H. J. & R. Barton had a capital of £470,000, while in 1847 Sir William Fielding had £360,000 and Robert Gardner £344,000.[20] However, during the course of the next half century, Rylands & Co. increased the momentum of their growth; by 1897 fourteen more mills had been acquired, branches had been opened in Paris and Rio, and 20,000 customers bought over £3m. worth of goods. Other home trade houses – Bannermans, S. & J. Watts, Richard Haworth and A. & S. Henry – could not maintain this pace, and Rylands shortly appeared in a class of its own.[21] Nevertheless, the firm offers a standard for comparison with the London firms, to which we may now return.

[17] B. of E, Manchester letters, 27 Feb. and 2 Mar. 1836.
[18] B. of E. Manc. ltr bks, v (1846) p. 146. [J. Mortimer], *Henry Bannerman & Sons Ltd* (Manchester 1891).
[19] B. of E. Manc. ltr bks, vii (1850) p. 150.
[20] B. of E. Manc. ltrs 4 Apr. 1829, ltr bks vi (1847) pp. 159, 165.
[21] D. A. Farnie, 'John Rylands of Manchester', *Bull. of the John Rylands Lib.*, lvi (1973). Guildhall Lib., Kleinwort Information Books, No. 184, p. 76. Records of Rylands & Sons Ltd at John Rylands Library.

THE GREAT WHOLESALE HOUSES

The first generation of the Industrial Revolution undoubtedly saw a vigorous expansion of the northern merchant manufacturers at the expense of London, but this expansion lost some of its drive by the later years of the French Wars. Overseas trade proved ruinous to many sanguine inexperienced northerners, and the slimmer profits of the post-war years prevented the accumulation of manufacturing fortunes.[22] Initiative now reverted to London, taking a new form appropriate to a period of overproduction and tumbling prices.

The new system was at first called the 'Todd system' after its most successful exponents, Todd and Morrison (later Morrison, Dillon & Co).[23] The most succinct account of James Morrison's technique appears in the autobiography of Sir John Bowring, and is worth quoting at length:

Morrison told me that he owed all his prosperity to the discovery that the great art of mercantile traffic was to find sellers rather than buyers; that if you bought cheap, and satisfied yourself with only a fair profit, buyers – the best sort of buyers, those who have money to buy would come of themselves. He said he found houses engaged with a most expensive machinery, sending travellers about in all directions to seek orders and to effect sales, while he employed travellers to buy instead of to sell: and if they bought well, there was no fear of his effecting and advantageous sales. So, uniting this theory with another, that small profits and quick returns are more profitable in the long run than long credits with great gains, he established one of the largest and most lucrative concerns that has ever existed in London, and was entitled to a name which I have often heard applied to him, 'The Napoleon of Shopkeepers'.[24]

In the post-war depression it would not have been difficult to locate manufacturers anxious to unburden themselves of excess stocks. Morrison was related to Flints who were described in his biography as 'great ready money haberdashers' in London, from whom he probably acquired initial knowledge of northern suppliers as well as an appreciation of the benefits of fast turnover.[25]

In 1834 the *Circular to Bankers* explained the development of the system in a little more detail:

[22] *Circular to Bankers* 15 Jan. 1836.   [23] *Circular to Bankers* 10 Oct. 1834.
[24] Quoted in R. Gatty, *Portrait of a Merchant Prince. James Morrison 1789–1857* (privately published, Northallerton 1981) p. 23.
[25] R. Gatty, *James Morrison*, p. 9.

Morrison has made a large fortune, some say more than £1m. sterling. There are a dozen or more firms on the same system in London and doing well. These houses were able to establish themselves in this line of business through breaking down of the manufacturers owing to changes in the value of money. When the manufacturers' property began to diminish they made very ready use of the credit being offered to them to obtain their raw materials. They could maintain themselves for years by vending their goods under prime cost at the low-priced warehouses of London. Some bankruptcy cases showed that goods had been sold in large quantities at 25%–30% below the fair ready money price. If goods could be purchased in this manner amounting to say one-fifth or one-seventh of a company's trade, and the total trade of the company was worth £1,200,000 to £1,500,000 this would be an abundant source of profit. This is how the first-established cheap-selling warehouses did it.[26]

The existence of credit on the supply side is confirmed by records of two smaller warehouses in the 1830s.[27] The Morrison system was evidently continued for a good many years after the founder had gained his fortune. Daniel Puseley's *Commercial Companion* (1860) maintains that Morrison, Dillon & Co. was the 'most extensive and most eminent wholesale house of its class in the City of London', though now conducted by the son of the founder. The confidence in the house, Puseley maintained, was 'exemplified by the simple yet striking fact that the house... is the only extensive one of its class that has never had occasion, or deemed it requisite, to be represented in the provinces or elsewhere by travellers or agents of any class'.[28] Actually the firm continued to have strong representation in the provinces, but by buyers ('confidential agents') rather than by salesmen. Giving evidence to the government's *Select Committee on the Trade Marks Bill* in 1862, John Dillon, the managing partner, explained that his marketing was now principally conducted by extensive mailing of circulars, and that he had sometimes sent out as many as 2,500 to advertise goods bought by tender of bankrupt stock.[29] No doubt the introduction of the penny post (1840) stimulated this kind of business.

It is not difficult to identify several of Morrison's early competitors. In 1828 the *Circular to Bankers* remarked that 'We hear of

[26] *Circular to Bankers* 10 Oct. 1834.
[27] N. B. Harte, *A History of George Brettle & Co. Ltd 1801–1964* (privately published, 1977) cites Moore, James & Co and Ward, Brettle & Ward as receiving and giving short periods of credit, apparently two months.
[28] D. Puseley, *Commercial Companion* (1860) p. 125.
[29] *Sel. Comm. on Trade Marks Bill*, Parl. Papers, 1862, XII, pp. 543–4.

warehousemen who deal in the more showy, ornamental or more petty articles of attire and not much in the substantial parts of clothing, who severally make returns in trade amounting to £1m. to £2m. per annum.'[30] This is an unmistakable reference to the two most energetic firms in the lace trade, James Fisher & Co. and Groucock, Copestake and Moore. Like most London warehousemen, James Fisher received his early training in retail drapery. He started on his own about 1800 and built rapidly on an early connection with John Heathcoat, the innovating entrepreneur in the manufacture of bobbin net lace. Despite this valuable advantage, it seems that he always employed a team of well-paid travellers. When Heathcoat's patent expired in 1823, Fisher built a large lace factory in Nottingham and in the 1830s contrived to dominate the trade by taking out a sequence of patents in the name of his chief mechanic William Crofts. His London business reached its apogee, it is said, about 1845.[31]

Copestake, Moore & Co. was established and energetically built up by two of Fisher's most able staff. His northern traveller, George Moore, another product of the draper's shop, is celebrated in one of Samuel Smiles's later biographies.[32] The history of the firm is evidently one of the growth of a sales force drilled by Moore, rising from four in 1830 to twenty-seven in 1852. Following Fisher's example, the firm built a factory in Nottingham in 1845. Notwithstanding the panegyric on Morrisons, Puseley wrote that Copestake, Crampton and Co. house was 'at present by far the largest of its class in the world'.[33] In the 1860s the firm employed over 300 men in their City warehouse, and comparison with I. & R. Morley (for which more complete data is available) suggests that annual sales may have exceeded £3.0m. a year.[34]

Evidently Morrison, Dillon & Co. were not slavishly followed by their closest rivals, and the few figures available suggest that Copestake, Moore & Co. drew substantially ahead in sales (Table 6.3). The available evidence suggests two possible reasons. One is that in the 1830s Morrison concentrated his attention on becoming

---

[30] *Circular to Bankers* 17 Oct. 1828.
[31] W. Felkin, *History of the Machine Wrought Hosiery and Lace Manufacturers* (1867) Ch. 22.
[32] S. Smiles, *George Moore, Merchant and Philanthropist* (1878).
[33] D. Puseley, *Commercial Companion*, p. 41. S. Smiles, *George Moore*, p. 287.
[34] I. & R. Morley employed 100 men for an annual turnover of £1.0m. (see below) while Copestake & Moore employed 300 men at a nearby London warehouse.

Table 6.2. *The City of London textile market in 1817*

	Hosiery & lace	Silk & ribbons	Man-chester goods	Woollen goods	Gloves	Other textiles	General merchants	Totals
Wood Street	35	24	3	6	5	2	10	85
Lawrence Street	2	2	8	1	—	2	14	39
Lad Lane	2	1	2	1	—	2	4	12
Cateaton Street	1	1	3	9	—	2	11	27
Alder-manbury	4	3	1	11	1	4	19	43
	44	31	17	28	6	12	58	206

Source: Johnstone's *Commercial Guide and Street Directory* (1817). 97 other tradesmen are listed in these fives small streets, including six carriers. The categories for occupations are variously given in the *Directory* eg. hosiery and lace includes firms describing themselves as manufacturers, Blackwell Hall factors, flannel warehouses etc. Manchester goods includes calico merchants, fustian manufacturers, cotton manufacturers and small-ware manufacturers.

a merchant banker but had to withdraw at the crisis of 1837, losing a great deal of capital.[35] The other is that in the long term the employment of commercial travellers proved more successful in generating new business than the cut-price system. In 1885, A. P. Allen, the author of an early and best-selling book on travellers, wrote:

Only a few years ago there were houses which prided themselves on doing a magnificent business without a single representative. This was no vain boast, but they, like others, have succumbed to the inevitable law, and I am not aware that there are more than one or two houses of any repute that can command any large amount of business without the aid of a commercial traveller.[36]

Unfortunately, very little is known about other London warehouses on the Morrison plan, beyond the fact that most emerged from the ranks of specialists. Among the leading houses, Cookes of St Paul's

[35] Guildhall Lib. MSS. 11, 705–7, Morrison Cryder letters.
[36] A. P. Allen, *Ambassadors of Commerce* (1885) p. 106.

were originally carpet manufacturers and warehousemen while Leaf & Co. specialised in silks and ribbons. By 1866, Cookes already had thirty-one departments, each dealing with a different type of fabric; in 1874 Leafs had four.

While many of the great London houses were founded at the end of the eighteenth century or in the early years of the nineteenth century, the impression gained is that they did not begin to grow rapidly until after mid-century. The growth of the railway network centring on London offers the most ready explanation, but relatively easy access to capital must also be considered. Certainly the London warehouses were amongst the earliest textile enterprises to take advantage of the opportunity of incorporation. Morrison, Dillon & Co. set the ball rolling by incorporating as the Fore Street Warehouse Co. in 1864, with a capital of £420,000. Only one of the original six directors bore either of the founders' names. Bradbury Greatorex & Co. followed in 1868, admitting 'a few gentlemen of capital and experience as shareholders'. Pawsons were incorporated in 1873, with the help of A. J. Mundella, who was I. & R. Morley's main rival in hosiery manufacture. Rylands incorporated in 1873 and the London Warehouse Co., led by John F. Pawson, the next year. Other firms remained private partnerships but saw amalgamations: I. & R. Morley took over Nevilles of Gresham Street in 1864 and the Midland Hosiery Co. in 1884, while Birkins, the leading Nottingham lace manufacturers, took over Fishers. At the manufacturing end, incorporation was scarcely considered before the Oldhams movement of the 1880s, and Lancashire firms characteristically remained short of capital. Leafs delayed incorporation until 1893 and later admitted they had been acutely short of capital since 1874.[37]

The fashion historian Sarah Levitt has suggested that the London textile warehouses were most prominent in the supply of the fashionable embellishments to the characteristically plain dress – and especially men's dress – of Britain's Victorian epoch. She rests her case mainly on the records of Welch, Margetson & Co., who specialised in the supply of neckwear, but it seems to fit the experience of the lace warehouses just referred to, and perhaps also the hosiery and ribbon specialists, at any rate in their earlier years.

[37] O. Blumenthal, *British, Foreign & Colonial Trade Marks Directory* (1866) p. 73. West Yorks R.O. C 149/958, Seyd & Co.s *London Commercial List*, 1877. C. M. Leaf, *Walter Leaf 1852–1927* (1932) p. 114. *Modern London. The World's Metropolis. An Epitome of Results* (c. 1887) p. 179, for Leaf & Co. Ltd.

However, the policy of the most successful house, Morrison, Dillon & Co. was evidently laid on quite different foundations, and we must see how it is possible to reconcile the two traditions.

Once again, evidence is inadequate but there are some indications of trends. The experience of Leaf & Co. is instructive. Not untypically of older houses, the firm started its life at the end of the eighteenth century as a haberdasher; a century later it specialised in silk, ribbons, velvet, crepe, dress goods, flowers and feathers. According to an advertisement article in *Modern London: The World's Metropolis* (c. 1893), 'The fashions of the day are the guiding influences of the firm's operations... It is with such firms as that of Messrs Leaf & Co Ltd that styles and fashions originate; and it is under their favouring influence and auspices that they reach the perfection of art and taste upon which we, of the present age, have a just right to pride ourselves.' This fulsome comment might be accepted as the last word on the subject but for the fact that Walter Leaf, the senior partner from 1874–1893, admitted in a posthumous autobiography that his firm spent these years struggling for survival and that Morrison Dillon & Co. were 'the great rival business'. This was no small concern; in 1879 the Bank of England recorded its capital as £500,000, which was quite as large as most merchant banks at the time. In 1891, and united with Pawsons, it was down to £354,000. No doubt much of the problem was the decline of the Spitalfields silk and Coventry ribbon industries, but Leafs had long had direct connections with silk factories in France, Germany, Switzerland, Italy and Austria, and there was time to adjust. The underlying cause was more likely the traditional commitment to the upper end of the market and the consequent need to find customers more akin to those served by Morrison and similar firms. Capital was short because of this major development.[38]

The burgeoning of departments in the leading houses, and the proliferation of lines in the trade catalogues of the later nineteenth century, can leave little doubt that the most successful houses aimed at the widest possible range of tastes and pockets. They liked to feature some of the latest modes, but the country drapers that they served represented a predominantly conservative market. The old-style drapers had to reach down the scale and the cheap-selling warehouses upwards, eventually serving much the same retail

[38] C. M. Leaf, *Walter Leaf*, pp. 111, 114, 146. *Modern London*, p. 179. Bank of England Discount Applications 1877–91, C 29/23, 24.

outlets, but there remained a long tail of smaller concerns, less ambitious or less ably conducted, that remained closer to one tradition or the other.

MERCHANT DOMINATION

In the later Victorian years the British textile industry was dominated by merchants. In two generations of rapid growth, from the 1820s to the 1880s, they had become the undisputed kings of the textile business. After all that has been written about the Industrial Revolution in cotton, and in textiles generally, it may seem almost reactionary to assert that merchants rather than manufacturers ruled Britain's premier industry. The idea certainly requires some explanation.

The economic power of the merchant class in this industry was the consequence of three factors. The disintegrated structure of the textile industry is well known. The British industry traditionally consisted of a large number of small (or small-to-middling) family firms with limited capital all making similar goods in conditions approximating to the economist's definition of perfect competition. Sporadic attempts to launch or forge integrated production (whether vertical or horizontal) made little impact on the overall scene before 1914,[39] and on hosiery and knitwear before the 1960s. As a result, power was retained by the entrepreneurs controlling credit and marketing.

The City of London textile market retained its leadership despite the rise of import trading centres in Manchester, Liverpool, Leeds, Bradford and Glasgow. Notwithstanding strong growth of financial specialisms in the City, merchanting continued to be more important until at least 1914, and within this sector textiles were much the most important single element.[40] When the process of integration of family firms began at the end of last century, all the well-known groupings (J. & P. Coats, Fine Spinners & Doublers, the Calico Printers Association, Tootal Broadhurst Lee and others) were horizontal combinations. All the home trade and shipping (i.e. export) houses remained independent.[41]

[39] The best bibliography of the extensive literature on the cotton industry in this period is in D. A. Farnie, *The English Cotton Industry and the World Market 1815–96* (Oxford 1979) pp. 329–84.

[40] S. D. Chapman, 'The Decline and Rise of Textile Merchanting 1880–1990', *Bus. Hist.* XXXII (1990).   [41] R. Robson, *The Cotton Industry in Britain* (1957) Ch. IV.

Merchant domination is not immediately obvious from the extensive literature because practically all the numerous writers on nineteenth and early twentieth-century textiles were primarily interested in production rather than trade and were based in the North of England rather than London. They regularly identified the fragmentation of the production process but scarcely anyone paused to consider finance and marketing. There are several biographies and a couple of histories of London textile merchant houses (more than of other centres) but they disclose little of how the system worked.[42]

Consequently most of the hard evidence must come from analysis of financial data. Table 6.3 assembles details of the capital of leading merchants at the apogee of their power about 1880. At this date there is nothing in manufacturing comparable in capital to the leading merchants, and when the great combines of Tootals, the C.P.A. and J. & P. Coats were assembled, it took some years for them to exploit their potential in marketing. In hosiery there was nothing on this scale until Wolsey was formed in 1920.[43] Indeed, the biggest City and Manchester merchant houses compared in size with all but the biggest of the merchant banks, which have been recognised as the most powerful group in City finance. This is confirmed by Rubinstein's tabulations of millionaires and half-millionaires, which contain scarcely any textile manufacturers but numerous merchants, especially in London.[44] The calculations in Table 6.4 suggest the average capital of cotton mills about 1880.

In a few instances we can focus instructively on particular merchant houses. I. & R. Morley's sales at the end of last century was about ten per cent of the total British production of hosiery and knitwear, and their capital was something like fifteen times that of the largest producer of knitted goods, N.M.C.[45] Morley's was not the biggest City textile warehouse (that was undoubtedly Cookes) but comparison with John Rylands (Manchester's biggest merchant)

---

[42] R. Gatty, *James Morrison*. S. Smiles, *George Moore*. E. Hodder, *The Life of Samuel Morley* (1888). C. M. Leaf, *Walter Leaf*. N. B. Harte, *A History of George Brettle & Co. Ltd. 1801–1964* (1977). F. M. Thomas, *I. & R. Morley, A Record of a Hundred Years* (1900). *Dict. Bus. Biography* articles on J. D. Allcroft, Sir George Williams.

[43] Manchester P.L., Tootal Broadhurst Lee minute books, C.P.A. minute books. J. Hunter, *History of J. & P. Coats* (forthcoming). Wolsey Ltd. was incorporated with a capital of £2.0m. in 1920 (private records).

[44] S. D. Chapman, *The Rise of Merchant Banking* (1984). W. D. Rubinstein, *Men of Property* (1981) p. 107.

[45] Lord Hollendon's estate office, Leigh, Kent: I. & R. Morley sales data and other records.

Table 6.3. *Capital of leading textile warehousesmen c. 1880*

	Year	£m.	Factories
London			
Cooke, Son & Co.	c. 1880	c. 2·0	1
I. & R. Morley	c. 1880	c. 1·4	7
Dent, Allcroft & Co.	1886	0·69	1
Copestake, Crampton & Co.	1880	0·65	1
Leaf, Sons & Co.	1879	0·5	
Fore Street Warehouse Co. Ltd,	1880	0·42	
Bradbury Greatorex & Co.	1894	0·4	
J. & C. Boyd	1880	0·39	
Pawsons & Co.	1880	0·31	
George Brettle & Co.	1882	0·25	1
Foster, Porter & Co.	1881	0·21	
Ward, Sturt & Sharp	1878	0·2	
Caldecott, Sons & Co.	1881	0·2	
Crocker, Sons & Co.	1881	0·15	
Devas, Routledge & Co.	1878	0·14	
London Warehouse Co. Ltd.	1874	0·11	
Dewar, Sons & Co. Ltd.	1876	0·10	
Baggalays & Spence	1881	0·10	
David Evans & Co.	1883	0·05	1
Welch, Margetson & Co.		nd	2
Provinces			
John Rylands & Son, Manchester	1876	1·3	15
A. & S. Henry, Manchester	1889	1·1	3
Arthur & Co., Glasgow	1878	1·2	3
Thomas Adams & Co., Nott'm	1877	0·13	1

Sources: Incorporated companies in Seyd & Co.'s *London Commercial List* (1877), copy in West Yorks R.O. C149/958. N. B. Harte, *A History of George Brettle & Co.* (1977) p. 103. John Rylands MSS, John Rylands University Library, J. F. Barclay, *The Story of Arthur & Co.* (Glasgow 1953) p. 50. *Dict. Bus. Biog.* 1, article on J. D. Allcroft.
Partnership capital in Bank of England R.O., Discount Applications C29/23.
Capital of Cooke, Son & Co and I. & R. Morley has been estimated from data on Cooke's sales and capital for 1920–40 (Courtaulds' Archives, Coventry) and Morleys' sales 1830–1926 (Lord Hollendon's Estate Office, Tonbridge, Kent).

shows the former were as large as and more effective in their operations (Table 6.5).

However, perhaps the most convincing evidence of the central role of the merchant is found in an account of the credit system. The leader of the London textile trade for many years was James

Table 6.4. *Average size of investment in British cotton mills (machinery only) c. 1880*

	1878	c. 1880
Spinning mills (1,159)		
Average spindles per mill	24,738	× 24s. (£1·2) = £29,685
Weaving mills (765)		
Average looms per mill	307	× £24 = £7,368
Combined mills (597)		
Spindles/mill	26,022	× 24s. (£1·2) = £31,226
Looms/mill	469	× £24 = £11,256
		£42,482

Sources: C. H. Lee, 'The Cotton Textile Industry', in Roy Church, ed., *The Dynamics of Victorian Business* (1980) Table 8.2, p. 173 (for calculations of average spindles and looms per mill). T. Ellison, *The Cotton Trade of Great Britain* (1886) p. 70 for value of machinery. Many firms rented space and steam power but if they owned both it may be supposed that an average fixed capital investment would be in the order of £35,000 for a spinning mill, £10,000 for a weaving mill and £50,000 for a combined mill. However, the relative weakness of the manufacturer vis-à-vis the merchant lay in shortage of working capital, S. D. Chapman, 'Financial Restraints on the Growth of Firms in the Cotton Industry', *Econ. Hist. Rev.* XXXII (1979).

Table 6.5. *Marketing organisation of Rylands and I. & R. Morley compared, 1897–1900*

	Morleys 1900	Rylands 1897
Warehouse staff	1,241	1,200
Travellers	77	70
Customers	9,000	20,000
Annual sales	£3·06m.	£3·0m. +
Average annual sales per customer	£333	£150 +

Sources: F. M. Thomas, *I. & R. Morley* (1900) pp. 22, 76, 85, 100. I. & R. Morley London Sales 1830–1926 (MS, Lord Hollenden). D. A. Farnie, 'John Rylands of Manchester', *Bulletin of the John Rylands Library*, LVI (1973) pp. 106, 112.

Morrison, who made his fortune at the cheap end of the market, buying at bankrupt prices and keeping costs low and turnover high by selling cheap to country drapers without employing travellers.[46]

[46] R. Gatty, *James Morrison*, p. 23.

There appears to be no explicit record in the British literature of the mature system, and no relevant business archives, but the biography of a New York merchant who learned his business in England appears to give substance to the sketchy material published on this side. This commission merchant advanced 50 per cent of the fair selling price of the goods to the manufacturer, charging interest at 6 per cent per annum, while commission on sales averaged 5 per cent. He sold to a multitude of small retailers, invoicing at 30, 90 or 120 days. The merchant had no doubt of the advantages of the system to his suppliers, his customers and himself:

Altogether, assuming that advances did not run for more than four months, the entire selling cost, including interest and expenses, did not exceed 10 per cent of the selling price, and in many cases was much less. In return, the mill was assured continuity of operation, ample working capital with which to purchase materials and pay its labour, and freedom from credit risk. On the other hand it was a safe and profitable business for the commission merchant, providing he exercised sound judgement and possessed an intimate knowledge of goods and credits.[47]

Of course, the merchants' suppliers and customers did not always see the system in such a favourable light. Dependent manufacturers spoke of the 'merchant's yoke' and being 'downtrodden', while the connection between the merchant and retailers was compared to the tied house system established by the brewers in the period. Heylin's *Buyers and Sellers in the Cotton Trade* (1913) maintained that 'It has not been uncommon for spinners to find that cloth agents or merchants, in addition to holding unsold stock of manufacturers, have had a lien on the manufacturer's business and practically controlled it.'[48]

MERCHANTS' PROBLEMS

During the last two decades of the nineteenth century serious problems appeared in the system. Growing international and domestic competition arrested the dramatic growth of earlier years and put pressure on profit margins.[49] Intense competition induced merchant houses to offer longer credits and put more and more travellers on the road.[50] This 'reckless' policy brought many new

[47] W. H. Hillyer, *James Talcott, Merchant, and His Times* (New York 1937) pp. 92–3.
[48] H. B. Heylin, *Buyers and Sellers in the Cotton Trade* (1913) pp. 122–3, 128. Marks & Spencer's archives, Sacher typescript history of the company.
[49] Guildhall Lib., Stock Exchange company files, especially those for Fore St Warehouse Co. (former Morrison, Dillon & Co.), Foster, Porter & Co., and Pawson & Co. I. & R. Morley sales data, loc. cit.   [50] A. P. Shaw, *Ambassadors of Commerce* (1885) p. 106.

Table 6.6. *Capital of some leading London retailers, 1895–6*

	Shares	Debentures	Total (£m.)
John Barker & Co.	0·28	0·15	0·43
Thos. Wallis & Co.	0·30	0·12	0·42
Harrods	0·28	0·10	0·38
D. H. Evans & Co.	0·20	0·06	0·27
Liberty & Co.	0·20	—	0·20

Source: The Statist xxxvii (1896–1), p. 332.

and old firms to grief in the 1880s, while some of the most eminent houses (like Morrisons and Leafs) struggled for survival. Several second and third generation leaders found it necessary to incorporate their family businesses, but limited liability was still widely distrusted in the City and dynasties were thought inherently superior to meritocracy in retaining the loyalty of customers, suppliers and workpeople. As we have seen, the two most successful City textile houses, Cookes and Morleys, remained family enterprises until after World War I.[51]

These problems were exacerbated as manufacturers and major retailers began to forge direct links. There had always been connections at the fashion end of the market, but they seem to have multiplied rapidly in the 1870s and 1880s. In the late 1880s the shareholders of Morrisons (now the Fore Street Warehouse Co. Ltd) were told 'Things are much changed now, those great retail houses go to the manufacturers and are larger purchasers than even wholesale houses can be of certain specialities.' Walter Leaf, whose City house specialised in fancy goods, said that the big retailers had already 'seriously damaged' the wholesale trade by 1874. Towards the end of the century the traditional piece goods trade with the drapers declined in favour of the ready-made garment trade, where the great retailers had the advantage of the wholesalers.[52] By the mid-1890s the leading London stores were already rivalling most of the wholesalers in capital assets (Table 6.6).

The history of Debenhams relates that Frank Debenham, the driving force of the firm from the 1860s to the 1890s, was always

[51] R. Spencer, *The Home Trade of Manchester* (1890) p. 45. C. M. Leaf, *Walter Leaf* p. 112. Fore St Co. annual reports.
[52] Fore St Co. report, 1888. C. M. Leaf, *Walter Leaf*, p. 114. H. B. Heylin, *Buyers* p. 122.

'determined to buy at source' and before 1870 was buying silks at Lyons, St Etienne and other places in France and Italy. When woollen underwear began to be made in hosiery factories, Debenhams bought direct from manufacturers in Leicester and Nottingham, and also ready-made clothes from manufacturers. It is not known how many other West End and provincial drapers followed this lead, but according to Walter Leaf, major retailers were able to go direct to the manufacturer and buy from him on as good terms as any wholesale houses; some of them grew large enough to compete with the wholesale houses in their own line.[53]

According to *The Statist* in 1897:

> The wholesale drapery trade is now a lean trade, with a tendency to become leaner as the big retail houses deal more and more directly with the manufacturers or their agents; and the little shopkeepers, finding it hard to earn a living at all in competition with the great 'store' shops, want more and more concessions from the warehouses in the way of making up small parcels, such as quarter dozens, one-sixth dozens, and perhaps now and then one-twelfth dozens, until it is hard to distinguish so-called wholesale from retail trade. In these circumstances it is not surprising that some wholesale houses do not feel bound to inquire very closely whether a ready-money customer is or is not in the trade, whilst some large retail houses carry on also a considerable business in supplying smaller shopkeepers.[54]

Various solutions were found to prolong the lives of the home trade houses. Samuel Morley's success seems to have stemmed from his financial control. 'He knew how to turn the capital of the firm to the best account, never keeping larger balances than were absolutely needful lying idle, and taking advantage of every favourable change in the money market to gain his discounts', his Victorian biographer wrote. ('Discounts' evidently refers to buying not selling.)

The accounts of the public companies show that they were already tightening credit in the 1880s. The clearest comments on this process come from Reuben Spencer of Rylands, writing in 1889. At that time some 40,000 commercial travellers were competing for the business of some 50,000 drapers, who were frequently tempted to overstrain their credit. He urged that a retailer should never allow his liabilities to trade creditors to exceed 2 to 2.5 times his capital, and that he should do a cash business. Spencer's moralising work seems to have been very popular.[55]

[53] M. Corina, *Fine Silks and Oak Counters: Debenhams 1778–1978* (1978) pp. 44–5, 71, 114.
[54] *The Statist* XXXIX (1897) p. 840.
[55] E. Hodder, *Morley* pp. 23–6. R. Spencer, *Home Trade* pp. 53, 76–7.

The most satisfying way for the manufacturer to break out of the system was to establish his own brand with consumers, which gave him the opportunity to increase his profit margin and establish his own marketing organisation. Before the end of the century several firms were establishing their names with the public, including Horrocks of Preston, Hollins (Viyella shirts), Wolsey (underwear), Cartwright & Warner of Loughborough (hosiery), Lyle & Scott of Hawick (underwear) and so on. Most appear to have opened their own warehouses in London or Manchester, or both.[56] However, it would be a mistake to suppose that the trade in branded goods was completely lost to the established wholesale houses. Their catalogues show them advertising a limited number of branded lines, while in press advertisements the branded goods manufacturers were often at pains to stress that they only sold through particular warehouses. Specific evidence is hard to come by, but Hollins' accounts show that in 1914 only one-eighth of its sales were made direct to retail. In other words, manufacturers' brands were not a strong challenge to the established merchants before 1914.[57]

Several of the great warehousing firms were also manufacturers, though it is not to be assumed that this was always a response to constraints on mercantile enterprise. Rylands, Dents and Morleys for instance, were manufacturers before they were merchants, and always maintained a strong presence at the factory stage of enterprise.[58] However, there were other firms that entered manufacturing later, for instance Cookes (at Chatham), Welch, Margetson & Co. (Londonderry shirt factory), and even the small David Evans & Co. who had a silk printing works at Crayford.[59] But there were problems of integration, even for I. & R. Morley; according to some reminiscences of the firm: 'It was only on rare occasions that any of the Fletcher Gate [Nottingham] managers met the Wood Street [London] buyers. Samples were sent up to London and stock orders were given... but it was left very largely to the Fletcher Gate managers to decide the quantities to be made in the various lines.' Further problems lay ahead.

Another anticipation of major future developments was merchant

---

[56] See women's and trade periodicals of the day eg. *Draper's Record, Woman, Woman's Journal. The Times*, 17 Jan. 1906 (Horrocks).

[57] Coats Viyella archives, records of Wm. Hollins & Co. (unlisted).

[58] F. M. Thomas, *Morley*. D. A. Farnie, 'John Rylands'.

[59] Cooke, Sons & Co., *Cookes of St Paul's. 150 Years 1807–1957* (1957). Welch, Margetson & Co., *Centenary Booklet* (1933). Ulster R.O., Belfast T1346/1 (A. & S. Henry). S. D. Chapman, 'David Evans & Co, the last of the Old London Textile Printers', *Textile History* XIV (1983).

investment in overseas production, for instance Rylands in the Dacca Twist Co. (India) and Morleys in continental centres of glove making.[60] The 'home trade' houses had sought overseas outlets from their earliest years. Todd, Morrison & Co., the pioneers of the system, had travellers on the Continent at the end of the French Wars but were frustrated by the inadequacy of British textile designers. Similarly the energies of George Moore (Copestake, Moore & Co.) led him to open warehouses in Dublin and Paris in 1846.[61] But the main development came later, with the concentration on the imperial market. I. & R. Morley, Leafs, Bradbury Greatorex and Welch Margetson opened a string of offices in the white colonies. Reuben Spencer of Rylands wrote that 'It is notorious that the colonial trade is the backbone of the Glasgow home trade houses' and believed that Manchester had been slow to respond to the opportunities beckoning there.[62] This shift in policy can be closely chronicled at Morleys because of Samuel Morley's prominent public profile (he was a leading Liberal MP and friend of Gladstone). As late as 1881, Morley was opposing the formation of a London Chamber of Commerce to press for protectionism at home and in the imperial market, but when the Chamber was launched a few months later he became Chairman of the Council.[63] At the turn of the century nearly a quarter of Morleys' travellers were employed overseas.[64]

It would be a mistake to see this search for overseas markets as simply the consequence of saturation of the home market and the nationalism of the age. As a result of the Franco-Prussian War, the City strengthened its position as the international centre of both finance and trade, not least the textile trade. The official biographer of Sir George Williams, the head of Hitchcock, Williams & Co. from 1863 to 1906, explained the commercial consequences of the war to the City:

---

[60] *Threads* [I. & R. Morley's house magazine], 1 (4), Oct. 1925, p. 4. H. B. Heylin, *Buyers* p. 122. F. M. Thomas, *Morley* p. 70. Heylin maintained that in 1913 there were 'many shipping firms in Manchester, London and Liverpool directly interested in spinning and weaving mills, especially in India', but gave no examples. For Rylands' overseas interest see Guildhall Lib., Kleinwort Information Books No. 184 p. 176.

[61] R. Gatty, *James Morrison* pp. 17–18. S. Smiles, *George Moore* p. 165.

[62] I. & R. Morley sales catalogues. *Modern London. The World's Metropolis* (c. 1893) p. 179 (Leaf & Co). *A Short History of Bradbury, Greatorex & Co.* (1970). R. Spencer, *Home Trade* p. 56.

[63] S. R. B. Smith, 'British Nationalism, Imperialism, and the City of London, 1880–1900', Ph.D. thesis, London 1985, pp. 35–7.

[64] Eighteen of seventy-seven travellers: F. M. Thomas, *Morley* p. 76.

It was largely owing to the sudden cessation...of supplies from the two great Continental countries that Britain held her position for so long as the one great market place of the world. For years Continental competition in the colonies and in America was crushed, while the British retail draper, who in some cases had begun to buy direct from the Continent...was forced to fall back on the home wholesale houses...The trade of the civilised globe passed of necessity through British hands...These were the golden years of English commerce.[65]

Similar entrepreneurial opportunism is evident in Manchester, where Rylands led an assault on the continental market in the 1870s.

The Wholesale Textile Association was formed in London in 1912 to resist the encroachments of the manufacturers and major retail houses.[66] It was always a very secretive organisation and not much is known about its activities. Its main offensive activity consisted, it seems, in blacklisting manufacturers who contracted directly with retailers. The leading light for many years was the head of I. & R. Morley, Lord Hollenden. The pressure of the W.T.A. is evident in the advertisements of branded goods manufacturers, in which they insisted that they sold only through the wholesalers; in reality many of them were simultaneously involved in subterfuges to sell direct to the chain stores.[67] So late as 1953, the W.T.A. were advertising in the *Draper's Record* that 'The Wholesaler ensures that only the cream of the world's production is presented to the retail trade. He enables the Shopkeeper to examine the products of hundreds of manufacturers under one roof...'[68] By such pressures, the old merchant houses were able to resist the tide of change for a couple of generations. It was not until the period of mergers and takeovers of the 1960s that the last of the old firms were incorporated into vertical combines.

---

[65] J. E. Hodder Williams, *Life of Sir George Williams* (1906) p. 257. Guildhall Lib., Kleinwort Information Books, No. 184, p. 176. Rylands made 'a great push in Paris' and also in Rio in the 1870s.

[66] J. F. Barclay, *The Story of Arthur & Co. Ltd.* (Glasgow 1953) pp. 123–4.

[67] John Millington and S. D. Chapman, *Four Centuries of Machine Knitting* (Leicester 1989) p. 34.

[68] *Draper's Record*, 21 Mar. 1953, p. 95.

PART III

Response to instant communication

Problems of restructuring mercantile enterprise

During the course of the nineteenth century, communications improved at an increasing pace, better roads, river navigation, canals, harbours, docks, and sailing ships being overtaken by the impact of the railways, steamships and the great international ship canals. The consequences were obviously far reaching for trade and merchant organisation, but change could be accommodated within the existing family business. The advent of the telegraph was quite another matter. It represented *instant* communication worldwide, and its effects were sometimes revolutionary. In principle there was now nothing to prevent direct communication between the manufacturer and his most distant customers, and the traditional chains of middlemen began to look redundant. The opening of the international telegraph lines broadly coincided with the intensification of competition in overseas markets from a rapidly industrialising Germany and the United States, and consequent pressure on mercantile profit margins. The last quarter of the nineteenth century was therefore a period in which British merchants were forced to rethink their strategies and to conduct very different kinds of business to those undertaken by their forebears in trade, or to withdraw into other activities.

THE TEXTILE TRADE

Though the telegraph is familiar enough to historians, its economic implications have never been fully explored, and there is no major study to fall back on to measure its impact. The full implications are evidently too large to embrace in this book, but it will be helpful to identify some direct consequences of instant communication for merchant enterprise.

The notion of direct communication between exporting manufacturer and local wholesaler or retailer is not a fanciful idea prompted by retrospective insight. The main barrier would be the exporter's need to understand the market in which his customers were operating, but where he was selling standard commodities to North America or the 'white colonies' there was not too much problem about this, particularly in the 1860s and 1870s when competition was less severe than it became later. Indeed, the most successful entrepreneur in the transatlantic trade in the middle decades of the century, Alexander Turner Stewart, built up an organisation that linked factories and an export warehouse in Britain with a vast US importing organisation, retail emporium in New York and a mail order business. Sharp, Stewart & Co. employed over 2,000 in the Manchester warehouse alone, and there was also a cotton mill in the area, a linen factory in Belfast and a hosiery and lace factory in Nottingham. The buying organisation had offices in every important textile and clothing centre in Britain and on the Continent, and agents as far away as India. In 1864 it was reported that the wholesale and retail organisation in Broadway was 'probably the most extensive and perfect in the US, every article accepted to the D.G. [dry goods] trade may be found here', and within the decade 2,200 people were employed there with others in New York clothing factories. Capital rose rapidly from $10·0m. (£2·0m.) to $50·0m. (£10·0m.) in the decade 1862–71, far outpacing anything previously seen on either side of the Atlantic.[1]

Stewart can fairly be regarded as the pioneer of vertically integrated and international trading organisations that have dominated the twentieth-century marketing scene, but in the nineteenth century his vast organisation had few authentic successors and it declined rapidly after his demise. The failure to follow his lead had more to do with the preconceptions of entrepreneurs in Britain and America then any physical restraints. In Britain vertical combines and transatlantic combines were long inhibited by the highly fragmented structure of the textile industries. In America the entrepreneurs who made great fortunes in dry goods at this period (for instance John & James Stuart & Co., J. Seligman & Co. and Geo. Bliss & Co.[2]) evidently preferred to shift to pure finance, where more money could be made with less effort.

[1] H. E. Resseguie, 'Alexander Turner Stewart and the Development of the Department Sotre 1823–76', *Bus. Hist. Rev.* xxxix (1965). W. F. M. Weston-Webb, *Autobiography of a British Yarn Merchant* (1929) pp. 60–76.

[2] S. D. Chapman, *The Rise of Merchant Banking* (1984) pp. 52–3.

If it was not possible to dispense with the merchant entirely, certainly the chains of middlemen characteristic of earlier generations of mercantile enterprise were no longer necessary. Taking the best-known case to illustrate the point, the movement of raw cotton from America to Europe, the chain included merchants or agents in the southern ports (Charleston, Savannah, New Orleans etc.), shippers, merchants at the British ports, cotton brokers in Liverpool and cotton dealers in Manchester, Blackburn and other centres, and buying brokers who represented the spinning mills.[3] In buying as in selling, large transatlantic trading and manufacturing organisations emerged in the 1860s and 1870s on the foundations of family businesses established in earlier years. The best known was De Jersey & Co, of Manchester, who were the British arm of Ludwig Knoop & Co., a German merchant with extensive mill interests in Russia. More will be said about this colossus in the next chapter, but for the present it is worth noting that in 1875 it was thought to be the largest cotton buyer in the world with branches in all the cotton markets in Europe and America. Julius Knoop began his New York career as a pedlar and sent his son for apprenticeship with De Jerseys. By 1882 the firm was thought to be worth over £1·0m., completely outclassing anything previously seen in the import–export trade in cotton.[4]

But in the 1880s profit margins in the cotton trade became so tight that it was almost impossible to build up a large integrated business from retained profits. The pressure on margins can best be illustrated from the experience of Baring Bros.' Liverpool branch which was largely (but not exclusively) engaged in cotton trade finance. The returns over four decades were as follows:

	turnover	commissions	% return
1850–9	£11·75m.	£164,000	1·4
1860–9	£22·35m.	£238,000	1·1
1870–9	£50.72	£218,000	0·4
1880–9	£94.64	£80,545	0·1

In 1890 the branch reported to London that since 1878 a very large proportion of the turnover had borne no commission at all, though

[3] M. M. Edwards, *Growth of British Cotton Trade* (Manchester 1967) Ch. 6.
[4] Dun, Charleston, 1 p. 393. S Thompstone, 'Ludwig Knoop', *Textile History* xv (1984).

it necessitated 'a responsible and expensive staff'. Meanwhile the old import merchants' consignment and shipping business had all but disappeared.

An even more graphic view of the changes in the Liverpool cotton trade appears in the autobiography of Samuel Smith MP, *My Life Work* (1902). He was the founder, in 1864, of Smith, Edwards & Co., Liverpool cotton brokers, and also a partner in James Finlay & Co. of Glasgow in the Indian trade. At the turn of the century Smith, Edwards & Co. with a capital of £500,000 was much the largest of the Liverpool cotton brokers (Table 7.1). As Smith recalled:

The principal business then was selling for [import] merchants, and buying for Lancashire spinners, and many fine businesses had sprung up with the growth of Lancashire trade, where commissions were large and regular, and where the brokers incurred little or no risk. Speculation in those days was trifling compared with what it is now. Nearly all the business was bona-fide transfers of cotton in warehouse, and it was quite an exception to sell a cargo afloat. A rigid distinction was drawn between merchants and brokers, and any attempt to combine the two would have caused expulsion from the Cotton Brokers' Association. All the old landmarks of those days have been swept away. The great mass of business done has long been in contracts for future delivery. Speculation has enormously increased. The distinction between merchants and brokers has virtually disappeared. I have seen change after change pass over the scene, till old men can scarcely identify the highly-complex system of to-day with the steady routine of the 'fifties. At each stage strong opposition was offered to the speculative and 'demoralizing changes' as they were then styled ... but it was useless to fight against them. The old firms who refused to move with the times were nearly all swept away or died of inanition, and few of the leading houses of half a century ago are now in existence. The great originator of this change was the United States of America. It was there that these novel methods of business were hatched, and their gigantic combinations soon forced other countries to adopt their tactics or be exposed to crushing losses. For many years our cotton and corn trades have been, I might almost say, puppets in the hands of American players, and unless our commercial men took full account of this they were soon stranded.

The allegations about American entrepreneurs as the puppet masters is not, however, entirely borne out by more contemporary evidence. According to Baring Bros.' Liverpool house, reporting to London head office in 1883, 'the business is conducted mainly by English houses' and 'there are now few prominent American cotton shipping houses and it is no longer possible to obtain consignments from

Table 7.1. *Capital of some major US and UK cotton merchants in the early twentieth century*

Major US houses	overseas partners or branches	capital ($£$)
McFadden, Philadelphia	Bremen (1881)	75,000 (1904)
	Liverpool (1881)	
	Le Havre (late 1870s)	
Sprunt, Wilmington (N.C.)	Bremen (1906)	250,000 (1905)
	Liverpool (1905)	300,000 (1907)
Weld, Montgomery (Alabama)	Liverpool	1,000,000 (1899)
	Boston	
	Bremen	250,000 (1907)
	New York	
Anderson Clayton, Houston (Texas)	Liverpool	200,000 (1914)
Major UK houses		
Smith, Edwards & Co., Liverpool	Calcutta	500,000 (1904)
Muir, Duckworth & Co., Liverpool	Alexandria	200,000 (1906)
	Savannah (Ga.)	
Alexander Eccles, Liverpool	—	250,000 (1906)
Dennistoun, Cross & Co., Liverpool	New York	200,000 (1904)
A. Stern & Co., Liverpool	St Louis, Dallas,	200,000 (1908)
	Oklahoma City	
Williams, Wilson & Co., Liverpool	Fort Worth	100,000 (1908)
	San Antonio	
	Oklahoma City	
W. H. Midwood & Co., Liverpool	Augusta (Ga.)	210,00 (1911)
J. Taylor & Sons, Liverpool	—	100,000 —
		150,000 (1911)

Sources: Guildhall Lib. Kleinwort Information Books; Baring Bros. Liverpool correspondence XLV; John Killick, 'Cotton Marketing in the late Nineteenth Century: Alexander Sprunt & Son 1884–1956', *Bus. Hist. Rev.* LV (1981).

them'.[5] Twenty years or so later, the pacemaking US houses were not significantly larger in terms of capital, than the Liverpool leaders (Table 7.1).

The substantial truth in Smith's remarks is that New York forced the pace of change after 1870 when the cotton market there was organised exclusively for futures trading (i.e. contracts were agreed for delivery of standard quantities and qualities of baled cotton at dates up to a year ahead), as distinct from the traditional commodity (or 'spot') trading. The relaying of the Atlantic cable in 1872

[5] Baring Bros. Liverpool MSS, HC3.35 esp. XXXVII, W. F. Gair report 27 Dec. 1890, XXX letter of 4 Aug. 1883. Samuel Smith, *My Life Work* (1902) p. 17.

extended the commercial influence of New York to Europe, but Liverpool responded by developing its own futures market to function alongside the spot market. Nevertheless, New York continued to be the more speculative centre; the decline of Welds from £1·0m. to £0·25m. in the early years of the century (Table 7.1) offers a striking illustration of the vulnerability of the richest firms. British firms pretended to keep aloof from such speculative habits and were closely monitored by their merchant bankers, but transatlantic partnerships and agencies sometimes brought down the most staid concerns. Turnover of Liverpool houses was, as Smith remarked, very high in the period. Of 202 firms who were members of the Liverpool Cotton Brokers Association in 1885, less than half were in business twenty years later, but new firms were formed so that there were 220 in the 1905 Directory. The American pacemakers confronted the established Liverpool system by bypassing the traditional buying agencies in the old plantation states and the selling agencies in Europe. McFaddens started this restructuring by opening branches in Le Havre in the late 1870s and in Liverpool and Bremen in the 1880s. Welds and Sprunts were not far behind. However, it was not until the interwar period that another American enterprise, Anderson Clayton, came to dominate the transatlantic distribution of cotton;[6] Liverpool mounted a determined rearguard action and under the leadership of men like Smith showed resilience until World War I.

The undermining and demoralisation of the Liverpool import merchants and cotton brokers would seem to have offered an opportunity for spinners to forge direct links with New York for importing raw cotton, and weavers and printers for exporting. Nicholas's model of the development of British multinationals envisages the merchant function being usurped as manufacturers gradually familiarised themselves with overseas markets, or as a result of some crisis (rupture) of relations between manufacturer and overseas agent. But the cotton industry was a highly disintegrated structure and the reality was much more complex than this, as H. B. Heylin's *Buyers and Sellers in the Cotton Trade* (1913) explains. To simplify his commentary we may represent six characteristic

---

[6] D. A. Farnie, *The English Cotton Trade and the World Market 1815–96* (Oxford 1979) p. 60. A. H. Garside, *Cotton goes to Market* (New York 1935) Chs. 9, 10. J. R. Killick, 'The Transformation of Cotton Marketing in the late Nineteenth Century', *Bus. Hist. Rev.* LV (1981).

developments in each of which there is cause (in italics) and possible response (after the colon), so suggesting an alternative model for this industry.

(1) *Increase in size of the representative producer*:
manufacturers held stocks until a period of better selling prices.

(2) *Growth in scale of retailing*:
manufacturers went straight to retailers for better profit margins.

(3) *Growth in mass media advertising (newspapers, billboards, etc.)*:
manufacturers appealed direct to consumers by branding and advertising.

(4) *Growth in ready-to-wear clothing and decline of traditional drapers' piece goods trade*:
manufacturers sold direct to clothing factories or (in a very few instances) launched their own.

(5) *The 'great depression' (1873–96) in prices and profit margins tightens margins allowed by merchants while orders become more erratic*:
manufacturers sought more regular trade, even if it meant higher selling costs.

(6) *Many shipping firms in Manchester, London and Liverpool diversify their investments by taking direct or indirect interests in spinning and weaving mills (especially in India) while several home trade houses built factories in the provinces*:
manufacturers tried to achieve the consistently good dividends declared by the large merchanting houses by adopting similar vertical integration policies.

Parallel tendencies have been discerned in the metal industries, except in this case the growth of consumer durables must be substituted for ready-to-wear clothing. By the 1870s the conventional wisdom of three generations of manufacturers was against the high risks of marketing overseas; they were pushed towards it only by an accumulation of circumstances they could not control.

Heylin's analysis suggests that most of the opportunities to respond to change lay with the manufacturers but the reality is that few of them grasped it, and when they did, it was because (as Heylin conceded) it was 'the outcome of being driven to desperation'.[7]

[7] Six stages based on H. B. Heylin, *Buyers and Sellers in the Cotton Trade* (1913) pp. 122–3. Cf. G. C. Allen, *Industrial Development of Birmingham and the Black Country* (1929) Pt IV, Ch. 5.

The point may be illustrated from the experience of Tootal Broadhurst Lee, who in the 1880s were Lancashire's third largest firm after Rylands and Horrockses. Following incorporation in 1888 the firm reviewed its overseas marketing organisation, which had hitherto consisted of appointing exclusive agents round the world, paying them 10 or 15 per cent commission on sales. It was reported from New York that in the years 1881–7 direct sales to a dozen retailers had risen from under 10 per cent to 63 per cent, with a corresponding fall in sales through merchants, jobbers and wholesalers. American producers were supplying more and more of the home market but there was scope for more sales in better and finer goods. Consequently it was decided to open a New York office, which was soon paying its way. However, the decision to make this change was only reached because it was argued that 'our present trade with the importers and jobbers has now fallen to such a figure ... that we run little risk of losing anything by the proposed change', and the system of agents was retained in other markets, including the Continent, Latin America and the Far East. Meanwhile Rylands took a strong initiative in Rio de Janeiro but this does not appear to have succeeded for long or invited replication in other overseas markets, for later we are told that the firm's exporting was done through Manchester merchants with good foreign connections or through foreign merchants.[8]

Reluctance to change the established marketing system by competing with merchants can be further illustrated from the experience of Horrocks, the Preston cotton manufacturers who had a capital of £2·0m. at the turn of the century and were shown in Chapter 3 to have taken an early lead as exporters. In 1903 a Barings' report on them noted:

Large concerns like Horrocks lost so much in South America in years gone by that they now employ a London intermediary who pays them at once for their goods and runs this risk with their buyers. This must be a very expensive way of working and there must be many concerns who cannot afford, or who would wish to dispense with the intermediary.[9]

In other words, the Latin American market for textiles was still controlled by merchants, and the same was said to be true of

[8] Manchester P.L., Tootal Broadhurst Lee records, board minutes 1 (1888–93), general management committee minutes 1 (1888–9) esp. p. 73. D. A. Farnie, 'John Rylands of Manchester', *Bull. of the John Rylands Lib.* LVI (1973). Kleinwort Information Books, UK 1 p. 76.   [9] Baring Bros. Liverpool letters HC3.35, XLVII, 23 Jan. 1903.

Birmingham and Black Country products.[10] The North American and colonial markets were of course much closer to the domestic one, and inasmuch as they continued to be supplied by British merchants (rather than by manufacturers or American merchants), it was often by shipping houses and home trade houses that had integrated back to mill production and forward to Empire and American outlets. The scale of the biggest of these concerns like Cookes, Rylands, A. & S. Henry and I. & R. Morley also shows a big leap forward in size and complexity of the organisation (Table 6.3).

The other large Lancashire organisation that considered overseas merchanting was the Calico Printers' Association, a 'lumbering leviathan' formed in 1899 out of seventy-three firms. The C.P.A. had 'branches' (factories) specialising in production for particular markets such as India and Ceylon, the Levant (Middle East), 'Persia and Bagdad', East and West Africa, Rangoon, and China and Japan, and from time to time senior representatives were sent out to report on the situation, but it seems that the existing system of overseas agents (commission merchants) was not seriously questioned until the mid-1930s. Stiff competition on the Continent was attributed to Steiner of Church Works, near Accrington, 'doing a direct trade', but no attempt was recorded to respond in like manner.[11]

Another consequence of instant communication was that it became much less necessary for merchants and producers to hold large stocks. Once again, the only good data is for cotton, but as it was the foremost commodity of British trade it will serve to illustrate stockholding well. At the close of the French Wars stocks were as high as half the annual UK import, but by mid-century this had fallen to a third and in the early 1880s to under a fifth.[12] A major contraction, that is to say, had taken place before the opening of the transatlantic cable, but instant communication reduced the percentage further while the appearance of the 'futures' market served to stabilise prices. However, the effects on the cotton trade were less dramatic than on some other world trading commodities, partly because the system of trading developed before the age of telegraph, was highly competitive, and also because the American Civil War

[10] G. C. Allen, *Industrial Development*, Ch. 5.
[11] Manchester P.L., C.P.A. board minutes 1899–1912. Simon Pitt, 'Strategic Change in the C.P.A.', Ph.D. thesis, London 1990, Chs. 2–4.
[12] T. Ellison, *The Cotton Trade of G.B.* (1886) Table 1.

caused major dislocation of the leading suppliers for some years and consequently delayed further change. Indeed, the system of US agents, importing merchants and mill buying brokers was still prominent in Liverpool and Manchester when Alston Hill Garside wrote his definitive *Cotton goes to Market* in 1935. However, by this time the bulk of the American cotton taken by Liverpool was handled by about a dozen merchants, and some of the largest spinning companies in Lancashire bought direct from the importing merchants through their own buying rooms in Liverpool while others bought direct from exporters in the United States through agents in the main British ports.[13]

THE GRAIN TRADE

The commodities which saw more novel forms of enterprise and dynamic growth were those which were relatively new to international trade (like crude oil and rubber) or those in which trade was rapidly expanded, most notably grains, and foodstuffs like tea, meat and sugar. Of these, grainstuffs were much the most important within the period and are the best documented, so will form a main focus in this chapter. The three-fold increase in British imports of grain, and the multiplication of exporting countries is shown in Table 7.2. Russia, which was the principal supplier in the middle decades of the century, was rapidly overtaken by the USA and equalled by India, with Argentina (including Uruguay) and Canada close behind, while Western Europe lost its significance as an exporter.

Taken together, the multiplication of sources, increase in trade, and constant fall in freight rates created a situation in which trade in any single commodity was highly complex, competitive and fast moving. It offered opportunities to the international specialist with rapid lines of communication who could quickly outmanoeuvre the general merchant. In the 1880s it was still possible for merchants to handle two or three complimentary commodities (like, say, wheat and cotton, where the main exporters were the USA and India) but this became less and less usual as major international operators took over.

So early as 1882 a London corn broker, William Harris, declared to a government commission that 'The man who used to be the

---

[13] A. H. Garside, *Cotton goes to Market* pp. 116–7.

Table 7.2. *Quantity of wheat and wheaten flour imported into the UK 1872 and 1903 (m. qrs.)*

Country of origin	1872	per cent	1903	per cent
USA	2·0	21·3	11·0	39·5
Russia	4·2	44·7	4·0	14·4
India	0·0	0·0	4·0	14·4
Argentina and Uruguay	0·0	0·0	3·6	12·9
Canada	0·4	4·3	3·4	12·2
Roumania and Balkans	0·0	0·0	0·8	2·9
Austria–Hungary	0·0	0·0	0·3	1·1
Western Europe	2·0	21·3	0·5	1·8
all other countries	0·8	8·5	0·2	0·7
total imports	9·4	100·0	27·8	100·0
total cost of freight	£3·04m.		£3·20m.	

Source: The Corn Trade Year Book (Liverpool 1904) p. 141.

middleman [i.e. the merchant] is hardly known now; he gets no living out of it... I have seen firms of merchants for years in the City who have confined their business to the wheat trade, but I have never seen them do any good at it.' By this time, he explained, brokers ('commission-men') were making the most profitable business. The London broker dealt direct with a broker in New York or Chicago on orders from millers or dealers in various parts of Britain, instructions being telegraphed through. Brokers' commissions on cargoes of wheat tumbled from 3 per cent to as low as 0.5 per cent. Wheat prices in Chicago and Liverpool converged until the difference seemed scarcely significant; in the mid-1880s the price differential was 85 cents a bushel ($17\frac{1}{2}$d.) but in the years 1910–13 it was only nine cents (2d.) Clearly gross bulk dealing was necessary to show any profit.[14]

Before the Crimean War (1851–5) the major part of British grain imports had come from Russia, either via the Baltic or the Black Sea. In the north the trade was led by a mixed bag of old Muscovy trading families (Egerton Hubbard & Co., Hills & Whishaw and others), Anglo-German families (Brandts in London and Blessig,

---

[14] *Royal Cmn on Agriculture*, Parl. Papers, XIV pp. 345–6, ev. of W. J. Harris. C. K. Harley, 'Transportation and the World Wheat Trade 1850–1913', *Explorations in Economic History* XVII (1980).

Table 7.3. *Leading importers of grain into Britain from St Petersburg,*
1878–80

	quantity	per cent
E. H. Brandt & Co.	4·375	20·75
Egerton Hubbard & Co.	1·417	6·72
Blessig Braun & Co.	1·287	6·11
Hills & Whishaw	1·150	5·45
Neuhaus & Sieskind	1·126	4·41
34 other merchants	11·728	51·22
	21·083	100·00

Source: Nottingham Univ. Dept. of Manuscripts and Special Collections, Brandt MSS, circulars of C. Prévost, grain broker. The quantity cited is for the three years 1878, 1879 and 1880. The quantities given are in millions of chetverts, except for rye which is in kools.

Braun & Co. in Liverpool) and Greeks (notably Scaramangas, the successors to Rallis) (Table 7.3). In the south the trade was dominated by Rallis, Rodocanachis and other Greek families described in Chapter 5, until Odessa ceased to be a free port in 1857. The two leading Greek houses shifted their interest to India and the Russian grain trade was taken over by Jews led by Leopold Louis-Dreyfus.[15] The Russian grain embargo during the Crimean War stimulated a search for alternative sources, and the USA, India and Argentina became major suppliers. Consequently the period from the 1860s to the end of the century saw a struggle between a dozen or so major international firms. In England, the development of America as a major grain exporter stimulated Liverpool to challenge London's traditional leadership in the grain trade. Liverpool was the home port of leading grain merchants like Ross T. Smyth (a partnership between a Londonderry factor and one of the Rathbone family) Sanday & Co. and Balfour, Williamson & Co. Meanwhile in London Rallis developed the import of grain from India. All these firms faced the challenges indicated in Harris's description of the trade, as well as formidable competition from continental competitors.[16]

[15] P. Herlihy, *Odessa. A History 1794–1914* (1986) p. 213.
[16] G. J. S. Broomhall and J. H. Hubback, *Corn Trade Memories* (Liverpool 1930) pp. 59ff. Baring Bros. Liverpool letters HC3.35 esp. xxxviii (1891), xlv (1899), xlvii (1903).

Table 7.4. *Some major grain merchants of the world in the early twentieth century*

Merchant house	Place and date established	Sector(s)	Capital (£m.)
1. Dreyfus	Basle 1852	Russia, Balkans, Argentina	0·6–1·0 (1903) 1·88 (1902)
2. Bunge & Born	Amsterdam 1818 Antwerp 1850	USA, Argentina	1·6–2·0 (1910)
3. Ralli Bros.	London 1818	Russia, India	3·0 (1902)
4. Balfour Williamson	Liverpool 1851	California, Argentina	0·4 (c. 1890) 1·0 (1909)
5. Ross T. Smyth	Liverpool 1839	USA, Balkans, India etc.	0·3 (+0·2) (1907–12)
6. S. Sanday & Co.	Liverpool 1880	India, USA, Argentina etc.	0·2–0·35 (1906–15)
7. Blessig, Braun & Co.	St Petersburg 1793 Liverpool c. 1830?	Russia	0·4 (1902)
8. Rodocanachi	London 1838	Russia	0·4 (1911)
9. E. H. Brandt	Archangel 1802 London 1805	Russia	0·75 (1904)

Sources: nos. 1–5, 8–9, see Appendix to Ch. 10. No. 6: Kleinwort, Sons & Co. Information Books, Goldman Sachs I p. 135, II p. 191. No. 7: Baring Bros. Character Book LIV 6.2.4.

The outcome, so far as estimates of size and success by partnership capital can measure it, is set out in Table 7.4. Ralli Bros. look the biggest firm but in fact they had interests in a range of other commodities (particularly jute, hessian sacks and rice) imported from India so their relative importance in grain may be exaggerated. According to Ralli Bros.' *Calcutta Handbook* (1888), 'we feel the advantage of our position is in contracting for very distant deliveries when naturally all sellers come to us in preference'; in other words the firm used its unrivalled capital to dominate the forward contract business and from London sold direct to millers.[17] As mentioned in Chapter 5, Rallis conducted their whole business on the basis of cash trading. The firm 'never issues "paper" [bills of exchange] but does a cash business to the extent of its available means, and its means are great', a spokesman boasted in 1902. By 1886 India could produce wheat cheaper than any other country in the world, and low cost

[17] Cambridge South Asian Archive, Ralli Bros., *Calcutta Handbook* II (1888) p. 55.

plus cash dealing made Rallis the most powerful force in the world grain trade at the turn of the century.[18] Bunge & Born were probably the most successful continental firm; they were a German partnership who operated mainly in Argentina after 1876. According to the historians of the organisation, 'the new enterprise was fostered by the absence of English enterprises interested in operating in this market'. To secure its position the firm opened collection centres in the interior and built grain elevators and silos at the ports, but its most important single advantage may have been the Bunges' close connections with the Antwerp and French Protestant banks. This backing also enabled it to develop interests in the Congo, Indonesia and Malaya, deliberately diversifying into rubber and colonial produce, which in the early years of the century lifted capital dramatically from £300,000 to the huge sum given in the estimate.[19]

Rather less is known about Louis Dreyfus & Co. but there appear to be a number of interesting parallels with Bunge & Born. Dreyfus originally based his activities in the south of Russia and opened branches in all the Black Sea and Azov ports, competing with German rivals Neufeld & Co. At the turn of the century it was reported that they had 'hundreds of branch offices all over Russia'. Their domination in the Ukraine reminds us of Bunge's ubiquitous operations in South America which earned it the sinister nickname of 'the Octopus'. Later in the century the attractiveness of the Russian grain trade declined, partly because it became easier for new Russian inland dealers to forge their own connections with markets in Western Europe. Dreyfus then moved into the Balkans, supported by his small fleet of steamers, and became a close friend of King Carol I of Roumania, exporting the best and highest yielding grain in Europe. Meanwhile Edouard Bunge became broker to King Leopold II of Belgium and a royal business associate, connections reminiscent of the tradition of the Court Jews. Dreyfus's Jewish connection was probably helpful in obtaining financial support from continental bankers; at any rate the correspondence of the Buenos Aires branch of the London & River Plate Bank indicates

---

[18] J. Gennadius, *S. A. Ralli* (1902) p. 24. *Royal Cmn on Depression in Trade*, Parl. Papers, 1886, XXII p. 82.
[19] R. Green and C. Laurent, *Bunge & Born. Puissance et secret dans l'agro-alimentaire* (Paris 1984) esp. pp. 23, 43, 52. Kleinwort Information Books, France, Belgium & Holland II p. 104. Dun, New York, vol. 341 pp. 148, 200R. Dan Morgan, *Merchants of Grain* (New York 1979) Ch. 4.

the firm were not short of credit. 'These people draw very largely on Europe...We quite agree...that care is necessary in dealing with people of this [Jewish] class...' Despite the anti-semitic note, a $300,000 overdraft was agreed, which was no doubt one means by which Dreyfus broke into the Argentinian trade on a large scale and were soon challenging Bunge & Born, who were also being supported by the British bank.[20]

The developments in Russia just outlined help to explain the position of British merchants there. The changes took place in the north a couple of decades after those in the south so that the northern leaders listed in Table 7.3 reflect the old system rather than new leadership. Bank capital was focused more strongly on the south because the export of grain was developing more rapidly there and the shorter distances to Odessa and more rapid turnover suggested better profits. Nevertheless there are clear signs of decline of the old order. Brandts and their Liverpool friends Blessig Braun & Co. had been diversifying out of Russian trade for some years, Brandts towards merchant banking and Blessigs towards being a Russian investment group with interests in shipping and textile factories. Egerton Hubbard & Co. tried to ride both horses at once, but with very limited success. Brandts tried to mount an operation financing Argentinian grain movements but at the turn of the century the commission business of its chief representative in Buenos Aires 'almost ceased to show any profits owing to the competition from the big international grain dealers' and it was finally abandoned. In Odessa, Rodocanachis survived as a small investment group, perhaps because of the family's merchant banking activities in London, but Scaramangas disappeared.[21]

The three Liverpool houses that replaced the old order (Smyth, Sanday, and Balfour Williamson) were moderately successful but scarcely world leaders. Balfour Williamson occupied the premier position in California after Isaac Friedlander, the German Jewish immigrant who became the 'Grain King', went bankrupt in 1877. Smyth looks a rather smaller operation but the senior partner

---

[20] Dan Morgan, *Merchants* pp. 34, 37. Kleinwort Information Books UK II p. 97. V. A. Zolotov, *Khlebnyy Eksport Rosii Cherez Porty Chernogo (Russia's Grain Exports through the Black Sea and Azov Ports) (1860–90)* (Rostov 1966) p. 239. University College London, BoLSA MSS D35/14 esp. pp. 503, 567 (4 Apr. and 16 May 1902).
[21] L. Jurowsky, *Der Russische Getreideexport* (Munich 1910) pp. 83–8. C. Amburger, *William Brandt and the Story of his Enterprises* pp. 62–3. See also below, Ch. 8.

(H. L. Smyth) was also Chairman of the Liverpool North Shore Mill Co. which had a capital of £210,000 (1897) and was claimed to be 'the largest and most perfect mill in the kingdom'. He was also a director of the Bank of Liverpool and two major insurance companies. The strategy of Smyths and their principal local rivals, Samuel Sanday & Co., was to open branches or agencies in all the main production centres of the world, including the Balkans, India, the USA and Argentina. The last seems to have been the most difficult source for them due to lack of outward cargoes except coal and convenient alternative inward cargoes if local crops failed. In most of these centres they did not need to invest in the transport and storage facilities with which Bunges and Dreyfus tried to entrench their position in Argentina.[22]

What conclusions can be drawn about British mercantile enterprise from this short survey of the leading international players? The grain trade was evidently a high-risk one requiring iron nerves, with high bankruptcy rates. As the trade became globalised there were few old British firms (in the sense of hereditary British) in it; it was largely left to immigrant Germans and Greeks, then to the Atlantic frontiersmen of Liverpool. The strategies of the remaining firms were to concentrate on the relatively safe ground of India, the USA and Canada, or to diversify by opening branches in several centres. It looks as if they avoided Argentina, and it may be that there were sound reasons for doing so. The infamous Baring crisis of 1890, which shook Argentinian credit through the decade, was another reason for wariness. The British approach was not necessarily less sensible or enterprising than that of Bunge and Dreyfus, and certainly the London banks were not so impressed by the continental houses; it was reported in 1910 that Bunge had lost 3m. Belgian francs on grain while Dreyfus's sons were brash and speculative.[23] However, there remains a suspicion that continental banking practices may have been more supportive to bold enterprise than the British ones, particularly for firms with good establishment connections. The US Federal Trade Commission reported in 1920–6 that Dreyfus and Bunge were making their substantial profits mainly with borrowed money.[24] The surviving records do not allow this

[22] G. J. S. Broomhall and J. H. Hubback, *Corn Trade Memories* pp. 244–7, 172–85, 156–9. R. Paul, 'The Wheat Trade between California and the U.K. 1854–1900'. *Mississippi Valley His. Rev.* LXV (1958).
[23] Kleinwort Information Books, France II pp. 8, 104, III p. 114.
[24] Dan Morgan, *Merchants* p. 73.

question to be investigated any further for the grain trade, but it prompts the wider issue of whether financial support was adequate to meet the rapidly changing needs of British commerce. This is a matter that must be given further attention, drawing evidence from the wider range of firms and trade sectors. But first it is necessary to focus on some more innovative branches of trade to examine the British record, and hence to finalise the verdict on grain.

SOME INNOVATIVE TRADES

The two sectors of trade so far surveyed present a rather different story. In textiles, the merchants managed to hold off any significant invasion of their territory by manufacturers. In the Far East and South Africa, the same merchant houses, as we saw in Chapter 5, also advanced into other branches of trade such as tea, jute, diamonds and rubber. In the grain trade, however, withdrawal was more in evidence than advance. Would it be fair to conclude that British mercantile houses were averse to the more high-risk, innovative areas of trade? To answer this question we need to examine the record in some new trade developments of the late nineteenth century.

It is not difficult to discover some striking British initiatives in new commodities. Marcus Samuel and Bowrings in oil, Harrison Crosfields and Heilbut Symons in rubber, Vesteys and Borthwicks in meat, and Fyffes in bananas come easily to mind. Less well-known names include Chalmers Guthrie in coffee, Thomas Drysdale & Co. in hardware and Wallaces in tea.[25] On the crude measure of size of capital around the turn of the century, the record of these firms seems no less impressive than the best-known names in more traditional areas, including foreign competitors like Bunge and Dreyfus (Table 7.5). The commodities in which they dealt were traded internationally from worldwide sources in much the same way, and with comparable risks, to grain. The conservative houses were those that declined to change their traditional ways of trading and can be seen declining. Thus the capital of the Rathbone dynasty fell from £600,000 (1871) to little more than £50,000 (1903–4), while Dennistouns declined from £770,000 (1857) to £200,000 (1903–4). Numerous other houses slipped into bankruptcy, including

---

[25] Bibliography of major firms appended to Ch. 8.

Table 7.5. *Some major merchants in new commodities c. 1910–14*

	dates	capital (£m.)	sources
Marcus Samuel, London (oil)	1897	1·8	Henriques p. 198
Heilbut, Symons & Co., Liverpool (rubber)	1910	1·25	B of E
Chalmers Guthrie, London (coffee)	1903	0·75	KS–UK II p. 47, III p. 121
Bowring & Co., London (oil)	1912	0·91	KS–GS II p. 188
Vestey Bros., London and Liverpool (meat)	1914	2·0	BB–CRD 3/3
Thos. Drysdale & Co., Buenos Aires (hardware etc.)	1906–8	1·01	KS–R.Plate, p. 95
C. Czarnikow & Co., London (sugar)	1911	nearly 1·0	BB–CRD 3/3
Harrisons & Crosfield, London (rubber)	1910	0·45 ⎫	Appendix to Chapter 8
Wallace Bros., London (teak)	1911	0·8 ⎭	

Sources: R. Henriques, *Marcus Samuel* (1960), p. 198.
KS Kleinwort, Sons & Co. Information Books. The main series used here are those for the UK (3 vols.) and the reports to Goldman Sachs (GS), 2 vols., 1899–1926. At Guildhall Library, London EC.
BB Baring Bros. 'Character Books'. At the Bank, London EC.
B of E Bank of England Discount office records. At the Bank, London EC.

some prestigious names like Bensons of Liverpool (see Chapter 3), who lost most of their £200,000 capital in 1875.[26] It is not possible to document all the firms that disappeared by this route but official statistics show merchant bankruptcy rates increasing after 1875.[27]

The development of shipping services provided the most obvious and perhaps the principal route out of general trade. Case studies of the Holts, the Booths and Sir William Jackson, all Liverpool merchants who created shipping lines, support this view. More substantial evidence comes from Dr Cottrell, who shows that steam tonnage registered at Liverpool increased a hundred times from the late 1830s to 1880, a rate of growth that offered strong inducements. An analysis of the sources of capital for Liverpool steamship

[26] Rathbones' capital in S. Marriner, *Rathbones of Liverpool* p. 6 and Kleinwort Information Books, Goldman Sachs I p. 161. Dennistouns' in D. M. Evans, *Commercial Crisis* (1858) p. 137 and Kleinwort G. S. I p. 131.
[27] Richard Seyd, *Record of Failures and Liquidations 1865–76* (c. 1876) and *1875–1884* (1885).

companies from 1851 to 1881 shows that merchants were much the largest investing group apart from the shipowners themselves. It was in this period that Britain built up much the largest mercantile marine in the world, and there was no evident lack of enterprise here.[28]

But the question remains, if mercantile enterprise is so much in evidence, why is it that most British grain merchants made such an apparently poor showing compared with Bunge and Dreyfus? The complaint is not one made only or most strongly in this present work; historians of Argentina and the US grain trade have made it several times before.[29] The answer must be central to this present research. The subject is a difficult one because international grain firms have deliberately kept their operations secret; Dan Morgan's *Merchants of Grain* (New York 1979) is written like an enquiry into C.I.A. activities while Green and Laurent's book *Bunge & Born* is appropriately subtitled *Puissance et secret dans l'agro-alimentaire*. It appears that British houses such as Ralli Bros., Sanday and Smyth lost out to European and (later) American firms because powerful British millers such as Ranks took a direct hand in the trade themselves, further reducing the role of middlemen.[30] The main effects of this development were felt in the 1920s and 1930s and so lie beyond the scope of the present study, but a substantial point has to be made here. It is that the strength or weakness of mercantile enterprise from the last quarter of the nineteenth century had a great deal to do with that of British manufacturing organisation; the stronger the manufacturing organisation the weaker the mercantile opportunity, even in a trade that lived on its wits and other people's capital. It was the fragmented nature of the old British staple industries, and their slowness in responding to the market opportunities of integration, that allowed and encouraged the merchant houses, old and new, to retain much of the initiative in Britain.

[28] C. A. Jones, *International Business*, pp. 142–8. P. L. Cottrell, 'The Steamship on the Mersey 1815–80: Investment and Ownership', in P. L. Cottrell and D. H. Aldcroft, eds., *Shipping, Trade and Commerce* (Leicester 1981). Sir William Jackson in S. D. Chapman, *The Clay Cross Co. 1837–1987* (privately printed, 1987) pp. 36–9.

[29] R. Gravil, 'The Anglo-American Connection and the War of 1914–18', *Jnl Latin American Studies*, IX (1977). J. R. Scobie, *Revolution on the Pampas. A Social History of Argentine Wheat 1860–1910* (Austin, Texas, 1964) pp. 101–5.

[30] Cited in Dan Morgan, *Merchants* p. 73n.

CAPITAL AND CREDIT

The provision of credit to suppliers and customers had always been an important dimension of mercantile activity, and merchant houses that chose to integrate into manufacturing, mining or plantations very frequently continued in finance. Many of the big international commodity merchants like Louis Dreyfus & Co., Ralli Bros., Heilbut Symons & Co. and Rodocanachis appear in the lists of private bankers in the standard reference work, Skinner's *The London Banks*. Merchants shifting to manufacturing appeared on the boards of the London-based imperial and international banks that proliferated from the 1860s when joint-stock registration became easy.[31] The connection between merchanting and finance continued to be an intimate one. There is thus no general evidence of shortage of credit, rather the contrary where sufficiently detailed records survive.

The evidence from the banking side suggests intense competition to grant acceptance credits on international commodity business. The grain trade, though subject to fluctuation and bankruptcy, was as keenly fought over as any. The old-established London merchant banks which were early in the business (Barings in the USA and Argentina, Brandts in Russia and Argentina) found themselves competing with the Crédit Lyonnais (which opened in Russia in 1877) and the Bank of London and South America on the River Plate.[32] In the 1880s the famous German–Jewish financier Bleichroder moved into 'large grain transactions', acting through Ladenburg & Co. in London and New York. This was in addition to Liverpool banks like Lloyds and the Liverpool Union Bank.[33]

The more detailed records of James Finlay & Co. allow us to penetrate the problem of funding trade rather further. In 1871 Glasgow head office advised the Calcutta and Bombay branches that the Royal Bank of Scotland would cover acceptances to the extent of £100,000, which would be largely for the piece goods trade at this date. Finlays also had accounts with the Bank of England and Baring Bros.[34], while Finlay, Muir & Co. (the Indian wing of the

[31] See Chapter 8 for mercantile investment groups.
[32] Barings Liverpool letters HC3.35 (note 16). C. Amburger, *William Brandt*. Jean Bouvier, *Le crédit lyonnais* (Paris 1968) p. 227. U.C.L. Archives, Bank of London & S. America D 35/13 pp. 476, 69, D 35/14 p. 503.
[33] Kleinwort Information Books USA 1 MS 22031/1 p. 162. Lloyds Bank Archives A/35, B/817.
[34] Finlay MSS UGD 91/141 pp. 7, 11–12, UGD 91/32, 91/268.

organisation) had two with London merchant banks, F. Huth & Co. and the Merchant Banking Co. In 1882–4, when the tea and jute side of the business began to develop, accounts were opened with the Bank of Bengal, the Chartered Bank of India and the Agra Bank in London. The practice of having separate accounts for the subsidiary companies and activities evidently multiplied. At the turn of the century the Champdany jute mill, which had a capital of £200,000, had no less than ten accounts, as follows:

Clydesdale Bank	£10,000
Williams Deacons Bank	10,000
Seligman Bros.	10,000
London, City and Midland Bank	10,000
Royal Bank of Scotland	10,000
British Linen Bank	10,000
Bank of Scotland	10,000
Arbuthnot Latham & Co.	10,000
National Bank of India (Rs 5 lakhs =)	30,000
Bank of Bengal (Rs 5 lakhs =)	30,000
	£140,000

The ten banks can be classified as three English clearing banks, three Scottish ones, two merchant banks and two imperial banks, a neat spread that looks as if it was carefully planned.[35]

The tea companies were evidently financed in a similar way, for in 1890 we find Finlays' Calcutta manager reporting that he was running as much as £40,000 or £50,000 of bills with different banks for each of the two major companies, but never exceeded £10,000 on any single bank. The sale of goods in South Africa was done mainly under credits supplied by five major merchant houses there, including Mosenthal & Co. (the biggest merchants there) and Steel, Murray & Co., later to be bought by Finlays.[36]

A similar policy was applied to major suppliers. Finlays bought their piece goods though a Manchester firm called Robert Barclay & Co. which, however, had other business interests, also selling in South America. The initial agreement between the two firms in 1872 included Finlays' view that 'It is understood that your finance arrangements will be confined to us', and a £20,000 credit was arranged. In 1879 a cash credit account was arranged with the

[35] Finlay MSS UGD 91/154.   [36] Finlay MSS UGD 91/109/3.

Royal Bank of Scotland to the extent of £25,000 in favour of Barclays under Finlays' guarantee.[37] In subsequent years other bank accounts were opened until in 1903–4 they stood as follows:

Merchant Banking Co.	£30,000
Fruhling & Goschen	15,000
F. Huth & Co.	5,000
Cunliffe Bros.	(closed)
International Bank of London Ltd.	25,000
Webster, Steel & Co. (= J. Finlay & Co.)	(unlimited)
Bank of Scotland	15,000
National Bank of India	(unlimited)
Chartered Bank of India	(unknown)

In this list, the first four were London merchant banks but only Huths could be counted an important firm.[38] Finlays had an early connection with Huths through another Manchester supplier, Hugh Balfour & Co., until this firm became bankrupt in 1879 and, most probably, the London accepting house lost money. However, competition was evidently intensifying, for in 1905 Ruffers opened an account for £10,000 with Barclays in respect of their Montevideo trade and in 1908 Schröders, having made overtures for two years, offered a limit of £30,000. The Anglo-German merchant banks were particularly pushing at this period.

It might easily be supposed that, while leading trading companies like Finlays could open any number of accounts for acceptance credits, smaller firms were not so fortunate. Certainly the banks graded their clients and potential clients, but there were so many banks and so few A1 and A2 customers that many other firms received a ready hearing. The financial records of one of the smaller Anglo-German houses described in Chapter 5 illustrate the point nicely. Simon, Meyer & Co. (now Simon May) were a Hamburg-Jewish partnership that opened an office in Manchester in 1813 and in Nottingham in 1849, apparently with a very modest capital. In the second half of the century their activities were concentrated in Nottingham, exporting lace to the Continent and Russia, and later to Latin America. Their trade and capital showed cumulative growth in the long period from the 1860s to World War I, when lace was highly fashionable and Nottingham emerged as the foremost international centre, particularly for lace curtains. A branch was

---

[37] Finlay MSS UGD 91/141, 91/268.   [38] Finlay MSS UGD 91/262/4.

opened in the French centre of the lace industry, Calais, in 1887. The acceptance credits negotiated by the partners from 1880 to 1914 were as follows:

date	bank	acceptance credits (£)	cumulative total (£)	capital of Simon May (£)
1881	Hardy Nathan & Sons	10,000	10,000	
1885	J. C. im Thurn & Sons	10,000	20,000	
1887	Horstman & Co.	7,000	27,000	77,413
1889	Wechslerbank (Hamburg)	2,000	29,000	52,299
1889	Fruhling & Goschen	5,000	34,000	
1889	Marcuard, Krauss & Co. (Paris)	15,000	49,000	
1890	Brenier (Bremen)	5,000		42,697
1890	Hardy Nathan	+5,000	59,000	
1890	Wechslerbank	+3,000	62,000	
1896	Bank of Winterthur	8,000	70,000	57,152
1897	Armstrong & Co.	3,000	73,000	61,903
1903	Swiss Bankverein	10,000	83,000	164,422
1903	Discontogesellschaft	5,000	88,000	164,422
1911	Fruhling & Goschen	+10,000	98,000	426,924
1912	Capital & Counties Bank	n.d.		

A dozen different banks were drawn on, largely continental or, like Horstman and Fruhling & Goschen, of continental origin. The partners' notes show that their banks were urging them to make more use of the credits, and during World War I three further firms (Kleinworts, Konig Bros. and the Colonial Bank) offered a total of £40,000 additional facilities to help them take German competitors' trade. Simon May's experience not only underlines the abundance of acceptance capital available to a firm with a good track record; it also serves to emphasise that London was not always the cheapest source.[39]

Of course, capital for acceptance credits was short-term (typically three months) and must not be confused with fixed capital investment in plantations, mills, mines and transport. Relatively few

[39] Records of Simon May & Co. Ltd., Nottingham. For further detailed examples of acceptance credits, see S. D. Chapman, *Merchant Banking*, pp. 115–21.

merchants were interested in farming or manufacturing, and the evidence of earlier chapters (particularly Chapter 4, the agency houses) suggests that those who integrated back were more worried about what to do with surplus capital than about raising capital. Under the managing agency system, relatively small amounts of capital were needed to secure mercantile control of its overseas suppliers (there is more detail about this in Chapter 8), while in the Orient and on the new frontiers of trade, established mercantile houses often carried large expatriot deposits. Apart from the ever present threat of illiquidity caused by sudden shifts in the trade cycle, or by war, established merchants were little restrained by financial shortages.

But this is not to say that there were no financial problems. Three at least can readily be identified. It was mentioned earlier that adequate facilities depended on the banks' credit rating, which should have been based on some objective standard and, in principle, was.[40] In practice there was a lot of conflicting information and prejudice so that religious and ethnic minorities like Jews and Greeks sometimes had to be financially self-sufficient within the group, or draw on more sympathetic foreign banks. The banks were constantly exchanging confidential reports with one another and it was easily possible for misinformation to spread. Two or three obvious instances of City prejudice must serve to illustrate the point.

In 1873 an American firm of German–Jewish extraction set up as cotton merchants in a large way of business in Liverpool. Dun & Bradstreet, the best-known US credit agency, reported soon after in warm terms. The firm 'are large operators in cotton; last year [1877] they handled 94,000 bales representing about one million sterling. Mr Newgass is estimated worth £20–25,000, is very popular and his simple word goes a long way on Change. He is hardworking and honest.'[41] However Baring Bros. in Liverpool took a very different view of the firm.

Started here recently with a reported capital of $300,000 [£60,000]. Lehmann Bros. of New York, with whom they were in connection, being partners *en commandite* with a further contribution of $200,000 [making £100,000 in all]. They have been *by far* the largest importers of cotton (over 84,000 bales) this last season [1873], besides operating extensively in 'arrivals' and the losses to themselves and their friends must have been

[40] BB HC 16 'Reports on Business Houses' defines credit categories 1 to 4.
[41] Dun, foreign registers II, p. 83.

considerable. We should certainly not give them documents against acceptance nor do we recommend clean bills on them to be taken as the Union National Bank N[ew] O[rleans] have recently done. The firm was started with a considerable amount of 'stir' and so far as we can make out have been doing a dangerous and unprofitable business.[42]

In subsequent years Newgass made and lost a fortune in London finance, but on the eve of World War I still appears in the directories as a private banker.[43]

The major London accepting houses appear to have had only limited interest in the imperial territories as such and the relatively few reports that appear in their surviving records are surprisingly critical. Thus Kleinworts, the leading accepting house after Barings' fall in 1890, wrote of Jardine Matheson, the most enterprising agency house in China: 'The name of the firm has always been regarded here with a certain amount of uncertainty, no doubt due to the fact that their business is of a highly speculative nature and that they take large interests in enterprises which have not always been successful',[44] and of Neumann, Lubeck & Co., the well-known South African trading and investment company:

Mr Neumann...has been mixed up for many years in the South African mining market...Several of the enterprises which he has promoted have been questionable properties and...a large proportion of the business is in connection with the management of the various mining propositions in which they are interested...bankers here are not disposed to give the same credit to a firm in this line of business as they would to a new firm of similar resources which devoted its whole attention to banking business.[45]

The explanation is of course that the accepting houses measured the merit of their clients by the liquidity of their assets rather than by their enterprise; the cardinal commercial sin was locking up capital in risky enterprises. This is made more explicit in comments on other firms. Thus of David Sassoon & Co. it was said that their capital was given as £500,000 (1908) but 'it is a question to what extent it is in the form of property, mills &c.'. Similarly, it was said of Chalmers, Guthrie & Co., capital is £750,000 (1908) 'but believed to have locked up a good deal of money in San Salvador Railways and therefore less highly thought of than formerly'.[46]

---

[42] BB Customer Reference Books II no. 2732.
[43] S. D. Chapman, *Merchant Banking*, p. 77.
[44] Kleinwort Information Books 22,033/2 pp. 2–3.   [45] ibid. 22,033/1 p. 159.
[46] ibid. UK III pp. 130, 121.

The attitude reflected in these quotations, and the abundant capital of many of the leading houses, evidently induced some firms to finance their seasonal needs from private resources to a very late date. David Sassoon was a case in point, as Kleinworts recognised:

> They do a very large business in the exporting of opium from China and this business is done in the ordinary way by merchants taking advances against the shipments...[they] never ask for any accommodation of this nature and we think it is due to the fact that the partners make the necessary advances in a private capacity and hold the opium as a special hypothecation, thereby obtaining a good rate of interest on their capital.

Ralli Bros., as already noticed, confined itself to a cash business to the extent of its available means.[47] Self-sufficiency in finance guaranteed safe business but must have inhibited growth in some periods of opportunity.

Another major financial problem in this period was the advent of joint-stock organisation under the legislation of 1862. This might appear to have been a splendid opportunity for established merchant houses, but few saw it that way at the time. The anxieties of the dynastic leadership of a typical City firm, Leaf, Sons & Co., was expressed in the autobiography of the third generation leader. As background it should be explained that the firm originated as a London haberdasher in 1790 and evolved into a 'home trade house' specialising in silks, velvets and ribbons. Their principal competitors were Morrison, Dillon & Co., incorporated as the Fore Street Warehouse Co. Walter Leaf's sensitive recollections are worth quoting at length:

> The great rival business of Morrison, Dillon & Co. had quite recently been converted into a limited Company, the 'Fore Street Warehouse Company', and the Morrison brothers had taken out of it and permanently secured three large fortunes. No doubt it would have been possible in the same way to convert Leaf, Sons & Co. into 'The Old Change Company Limited'. As things turned out, it is clear that this would have been the wisest course. But my father chose the other.
> His motives were various. In the first place, the principle of limited liability was a new one and was still looked upon with suspicion. It was not certain by any means that a limited company would be able to retain the connexion which had been formed by personal contact between partners and customers; it was too early to see how the Fore Street Company would

---

[47] ibid. UK iii p. 129. J. Gennadius, *Ralli*, p. 24.

prosper, but the signs for the maintenance of its old reputation were none too favourable. Thus the security for the recovery of capital was not unassailable. Then my father, who was devoted to the memory of his dearly loved elder brother, William, could not bear to think of a step which would cut his sons out of a career to which they had been devoted; to keep it still open to them seemed an act of duty to the family. And then there was the strong element of pride in the achievements of his ancestors and himself in building up one of the finest businesses in the City of London. It was, I think, at his last interview with my father, just before his death, that my grandfather had implored him to stick to the old business. As I have already said, the business had reached a climax of prosperity in the last two or three years. There seemed to be no reason why, with my father at the head with his experience, ability and capital, supported by a new generation of partners, the prosperity should not continue and the deceased partners' estates paid off, while fresh fortunes were being made for the young. And finally I do not doubt, though I cannot recollect that my father ever expressed it, that there was in his heart the sense which is felt by those who have been in 'big business' that it is one of the finest sports in the world; that quite apart from the making of money it is a splendid exercise for the human intellect, and that it is a real contribution to the general advance of mankind; in short, that from the moral side it is a worthy line for the self-expression of the individual, and may be carried on with all dignity and honour. When, therefore, my father began to suggest to me that not only for the sake of himself and the family, but as a fine opening of a career, I might think of taking upon me the succession to the business, I was quite ready to entertain the suggestion. But it was the sense of duty which appealed most to me; I regarded it from the first as a disagreeable duty.

In fact, it took Walter Leaf '18 strenuous years' – 1875 to 1893 – to pay out capital to the families of deceased partners, and consequently throughout this difficult period of trade he was short of capital. In this period Leafs were more typical than Morrisons in the sense that only a handful of City warehousing firms followed the latter into incorporation.[48]

Another striking instance of resistance to incorporation was provided by F. G. Dalgety, a leading merchant in the Australian wool trade. He suffered 'the greatest anxiety' from shortage of capital in 1848–9 when two partners withdrew. The solution he found was in interlocking partnership spanning London and his colonial bases. This arrangement lasted well until the 1870s, when he ran into intense competition from the colonial banks and wool

[48] C. M. Leaf, *Walter Leaf 1852–1927* (1932) pp. 112–13. (Anon.) *Modern London. The World's Metropolis* (c. 1893) p. 179.

finance houses. A new partner pressed for incorporation to augment the capital but Dalgety refused to consider the change because, as he wrote: 'From my experience of companies I have a horror of them – and know full well that they cannot be managed to compete with private firms where partners act in accord and common prudence and energy are expressed.' A long feud within the partnership finally resulted in incorporation in 1884, which allowed the firm to survive as one of the leading firms in the Australian wool trade. However there was nothing inevitable about this decision and Martin Daunton, the author of the research on Dalgety cited in this summary, believes that many merchant houses in the same position chose the path of decline and ultimate disappearance rather than adopting company status.[49]

The problems and opportunities of companies were most keenly felt by the agency houses. For most of the time they appeared to have the best of both worlds by maintaining the advantages of private partnership for their original enterprises in London, Liverpool or Glasgow while claiming the advantages of limited liability for their partly owned overseas plantations, manufacturing, mining and transport companies. The device of managing agency meant that, strictly speaking, these enterprises were independent flotations, but in practice they functioned just like subsidiary companies, financially responsible to and dependent on the holding company. The subservience of these numerous companies, representing the larger part of the modern Indian industrial economy, must seem surprising.

The explanation offered by P. S. Lokanathan, whose *Industrial Organisation in India* (1935) is the most sensible of several commentaries by Indian academics and has a historical perspective stretching back half a century or so, was that the general prevalence and continuance of the managing agency system was because it was so difficult to recruit *local* capital to start or credit to maintain major enterprises in the country. So late as 1929–30, managing agents were providing more capital for cotton mills than the banks were. In the early years of company promotion in India, the capital was invariably raised by the agents and their connections. The banks supported the agency system 'and indeed practically forced join-stock companies to take agents as the system gave them two

[49] M. J. Daunton, 'Firm and Family in the City of London in the Nineteenth Century: the Case of F. G. Dalgety', *Historical Research* LXII (1989). For further examples see Hilton Brown, *Parrys of Madras* (1954) p. 198; C. A. Jones, *International Business* p. 105.

signatures for all loans'.[50] In other words, the agency house system in India owed its continuity to the paucity of indigenous capital for industrial development as well as the scarcity of managerial experience.

However, this does not mean that profit margins were always high or that there were no problems with the shareholders. Oral testimony and general historical accounts suggest that the annual general meetings of the managed companies were invariably formalities, rubber stamping the results of the managing agents, but shareholder revolts were by no means unknown.[51] Indeed, it could be argued that tension was inherent in the system, as the managing agents took a fixed fee for their services and could therefore afford to take the long view, while the shareholders looked for maximum return on their investment at an early date. In practice, there was often also tension between the partners in Britain and the local managers in Calcutta, Bombay, Rangoon or wherever the house functioned; the local men inevitably had a more immediate appreciation of the problems while their seniors in London or Glasgow claimed to have a superior sense of strategy deriving from longer experience and direct contact with the capital markets.

The various house histories that remain the principal source for particular agency houses seldom reveal anything of such tensions, so specific details are hard to find. However, the abundant records of Finlays record a striking case of open conflict between the principal partner (Sir John Muir) and the shareholders of the Champdany jute mill, which was registered in 1873 and one of four managed by the Glasgow firm in the period down to World War I. In the early 1890s it was said that the best jute mills were paying a dividend of 15 per cent, and in the next decade the *Investors Indian Year Book* (1911) reported the average rate of dividend exceeded 12 per cent for good companies. Over a period of thirty years, Champdany paid nothing for fourteen years and ten per cent in only four years. Sir John Muir blamed poor local management and some of the shareholders blamed Sir John. One of them wrote to him in 1893:

There is no public confidence in your management. There is a feeling you have a double interest in such an undertaking [as Champdany] and that your interests as shareholders are largely subordinate to your interests as

[50] P. S. Lokanathan, *Industrial Organisation in India* (1935) pp. 181, 214–29.
[51] See e.g. Vera Anstey, *The Economic Development of India* (1942) p. 114.

Managers, Agents and Financiers...The interests your senior resident partner has to supervise and control are so varied and so vast that the affairs of the Champdany Co. can only receive a small share of his time... the way in which the Champdany Co. has managed its purchases of jute has made it the laughing stock of the business community.

The Calcutta man in charge, the future Sir Allan Arthur, said the reason was 'antiquated' machinery and inadequate assistants, 'all to save a few thousand rupees annually in salaries...a most short sighted policy'. When Muir then proposed to acquire another jute mill by drawing on Champdany's reserves, another shareholder sued Finlays. In *Maxwell Hannay v. James Finlay & Co.* (1895), fraudulent management practices, including the payment of dividends out of capital to cover exchange rate (rupee–sterling) losses, were alleged. The main outcome was that Muir stormed out to India and sacked Arthur, though this did not prevent the latter from obtaining his knighthood and taking a leading role in Ewings for many years.[52] This was certainly not a unique case, for in 1899 we find one of the Gladstones confessing to a similar position in Ogilvy, Gillanders & Co. Their jute mills, he wrote, had been a disappointment from the shareholders' point of view but 'have been extremely lucrative to the firm'.[53] The majority of cotton mills in India were started by native merchants but run on the managing agency system. Japanese competition in the Chinese market shrank the profits to practically nothing at the end of the century. The situation was aggravated by lax management and the protests from shareholders and financial difficulties of the agents forced the winding up and reconstruction of several concerns.[54] In this instance the main beneficiaries, apart from the Japanese, were European firms (and especially machinery agents) who took over the managing agencies. Change was inaugurated by one of them, Greaves, Cotton & Co., in 1886 by projecting a cotton mill on the basis of a commission of ten per cent on profits. Tea and mining companies soon followed cotton. Nevertheless, a minority of companies were still managed on the original system when Lokanathan reviewed the problem (1935), and

---

[52] Finlay MSS UGD 91/178/4, 91/274, 91/110. R. E. Stewart, 'Scottish Company Accounting 1870 to 1920', Ph.D. thesis, Glasgow 1986, pp. 273, 341–6.
[53] Clwyd R. O., Gladstone MSS, GG 2591, Steuart Gladstone to Robert Gladstone 4 June 1899.
[54] The problems of the Indian textile industry are elaborated in Chapter 9.

it is quite clear that the unresponsiveness of the old agency system to the financial pressures inhibited the usual market mechanisms.[55]

MANAGEMENT CONTROL

In his book on *International Business in the Nineteenth Century*, Charles Jones identifies the most characteristic mercantile response to the challenges of the later part of the century as convergence on London. Given the easier communications of the period, he sees the capital market of the City as being the most decisive factor in control, though in fact he writes more about the social and political attractions of the metropolis than about recruitment of capital.[56] There is no question that merchants who became financiers invariably migrated to the City, or that some merchants had to draw on City resources to effect necessary transitions, but the problems of effective managerial control from Britain were scarcely solved before the inter-war period and the limitations of any such strategy have to be recognised. The argument of this chapter is that finance imposed few restraints on new strategies for established merchants but that attempts to centralise often took them into deep water. If this has not always been obvious from the various house histories it is because few are candid about their failures or about conflicts between the home partnership and the overseas branches.

Dr Jones's detailed examples are not always convincing on this point. Wernher Beit needed many millions to develop their Rand mines (see Chapter 9) and so established an investment banking operation in London, but effective leadership on the Rand was exercised by F. Eckstein & Co. Dalgety moved to London from Australia to run a more effective mercantile operation with local partners (not agents or employees) to maintain the close connection with the wool growing areas. Most telling of all, the Sassoon Brothers split up, one centring in London, the other continuing to live in Calcutta; the latter was much the most successful. That is, the migration to London had little to do with access to capital and a lot to do with social advancement.[57] To understand the problems it is necessary to focus more closely.

[55] S. M. Rutnagur, *Bombay Industries: the Cotton Mills* (Bombay 1927) pp. 25, 52, 62. P. S. Lokanathan, *Industrial ... India* pp. 338–9.
[56] C. A. Jones, *International Business*, Ch. 5.
[57] H. Sauer, *Ex Africa* (1937) p. 174. M. J. Daunton, 'Firm and Family'. C. Roth, *The Sassoon Dynasty* (1941).

Perhaps the easiest way of doing this is to quote one of the titans of Victorian trade, Sir John Muir of Finlays. In 1895 he told a management meeting in Calcutta that whether he was in India or Glasgow, he was always to be regarded as the senior managing partner of the firm, 'and that everything in connection with the business of the Calcutta and Colombo firms was to be conducted exactly as the managers believe he would wish to have it done if personally present with all the facts before him'. The ideal system, he suggested, was that of the senior partner of Webster, Steel & Co., whose Rangoon managers had to send a weekly diary to London. The reality was that, far from such intimate control. Sir John's accounts were *five years* behind schedule at that time. In fact, as his conflict with the shareholders shows, he was scarcely able to keep himself adequately informed of conditions in Britain. Yet Finlays were one of the most successful British firms in India, and much the largest in the tea trade, a position that could only have been maintained by *de facto* decentralisation combined with sound central strategy for marketing the tea in Europe and America.[58]

Another interesting case is offered by Ralli Bros. According to the hagiography that followed the death of Stephen Ralli in 1902, the principles of the firm included the rule that no partner or employee was allowed 'to lead a life unduly luxurious or extravagant', while 'A second rule was established in the iron discipline which regulates the relation of superiors and inferiors, and which, indeed, pervades the entire organisation.' The assistants in India were governed by three tomes called 'handbooks' which were packed with details about the rules, conditions and opportunities of trade. The tone of these volumes can be illustrated by a single quotation:

We must work in jute as extensively as we can because inactivity costs us still dearer than in other articles. Owing to the extent of our standing and to the additional risks inherent in this article, it is of vital importance that our organisation should be very efficient and that our home firms should be made thoroughly acquainted by us with the position and prospects of affairs on this side... The position and prospects of the crop, information about supplies and shipments &c must be promptly telegraphed home and must be the result of careful enquiries in Calcutta and in the interior on the part of our Agencies. As our business is greatly based on such information,

---

[58] R. E. Stewart, 'Scottish Accounting', p. 221. By 1924 Finlays were responsible for 40 per cent of tea plantations in India UGD 91/141.

any change must be reported without delay, and our telegrams must be clear and explicit.[59]

It was no doubt on the basis of such meticulous organisation that Rallis became the premier firm in the Indian jute trade, much as Finlays were in tea. Not much information leaked out from the Greek firms, but there is evidence that even in the tightly organised Rallis central control was far from complete. So late as 1938, a confidential report on the firm's organisation disclosed that 'In effect *India and London appear to be trading somewhat independently.*'[60]

The cable system to the Far East was inaugurated in 1865 but two generations later, in the 1920s, understanding between London and the trading centres was still basic and there was frequent tension between the two. The unpublished reminiscences of a former head of Bousteads, one of the leading British houses in Singapore, serves to make the point:

> London controlled the produce business, and turnover [rather than mark-up] was the prime object to provide cargo for the ships. The East was not expected to make a profit – in fact if one did you got ticked off as it was probably at the expense of turnover, so one traded at a loss without ever being told whether London made a compensating profit. The weekly produce letters from London were nearly always rude and scathing, and it was a saying that the ink turned to vinegar as it passed through the Red Sea.[61]

Excessive centralisation simply stifled mercantile enterprise in its satellite locations. It is easy to see that the success of some of the most dynamic mercantile enterprises of the pre-1914 period, such as Yules in India, Knoop in Russia and De Beers in South Africa, was based on *de*-centralisation – i.e. the titans of these organisations (David Yule, Ludwig Knoop and Cecil Rhodes) insisted on spending their careers 'in the field'. In Rhodes' case, this was based on aggressive repudiation of London financial interests, not least Rothschilds.[62] At Morgan Grenfell's, Yule's merchant bank in the City, it was reported that Sir David's 'sole idea was Calcutta and he entirely ignored the London office', a comment that was perfectly consistent

[59] J. Gennadius, *Ralli*, p. 23. Cambridge South Asian Archive: Ralli Bros. *Calcutta Handbook* II (1888). Vols. I and III are lost.
[60] Guildhall Lib. Ralli Bros. MS 23,834, Report on Organisation (typescript c. 1938) p. 27.
[61] G. R. Roper-Caldbeck, 'A Boustead Chairman looks Back' (unpublished history, 1978). See also Owain Jenkins, *Merchant Prince* (1987) pp. 15, 20, re tensions at Balmer Lawrie & Co.
[62] S. D. Chapman, 'Rhodes and the City of London', *Historical Journal*, XXVIII (1985).

with his lifelong absorption in Indian business.[63] Ludwig Knoop was a rather more complicated story; son of a Bremen small trader, he was apprenticed to De Jersey & Co. in Manchester and effectively took over the firm when it became insolvent. De Jerseys were in fact the British arm of his Russian cotton spinning mills and huge American cotton exporting organisation, and never controlled or led it. The 'centre' (Manchester), that is to say, never controlled the 'periphery' (Russia).[64]

It is equally familiar – or certainly was to contemporaries – that some of the major disasters and near-disasters in the mercantile history of the period were caused by excessive centralisation. The Kleinwort report on Jardine Matheson cited earlier is an obvious case in point. Even the 'princely hong's' closest allies, Jardine Skinner, were critical of the London principal: James Keswick 'seems poor chap to have made a mess of things both in business and in a private way', and the mismanagement of their finances represented a 'near-miss' for Britain's leading house in China.[65] The most spectacular crash between the Baring crisis (1890) and World War I was that of Arbuthnot & Co., merchants and bankers of Madras, caused by ruinous speculation in London nourished with funds from Madras. Their closest rivals in the South Indian trade and finance, Parrys, did not miss the point. 'A London office was not a wholly unmixed blessing... there was always the risk that the London office might take the bit in its teeth and from the representative might become the ruler', Parrys' historian wrote.[66] Instant communication opened up the possibilities of global organisation but did not prescribe how control could effectively be maintained.

The most effective challenge to the major British merchants, apart from European competitors, therefore came from the local (indigenous) traders, who gradually benefited from easier credit and faster communications. The case of the south Russian grain trade is unusually well documented. The Russians were so impressed by the far-reaching changes in the organisation of this trade from the 1870s that they liked to talk about the 'democratisation' of the trade. The extension of the railways from Odessa and the Black Sea ports and

---

[63] Morgan Grenfell records, Calcutta business, Misc. 2 file, Vivien Hugh Smith to T. S. Catto 3 Nov. 1921. Obituary of Sir David Yule in *The Times* 5 July 1928.
[64] S. Thompstone, 'Ludwig Knoop'.
[65] Jardine Skinner Guard Books No. 1, 29 Mar. 1892, Blue folder 1, 16 July 1891.
[66] Hilton Brown, *Parrys of Madras* pp. 132, 175–7.

the development of a credit system by the state bank, the private banks and the railways encouraged Russian dealers to send their own employees to the plains to buy direct from the peasants or local dealers, ousting the Jews and Greeks who had controlled the system in earlier years. Much less capital was now required as grain was moved faster; in the 1860s a handful of rich Russian wholesalers might have a capital of as much as a million roubles (£100,000) but by 1910 200,000 roubles (£20,000) was considered very rich. However, in the north of Russia, where the trade focused on St Petersburg, the grain still had to be carried great distances (500–3,500 km), so the old system continued much longer. The leading northern traders about 1880 were still London-based (Table 7.3); indeed the old form of trading organisation continued until 1890–5 and firms were able to diversify into other activities down to World War I.[67]

China provides another striking example of the resurgence of indigenous enterprise in the period. In 1873 the British Consul at Canton noted that 'a trade which was in the hands of the few has drifted into those of the many' because the need for a large capital had been removed by improvements in banking facilities. The telegraph and better mail service led to the replacement of these commission agents by Chinese traders and compradores in the next generation so that, by the end of the century, British merchants were limited to a few major ports, where piece goods were sold to those who came from the interior.[68]

The transition period in the cotton trade was spread over a longer period of time, but a variation on the same theme is discernible. In the 1880s it was obvious that many of the old merchant firms engaged in general Atlantic trade were collapsing and the trade fell into the hands of much smaller enterprises often with a capital of only £10,000 or £20,000, who cut costs by running a simple organisation based on close transatlantic ties. The first decade or two of this century saw the four or five US-based firms with European branches and a network of collecting points and presses on the cotton belt

---

[67] L. Jurowsky, *Der Russische Getreideexport* (Munich 1910) esp. pp. 46–62, 85–9. C Amburger, *William Brandt*. C. Prévost, *Export of Grain* (St Petersburg 1878–80), printed broker's lists in Brandt MSS, Nottingham Univ. Lib.

[68] C. A. Jones, *International Business* p. 107. F. S. A. Bourne, *Report of the Mission to China* (Blackburn 1898) esp. pp. 22–3, 36–7. Bourne emphasised that his remarks on the decline of British commission agents did not apply to major firms like Jardine Matheson (pp. 127–8); developments in these firms are examined in Chapter 8.

begin to pull ahead of European rivals and associates (Table 7.1).
The most successful of these American firms, Anderson Clayton, was
formed at the Liverpool end by a linking partnership with an old
firm of brokers, Pennefather & Mills, while another leading house,
Albrecht Weld & Co., was reported to work closely with Ralli Bros.
for Indian cotton.[69] Expressed in terms of the relationship between
London, Liverpool, New York and the US cotton belt, this change
must surely be identified as one of decentralisation to those in close
touch with the producing areas.

The grain trade is particularly interesting because some of the
leaders that emerged in the early years of this century (Table 7.4)
still retain their position.[70] The secrecy of their operations prevents
any decided view, but it appears that both Dreyfus and Bunge &
Born maintained their dominant positions from their strong
decentralised bases in Argentina, and Rallis occupied a comparable
position in India and Balfour Williamson in California. By contrast
Ross T. Smyth and Sanday & Co. adopted a deliberate strategy of
not committing themselves to any single grain supplying country
and limited evidence available to researchers prevents us from saying
they were wrong, for capital is not the same as profitability.
However, it can surely be said without fear of contradiction that, in
South America as in the American plantation states, the continuance
of strong local representation was a prerequisite of success.

The common factor in these three examples is that British
merchants (and foreign nationals generally) had less opportunity
than local enterprise to integrate back to their sources of supply or
to their markets. Where there were opportunities to restructure in
this way, as in the imperial territories, British enterprise could be
impressive. This is a theme that must be explored in the following
two chapters.

CONCLUSION

This chapter has highlighted some of the difficult problems for
merchants in a period of transition. It is clear that instant
communication caught traditional mercantile practice in a scissor
movement between the pressures of shrinkage of middleman
activities on the one side and the opportunism of indigenous traders

[69] S. D. Chapman, *Merchant Banking* p. 138.
[70] John Killick, 'Cotton Marketing'. Kleinwort Information Books, N.S.II pp. 57–8. BB CRB
   3/2 p. 19.

overseas on the other. The most vulnerable British group were the scores of overseas commission agents, many in a small way of business, identified in Palmerston's survey. Like so many small businesses, their life was characteristically short and their fate unknown. Most middlemen brokers were quickly forced out, if the experience of the Liverpool cotton brokers is any guide. The international houses were subject to additional pressures as the continental countries and the USA industrialised and their importance declined sharply in the later decades of the century. The home trade houses were squeezed by the rise of major retailers and looked overseas for outlets, intensifying competition with established merchants.

The well-known strategies available to the survivors were fraught with difficulties. Manufacturer-to-retailer operations were complex and expensive, and even leading merchant–manufacturers were compelled to withdraw. Commodity broking was a growth area, at any rate until the end of the century, but, as global sourcing emerged, became a highly complex operation where intimate knowledge of one or more producing areas (and not least the local trading community) seems to have been the key to success. Finance was a possibility on the City's lower rungs, but as London became the Mecca for world financial interests and leading bankers from Frankfurt, New York and Paris opened branches, this was no easy option and there were few successes to point to. Credit was easily accessible to all established firms, but merchants enjoyed no particular favour in this. *Instant* communication did not mean *easy* communication between the centre and the periphery, except in matters of routine ordering of standard commodities. Some form of agency was still easiest for both manufacturer and merchant. If merchants were to have a future, a solution had to be found which could exploit the name, experience and credit of the established house, and move into new sectors of trade without assuming all the risks involved in excessive centralisation or 'lock-ups' of capital. The outcome of the search for a new strategy is examined in the next two chapters.

Meanwhile it is important to emphasise that the survival of mercantile enterprise in manufactured goods or produce was dependent on the structure of the industry served. The new science-based industries that generated multinational companies were relatively late arrivals in Britain (at any rate compared with the US) and the only significant examples in Britain's main export commodity (textiles) were J. & P. Coats (sewing thread) and Courtaulds (viscose fibres), both peripheral specialisms. Other textile manufacturers and combines failed to make a significant impact on overseas markets so that the growing international business continued to be dominated by merchants. The maintenance of this traditional business allowed those in imperial areas time to develop agencies for more sophisticated products, to shift over to investment in local industries, and even to move to the service of some more effective foreign competitors of British producers.

CHAPTER 8

British-based investment groups before 1914

Research by economic historians into new forms of business organisation in the nineteenth century has cast the British role in a poor light. The British had shown little enthusiasm for joint-stock organisation for much of the century or for the credit-mobilier type of financing of industrial development. The multinational corporation was, it appears, largely an American phenomenon, with only late and limited indigenous development in Britain. The multi-divisional corporation was again entirely a creation of American managerial creativity. The trust was, as we have long known, an outcome of German dynamism.[1] Even the British banking scene continued to be dominated by family dynasties, while overseas investment in business enterprise, both colonial and foreign, was more restrained than historians had long thought.[2] The consequence appears to be that the small-to-middling business remained the most characteristic form of enterprise, even in the 'leading sectors', for longer than the early writers led us to suppose. In a wide range of manufacturing and service industries the characteristic structure featured a multiplicity of diverse specialists whose leadership was addicted to family and (if possible) dynastic control.[3]

The evidence for this situation has been extensively researched and is quite convincing. Yet, so far as the British position in the world economy is concerned, some misgivings must be allowed to surface. Could the world's largest and most dispersed empire,

---

[1] There is a large literature on this subject but see especially, P. L. Cottrell, *Industrial Finance 1830–1914* (1980); J. M. Stopford, 'The Origin of British-based Multinational Manufacturing Enterprise', *Bus. Hist. Rev.*, XLVIII (1974); A. D. Chandler, 'The Growth of the Transnational Industrial Firm in the US and UK', *Econ. Hist. Rev.*, XXXIII (1980) pp. 396–410; and H. W. Macrosty, *The Trust Movement in British Industry* (1907).

[2] D. C. M. Platt, 'British Portfolio Investment Overseas before 1870: Some Doubts', *Econ. Hist. Rev.* XXXIII (1980). S. D. Chapman, *The Rise of Merchant Banking* (1984).

[3] See e.g. L. Hannah, *The Rise of the Corporate Economy* (1976) Chs. 1, 2.

created – so we are persuaded – primarily from economic motives,[4] be entirely sustained, in all its diverse activities, by traditional entrepreneurial and family enterprise? Was there nowhere any increase in scale commensurate with the mighty growth of empire and world markets? Most research has been focussed on manufacturing industry, yet the traditional British genius was said to be mercantile rather than manufacturing, a sector that has attracted relatively little attention or research money, and it would be sensible to look for evidence of new kinds of organisational response to the boundless opportunities of the great age of imperialism.[5]

The far-reaching changes in mercantile organisation in the last quarter of the nineteenth century have been sketched in this book. We have seen that the introduction of the telegraph revolutionised international communications and that in London and Liverpool the general merchant and the commission merchant were superseded by specialised commodity brokers acting as principals. Unfortunately the standard works on this subject do not attempt to analyse market membership, though they leave some impression of family firms and dynasties.[6] Deficiencies in British entrepreneurship were offset by the migration of foreign entrepreneurs – especially Germans, Greeks and Americans – to British commercial centres.[7]

This outline probably accounts for the more important part of the British response, but not the whole of it. The specialised commodity brokers were in direct and daily contact with world suppliers, but they were not themselves suppliers from foreign and colonial sources, much less the generators of materials of international trade. That fraction was originally performed by general merchants and commission agents, but as the chain of middlemen contracted they were often under pressure to look elsewhere for business. At the same time, the overall demand for raw materials and foodstuffs was increasing by leaps and bounds. In this situation, a number of general merchants and original suppliers with established

---

[4] A. Hopkins and P. J. Cain, 'The Political Economy of British Expansion Overseas 1750–1914', *Econ. Hist. Rev.*, xxxiii (1980).
[5] The main exception to this generalisation is Blair King, 'Origins of the Managing Agency System in India', *Journal of Asian Studies*, xxvi (1966).
[6] T. Ellison, *The Cotton Trade of Great Britain* (1886). G. L. Rees, *British Commodity Markets* (1964). P. Chalmin, *Négociants et chargeurs: La saga du négoce international des matières premières* (Paris 1983). Sir P. Griffiths, *The History of the Indian Tea Industry* (1967) Ch. 43.
[7] Ch. 5, above.

reputations evolved into investment groups, a form of organisation defined neither by contemporaries, nor by the writers of numerous commissioned histories, nor indeed by economic historians. Historically, an investment group is simply an entrepreneurial or family concern whose name and reputation was used to float a variety of subsidiary trading, manufacturing, mining or financial enterprises, invariably overseas and often widely dispersed. The real economic strength of the group was concealed from the public, and is still largely concealed from historians, by the practice of preserving the parent organisation as a partnership or private company, while the activities it owned or controlled were often registered abroad and run by junior partners or managers there, sometimes under quite different names and local legislation. It was a device that developed from various starting points to maintain effective economic power in a few hands, but its very size and diversity made it much more than a family business in the accepted sense. At the same time, it was able to avoid the clumsy leadership of such manufacturing giants as Imperial Tobacco and C.P.A. that were federations of factious family interests.

This chapter attempts to assemble the little that is known about this phenomenon by surveying some of the major sectors of international trade, India, China and the Far East, Russia, South Africa, Latin America and Australia. Leaving the details aside for a moment, it is not difficult to identify the economic logic behind the organisation of trade. In the course of the revolution in communications that extended worldwide during the last three decades of the nineteenth century, general merchants were increasingly caught in a scissor movement, for while the chain of mercantile links contracted, the financial sector (the traditional escape route of successful merchants) was dominated increasingly by the merchant and international banks in which the great merchant houses were themselves partners or investors. Several prominent first-class houses disappeared in the 1870s and 1880s. Meanwhile, the rate of interest continued at higher – often much higher – levels abroad than in Britain. The old-established firms were familiar with local investment conditions and opportunities in the countries in which they had won their fortunes and reputations, while London merchant banks, company promoters, stockbrokers and the investing public at large were wary of unproved foreign and colonial ventures, especially those in mining and manufacturing.[8] Partners who accumulated capital during their years of overseas service would leave it invested in the organisation, and when they were promoted to the home partnership or retired from business it was invariably more profitable to leave it there than take it out. The business also attracted the loyalty and capital of family connections, friends and a wider circle of adherents both at home and in the overseas bases.

A more specific reason for the investment group, later rationalised in South Africa, was that of spreading high-risk investments. It was widely accepted that the risks of deep-level mining were so high in relation to fluctuating market demand, and capital needs so immense, that the initial burden had to be shouldered by an exploration company or financial group. Having proved an economic reef, the finders might then appeal to a wider investment public, in practice rewarding themselves by maintaining control over groups of mines and other properties they did not own.[9] However, South African investment groups were by no means the first or only such concerns, as we shall see, to promote investment groups.

This identification must be related to the exploration of other historians in this jungle. The activities of mercantile investment groups should be distinguished from portfolio investments overseas.[10] The present chapter deals with the diversification and redeployment or mercantile capital, most characteristically in the course of the evolution of the business, or when assets were acquired by default of debtors, or to find an outlet for surplus capital. Portfolio investment simply represents wealthy individuals or firms seeking optimum returns from diversified shareholding. Focus on trading, manufacturing and mining interests in a firm with merchant origins does not, of course, deny the existence of other types of mixed enterprise emerging in the period. Multinationals have already been noticed several times and mining exploration companies and the so-called free-standing overseas investment companies were also important. Their roles will be compared to those of mercantile investment groups in the final chapter. The phrase 'British-based' in this

[8] S. D. Chapman, *Merchant Banking* esp. Ch. 1. J. W. McCarty, 'British Investment in Overseas Mining 1880–1914', Ph.D. thesis, Cambridge 1961.
[9] S. H. Frankel, *Investment and the Return to Equity Capital in the South African Gold Mining Industry 1887–1965* (Oxford 1967) p. 23.
[10] Charles Jones, 'Great Capitalists and the Direction of British Overseas Investment in the late Nineteenth century', *Bus. Hist.* xxii (1980).

analysis also needs a word of explanation. By no means all the firms listed were British, but all had a base in Britain and conducted a large part of their trade or financial operations (or both) through London. Since foreign-born merchants made such a major contribution to British overseas trade and finance in the nineteenth century, their exclusion from consideration would result in gross distortion.[11]

INDIA, CHINA AND THE FAR EAST

The investment groups originated in the Orient in the special circumstances that surrounded British trade to India, China and the Far East. The monopoly of the British East India Co. began to be eroded in the 1780s, when various former employees began to trade on their own account. In course of time the most successful of these concerns was Paxton, Cockerell, Trail & Co., which was started about 1781 in Calcutta, and presently fell under the control of an ex-naval officer called John Palmer. The abundance of money in Calcutta in 1822 caused the interest on the Company's debt to be progressively reduced from 8 to 4 or 5 per cent and led investors to deposit large sums with the agency houses, to which they responded by taking deposits only on fixed terms. Overflowing with deposits, the agency houses invested heavily in indigo factories, sugar plantations, ships, agricultural and building speculations, docks, and loans to mercantile firms in Singapore, Java, Manila and other places, as well as to their local customers. It was estimated that by 1830 the total liabilities of the six agency houses amounted to £17m., of which £5m. was accounted for by Palmers.[12]

As is well known, Palmers became bankrupt in 1830, followed at intervals by the five other leading houses possessing similar investments. However, the system they created was too useful to perish and never lost the respect of the Indian communities. The partners carried on their bankrupt firms for many years afterwards, and in the course of the next generation the system was taken up by other British merchant houses, including some based in Liverpool and Glasgow.[13] Experience showed that because of the risks connected with distance, war and financial crises in the India trade,

[11] Ch. 5, above.
[12] *Sel. Comm. on Foreign Trade, Third Report*, Parl. Papers, 1820, II, p. 218. Bodleian Lib., Palmer MSS, esp. D107. J. W. Maclellan, 'Banking in India and China: A Sketch', *Bankers Mag.*, LV (1893). [13] Ch. 4, above.

Table 8.1. *Agencies of Andrew Yule & Co. in India, 1899*

Jute mills		
Budge Budge	£330,000	
Central	140,000	
Delta	127,000	
National	100,000	£697,000
Cotton mills		
Bengal Mills		£200,000
Coal mines		
Adjai Coal Co.	Rs 350,000	
Bengal Nagpur	225,000	
Katras	500,000	
	1,075,000	= £100,000
Tea estates		
Assam Tea	£40,000	
Banaharat	50,000	
Choonbutti	20,000	
Mirzapore	8,600	
New Doars	15,000	
Selim	30,000	
Singtom	16,000	£179,600
Flour mills		
Howrah		£25,000
Other interests		
Mirzapore carpet factory	n.d.	
Eagle Soap and candle works	n.d.	
Total		£1,201,600

Source: Thacker, Spink & Co., *Directory of the Chief Industries of India...and...Tea, Coffee and other Estates* (Calcutta 1899). See also (anon.) *Andrew Yule & Co. Ltd. 1863–1963* (privately published, 1963) and *Thomas Sivewright Catto (1879–1959). A Personal Memoir and a Biographical Note* (privately published, 1962).

satisfactory trading results could only be achieved by employing a large capital and 'a very extended range of operations'. Given a large capital and high degree of liquidity, it was easy to make money by accepting deposits at 6 per cent and lending to planters and manufacturers at 10 per cent.[14]

At the turn of the century the largest and most diversified of the Indian managing agencies evolving into investment groups was most

[14] *Sel. Comm. on Manufactures*, Parl. Papers, 1833, VI, pp. 138, 196, ev. of G. G. de H. Larpent.

probably Andrew Yule & Co. It was directed by (Sir) David Yule, whose single-minded business career was referred to in Chapter 4. The Yules came of a Manchester textile trade background and opened an agency in Calcutta as an outlet for piece goods in 1863 but already in the early 1870s were investing in a coal mine and cotton mill. The concentration on jute mills only appeared in the 1890s when David Yule took command. Yules' range of interests – jute, cotton, coal and tea – was pretty representative of the Indian houses at large. The only specific advantage of the firm, apart from the principal's capacity for work, was his personal connection with Vivian Hugh Smith, a partner in the London merchant bank Morgan Grenfell & Co. The American parent of this firm was of course the foremost among investment bankers committed to industrial development, and Morgan Grenfell were early into what is now called corporate finance, but the benefits for Yules are not on record. Table 8.1 shows that Yules controlled assets in excess of £1·2m., but their actual capital was evidently much less; in 1918, when the business was twice the size, it was sold to Morgan Grenfell for £0·6m.

Possibly the most successful investment group operating in the Far East was the Scottish house Matheson & Co., which for many years was closely associated with, and in 1912 entirely bought out by, Jardine Matheson & Co. of Hong Kong and Jardine Skinner & Co. of Calcutta. Jardines' fixed capital investments began with a silk filature in Shanghai in 1870 and a sugar refining plant in Hong Kong in 1878. In the same decade they were employing mining engineers to test and report on potential sites in China, Malaya and Korea and built the first railway line in China. In the 1880s they set up and ran a shipping line and controlled Hong Kong's dockyards. Meanwhile Mathesons bought Rio Tinto mines (1873) and pioneered gold mining in the Transvaal. Several copper mines followed. In the 1890s, acting as agents of Platt Bros. of Oldham, Jardines built cotton spinning mills at Shanghai and Hong Kong to meet the incipient Japanese competition. Along the way they regularly extended their banking and insurance interests. When Matheson & Co. was incorporated in 1908 the issued capital was given as £200,000, but the capital invested in the various subsidiary companies controlled by them was many times that amount; the mining interests in which they shared alone mounted to at least £7m. Most of this capital, so far as is known, was subscribed to joint-stock companies managed by Matheson such as the Indo-China

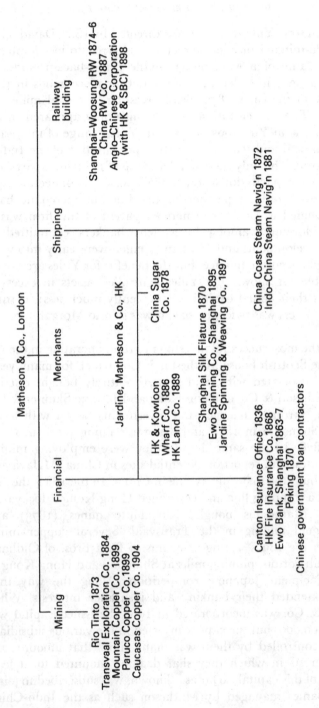

Mining | Financial | Merchants | Shipping | Railway building

Matheson & Co., London

Jardine, Matheson & Co., HK

Rio Tinto 1873
Transvaal Exploration Co. 1884
Mountain Copper Co. 1899
Paruco Copper Co. 1899
Caucasas Copper Co. 1904

Canton Insurance Office 1836
HK Fire Insurance Co. 1868
Ewo Bank, Shanghai 1863–7
Peking 1870
Chinese government loan contractors

HK & Kowloon
Wharf Co. 1886
HK Land Co. 1889

Shanghai Silk Filature 1870
Ewo Spinning Co., Shanghai 1895
Jardine Spinning & Weaving Co., 1897

China Sugar
Co. 1878

China Coast Steam Navig'n 1872
Indo–China Steam Navig'n 1881

Shanghai–Woosung RW 1874-6
China RW Co. 1887
Anglo–Chinese Corporation
(with HK & SBC) 1898

Key: HK = Hong Kong

Figure 8.1. Structure of the Matheson Investment Group c. 1914.

Steam Navigation Co. (1881), the Ewo Bank of Peking (1870), the Hong Kong Fire Insurance Co. (1868), the Jardine Spinning & Weaving Co. (Hong Kong, 1897) and the British & Chinese Corporation (1898), a joint venture with the Hong Kong & Shanghai Bank (in which Mathesons were major shareholders) formed to build railways in China.

There are at least three substantial business histories devoted to Jardine Matheson & Co., but none of them make a serious attempt to analyse the policy behind this proliferation of enterprise or to estimate its overall value. The financial records of the Jardine Matheson & Co. deposited at Cambridge tail off in the 1880s, and the present company declines to release further information. However, some notion of the size and diversity of the organisation may be conveyed by the adjacent figure showing Matheson & Co.'s investments on the eve of World War I.[15]

Fortunately other business histories are a little more forthcoming, particularly that on Matheson's principal rival, Butterfield & Swire. The historians of this aggressive firm confirm that the difficult trading conditions in the Far East in the 1870s acted as the major stimulus to the development of a diversified business in which the components would feed each other. John Swire's extension from China shipping to sugar refining, insurance and dockyard development was prompted not only by the example of Jardine Matheson, but by the need to sustain his fleet at work. For most of his career he was short of capital so drew in friends as shareholders; in 1876 the partnership capital was £0·75m. but over £4·0m. was committed to the other interests.

The agency houses whose main interests were in India evidently followed a different course from those whose primary links were with China. Probably the best documented case is James Finlay & Co., a Glaswegian house founded in 1745 and originally strong in the cotton trade and industry. When Sir John Muir took over the leadership in the 1860s, the traditional policy underwent dramatic revision. Muir decided that cotton gave insufficient employment to

---

[15] The full bibliography of Mathesons and 29 other investment groups included in this study is contained in the Appendix. Subsequent footnotes are therefore limited to supplementary references. Capital invested in mining has been calculated as follows: RTZ £3·5m., Transvaal Gold Co. £0·3m., Mountain Copper Co. £1·2m., Panuco Copper Co. £0·33m., Caucasas Copper Co. £1·3m. C. E. Harvey, *Rio Tinto Co.* (1981) p. 19. Standard Bank Archives, Jo'burg, Inspection Reports, Pilgrim's Rest, 1884–90; J. W. McCarty, 'Overseas Mining', Ch. 5.

the partners' capital and turned to tea as a trade with more growth potential. Another agency house, Cockerell & Co., had already demonstrated the possibilities with the £0·5m. Assam Tea Co. (1839) so the investment was in no way a speculative one.[16] From the tea estates the Finlay partners went on to investments in Indian jute mills (from 1873), shipping (from 1882) and cotton mills (from 1902). In much the same way, when Henry Neville Gladstone, a son of the prime minister, took over Ogilvy, Gillanders & Co., another old Scots house, in the 1880s, he saw that the old shipping agency and consignment businesses could no longer be relied on as a mainstay of the business, and the firm shifted its capital to the development of Indian industries, particularly indigo factories, jute mills, railway development, coal mining and syndicates for the mining of copper, diamonds and gold. In the early years of this century they spread their interests to include two Russian petroleum companies and the Russian Collieries Co. It is interesting to note that a leading merchant bank characterised the senior partner as a representative rather than outstanding business man. Similar details are available on Wallace Bros, who floated a string of subsidiary joint-stock companies beginning with the Bombay-Burma Trading Co. in 1863 (intended to exploit the teak business) and from this success moving on to Arracan Ltd. (Siamese trade) in 1885 and the Indo-Java Rubber Planting and Trading Co. (1906). The Company's official history records that the Dutch East Indies and Malaysia were explored for investment possibilities in oil, gold, coffee and rubber. Rather similar but less well-documented investments can be found in the development of Mackinnon, Mackenzie & Co. and Binny & Co. (now the Inchcape Group), E. D. Sassoon & Co. (Anglo-Persian Jews originally competing with Mathesons for the opium trade), R. & J. Henderson, the Borneo Co. agents, and Guthrie & Co., who borrowed £200,000 from the King of Siam to sustain their rubber estate investments. A careful analysis of British investment in Malayan plantation rubber in its main period of growth between 1904 and 1922 shows the major role of the agency houses.

However, by this time the local depositors in India and the Far East had evidently given way to much stronger financial support from the home country, at any rate in secure investments in the British colonies. Few partnerships that were running in the

---

[16] H. A. Antrobus, *A History of the Assam Co.* (Edinburgh 1957).

traditional way might now be regarded as something of a curiosity in the City. The transition from the old system to the new was eased, at least among firms in the vanguard, by the growing size of partners' capital left in the business, and by the growing flow of funds from the agency, banking and insurance business.

Certainly investment groups came in various forms and guises from around the turn of the century. Arthur Lampard of Harrisons & Crosfield, originally a firm of tea importers, became a leader in the development of rubber plantations when his Far Eastern tours opened his eyes to the potential. His firm had only modest capital and, initially, limited interest, so most of a long series of issues were made through the Stock Exchange. Marcus Samuel launched his Shell Transport & Trading Co. with the support of seven other Far Eastern trading houses to form what was originally called the 'Tank Syndicate'. The Samuels subscribed £1·2m. out of the original (1897) capital of £1·8m. but reserved entire control to themselves, a characteristic feature of investment groups. Though Shell's assets reached £11·0m. in 1918 they still had entire control.

LATIN AMERICA

Although the investment group is most familiar in India, China and the Far East (albeit disguised by the phrase 'agency house'), it also appeared in most other sectors of British overseas trade. Latin America and Australia were not the most fertile ground for this form of capitalism but, perhaps because of the difficulties, the surviving records and literature relating to the groups operating there are rather more informative.

The best-known name was of course Antony Gibbs & Sons, originally a small merchant house exporting textiles to Spain and South America, then, from the 1840s to 1860s, holders of the well-known Peruvian guano monopoly. The development of the business is most strikingly epitomised in the words of Vicary Gibbs, who was senior partner at the turn of the century. Leaving aside the period from 1808 to 1845, when he wrote 'the business was being gradually worked up', Gibbs divided his firm's history into two periods. In the first, from 1845 to about 1870, he believed that the business was still concentrated on a very few lines, 'all who were engaged in it, both chiefs and juniors, were active working partners', most of the business was simply consignment trade which was 'enormously profitable' (£80,000–£100,000 p.a.), so that 'the borrowed capital formed only a small proportion of the capital of the firm'. In the second period, which he knew better from personal experience, he saw great contrasts:

> The business became extraordinarily various and widespread. There was no active working head, and latterly even junior members went into Parliament. Consignment business had practically ceased and the firm was forced into all sorts of enterprises of which it had no experience. But for the one business left which the firm understood viz. Nitrate, the business as a whole was extraordinarily speculative and unprofitable. The borrowed capital formed a very large proportion of the capital of the firm...[17]

The variety of business developed in the second period has not yet been fully written up (though there is ample documentation), but it certainly included nitrate factories and railways (in Chile), shipping, copper mines, various Australian interests and a large portfolio of stocks and securities. Vicary Gibbs thought the business had come to closely resemble a trust company.

Gibbs' experience in South America was in itself unique, yet it exhibits features that were familiar to many established merchant houses at the period. Prosperity and high profits in the middle decades of the century were succeeded by severe competition in which a new generation, casting about for easier ways of supporting its gracious life-style and public service, was willing to defy the conventional wisdom of mercantile forebears by making long-term commitments to new ventures in developing countries. Living beyond their means or aspirations, the new merchant adventurers used their name to recruit capital from connections and clients to float a variety of overseas development projects. In general, only the success stories have (so far) been recorded, but in Gibbs' case, liquidity crises are on record in 1876, 1884, 1890, 1894 and 1920. Australia in particular swallowed up more capital than the partners and their clients could easily afford.[18]

Other British investment groups active in South America appear to have been less speculative and to have initiated joint-stock enterprises in a more formal way. Balfour, Williamson & Co., founded in Liverpool as forwarding agents in 1851, and subsequently prominent in the grain trade with California, set up the Pacific Loan & Investment Co. in 1878 to extend their interests on the west coast of the USA, and in Chile and Peru. Initially most of the investments were connected with the grain trade (flour mills, warehouses,

[17] Guildhall Lib., Antony Gibbs & Co. MSS 11,024/1, memo of Apr. 1902.
[18] Anthony Gibbs & Co. MSS 11,042/2, 12 Dec. 1883, 8 Jan. 1891.

elevators and wharves) but interests were also taken in fruit farms, a coal mine and iron ore deposits. Trading connections were encouraged to deposit money with the London house, which in turn advanced credits to Chilean nitrate companies on a large scale. 'No matter where the ownership lay, management was always the responsibility of Balfour Guthrie', the US organisation, according to the firm's official historian Wallis Hunt. The Chilean operation (Williamson Balfour) made issues for the South American companies and accepted seats on their boards. In the first decade of this century, these investment activities were greatly increased to include petroleum and cement, and the flour milling side was built up. The partners' 'responsible capital' in 1913 was £2·0m., but figures scattered through Hunt's book indicate that they controlled investments worth at least £4·475m. in 1913.

The evolution of Knowles & Foster seems to have followed a similar pattern but on a much more limited scale. The firm started in the Brazilian trade in 1826 and diversified in the period when Thomas Foster Knowles was the most active partner (1878–1939). The best-known venture was the Rio Flour Mills Co., incorporated in 1886 with an initial capital of £0·25m. The mill company, part of whose capital was owned in Brazil, in time launched its own subsidiary shipping company and cotton mill; the capital reached £0·6m. in 1912 and £0·8m. in 1919. It is an interesting commentary on the source material that while Gibbs and Knowles & Foster were included in W. Skinner's standard work *The London Banks*, Balfour Williamson was not.

RUSSIA

During the first three-quarters of the nineteenth century a large part of British overseas trade, especially that to the Continent, was conducted by continental merchant houses with branches in London, Manchester, Leeds, Liverpool and other commercial centres (Chapter 5). The 'international houses', as they have been called, provided a great deal of the enterprise, capital and specific expertise needed to translate British production techniques into commercial success, especially in the markets of Europe and Asia Minor. They were largely of German and 'Greek' (Ottoman Christian) origin, but included a sprinkling of Dutch, French, Italian and other merchants. One of their most singular achievements, still uncharted, was to link the UK economy with the great Russian market which, for very different reasons, was short of the

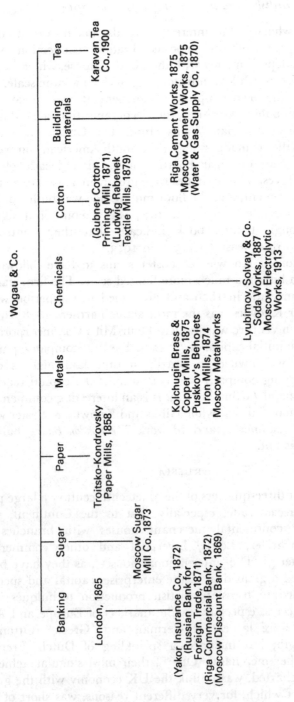

Note: firms in brackets are those in which Wogaus had a participation rather than full ownership.

Figure 8.2. Structure of Wogau & Co., Moscow and London, in 1914.

Wogau & Co.

Banking — London, 1865

Sugar — Moscow Sugar Mill Co., 1873
(Yakor Insurance Co., 1872)
(Russian Bank for Foreign Trade, 1871)
(Riga Commercial Bank, 1872)
(Moscow Discount Bank, 1869)

Paper — Troitsko-Kondrovsky Paper Mills, 1858

Metals — Kolchugin Brass & Copper Mills, 1875
Puskkov's Behoiets Iron Mills, 1874
Moscow Metalworks

Chemicals — Lyubimov, Solvay & Co. Soda Works, 1887
Moscow Electrolytic Works, 1913

Cotton — (Gubner Cotton Printing Mill, 1871)
(Ludwig Rabenek Textile Mills, 1879)

Building materials — Riga Cement Works, 1875
Moscow Cement Works, 1875
(Water & Gas Supply Co, 1870)

Tea — Karavan Tea Co.,1900

indigenous mercantile enterprise. Many of the German houses originated in Hamburg where they had traditional trading links with the Baltic ports as well as England, while the Greeks had long-standing connections with the Russian Black Sea ports.[19]

As France, Germany and other parts of the Continent industrialised their potential as export markets fell away, and the merchant houses that had prospered in European trade shifted their interests further afield.[20] But Russia continued to be a major sector for capitalist development, and several of the most successful merchant houses promoted investment groups there. The most diversified of these was probably Wogau & Co., whose structure was so complicated by 1914 that it seems best to represent it in a diagram. The firm was founded in Moscow in 1839 by M. M. Wogau of Frankfurt, and the London branch was opened by his partner E. A. Schumacher in 1865. In its early years the firm was largely interested, it seems, in the trade in tea, sugar, cotton and other commodities of international trade, but in the last quarter of the century it joined the vanguard of Russian industrialisation by investment in a remarkable range of industries, including sugar refining, paper milling, metals, chemicals and building materials. In 1914 the concern in all its diverse activities was still run entirely by the descendants of the founders, but a large part of the capital consisted of deposits left in the business by relatives at 6 per cent interest. The London branch had now evolved to the status of a leading merchant bank with a capital of about £1·0m., a median figure for accepting houses whose bills were regarded as first class.[21]

However, the largest investment group active in Russia was undoubtedly that built up by Ludwig Knoop, 'the Arkwright of Russia' (Chapter 7). Knoop came from Bremen but began his career with De Jersey & Co., a Manchester firm that specialised in the export of yarns and (later) machinery to Russia. When they went bankrupt in 1847, Knoop effectively took over the organisation along with the Russian agency for Platt Bros., the textile machine builders. Most of his enterprise was focussed on building, equipping and managing cotton mills in Russia, but he was also active in the cotton trade with the US and in banking. It is said that Knoop was

---

[19] Ch. 5, above.
[20] Eg. Ralli Bros. to India, Kessler to the USA, Reiss Bros. to Indonesia. Further examples are given in the author's 'International Houses'.
[21] Capital of accepting houses in S. D. Chapman, *Merchant Banking* p. 55.

instrumental in setting up some 122 spinning concerns in Russia by the 1890s, and that at the end of the century the Knoop family were on the boards of ten manufacturing companies and in addition held shares in another fifteen undertakings. The house's capital in 1914 was £1·2m. but an attempt to embrace all their interests in one concern envisaged a capital of £8·0m.

Wogaus and Knoops were the pacemakers, but a number of other firms evidently had comparable interests, albeit on a more modest scale. Brandts, best known in London as merchant bankers, had interests in sugar and cotton mills as well as shipping and a meat refrigeration plant in Argentina. Hubbards, one of the few survivors of the old Anglo-Russian merchants, were also interested in cotton mills, forestry and other ventures. The Russian petroleum and mining industries attracted a good deal of West European capital in the first decade of this century, but to maintain a balanced view, it should be added that this was more often raised by financial syndicates.[22]

The Anglo-Russian grain trade was originally in the hands of Greek firms with offices in London, such as the Rallis, Rodocanachis, Scaramangas and Negropontis, but in the second half of the last century their leadership in this sector flagged. In *Merchants of Grain* (1979), Dan Morgan suggests this was because Dreyfus and other Jewish merchants had easier access to the capital required for warehouses, docks and ships to conduct the fast-growing trade. This is not convincing because the leading Greek houses were much richer than the firms that superseded them: by the turn of the century Rallis had a capital of £4·2m. in the Far Eastern trade. However, the only clear evidence of a Greek firm creating an investment group in Russia refers to Rodocanachis who ran cotton spinning and weaving factories, a flour mill, brewery, pottery, wire factory and steamship company. The explanation for the change of course by the Greeks seems to be the rise of Jewish middlemen in the Russian grain trade who built a closer relationship with their co-religionists.

SOUTH AFRICA

At first glance the South African mining investment groups may appear an entirely different species to those considered in the Far East, South America and Russia, but on closer inspection there are

[22] For British examples of such syndicates see eg. Gibbs MSS 11,117, and J. W. McCarty, 'Overseas Mining', Ch. 5.

some close connections and parallels. It was not simply that investment groups in the sectors already discussed were moving into mining and real estate, and would have moved further faster if their geologists had made more economic discoveries. Nor was it just a matter of South African adoption of the practice of a partnership or private company controlling a range of private companies whose total capital far exceeded that of the parent. Even more significantly, the earliest effective gold mining company in South Africa, the Transvaal Gold, Exploration & Land Co., was initiated, financed and controlled by Matheson & Co. The London partners were encouraged by the success of Rio Tinto Copper, which they had floated in 1873, and made them the biggest importers of copper. The new venture started at Pilgrim's Rest in 1882 with a capital of £100,000, which had built up to £300,000 before the end of the decade. We have seen that initially Mathesons were merchants, and so also were other firms that became prominent in South African mining in the early years, notably Jules Porges & Co. of Paris, Barnato Bros. and J. B. Robinson. As these firms grew wealthy, they became even more like other major merchant houses, with offices in London and increasingly diversified investments, including banking.[23]

Only Rhodes always insisted he was a 'digger' but his enterprise also owed something to the influence of British business in India, at any rate by way of exemplar. In a triumphant letter written in 1888 just after the consolidation of the Kimberley diamond mines into the De Beers' Company, he wrote 'we have now got the powers we required, and with the enormous back country daily developing we have every chance of making it another East India Company... Africa is on the move. I think it is a second Cinderella.'[24] Rhodes' subsequent career shows that the vision was not simply imperial flag-waving; rather was it recognition of the possibility of using De Beers' profits and the almost unlimited legal powers conferred in the articles of association to insure against further discoveries and to create a diversified investment group. At the very same period that Rhodes was forging De Beers, his partner Rudd was raising capital for the launch of Consolidated Gold Fields of South Africa, intended as a holding company to develop Rand mines, but in 1888 also used

[23] On Mathesons' Transvaal interests see A. F. Williams, *Some Dreams Come True* (Cape Town 1948) pp. 492–3 and Standard Bank Archives, Jo'burg, Inspection Reports, Barberton, 10 Sept. 1888, 21 Nov. 1889 etc.
[24] Rhodes House Library, Oxford, MSS Afr. t14, 317–20.

to support De Beers. As one of his associates wrote, Rhodes 'disliked the feeling of not having a finger in every pie; besides, he was never averse from making money whenever there was a chance'.[25] If his attempts to diversify do not look so impressive in the formal records, this is largely because the London board of De Beers repeatedly vetoed his bold projects, the City financiers fearing that he would pour their investors' money into unproven and open-ended projects such as those in Rhodesia and German South-West Africa.[26]

Apart from the emphasis on mining, the principal difference between South African investment groups and those operating in other sectors of international trade was the source of capital. In India, China, Russia and some of the Latin American republics, British firms made considerable use of local capital deposited with them, and it is easy to suppose that this was not available in empty countries like the Transvaal, Cape Colony (Kimberley), Rhodesia and Namibia. In point of fact, British investors were for long wary of mining shares, and the initial capital for the Rand gold mining industry was, with few exceptions, generated internally.[27] However, this capital was inadequate to sustain the sinking and equipping of deep level mines – estimated in 1889 at £0·5m. each – and Alfred Beit (the financial genius behind both De Beers and Rand Mines Ltd.) turned to the Continent. As a result of the popularity that De Beers shares had enjoyed in Paris, Berlin and Vienna, the same groups that had introduced these shares to the respective stock exchanges were glad to father the gold shares offered to them by Wernher, Beit & Co. Indeed, these stockbrokers were so eager to participate in the Rand promotions that Wernher Beit did not have to resort to issuing prospectuses and soliciting public subscriptions. Other promoters also found themselves on an easy wicket; Barnato boasted at a civic reception in London in 1895 that he had never issued a prospectus. The shareholders were more like holders of bank deposits than of franchises under a constitution.[28]

From the earliest years of South African diamond and gold mining, the group system and the autocracy of a handful of pioneer financiers together conspired to create a situation in which a few

[25] Consolidated Gold Fields of S. A. Ltd, *The Gold Fields 1887–1937* (1937) p. 20. J. B. Taylor, *A Pioneer Looks Back* (1939) p. 122.
[26] S. D. Chapman, 'Rhodes and the City of London: Another View of Imperialism', *Historical Journal* xxvii (1985).
[27] A. C. M. Webb, 'Witwatersrand Genesis: A Comparative Study of some early Gold Mining Companies 1886–94', PhD. thesis, Rhodes Univ. 1981, Ch. 1.
[28] J. B. Taylor, *A Pioneer*, pp. 109–10. S. Jackson, *The Great Barnato* (1970) p. 170.

familiar names controlled chains of mining, land, transport and other combines. The problem is to put figures on this situation and to identify the exact nature of control, partly because of the usual problems of business secrecy, but also because of the extraordinarily volatile nature of the market in mining shares. The most reliable group figures seem to be those assembled by the General Manager of the Standard Chartered Bank in 1895. Admittedly that was a boom year, but the £8·om. entered for Barnato Bros. seems a sober figure when compared with Barnato's own estimate of £20m. at this date. J. B. Robinson was reckoned to be of equal size and Neumann, Lubeck & Co., who were generally stock dealers, rather smaller.

The only significant difference between the South African investment groups and those surveyed in other sections of this chapter is that in general, the former were founded later and their development was telescoped into a much shorter period of time. Perhaps their most interesting feature as investment groups, apart from precocious development, is that they brought together British enterprise, French and German capital, and American engineering expertise, an unusual if not unique combination in this period. The view that the mines of Kimberley and Johannesburg were somehow controlled by Rothschilds and other London financial interests is, in the light of recent evidence, no longer tenable; South African investment groups were as much the product of specific local trading conditions and decisions as others mentioned in earlier sections.[29]

BRITISH CONTEXT OF INVESTMENT GROUPS

Clearly the information assembled in this survey is incomplete; it is based on the records of only thirty investment groups and few of them are well documented. Nevertheless it is felt that most of the leaders of this development have been identified and a fairly wide geographical coverage achieved so that it is possible to make some assessment of the significance of the phenomenon. At least, recognition of the species should lead to the identification of further and perhaps more telling examples and consequent revision or refinement of the features that can be described at this stage.

The sources cast little light on the problems of management and organisation, but there can be no serious doubt that the investment group was primarily a device to maintain the wealth and power of the family (or families) that controlled the particular business.

[29] S. D. Chapman, 'Rhodes'.

Nevertheless outside expertise was introduced, sometimes with far-reaching results – for instance James Bryce in Wallace Bros. (for his unique knowledge of Burma), William Keswick in Mathesons for his managerial ability, and Herman Eckstein to promote the development of Wernher Beit's Rand Mines Ltd. The traditional development of the successful merchant house featured young partners investing their early careers in overseas stations, returning to a 'home' partnership as they attained entrepreneurial maturity. This arrangement, evidently assumed by investment groups, assured a regular testing and turnover of the partners (or directors). Management recruitment within the family was not always a narrow choice, for Victorian families were large and selection was not confined to sons and sons-in-law of the partners.[30]

Historians of particular houses have noted some positive virtues of the system from the management point of view. Thus Sir Percy Griffiths writes in his attractive survey of the Inchcape Group that 'Managerial expertise in India was in short supply and the system enabled a limited number of experienced managers to apply their professional skill in more than one field. There can be little doubt that such a system was almost essential to the economic growth of nineteenth-century India.' The historian of Wallace Bros. offers some insights, recording that from 1878 'the management was so constituted that the responsibility of the several managers in any branch was in the nature of a partnership', while the central partnership kept detailed records on the recruitment and progress of all its staff. But there are also clear indications of management weakness in comparable firms. So early as 1891, Jardine Skinner's were complaining of management recruitment problems, adding 'you may find that you have ultimately to recruit Germans, of whom there is an almost unlimited supply'. Incompetent management carried another agency house (Binnys) into bankruptcy in 1906, while at different times Hubbards, Gibbs, Butterfield & Swire and the British & Chinese Corporation (Jardine Matheson) are known to have suffered from inadequate management. In South Africa there was no shortage of young upper-class adventurers from England, but many of the mining engineers had to be drawn from the USA, and

[30] Wallace Bros. records, Guildhall Library, contain the only full record of staff recruitment and promotion for an investment group. There are stray comments on recruitment in various works eg. in M. Keswick, ed., *The Thistle and the Jade* [Mathesons] p. 38; R. Henriques, *Marcus Samuel* (1960) pp. 63–6, C. Drage, *Tai koo* [Butterfield & Swire] (1970) p. 224, and Hubbard (Anglo-Russian Mills) MSS at Guildhall Library.

the 'problem of finding competent managers proved an enduring one'.[31] Nevertheless, this does not significantly change the overall conclusions of Chandler and others about the managerial consequences of British business nepotism; rather do they reinforce the American interpretation, showing how the traditional system was maintained through a period of rapid growth in the scale of international trade and investment.

However, it may be necessary to modify another accepted interpretation of British business history in the Victorian age, that of antipathy to the joint-stock company, for the investment group system evidently allowed the traditional family control to acquire many of the advantages of the joint-stock system without losing control. Like so many others in British economic history, this interpretation is largely based on manufacturing industry, and finance and trade often proceeded from rather different assumptions – if only because the family owners were often of Scots or foreign origin. But the important factor was that the English legal framework for the creation of joint-stock companies was generous after 1865 and colonial legislation or case law made it even more so. This is most evident in the case of South Africa, where Cecil Rhodes was able to do much as he liked, but is also significant in the important case of China.[32] For ambitious entrepreneurs on the new frontiers of economic development, whether in India, China, Argentina, Russia or South Africa, the opportunities were often too good to miss; the family name attracted (or retained) the necessary capital while the joint-stock system contained any possible loss. The art of the controllers of the investment group was that of knowing how to use other people's money profitably. They also offered advantages to the investor, for the Stock Exchange was not much interested in developments in distant parts of the world, and the family business offered a relatively cheap and secure way of acquiring the high rates of return from foreign investments.

But probably the most interesting finding in this area of research relates to the scale of business at the time. One of the most striking

---

[31] In addition to the bibliography in the Appendix, see C. B. Davis, 'Financing Imperialism', *Bus. Hist. Rev.* LVI (1982) pp. 244–9; R. P. T. Davenport-Hines and Geoffrey Jones, eds., *British Business in Asia since 1860* (Cambridge 1989) esp. Ch. 1; J. T. Hammond, *Autobiography* (New York 1935) p. 231 and A. C. M. Webb, 'Some Managerial Problems faced by Early Witwatersrand Mining Companies' (forthcoming).
[32] Rhodes House MSS, loc. cit., and *Economist*, 25 Feb. 1893 (article on 'vendors' shares). A. Feuerwerker, *China's Early Industrialisation* (New York 1970) pp. 18–19.

features of the investment group system is that it deliberately concealed the true magnitude of its operations behind the modest financial data of the parent company, and this has also deceived historians. The data on investment groups assembled in the Appendix to this survey have many gaps, and experience suggests they will be difficult to plug, but the figures are sufficient to make an initial comparison. Hannah's list of the fifty largest companies of 1905 includes two dozen firms with a capital of £4·0m. or more, mostly in beer, textiles and shipbuilding, and all in manufacturing.[33] The preliminary survey in this work already offers more than half that number and comparisons between firms hint at several more that might qualify for this division. Peering into the future of research in this area, it is not too much to suppose that the 1905 manufacturing list might be equally matched in scale by a list of overseas investment groups based in or partly conducted from Britain. When we add the African chartered companies,[34] it is clear that the growth of scale of British enterprise in the period has already been seriously underestimated.

Unfortunately the sources available at present do not allow any calculation of the economies of scale of such investment groups, but the published work contains some indications that size and integration would be cost-saving.[35] We may surmise that trade generated the work for shipping, warehouse and financial services on the one side, and, through agencies for British engineering and machinery manufacturers, unrivalled appreciation of investment opportunities in the overseas countries in which they operated. No doubt there was, in some group or other, 'empire building' for its own sake or to flatter the founder, but no evidence of this has emerged so far. The emphasis, rather, is on necessary decentralisation and decision making, a system of organisation that was no doubt more efficient than the factious federations of family firms characteristic of many large industrial giants of this period.

It might easily be supposed that a strong growth in investment groups would soon carry them out of the control of the founding families, partly as a wider variety of experience and expertise was appointed to the boards of directors, partly as control increasingly centred on London. In fact, most of the investment groups evolved

---

[33] A. G. Hopkins, 'Imperial Business in Africa', *Journal of African History* xvii (1976) pp. 29–48, 267–90.   [34] L. Hannah, *Rise of the Corporate Economy*, p. 183.
[35] Eg. in S. Marriner & F. E. Hyde, *The Senior* (Liverpool 1967) and the bibliography of South African investment groups.

rather slowly and clung to family control. The only significant exception to this generalisation was the South African mining groups where capital requirements were so much greater than elsewhere, but even these were not ruled by the City. The diamond mining organisation has been closely studied by Colin Newbury whose book *The Diamond Ring* (1989) shows that merchants were represented on well over half the company boards and that the influence of merchants investors has been underestimated in the developing strategy of the industry and trade. During the most dynamic period of enterprise in gold mining on the Rand, from 1884 to the end of the century, there can be no doubt that initiative and control was local.[36]

The tensions between the London office and overseas bases of some leading agency houses recorded in Chapter 7 leave no doubt that local enterprise was a continuing feature of the system. City finance was not a prerequisite of new developments. Sir Ernest Cable of Birds made the point most dramatically when he wrote in 1903 that 'In the prosperous times of a boom, we can "off our own bat" float a jute mill in three hours'; at other times the City showed little interest in small colonial issues. Despite much larger issues for South Africa, not even Rothschilds could impose their control. Investment groups that centralised strongly, notably Antony Gibbs & Co. (Latin American trade), John Hubbard & Co. (Russian trade) and David Sassoon & Co (Indian trade) are known to have run into deep water.[37] The success and reputation of the investment groups, wherever they operated overseas, depended on the continuation of their 'local' expertise and day-to-day independence.

The final point must relate to investment groups and the City of London financial establishment at large. In one sense the families who owned these concerns *were* the City establishment, for twenty out of the thirty examined appear in W. Skinner's *The London Banks* (1914), and the others were closely connected with the same interests, for instance Balfour Williamson & Co. called themselves merchant bankers, Harrison & Crosfield were a leading issue house, and De Beers' London board was dominated by Lord Rothschild's

---

[36] Colin Newbury, *The Diamond Ring. Business, Politics and Precious Stones in South Africa 1867–1947* (Oxford 1989) esp. pp. 57, 361, 371. M. Fraser and A. Jeeves, *All that Glittered... Correspondence of Lionel Phillips 1890–1924* (Cape Town 1977). A. C. M. Webb, 'Witwatersrand Genesis'.

[37] Cable cited in A. K. Bagchi, *The Presidency Banks* p. 24. S. D. Chapman, 'Rhodes'. For the other firms see the Appendix to this chapter.

right-hand man, Sir Carl Meyer. Moreover, various partners or directors of these groups also appeared as directors of imperial, international and clearing banks and of major insurance companies.[38] There was no clear line demarcating investment groups with financial functions from merchant banks active in the promotion of public utilities and overseas shares.[39] Indeed, the only realistic distinction seems to be between them and what may be called the English *haute banque* – Rothschilds, Barings, Kleinworts, Schröders, Morgans and other leading accepting houses, whose reputation depended on their liquidity.[40] Most of these firms were also active as issuing houses, but limited their interest to safe stock, which in the context of this chapter often meant investments whose value had been demonstrated by the investment groups. In other words, the groups still performed a mercantile function in the sense that they were the 'local' experts with capital and supporting services in the countries or sectors of world trade in which they specialised.

APPENDIX *Investments and capital (in £m.) of 30 leading British-based investment groups c. 1900–14*

Group	Overseas base	Activities	Partners' capital	Group capital
Far East				
Palmer & Co.	Calcutta 1781	B, H, Im, S, Sm	0·4 (1830)	5·0 (1830)
Binny & Co.	Madras 1799	Co, Cm, K, Sm, Su, Wm	0·12 (1906)	
Ogilvy, Gillanders	Calcutta 1824	Cu, Dm, G, Jm, K, Rw, Su, S	0·75 (1907)	
Matheson & Co.	Canton 1832	(see Fig. 8.1)	0·2 (1906)	1·72 (1891)

---

[38] Directors' and partners' names appear in W. Skinner, *The London Banks*, and these names may then be checked in W. Skinner, *Directory of Directors*.

[39] E.g. Erlangers were active in promoting railways in South Africa and Rhodesia in partnership with Paulings, the railway contractors, G. Pauling, *The Chronicles of a Contractor* (1926); Speyers were said to control the whole of London's omnibus service and the underground electric railways, A. Moreton Mandeville, *The House of Speyer* (1915); Guildhall Lib. MS, 21,799, E. C. Grenfell's notebook pp. 106–7.

[40] S. D. Chapman, *Merchant Banking*, esp. Ch. 5.

APPENDIX (*contd.*)

Group	Overseas base	Activities	Partners' capital	Group capital
E. D. Sassoon & Co.	Bombay 1833	B, Br, Cm, Pm, S, Tw	1·25–1·50 (1909)	6·7 (1920)
Boustead & Co.	Singapore 1831	B, P, R, T	0·3–0·5 (1908)	
Finlay & Co.	Bombay 1862	B, Cm, Jm, K, S, Su, T	1·0 (1909)	4·36 (1898)[1]
Guthrie & Co.	Singapore	B, Op, R, Tin	0·45 (1912)	
Jardine, Skinner	Calcutta 1840	Im, Jm, Pm, K, Sm, T	1·3 (1892)	
Mackinnon Mackenzie	Calcutta 1847	Jm, K, S, T		1·66 (1914)
Wallace Bros.	Bombay 1847	B, Cm, H, F, R, Rw	0·8 (1911)	3·2 (1909)
Ralli Bros.	Calcutta 1851	B, Cm, K		4·2 (1902)
Henderson	Singapore 1856	F, G, K, Jm, Pm, R	0·5 (1908)	0·3 (1913)[2]
Butterfield & Swire	Shanghai 1867	H, S, Su	0·75 (1896)	5·14 (1900)
M. Samuel & Co.	Yokohama 1878	B, P, S	1·29 (1903)	3·0 (1903) 11·0 (1918)
Harrison & Crosfield	Malaya 1899	R, T, To	0·2 (1901)	
Latin America				
Antony Gibbs	Lima 1822	B, Rw, S, Z	0·44 (1900)	2·0 (1900)
Bunge & Co.	Buenos Aires 1858	Fm, P, R, S, W	1·6–2·0 (1910)	
Dreyfus & Co.	Buenos Aires 1880	B, S, W	0·6 (1903)	1·9 (1902)[3]
Balfour Williamson	Valparaiso 1878	Ce, Fm, Fe, K, P	2·0 (1913)	4·5m. + (1913)
Knowles & Foster	Rio de Janeiro 1886	B, Fm, K		0·6 (1912)[4]
Russia				
Brandt	Archangel 1805	B, Cm, Sm	0·75 (1904)	
Hubbard	St Petersburg 1816	B, Cm, F, K, P	0·3 (1900)	0·73 (1900)

APPENDIX (*contd.*)

Group	Overseas base	Activities	Partners' capital	Group capital
Wogau	Moscow 1839	(see Fig. 8.2)	1·0 (1915)	3·67 (1915)
Knoop	Moscow 1840	B, Cm	1·2 (1915)	8·0 (1915)
Rodocanachi	St Petersburg 1851	B, Br, Cm, Fe, Fm, S	0·4 (1913)	
South Africa				
Robinson	Kimberley 1871	B, Dm, G	8·0 (1895)	
Wernher Beit	Kimberley 1873	B, Dm, G		13·0 (1895)
Barnato Bros.	Kimberley 1873	B, Dm, G	0·96 (1897)	8·0 (1895)
De Beers	Kimberley 1874	Dm, G, Rw	3·95 (1896)	14·4 (1896)
Neumann, Lubeck	Johannesburg c. 1888	B, Dm, G		2·5 (1895)

Notes: (1) Overseas base refers only to the earliest or principal overseas location; in fact almost all investment groups operated simultaneously from several overseas centres of trade. (2) Much information on capital is drawn from bank records and must be read as an order of magnitude possibly erring on the conservative side rather than precise data.

Key to investment group activities:

B	Banking	Op	Oil palm plantation
Br	Breweries	Pm	Paper mills
Ce	Cement works	P	Petroleum
Co	Coffee plantation(s)	R	Rubber estates
Cm	Cotton mill(s)	Rw	Railway(s)
Cu	Copper mine(s)	Sm	Sugar mills
Dm	Diamond mine(s)	S	Shipping
F	Forests	Su	Silk mill(s)
Fe	Iron works	T	Tea estates
Fm	Flour mill(s)	To	Tobacco plantation
G	Gold mine(s)	Tw	Tramways
H	Harbours and/or docks	W	Warehousing
Im	Indigo mills	Wm	Woollen mill(s)
Jm	Jute mill(s)	Z	Soda factories
K	Coal mine(s)		

References

1. Tea estates only.
2. Borneo Co. only, nominal valuation.

3. Russia only, Argentinan interests probably much greater.
4. Rio Flour Mill Co. only.

SOURCES ON FIRMS

(order of appearance in text)
Abbreviations: KB Info Bks = Kleinwort Benson Information Books, Guildhall Lib. Skinner = W. Skinner, *The London Banks (1865–1914), Directory of Directors.*

INDIA, CHINA AND THE FAR EAST

Palmer & Co.

J. W. Maclellan, 'Banking in India and China, A Sketch', *Banker Mag*, LV (1893), p. 52.
Bodleian Lib., Palmer MSS, D107 (bankruptcy).
A. Tripathi, *Trade and Finance in the Bengal Presidency 1793–1833* (Calcutta 1956).

Matheson & Co.

E. Lefevour, *Western Enterprise in Late Ch'ing China. A Selective Survey of Jardine Matheson & Co.'s Operations 1842–95* (Harvard 1968).
Maggie Keswick, ed., *The Thistle and the Jade* (1982).
Cambridge Univ. Lib., Jardine Matheson MSS, Jardine Skinner MSS.
J. W. McCarty, 'British Investment in Overseas Mining 1880–1914', Ph.D., Cambridge 1961, Ch. 5.
C. E. Harvey, *The Rio Tinto Company 1873–1954* (1981).

Ogilvy, Gillanders & Co.

J. S. Gladstone, *History of Gillanders, Arbuthnot & Co. and Ogilvy, Gillanders & Co.* (1910)
KB Info Bks UK II p. 165.

James Finlay & Co.

[C. Brogan], *James Finlay & Co., 1750–1950* (Glasgow 1951).
John Scott and Michael Hughes, *The Anatomy of Scottish Capital* (1980), Ch. 1.

E. D. Sassoon & Co.

Cecil Roth, *The Sassoon Dynasty* (1941).
Stanley Jackson, *The Sassoons* (1968).
KB Info Bks UK III p. 131.
Brandt Circulars, Nottingham Univ. Lib.

Wallace Bros.

A. C. Pointon, *Wallace Bros.* (Oxford 1974).
R. H. Macaulay, *The Bombay Burma Trading Corporation* (1934).
Wallace Bros. MSS, Guildhall Library.

Guthrie & Co.

KB Info Bks UK II pp. 47, 121, 151. Skinner.
G. C. Allen and A. G. Donnithorne, *Western Enterprise in Far Eastern Economic Development; China and Japan* (1954).

R. & J. Henderson

KB Info Bks UK III p. 166.
Sir P. Griffiths, *A History of the Inchcape Group* (1977) pp. 130–36.
Borneo Co. MSS, Inchcape Group, London.

Harrisons & Crosfield

Harrisons & Crosfield, *One Hundred Years as East India Merchants 1844–1943* (1943).
KB Info Bks UK I p. 98.

Edward Boustead & Co.

KB Info Bks UK II p. 46.
Eric Jennings, *Boustead History* (unpublished MS, 1978).

Butterfield & Swire

S. Marriner and F. E. Hyde, *The Senior. John Samuel Swire 1825–98* (Liverpool 1967).
C. Drage, *Taikoo* (1970).

M. Samuel & Co.

R. Henriques, *Marcus Samuel* (1960).
F. C. Gerretson, *History of the Royal Dutch (1953–7)* II, pp. 145–6.
KB Info Bks UK II pp. 170–1, gives £1·2m. as partners' capital.
Antony Gibbs & Co. Info Bks, Guildhall Lib. MS 11,069C gives Shell's capital as £1·8m. in Oct. 1897, £2m. in June 1900, £3m. in Feb. 1903.

Jardine, Skinner & Co.

Jardine Skinner MSS, Univ. of Cambridge.

Mackinnon, Mackenzie & Co.

Sir P. Griffiths, *A History of the Inchcape Group* (1977).
G. Blake, *B. I. Centenary* (1956).
Inchcape Group Archives, London.

Binny & Co.

Sir P. Griffiths, *A History of the Inchcape Group* (1977).
Binny & Co. MSS, Inchcape Group, London.

Ralli Bros.

[Jack Vlasto], *Ralli Bros. Ltd.* (1951).
S. D. Chapman, 'The International Houses', *Jnl Eur. Ec. Hist.* vi (1977).
Baring Bros. 'Characters Book 1' pp. 131–2.
Jardine Skinner MSS In Letters 13.

LATIN AMERICA
Antony Gibbs

J. A. Gibbs, *The History of Antony & Dorothea Gibbs* (1922).
W. Maude, *Antony Gibbs & Sons Ltd* (1958).
Guildhall Lib., Papers of Antony Gibbs & Sons, esp. 11,942/1, 11,042/2, pp. 1–29.
John Mayo, 'British Commission Houses and the Chilean Economy 1851–80', *Journal of Latin American Studies*, xi (1979).
W. M. Matthew, *The House of Gibbs and the Peruvian Guano Monopoly* (1981).

Knowles & Foster

[Anon.], *The History of Knowles & Foster 1828–1948* (1948).
R. Graham, 'A British Industry in Brazil', *Bus. Hist.* viii (1966).
The 'group capital' entered for this firm refers only to Rio Flour mills.

Balfour, Williamson & Co.

Wallis Hunt, *Heirs of Great Adventure. The History of Balfour, Williamson & Co. Ltd* (1951).
Balfour Williamson MSS, University College London.

RUSSIA AND LATIN AMERICA
Bunge & Co., Louis Dreyfus & Co.

J. R. Scobie, *Revolution on the Pampas* (Austin 1964).

Dan Morgan, *Merchants of Grain* (1979).
M. P. Federov, *Khlebnaya Torgovlya u Glaneyshikh Russkikh Portakh i Kenigsberge* (The Grain Trade in the Main Russian Ports and in Konigsberg) (Moscow 1888).
P. Chalmin, *Negociants et chargeurs: La saga du négoce international des matières premières* (Paris 1983).
Brandt Circulars, Nottingham Univ. Lib.
KB Info Bks, France, Belgium and Holland II, pp. 8, 104, III p. 114, UK II p. 97.

RUSSIA

Wogau

Documents on Monopoly Capitalism VI (Moscow 1959) pp. 597–706.
Brandt Circulars, Nottingham Univ. Archives.
Bank of England Discount Office records (unlisted).

Knoop

S. Thompstone, 'Ludwig Knoop, The Arkwright of Russia', *Textile History*, XV (1984) pp. 45–73.
Brandt Circulars, Nottingham University Archives, for financial details.
Baring Bros. Character Books VIII (1870–83) p. 189.

Brandt

C. Amburger, *William Brandt and the Story of his Enterprises* (typescript n.d., c. 1950).

J. Hubbard & Co.

T. H. S. Escott, *City Characters under Several Reigns* (1922) Ch. XIV.
Guildhall Lib., Anglo-Russian Cotton Co. MSS 10,361/1, 2.
J. Mai, *Das Deutsche Kapital in Russland* (Berlin 1970) p. 70.
KB Info Bks UK III, p. 139.

Rodocanachi, Sons & Co.

P. Herlihy, 'Greek Merchants in Odessa in the Nineteenth Century', *Harvard Ukrainian studies*, III/IV (1979–80) pp. 399–420 and information from Dr Herlihy.
S. D. Chapman, 'The International Houses', *Jnl Eur. Econ. Hist.*, VI (1977).
Bank of England Discount Office records (unlisted).

SOUTH AFRICA

De Beers

R. V. Turrell, 'Rhodes, De Beers and Monopoly', *Journal of Imperial & Commonwealth History*, x (1982).
C. Newbury, 'Out of the Pit: the Capital Accumulation of Cecil Rhodes', ibid. x (1981).
Consolidated Gold Fields of S. A. Ltd., *The Gold Fields 1887–1937* (1937).
J. B. Taylor, *A Pioneer Looks Back* (1939).

Wernher, Beit & Co.

A. P. Cartwright, *The Corner House* (Cape Town 1965).
R. V. Kubicek, *Economic Imperialism in Theory and Practice. The Case of South African Gold Mining Finance 1886–1914* (Duke 1979).

Barnato Bros.

H. Raymond, *B. I. Barnato: A Memoir* (1987).
S. Jackson, *The Great Barnato* (1970).
Statist, XLII (1898) p. 457 for Barnato family wealth.

Robinson

L. Weinthal, *Memories, Mines and Millions* (1929).

Neumann, Lubeck & Co.

R. V. Kubicek, *Economic Imperialism in Theory and Practice. The Case of South African Gold Mining Finance 1886–1914* (Duke 1979).
Standard Bank Archives.
Skinner.

CHAPTER 9

Imperialism and British trade

In the introduction to this book some initial reference was made to mercantile strategies in relation to the development of the British Empire. Professor D. C. M. Platt, a specialist on Latin America, sees the concentration on trade and investment within the bounds of Empire as a perfectly rational strategy, given the low returns and high risk associated with enterprise in that continent.[1] British trading interests there gradually declined in relative importance as the century advanced, and the revival of investment interest in the 1870s and 1880s suffered a severe setback with the infamous Baring crisis of 1890, which brought the most prestigious gentile merchant bank in London to its knees.[2] A comparable withdrawal from trade in Tsarist Russia has also been seen as inevitable.[3]

The Platt thesis has found support in earlier chapters of this book to the extent that it has been recognised that the major British trading houses were increasingly to be found in India, British colonies in the Far East, South Africa, Australia and other Empire countries. The case histories of particular commodities have also revealed shifts towards Empire trade. Grain, once drawn from the Baltic and Black Sea, was increasingly imported from North America and India, and there were various attempts to promote cotton cultivation in India. Tea and rubber were transplanted to appropriate imperial territories, while the most vigorous arm of the export trade in textiles, the City warehouses, marked out a chain of imperial stations (see Chapters 3, 5). However, it would be quite unrealistic to suppose there was no competition in these sectors of overseas trade; rivalry was particularly keen in the non-imperial countries adjacent to British spheres of interest, for instance in China

---

[1] D. C. M. Platt, *Latin America and British Trade* (1972) Ch. VII.
[2] See above, Chapter 1.
[3] S. Thompstone, 'The Organisation and Financing of Anglo-Russian Trade before 1914', Ph.D. thesis, London 1992.

and in the Transvaal (South Africa). A systematic assessment of British mercantile performance must therefore focus on some of the areas in which our merchants chose to concentrate, rather than on those from which, by degrees, they made a tactical withdrawal.

Clearly it is not possible to examine the trade of all the imperial countries. In this chapter two sectors are chosen for close examination, the Far East and South Africa, which feature respectively the competition with the Japanese and with the Germans. In both cases there is good local evidence which has not been picked up by British scholars so that we do not have to rely on consular reports or London interpretations. Clearly British enterprise did have real advantages in the imperial territories, but the 'local' view of how it matched the challenge and opportunities must offer another perspective from which we may hope to obtain a more rounded assessment.

BRITAIN AND JAPANESE COMPETITION IN THE FAR EAST

In recent years British scholars have rather lost interest in the later economic history of the Empire and the initiative, at any rate so far as India and the Far East is concerned, has been taken up with characteristic thoroughness and dedication by Japanese scholars, who are particularly keen on comparative studies. However, the Japanese are by no means unanimous in their interpretation, so that an examination of their various views provides an instructive external debate on the commercial consequences of British imperialism.

It must be observed initially that it was inevitable that Britain's pioneering role should face new rivals and lose relative place as other European countries and the USA entered the trade and as commerce within Asia was promoted. The decline of both the British and western shares of trade is reflected in the figures assembled in Tables 9.1 and 9.2. Dr Sugihara has calculated that the annual average rate of growth of intra-Asian trade during the 30 years 1882–1913 was significantly greater than the growth of Asia's exports to the West.[4] However, given the lowly starting point of the level of Asian trade, the catalytic effect of European textiles, and the greater ease of sectoral (as distinct to global) trade, this could scarcely be counted as evidence of any failure by Britain or the West. In absolute terms,

[4] K. Sugihara, 'Patterns of Asia's Integration into the World Economy 1880–1913', in W. Fischer, R. M. McInnis and J. Schneider, *The Emergence of a World Economy* (Wiesbaden 1986).

Table 9.1. *The British share of Chinese trade 1870–1891*

	share of overseas trade	percentage of total foreign residents in China	percentage of total foreign firms in China
1870	95% of imports	n.d.	n.d.
	74% of exports		
1882	62% of total trade	49	69
1891	59% of total trade	42	63

Source: G. Kurgan-van Hentenryk, *Leopold II et les groupes financiers belges en Chine …1895–1914* (Brussels 1972) pp. 25–6, citing Belgian consular sources.

Table 9.2. *Geographical distribution of Asia's trade (per cent)*

		1883		1913	
		to the West	to Asia	to the West	to Asia
China	exports	76	17	56	49
	imports	47	51	56	42
Japan	exports	80	18	47	50
	imports	71	29	44	53
S.E. Asia	exports	58	26	52	41
	imports	57	35	56	39
India	exports	68	26	63	27
	imports	85	13	75	22

Source: K. Sugihara, 'Patterns of Asia's Integration into the World Economy 1880–1913' in W. Fischer, R. M. McInnis and J. Schneider, eds., *The Emergence of a World Economy* (Wiesbaden 1986).

the trade of the West increased three times over the period and that of Britain doubled. Such broad orders of magnitude, though valuable as a guide to trends in trade, offer no real guidance to consumer preferences or the response of those who supplied them. They show growing opportunity but cannot measure entrepreneurs' awareness of it or capacity to meet it.

On consumer preference in oriental markets we now have the penetrating work of Dr Kawakatsu of Tokyo. His analysis of the main British export commodity, cottons, shows that the quality of British goods was superior and the price much lower than the nearest equivalent Japanese product. His conclusion is broadly supported by other Japanese scholars.[5] Nevertheless, British cottons failed to penetrate eastern Asia to any significant extent despite Lancashire's eager expectations. One reason is that Lancashire mills concentrated on the finer yarn counts and fabrics for which there was little *popular* demand in this huge market. The coarser yarns and thick texture fabrics were the speciality of Bombay mills whose output was deliberately made to compliment that of Lancashire rather than compete with it. This complementarity extended back to the source of supply as the Indian mills processed locally grown short-staple cottons while the Lancashire industry was founded and based on the long-staple variety grown in the US and West Indies. The Chinese were accustomed to the thick cotton cloth made from low-count yarns while Japanese preference was very similar. Consequently the Japanese textile industry not only survived the onslaught of western technology but home-made goods maintained a preference in the vast Chinese market. Lancashire recognised the potential of the Chinese market as early as the 1830s but the vision never materialised.

From this basic analysis of the market situation we may turn to the implications for British traders. The traditional British export to India from the early years of the nineteenth century was the Lancashire piece goods that had first imitated then superseded the best Indian products. The very real difficulties of extending the trade further east only slowly emerged and the Treaty Port system confined exports to China to a few channels. The Japanese were quick to learn western technology and used it to take the initiative in their 'local' markets.

Early in the century British traders in the Far East had it all their own way, as a letter from an American merchant in Singapore reminds us. In 1836 he wrote to his London merchant banker:

England furnishes the greater part of European articles such as Long Ells, Red cloth, cotton fabrics, Iron and Ironmongery as they cannot be imported from the Continent at as low prices. Indeed except on American Brown Shirtings & Jeans which are in great demand, G.B. may be considered to monopolise the supplying of this market with all European manufactures and these of the cheaper sorts respectively. Sales are made payable in Spanish Dollars, on delivery or at a credit not exceeding three months... The Commissions charged by British Houses here are five per ct,

---

[5] H. Kawakatsu, 'International Competition in Cotton Goods in the late Nineteenth Century: Britain versus India and East Asia', in ibid. T. Nakaoka, 'The Role of Domestic Technical Innovation in Foreign Technology Transfer: the Case of the Japanese Cotton Textile Industry', *Osaka City University Economic Review*, XVIII (1982).

on Sales, two and a half on remittance and other charges which in the aggregate make as totals sums of ten per cent...Bills on London may always be had at usually 4/6 p ct, for 6 mths, sight, and as there are constantly ships on the berth for London, Liverpool and Glasgow, produce finds a ready conveyance to those places...

However this pre-eminence was clearly slipping within a generation. Professor Sugiyama of Tokyo has drawn attention to the imperial factor in the negative sense that he has identified the consequences of mere peripheral contact with great markets like those of China and Japan. The Treaty Port system, he writes:

Far from promoting and protecting the activities of Western merchants... acted as a non-tariff barrier to prevent their economic penetration. In both China and Japan, well-developed markets already existed with their own commercial credit and distribution networks. Indigenous merchants controlled the trade and distribution of goods for both selling and buying and it was very difficult for complete outsiders to enter into or develop the market.

This goes a long way towards explaining the resilience of the Japanese to the western economic onslaught, but says nothing of the rapid advance of German merchants in the Far East. Indeed Sugiyama, though seemingly an Anglophile, adds that the marketing of British goods was 'also hampered by the inflexibility of the agency house system'. However Dr Jenkins, in a paper on West Riding woollens in Japan, develops the point by quoting a contemporary (1886) Tokyo report that many British merchants were 'content to work along the old lines and do not seem to keep up with all the progressive movements in Japan, and thus find themselves at a disadvantage in business transactions with the Japanese'. It was this conservatism that also gave German competitors the opportunity to take an increasing share of the market, much to the jealousy and annoyance of the established British interests. A handful of continental firms in the East attained the capitals of typical British firms, for instance Carlowitz & Co. with £300,000 (1905) and Volkart Bros. with £400,000 (1913). The whole issue of British mercantile performance in the Far East seems to focus on the organisation and entrepreneurial qualities of the agency houses, the form of enterprise born and fostered in British India.[6]

The leading British agency house operating in China was undoubtedly Jardine Matheson who from the 1840s were active in

---

[6] S. Sugiyama, 'Textile marketing in East Asia', *Textile History*, XIX (1988).

the piece goods trade.[7] In what might be seen as the great period of opportunity before the Japanese imbibed western technology, Jardine Matheson's profits were in the doldrums. The 1860s, 1870s and 1880s, far from being a golden age for the 'princely hong', were a period when their fortunes were at a nadir and in 1892 even their closest friends could find few kind words for them.[8] Jardine Matheson was closely related by family ties and trading and financial interests to Jardine Skinner, who concentrated on India and grew much faster in this period if the estimates assembled in Table 9.4 can be accepted.[9] Certainly the British firms who ran the tea plantations in India did much better in this period. It is significant that in the 1880s Jardine Mathesons found it necessary to form a shipping cartel with their traditional rivals Swires, for the need to protect limited profits had become paramount.[10]

A logical British response might have been to have invested in Bombay cotton mills and directed the output to the Chinese market but in fact, following the crisis of 1870, this was an area largely taken over by Indian enterprise, with British merchants apparently content to control the cotton trade with the West.[11] Only a handful of British agency houses were interested in Indian cotton mills (at one time or another Sassoons, Finlays, Greaves, Cotton & Co. and Binnys) and these seem to have concentrated on the quality and 'high-tech' (ring spinning) end of the market. In 1914 only 15 out of the 95 cotton mills in Bombay were in European hands and Greaves, Cotton & Co., whose capital was only about £0·5m., were said to control a dozen of them.[12] Two or three mills at Madras, the minor Indian centre, were controlled by Binnys. The British agency houses formed a sort of élite cousinhood in the Far East and it seems probable that Jardine Matheson's disappointing results were well marked by them. In other words, the lack of interest in manufacturing for the Chinese market and its Japanese 'overspill' looks more like sensible

---

[7] E. Lefevour, *Western Enterprise in Late Ch'ing China... 1842–95* (Harvard 1968) Ch. 2. John McMaster, *Jardines in Japan 1859–1867* (Groningen 1966).

[8] See Appendix pp. 282–3. Jardine Skinner MSS, Guard Books No. 1, 29 Mar. 1892. Cf. S. Marriner and F. E. Hyde, *The Senior*, p. 86.

[9] Unfortunately there is no comparable data for other firms. Jardines' principal rivals were Swires, whose results in the China shipping trade look better: S. Marriner and F. E. Hyde, *The Senior* pp. 75, 84–9.

[10] H. A. Antrobus, *History of the Assam Co.* (Edinburgh 1957) pp. 407–12. Records of James Warren & Co. (the Planters' Stores). S. Marriner and F. E. Hyde, *The Senior*, Chs. 4, 5.

[11] M. Vicziany, 'The Cotton Trade and the Commercial Development of Bombay 1855–75', Ph.D. thesis, London 1975. Ch. 5.

[12] D. Kumar, ed., *Cambridge Economic History of India* II (1983) p. 579.

Table 9.3. *Cotton mill agencies classified by ethnic groups. Bombay 1895–1925*

Communities	1895		1915		1925	
	Agencies	Mills	Agencies	Mills	Agencies	Mills
Parsis	15	22	14	25	13	22
Hindus	27	30	11	18	17	19
Mohamedans	4	4	7	11	3	15
Jews	1	8	5	17	3	14
Europeans	3	6	3	12	5	11
Totals	50	70	40	83	41	81
European share	6%	8·6%	7·5%	14·5%	12·2%	13·6%

Source: S. M. Rutnagur, *Bombay Industries: the Cotton Mills* (Bombay 1927) p. 54.

and well-informed strategy than lethargy. Conceivably UK merchants were restrained by their Indian creditors, the Parsi merchants who owned most of the Bombay mills (Table 9.3).

Both Indian and Japanese scholars have blamed the shortcomings of the Bombay cotton industry on the agency house system. Professor Kiyokawa, who has made the closest analysis of the desultory performance of Bombay cotton, blames poor technical education in middle management, and directors whose main aim was 'to employ cheaper managers and masters [supervisors] without themselves understanding a bit of textile technology'. The Parsi and Hindu merchant owners, that is to say, were interested in early profits rather than long-term investment benefit, and several paid the price for the short-sightedness in bankruptcy or gaol sentences. There is no reason to take exception to this indictment but on present evidence we must distance the British houses from it. Indeed, as Kiyokawa recognises, the agency houses involved in the cotton industry were the principal innovators in India: Greaves, Cotton & Co. with ring spinning, Binnys with automatic looms and Finlays with electric drive, to mention only a few key developments.[13]

[13] T. Kiyokawa, 'Technical Adaptations and Managerial Resources in India: A Study of the Experience of the Cotton Industry', *The Developing Economies* (Tokyo), XXI (1983) esp. pp. 130–1. This source does not name the British owners; such details are available in the *Indian Industrial Commission Report*, XIX (1919) pp. 204–7 and in Greaves, Cotton & Co., *A Century of Progress* (Bombay 1959) pp. 6–7.

In the final analysis, the objectionable feature of the agency house system was that the managing agents took a commission determined by output or sales rather than company profits. The notion of a commission based on profits was introduced by Tatas (the leading Parsi merchant house) in the 1870s and Greaves, Cotton & Co. in the 1880s, but was slow to find general acceptance.[14] The position of Greaves must however have been a significant force for change, for before World War I 97 per cent of cotton textile machinery imported into India came from Britain, and the firm were Indian agents, first for Platt Bros. (1870–80), then for Howard & Bullough, two of the leading Lancashire machine makers of the period. Some other agency houses were technical innovators in other sectors of the Indian economy, for instance Steel Bros. in rice milling and Martins in the iron and steel industry.[15]

The leading work in Japanese on the agency houses is still Kenji Koike's *On the Managing Agency System* (1979). From the point of view of the present book the value of Koike's work is marginal because his earliest data on firms refer only to the period of World War I, which is where our story ends. Nevertheless, his tabulations have the merit of showing that the leading British agency houses in India and Malaysia not only survived but continued to grow through the difficult interwar years, when trade with Japan intensified (Tables 9.5 and 9.6). No doubt the houses were sheltered by the Empire as well as the legal advantages of the agency house system, and the assets of the German houses were sequestrated at the opening of World War I. But it is worth emphasising that the British houses must not be placed in the same category as the Indian houses that saw such a high turnover and were deservedly associated in the Indian mind with exploitation and inefficiency.[16]

Koike's most stringent criticisms are reserved for those who would treat the agency houses as a homogeneous system, and rightly so, for in the post-imperial period Indian historians have too often written almost as if the system was some debilitating oriental disease with

[14] S. Yonekawa, 'Public Cotton Spinning Companies and their Managerial Characteristics 1870–1890: A Comparative Study of Four Countries', *Hitotsubashi Journal of Commerce and Management* XXI (1986) pp. 77–82.

[15] Robert Kirk and Colin Simmons, 'Lancashire and the Equipping of the Indian Cotton Mills: A Study of Textile Machinery Supply 1854–1939', *Salford Papers in Economics* No. 6, 1981, pp. 17, 27. India Office Library MSS, Indian Industrial Commission Confidential Inspection Notes 1916–18, pp. 24–6, 72–4. See also H. E. W. Braund, *Calling to Mind. An Account of the first 100 years of Steel Bros. & Co.* (1975) p. 39.

[16] Kenji Koike, *Keiei Dairi Seido Ron* (Tokyo 1979) (*On the Managing Agency System*).

Table 9.4. *Capital of the leading British agency house group, Jardine Matheson and Jardine Skinner (£m.)*

	JM	JS	total
1848	1·41	0·10	1·51
1860	3·00	0·66	3·66
1870	2·17	0·76	2·93
1880	1·34	0·99	2·33
c. 1890	1·70	1·34	3·04

Source: Jardine Matheson: Appendix, pp. 282–3.

Jardine Skinner: the JS Archive in Cambridge Univ. Library contains no accounts but occasional figures for capital are mentioned in the correspondence, in particular £100,000 in 1848 and £1·34m. in 1890. The other figures are interpolated between these two following the path of JM's profits; they are therefore crude estimates which for the years between 1848 and 1899 may err on the low side.

Table 9.5. *Growth of British agency houses in India 1916–39*
(nos. of agencies + capital controlled, in mn. rupees)

| agency house | 1916 | | 1939 | |
	nos.	value	nos.	value
Tata	7	60·2	9	216·3
Birds and Heilgers	26+8	33·0 +9·6	30	56·3
Gillanders Arbuthnot	9	40·0	16	36·5
Killick Nixon	10	38·4	13	63·7
Andrew Yule	36	28·6	51	68·0
Martin Burn	15	22·6	28	102·5
McLeod	17	17·5	17	22·5
Jardine Skinner	15	15·9	13	25·2
Macneill Barry	8	10·3	12	32·0
Shaw Wallace	17	9·0	17	11·0
Begg Dunlop	12	6·6	15	16·3
Duncan	13	5·4	25	19·2
Octavius Steel	12	4·5	23	13·2
Williamson Magor	10	4·8	14	7·0
James Finlay	3	3·1	8	17·2

Source: Kenji Koike, *Keiei Dairi Seido Ron (On the Managing Agency System)* (Tokyo 1979) pp. 72–3, based on the *Investors India Year Book,* 1917, 1939–40 and other sources.

Table 9.6. *Growth of British agency houses in Malaysia, 1913–1940*
(agencies + acreage controlled in 10,000s acres; the first figure is the total
acreage owned, the second the acreage planted)

	1913		1940	
	nos	acreage	nos.	acreage
Barlow	31	8·3; 4·7	21	7·8; 6·0
Cumberbatch	27	3·8; 2·6	67	13·4; 11·7
Whittall	27	6·1; 3·1	29	5·6; 4·8
Harrisons & Crosfield	26	10·5; 4·4	78	39·3; 25·6
F. W. Barker	24	7·6; 2·6		
Guthrie	25	15·7; 4·7	33	30·4; 21·4
Boustead	22	8·1; 3·8	53	20·1; 15·7
Sime Darby	12	2·0; 1·1	34	11·1; 9·5
Kennedy	9	1·9; 1·3	29*	5·9; 4·6

*incorporating Burkill.
Source: K. Koike op. cit. p. 141.

uniform symptoms endemic to the British business community at large. But having recognised the variety and flexibility characteristic of the species, it must be admitted that some part of the indictment still sticks. Undoubtedly the power and persistence of the British agency houses was at least partly due to the legal fiction of agency. In reality, the agency houses were not agents at all but private partnerships that contrived to control public companies by the device of using the prestige of their name and the British legal system to have permanent control written into the articles of association of various companies. In Malaysia and Burma their economic power was more to do with vast land ownership (plantations) that followed imperial control (Table 9.6). Where shareholders had a free hand (as in the Finlay case cited in the last chapter) they were ready to protest management inadequacy, but it happened all too rarely; company A.G.M.s were invariably formalities.[17]

It also remains true that, while technical leadership was recruited in Dundee, the coalfields and elsewhere in Britain, top management continued to be overwhelmingly oriented to trade and finance and resistant to technical expertise at the highest levels (Table 9.7). In

---

[17] According to Sir Alec Ogilvie, a former head of Andrew Yule & Co., this remained true to the period when most of the old agency houses disappeared in the 1960s (conversation with the author, Dec. 1987).

Table 9.7. *Professional qualifications of cotton mill directors in Bombay in*
1925

	Agency directors	Outside directors	Total directors	Percentage of all directors
Merchants	86	63	149	85·1
Technical	7	4	11	6·3
Lawyers	3	12	15	8·6
Totals	96	79	175	100·0

Source: S. M. Rutnagur, op. cit., pp. 249, 257.

the late nineteenth century most of the houses whose histories we
know were completely controlled by martinets like Sir Alexander
Muir (Finlays), Sir David Yule (Andrew Yule & Co.), Sir James
MacKay (Mackinnon, Mackenzie & Co.), Sir Ernest Cable (Birds),
Sir John Anderson (Guthries) and William Keswick (Jardine
Matheson). In most cases their families seem to have maintained
control down to the early 1960s. Long survival was the consequence
of a subtle combination of factors, some of which are outlined in the
last chapter, but if one were compelled to chose the most important
single factor, it might be the tradition of short careers and early
retirement from service in the tropics, which regularly made
opportunities for ambitious, loyal and hardworking young men.

　　The long resistance to the entry of the indigenous population
(Indians, Malays etc.) to the upper echelons of management only
crumbled after Indian independence in 1948. The exact position at
the end of our period was recorded by the Indian Industrial Census
in 1911 (Table 9.8). It appears that British and indigenous enterprise
kept to their separate paths, particularly when one takes into
account specialisms within an industry like that in cotton. As late as
1946, just two years before independence, the leading British agency
house Andrew Yule & Co., took a case as far as the Privy Council to
maintain complete control of their so-called agencies.[18] The British
agency houses were evidently most tenacious in keeping their power
but less far-sighted when it came to such other long-term
considerations as sponsorship of technical education, recruitment of
meritocracy, racial equality and genuine competition. But then,
those were scarcely the values the Raj had stood for.

[18] Information from Sir Alec Ogilvie; I have not traced this legal case.

Table 9.8. *The share of Indian and British ownership in factories in India, 1911*

	number of factories	Companies of which directors are		
		European	Indian	both
Cotton mills	168	14	98	25
Tea plantations	927	681	32	0
Jute mills	50	59	0	0
Collieries	331	133	17	26
Cotton presses	631	18	180	14
Jute presses	109	50	16	0

Source: N. Z. Ahmed, 'Some Aspects of the History of British Investments in the Private Sector of the Indian Economy 1875–1914', M.Sc. Econ. thesis, L.S.E., 1955, p. 37. The smaller group of private firms has been omitted as the agency houses characteristically limited their liability by operating through companies.

THE BRITISH AND GERMANS IN SOUTHERN AFRICA

The structure of mercantile enterprise in southern Africa differed from that in India and the Far East in a number of ways. There were a handful of German houses active in Calcutta, Singapore and other oriental ports but they were scarcely of any consequence compared with the British presence. An Indian writer employed by one of the British agency houses maintained that there were as many as 30,000 Germans in Calcutta in 1900, but if this is true the men were there as clerks rather than entrepreneurs.[19] In Cape Colony, by contrast, there was a large non-British trading group active from the earliest years. From the 1840s to the 1870s, Mosenthal Bros. of Port Elizabeth and Cape Town emerged as the strongest house, with Lippert Bros. not far behind. The Mosenthals came from Hesse where the family had been active as Court Jews while Lipperts were based in Hamburg.[20] One explanation of the success of such houses is the settlement of German soldier farmers in the Eastern Cape, several of whom became agents of Mosenthals, Lipperts and their

[19] Clwyd R. O., Glynne-Gladstone MSS G–G 2744; M. N. Mookerjee, *Private Diary for…Gillanders Arbuthnot & Co.* (privately printed, Calcutta 1900) p. 23. No doubt the estimate is much exaggerated, but it is significant that the firm (which belonged to H. N. Gladstone, eldest son of the Prime Minister) should accept and print it.
[20] D. Fleischer and A. Caccia, *Merchant Pioneers. The House of Mosenthal* (Johannesburg 1984) pp. 38–40.

British competitors as up-country store keepers. However, the more important factor was that Mosenthals themselves ran a chain of country stores in the early years, and such stores were the very life blood of the early settler economies. In this matter at least, the farming economies of the Cape, Natal and the Transvaal were more akin to the economies of Latin America studied by Platt than the already established mercantile networks of India and China.

The Mosenthals moved to London in 1835 and opened their first store in Cape Town in 1837. In the early years they sold drapery, hosiery, ironware, cutlery, hardware, glassware, stationery and jewellery and in 1840 extended to pedigree sheep. Purchases were mainly wool and ostrich feathers. Branches were opened in small towns in the Eastern Cape which was sheep rearing country and still very much a frontier economy. Storekeeping involved the granting of credit to customers, so that Mosenthals soon found themselves financing the wool trade by granting long-term credits to farmers.[21] When the Kimberley diamond fields were opened up in the late 1870s, initially by local (Cape Colony and Natal) enterprise and capital, it was but a short step to financing this enterprise; indeed the earliest discovery of a giant stone was made on an advance by Mosenthals.[22] Rather less is known about Lipperts because the business went bankrupt in 1883, but the pattern was evidently similar to that of Mosenthals, beginning with the migration of one of the family to the Cape in the early 1840s. After running frontier stores in the wool economy for some years they moved into diamonds and banking before the crash.[23]

The grip of the various merchants on the economy of southern Africa can be judged from the difficulty that the Standard Chartered Bank, the most successful imperial bank operating in the area, found in penetrating the country areas. The General Manager in Cape Town wrote to his London directors in 1870 that the branches were being instructed to advance up to 75 per cent current values but he did not expect to obtain much business on this basis 'as the farmers are too much in the hands of the storekeepers to whom they owe money, and the storekeepers in turn are in the power of the

---

[21] D. Fleischer and A. Caccia, *Merchant Pioneers*, p. 122. S. Dubow, *Land, Labour and Merchant Capital... the Cape 1852–72* (Cape Town 1982) pp. 25–6.

[22] Standard Bank Archives, Johannesburg (hereafter SBA), General Manager (Cape Town) to London Office (hereafter GM/LO) 31 Mar. 1867.

[23] *Dict. S. African Biog.* IV, article on Edward Lippert; SBA Inspection Reports (hereafter Insp. Rep.), Cape Town 1880. GM/LO 29 July 1870, 27 June 1879, 13 Sept. 1884.

merchants'.[24] The Standard Bank began in 1864 with a nominal capital of £1·0m., but Mosenthal's capital of half-a-million (1876) was already the equal of the typical City merchant bank operating at this period. The next largest merchant house was possibly Malcomess & Co., which had numerous stores but focussed on King William's Town, the centre of the German community. Their capital was £400,000 in 1896, though this may have been boosted by sale of property in Johannesburg. The largest firm of British origin in Cape Colony at this time was probably Blaine, MacDonald & Co. with £200,000; Lipperts were thought to be worth £80,000 in 1880.[25]

By the time that diamonds and gold were being discovered in South Africa, some agents and former agents of the great merchant houses were in command of considerable capitals. Two examples come from Mosenthals. Lilienfeld Brothers of Port Elizabeth, who were cousins of Mosenthals, were still in the store trade in 1876 when their capital was estimated by the Standard Bank at £100,000, plus the facility of settlers' deposits. 'Some of the wealthier Boers have for years been in the habit of depositing money with them at I believe six per cent interest', the Bank reported.[26] For another such firm, Teich Brothers of Philips Town, we have a very revealing balance sheet for 1882:

Assets		Liabilities	
Property in Philipstown	£8,000	To A. Mosenthal & Co.	£30,000
Merchandise	6,000	To customers	
Live stock	10,000	[deposits?]	3,000
Bonds, shares, cash	5,000	Partners' capital:	
Outstanding debts	28,000	Herman Teich	
Rietput branch	10,000	Hugo Teich	21,000
		Reserve	13,000
	67,000		67,000

[24] SBA GM/LO 14 May 1870.
[25] SBA Insp. Reps., Port Elizabeth, July 1876 (Mosenthal), East London Jan 1886, July 1896 (Malcomess), Kimberley Mar. 1879 (Blaine). W. H. Worger, 'The Making of a Monopoly: Kimberley and the South African Diamond Industry 1870–95', Ph.D. thesis, Yale 1982, p. 46 (Lippert).
[26] SBA Insp. Rep., Hope Town, May 1875, Aug. 1876. Mosenthals had sold their Hope Town store to Martin and Gustav Lilienfeld in 1861: D. Fleischer and A. Caccia, *Merchant Pioneers* pp. 214–16.

In this instance, which may be fairly typical, half the capital of the company was provided by a great merchant house and by local depositors. In both cases outside connections and local confidence were crucial to the storekeeper.[27]

When diamonds and gold were discovered the German presence was reinforced by new arrivals. Among the well-known names of the pioneer years, Mosenthals appointed Anton Dunkelsbuhler to represent them at Kimberley, Lipperts sent their cousin Alfred Beit, and Jules Porges (a German Jew originally from Prague) came with Julius Wernher. Other early arrivals included the future London merchant bankers Sigismund Neumann and Erlanger.[28] All were trading in diamonds and company shareholdings, though Mosenthals conducted the biggest share of the trade. In the numerous reminiscences and records that were published in later years, Rhodes was the only one to insist that he was a 'digger', but his partner C. D. Rudd was previously a country storekeeper, though with much less capital than those just used for illustration.[29]

The subsequent importance of the German group can be measured in the composition of the syndicate of diamond merchants that purchased the output of the De Beers monopoly. The group of dealers early in 1890 were Beit (25%), Barnatos (20%), Joseph Bros. (10%), Dunkelsbuhler (now independent) (10%), H. J. King (10%), Gervers (2.5%) and Hertz (2.5%). The first two names and Dunkelsbuhler are familiar, Barnato was an East End (London) Jewish dealer whose meteoric career in South Africa ended in suicide in 1894. King is the only British surname in the list. However, it is important to add that the syndicate was operating through the London market (rather than any continental base) and the Mosenthals family had now made London their home. During the next few years a few small firms were admitted to small shares, but most of the production was taken by three or four great merchants. In 1913–14 these were Wernher Beit & Co. (30%), Barnato Bros. (37%), Dunkelsbuhler (10%) and Mosenthals (12.5%); the former German houses were still taking more than half between them.

[27] SBA Insp. Rep., Hope Town, May 1875, Aug. 1876.
[28] T. Gregory, *Ernest Oppenheimer and the Economic Development of Southern Africa* (Oxford 1962) p. 47. SBA Insp. Reps. Kimberley, June 1875, Dec. 1877.
[29] SBA Insp. Rep., Kimberley, Dec. 1877. Rudd's capital was only £1,000 at this time as an earlier venture had ended in bankruptcy; in 1877 Rhodes was described as a 'contractor' engaged to dry out mines and worth £3,000. Clearly neither were in the same league as the greater or lesser merchants.

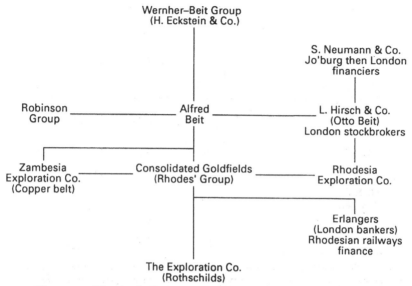

Figure 9.1. The Anglo-German financial connection in South Africa.

Neumann presented the earliest effective challenge to the syndicate by buying diamonds from newly opened Transvaal sources in 1903.[30] The complex Anglo-German financial connection on the Rand goldfield is illustrated in Figure 9.1.

There were indeed so many Germans that flocked to Kimberley and the Rand that the journalist Louis Cohen maintained in his *Reminiscences* that the 'principal company promoters and share producers' in Johannesburg in the early years were 'mostly Germans', while a partner of the leading gold mining firm on the Rand (Wernher Beit) maintained that German capital was critical to the development of the region:

> It was never out of Rhodes' mind that it was [Alfred] Beit's money, and the money interests that Beit could 'influence', that were the chief props of the diamond industry. He realised that Beit's following among the German, Austrian and French bankers was very strong, and that through these sources almost unlimited capital was at Beit's command.

Kubicek, in a close study of these years, reckoned that by 1890 there was probably more German capital invested in South African gold mining shares than by British investors, though this interest was

[30] SBA GM/LO, 13 Feb. 1890. Colin Newbury, 'The Origins and Function of the London Diamond Syndicate 1889–1914', *Bus. Hist.*, XXIX (1987).

Table 9.9. *Britain and continental shareholding in the Rand mining companies, April 1900*

Group	Market valuation	British shareholding valuation	%
Wernher Beit	£73·75m.	£57·53m.	78
Consolidated Gold Fields	38·80	36·86	95
J. B. Robinson	16·43	13·64	83
Barnato	8·83	8·47	96
Farrar	13·38	10·30	77
Neumann	11·14	8·80	79
G. & L. Albu	5·30	1·59	30
A. Goerz	6·15	1·85	30
Sundries	14·57	13·40	92
	188·35	152·44	81

Source: Barlow Rand Archives, Johannesburg, HE 305, Private Notes on Companies and Syndicates. The survey by F. Eckstein was based on careful analysis of the shareholders' registers. It is reported with approval in Standard Bank Archives, General Managers' reports, 8 Aug. 1900.

gradually reduced.[31] Edward Lippert, backed by President Kruger, increased contemporary British paranoia by starting a National Bank in the Transvaal in 1896 explicitly to strengthen Dutch and German interests there. However by 1900, when we have the first exact information, British firms and investors were evidently so well ahead of the German firms on the Rand (Goerz and Albu) that it is difficult to suppose that they were ever anything else but in the lead (Table 9.9). Even Alfred Beit, notwithstanding his close financial connections on the Continent, had to cultivate links with the City.[32]

This, of course, raises the question of definition of nationality as Wernher, Beit and Neumann were earlier identified as of German origin. In 1888 Wernher Beit was established as a London-based investment group with F. Eckstein deputed to take charge of the

---

[31] L. Cohen, *Reminiscences of Johannesburg* (1924) pp. 46, 99, 104. E. Rosenthal, *On Change through the Years* (Johannesburg 1968) p. 224. J. B. Taylor, *A Pioneer Looks Back* (1939) p. 123. R. V. Kubiceck, *Economic Imperialism ... The Case of South African Gold Mining Finance 1886–1914* (Durham, N. C., 1979) p. 153.

[32] SBA GM/LO 6 June 1888, 26 Aug. 1896. Lippert was evidently exploiting Boer anti-British sentiments in an endeavour to restore his family fortune. Roy Macnab, *Gold their Touchstone. Goldfields of South Africa 1887–1987* (Johannesburg 1987) p. 35 suggests that Beit needed Rhodes for his London links.

firm's Johannesburg operation. Wernher bought a famous English country house (Luton Hoo) while Beit became Rhodes's most fervent admirer and imperial disciple. Neumann increasingly focussed on London and opened an office there (Neumann, Lubeck & Co.) soon after Wernher Beit. The leading stockbrokers for South African mining shares (or 'Kaffirs') were L. Hirsch & Co., who were established in London in 1887. The partners included Alfred Beit's younger brother, Otto, and Neumann's brother Ludwig; another stockbroker in this line was Singer & Friedlander whose junior partner had been with Neumann on the Rand. In other words, the most successful group of German–Jewish merchants and speculators very quickly translated their loyalty to London where they became rich members of the cosmopolitan community and won a strong following of British shareholders.[33]

There was of course always a strong contingent of British at Kimberley and on the Rand. Rhodes (Consolidated Gold Fields) needs no further comment except to stress that his partner (Rudd) came of the Cape mercantile tradition; Robinson had been a Cape wool merchant, Barnato an East End trader, and there was also Farrar, who emigrated as representative of his family engineering firm. But despite Rhodes's alleged anti-semitism, the men were not separated from the German–Jewish cousinhood. Rhodes enjoyed the admiration, not only of Beit, but also of Erlanger and Mosenthal, and the financial support (despite some conflict) of Rothschilds. Farrar's financial activities were fuelled by such London stockbrokers as Mocatta and Helbert, Wagg & Co. A large part of Robinson's shares were sold in Paris at one period.[34] The high risk of mining on the Rand necessitated a wide diversification of shareholdings.

The situation in South Africa, that is to say, was more complex than that postulated by Professor Platt and Charles Jones on the basis of their research in Latin America. British imperialism certainly conferred significant advantages on white developers, particularly in

[33] A. P. Cartwright, *The Corner House. The Early History of Johannesburg* (Cape Town 1965) Ch. XIII. Sir P. Fitzpatrick, *South African Memories* (1932), pp. 29–37, *Dict. S. African Biog.* articles on Sir S. Neumann and Sir Otto Beit. R. V. Kubiceck, *Economic Imperialism* p. 155.

[34] Leo Weinthal, *Memories, Mines and Millions...the Life of Sir Joseph Robinson* (1920), pp. 33, 45, 58. S. Jackson, *The Great Barnato* (1970). R. V. Kubiceck, *Economic Imperialism* pp. 129, 133 (Farrar). Leo Weinthal, ed., *The Story of the Cape of Cairo Railway and River Route 1887–1922* I, pp. 638, 641, 653–5 (Erlanger). D. Fleischer and A. Caccia, *Merchant Pioneers* p. 197 (H. Mosenthal). S. D. Chapman, 'Rhodes and the City of London: another view of Imperialism', *Historical Journal* XXVIII (1985).

respect of local government institutions, the mining boards, the press and the recruitment and employment of labour, but German emigrés enjoyed such rights as much as those from Britain, the Cape and Natal did.[35] When Johannesburg became a financial satellite of London, the continentals found no difficulty in changing into London-based international houses, much as other successful merchants had been relocating in London throughout the century. There had been no separation of white financial interests in Johannesburg and there was none in London – except, of course, between the successes and failures. British imperialism and the Pax Britannica created a congenial area for *all* European capitalist enterprise, and in some sectors Asian enterprise was as active commercially as British. It was the exclusive advantages for long conferred by the East India Co. in India and China that made those vast countries different from other areas of British settlement and sovereignty.

This is not to suggest that wealthy continentals were immediately absorbed into the British establishment. Bismarck's imperialist ambitions in southern Africa and Kruger's policy to keep the Transvaal free of the British, if necessary with Dutch or German support, inevitably created tensions and prejudices which were exacerbated by widespread fraud during the 'Kaffir booms' and by the Jameson Raid.[36] Alfred Beit was eventually the most successful entrepreneur on the Rand but when he arrived in Kimberley in 1877 the Standard Bank noted 'Mr Beit's name is of little or no value to us.'[37] Neumann's unpleasant reputation in the City was cited in Chapter 7, but this did not prevent him from becoming part of King Edward VII's horse-racing circle and an active member of the Berkeley Synagogue in London.[38] However, the most instructive case study is that of Emile Erlanger & Co., the pioneers of Rhodesian Railways also alluded to in the last chapter. At the time the savage criticisms were made by Kleinworts (the leading accepting house), Neumann's had a capital of £1·0m. or more, Erlangers perhaps £0·5m.[39] It is clear that money did not always buy respect in the City; liquidity, probity and adherence to what were regarded as the

[35] C. Newbury, 'Technology, Capital and Consolidation: the Performance of De Beers Ltd, 1880–89', *Bus. Hist. Rev.* LXI (1987).
[36] D. M. Schreuder, *The Scramble for Southern Africa* (Cambridge 1980).
[37] SBA Insp. Rep. Kimberley, Dec. 1877.
[38] *Dict. S. African Biog*, article on S. Neumann.
[39] Bank of England Discount Office files. SBA Insp. Rep. Johannesburg 1898.

City standards were necessary. On these grounds, Beit won early acceptance, but Erlanger took longer and Neumann never really made it. In the final analysis, the situation was not so different from that in India, where the outstanding successful merchants presently found acceptance at the heart of the Empire. The best-known names are Sassoons (originally Persian Jews) and Tatas (the leading Parsi family), but we should add Rallis, the Greek family who successfully shifted the focus of their trading interests from the Middle East to India in the 1860s and by 1914 were the largest mercantile undertaking there.[40] The Empire offered its successful 'provincials' access to the world's mercantile and financial metropolis, thereby enriching the diversity of talent that had for so long been characteristic of the City of London.

CONCLUSION

Evidence collected from the principal British trading areas, India and South Africa, suggests that the Platt thesis on imperial trade needs modification or refinement in two ways. The concentration of the British on a few sectors of world trade as the century advanced must not be taken as some implicit recognition of economic spheres of interest by other trading nations. In particular, the Germans and the Japanese were active on the periphery of the Empire soon after mid-century and gradually encroached on the growing imperial area. The Germans appear to have benefited from British domination almost as much as the imperial power did, at any rate in South Africa and China. The main thing that restrained a *national* German advance in these areas was that Anglomania won over numbers of leading Germans, not always because they were Jewish. This crucial change of allegiance, not unfamiliar in the annals of the international houses, was most striking in South Africa and in the City of London. During World War I German property was sequestrated, terminating significant German enterprise in both southern Africa and India. Neither the British Empire nor the war had such effects on the Japanese; after the Russo-Japanese War (1905) they benefited increasingly from the focussing of European interests on other parts of the world.

The specifically British institutions connected with mercantile developments were the agency house system and the imperial banks.

[40] See above Chs. 3, 5.

Both had solid virtues which have been acknowledged in this and earlier chapters, but they also had serious limitations which affected opportunities to rival interests. Taken as a whole, the agency houses were slow to exploit the opportunities of industrialisation of India; the British ones were not most culpable but suffered from the consequences of an often inefficient system. The Standard Bank shortly came to dominate banking in South Africa,[41] but, like the domestic system (the so-called 'clearing banks'), the merchant banks and British overseas banks generally, was no exception to this generalisation. On present evidence, there is no reason to suppose that the various imperial banks that were active in India and China drew any closer to a *credit mobilier* concept of banking.[42] The much more active interest of French and German banks in South Africa offered greater security to continental merchants venturing into a new and difficult trading area and made even Rhodes feel vulnerable to continental pressures.

APPENDIX. *Capital and profits of Jardine Matheson & Co., 1836–1891*

	total capital (HK$m.)	net profit (HK$m.)	total capital (£m.)	rate of profit (%)	exchange rate HK$ = 31
1836	6·47	n.d.	1·47	—	—
1837	5·87	0·67	1·33	11·4	4·4
1839	5·76	0·24	1·28	4·2	4·5
1840	7·36	1·04	1·67	14·1	4·4
1846	6·5	n.d.	1·44	—	4·5
1847	4·68	(0·18)	0·98	—	4·8
1848	6·61	0·21	1·41	3·2	4·7
1849	6·00	0·61	1·28	10·2	4·7
1850	5·38	0·40	1·12	7·4	4·8
1851	5·65	0·27	1·22	4·8	4·6
1852	6·2	0·38	1·48	6·1	4·2
1853	6·00	0·32	1·40	5·3	4·3
1854	6·57	0·40	1·64	6·1	4·0
1855	7·61	0·14	1·77	1·8	4·3
1856	8·09	0·87	2·61	10·8	3·1
1857	10·24	1·43	2·93	14·0	3·5
1858	10·89	0·06	3·51	0·6	3·1

[41] SBA GM/LO.
[42] S. D. Chapman, 'Venture Capital and Financial Organisation: London and South Africa in the Nineteenth Century', in Stuart Jones, ed., *Banking and Business in South Africa* (1988). J. W. MacClellan, 'Banking in India and China', *Bankers Mag.* LV (1893).

APPENDIX. (*cont.*)

	total capital (HK$m.)	net profit (HK$m.)	total capital (£m.)	rate of profit (%)	exchange rate HK$ = 31
1859	10·73	0·95	2·82	8·9	3·8
1861	13·29	0·46	3·16	3·5	4·2
1862	12·24	0·97	2·91	7·9	4·2
1863	12·90	0·68	2·87	5·3	4·5
1864	15·08	0·16	3·67	1·1	4·1
1865	16·12	0·05	3·93	0·3	4·1
1866	16·05	0·44	3·73	2·7	4·3
1867	17·09	(0·03)	4·17	—	4·1
1868	14·75	0·13	3·28	0·9	4·5
1869	12·78	(0·20)	2·84	—	4·5
1870	9·77	0·42	2·17	4·3	4·5
1871	7·70	0·30	1·71	3·9	4·5
1872	6·78	0·36	1·47	5·3	4·6
1873	7·18	0·18	1·60	2·5	4·5
1874	7·01	0·25	1·56	3·6	4·5
1875	7·23	0·27	1·54	3·7	4·7
1876	7·49	0·24	1·53	3·2	4·9
1877	9·24	0·46	1·89	5·0	4·9
1878	7·71	0·59	1·54	7·7	5·0
1879	7·69	0·24	1·45	3·1	5·3
1880	7·65	0·44	1·34	5·8	5·7
1881	7·41	0·46	1·37	6·2	5·4
1882	7·81	0·51	1·40	6·5	5·56
1883	8·98	0·24	1·69	2·7	5·3
1884	8·58	0·02	1·62	0·2	5·3
1885	8·28	0·26	1·56	3·1	5·3
1891	8·60	n.d.	1·72	—	5·0
1906	10·02	n.d.	2·00	—	5·0
1910	—	—	2·20	—	—
1913	—	—	2·50	—	—

Sources: Capital: Jardine Matheson Archive, Cambridge University, ledgers (A1/35–75), as tabulated in Mayako Ishii, 'Activities of British Enterprise in China in the Latter Half of the Nineteenth Century', *Socio-Economic History* (Tokyo), XLV (1979), Table 1.

Profits: Jardine Matheson Archive as above, but drawn from data assembled by Lord Blake for his forthcoming history of the firm. The author is indebted to Lord Blake for his generous help. The 1891 figures come from E. Lefevour, *Western Enterprise in Late Ch'ing China* (Harvard 1968) p. 123, those for 1906–1913 from Kleinwort Information Books, Goldman Sachs series, II, p. 2. The last two figures include the paid-up capital (£0·2m and £0·5m.) for Matheson & Co. of London.

Losses are shown in brackets.

PART IV

Conclusions

CHAPTER 10

Performance of British mercantile enterprise

Through the various chapters of this book it has become increasingly clear that the data available are far too patchy to reach any precise conclusions on the quality of British mercantile enterprise in the heyday of the country's overseas trading operations. However, it is possible to make some objective judgements from three angles. The role of ethnic, religious and cultural minorities has been a recurrent topic and some final assessment of their contribution is necessary. Secondly, it is possible to assess mercantile enterprise by comparing its achievements with those of other kinds of overseas marketing operations active in the period such as manufacturers selling directly abroad, free standing companies, exploration companies, and other forms of organisation traced by historians in the course of recent research. Finally, we should make a critical assessment of the one distinctive form of mercantile enterprise that emerged in the period, the managing agency system, in the context of other assessments of British economic performance in the nineteenth century.

COSMOPOLITAN MERCANTILE ENTERPRISE

The achievements of British mercantile enterprise in London and the outports in the eighteenth and nineteenth centuries were undoubtedly a consequence of the rich ethnic and cultural mix. As London superseded Amsterdam the cosmopolitan commercial bourgeoisie shifted to the new metropolis of trade, and as Manchester emerged as the 'metropolis of manufactures' it too attracted an international trading community. In Chapter 1 it was noticed that in London in 1763 more than three-quarters of merchants were of foreign origin or descent. In 1914 twelve out of the twenty leading accepting houses (merchant banks) – the very *crème de la crème* of merchant enterprise – were of foreign origin, and numerous other names in Skinner's *London Banks* were of German, Greek, American and other foreign extraction.[1] In Manchester, as Chapter 5 showed, two-thirds of the capital for the continental trade in 1833 was provided from abroad, evidently for the most part by firms of German and Greek origin, and very largely the former at this early date. At this date, cotton represented some 48·5 per cent of British exports, of which the Continent took 47 per cent,[2] so it is not too much to suggest that the role of the German international houses played a crucial role in sustaining the rapid growth of British textiles during the later decades of the Industrial Revolution. In the middle decades of the century the Middle East succeeded the Continent as an important market, and the large number of Greek traders played a similar role in sustaining the momentum of textile growth. The numbers of American merchants active in Britain was rather less significant, but a few of them were clearly pacemakers – for instance Brown Shipley in the Liverpool cotton trade and transatlantic finance, A. & S. Henry as a Manchester shipping house and A. T. Stewart in both centres. Such evidence as we possess suggests that merchant houses of foreign origin were as well-capitalised as their indigenous British competitors.[3] In the later decades of the century the relative importance of this overseas enterprise *may* have declined as Germany and the USA industrialised, but the evidence is not conclusive for both nationalities were very active in British imperial territories in South Africa and the Far East. German Jews provided much of the enterprise and American engineers much of the engineering expertise on the Rand[4] while Ralli Bros. boasted that they held the premier place in Indian trade: 'neither English nor German firms can compare with its ascendency there,' the biographer of Stephen Ralli claimed in 1902.[5] W. E. Gladstone, one of whose sons headed a leading agency house, was worried about the large numbers of Germans in India.[6]

The numbers of foreign-born merchants were too large and their origins too diverse to venture any overall generalisations about their training, motivation or business ethics. However, it was generally believed that German commercial education was superior to that

[1] S. D. Chapman, *The Rise of Merchant Banking* esp. Chs. 1–3.
[2] R. Davis, *The Industrial Revolution and British Overseas Trade* (Leicester 1979) p. 15.
[3] See above, Chs. 5, 6.   [4] See above Ch. 9.
[5] J. Gennadius, *Sephen A. Ralli* (1902) p. 28.
[6] Clwyd R.O. Glynne–Gladstone MSS 2744, N. M. Mookerjee, *Private Diary* (Calcutta 1900) p. 23.

available in Britain, and some Anglo-German merchants were in the vanguard of the movement to improve technical education in England.[7] The consequences of the neglect of technical education appear most strikingly in India, where the agency houses lost the Chinese market to the Japanese not so long after Japan based its university system on the German model.[8]

However, education was probably less important than motivation. The search for social acceptance is evidently a key to understanding such diverse elements as German Jews, American Puritans and Greek Orthodox settlers. It represented the prime element in the careers of such racial minority leaders as N. M. Rothschild, Joshua Bates of Barings ('the first merchant in London' in 1833) and Stephen Ralli. The English were not exactly intolerant of foreigners and Scots, but social ostracism kept the newcomers struggling for greater wealth and hence recognition.[9]

In the final analysis, what is most important is not the education, culture, religion or aspirations of any particular ethnic group so much as the total social mix and the competition in a great trading centre. London, Manchester, Bradford and other British cities attracted a cosmopolitan mixture of enterprise, experience and connections which was unrivalled anywhere in the world in the Victorian age, and it was the *mélange* of diverse cultures that generated much of the restless energy of British-based trading activity in the period.

One point implicit in this conclusion must be emphasised. Just as it is scarcely realistic to speak of 'British' mercantile enterprise in this period, so also it does scant justice to the facts for historians to write as if there were one predominant culture in London, Liverpool, Manchester, Glasgow and other centres of trade in the period. There were in fact a whole range of competing ethnic and religious cultures. The successful might buy country estates, send their children to public schools, and intermarry with indigenous wealth, but the evidence of this book and other work suggests that such a retreat into 'gentlemanly capitalism' was only one option chosen. Ideologies drawn from other cultures were often cherished to the second and third generations, and prescribed quite different lifestyles

---

[7] E.g. Sir Jacob Behrens, Caesar Czarnikow. [8] See above, Ch. 9.
[9] S. D. Chapman, 'Merchant Ideologies: Alien Cultures in British Commerce in the Nineteenth-Century' (forthcoming article).

and attitudes to business.[10] This brings us to the complex subject of cultures and business behaviour.

ENTERPRISE AND CULTURE

The first half of the nineteenth century is the period of merchant activity on a small scale, with hundreds of commission agents scattered round the world, as Palmerston's surveys of 1842 and 1848 confirmed. The economic stability of the period was gradually attained by the control of strong financial houses (though the crises of 1825, 1836–7 and 1848 paralysed the system for months), and by the trading networks that had been characteristic of European commerce since the middle ages. Some of the strongest merchant houses were based on capital migrating from the Continent and America to take advantage of British leadership in textiles; such were Schunk, Souchay & Co., Ralli Bros. and Brown Shipley, to mention only the wealthiest of the German, Greek and American migrants. Many of the houses that were subsequently to grow to great size, like Rylands, Cookes and Morleys among the home trade houses and Jardine Matheson and Finlays among the agency houses were laying extensive foundations in this period, but others, ultimately just as successful, were not founded until the second half of the century; Czarnikow, Wogau, John Swire & Co., Birds, Duncans, Shaw Wallace and the Planters' Stores & Agency Co. among others did not appear until the 1850s and 1860s.[11]

The second half of the century, and particularly the half century from 1860 to 1914, saw a growth in houses that were able to respond to the opportunities and challenges of the rapid growth of the international economy. Table 10.1 assembles data to illustrate the rapid growth rates and large size attained by some of the most successful concerns. (It is possible to show only a score of firms because financial information is so difficult to obtain, few records having survived.) Numbers of other trading houses are known to have topped £1·0m. capital by 1914: Sassoons, Binny and Yules in India, Mosenthal, Robinson, Rudd and others in South Africa, Knoop, Czarnikow in European trade, and Arthurs, Cookes and Morleys among the home trade houses come easily to mind. To these can be added more dispersed trading enterprises like Marcus Samuel

---

[10] S. D. Chapman, 'Aristocracy and Meritocracy in Merchant Banking', *Brit. Jnl Soc.* xxxvii (1986).   [11] See above, esp. Chs. 3, 4, 5.

Table 10.1. *Capital growth of some leading international merchants c. 1860–c. 1910*

	period	capital growth (£m.)	p.a.(£)
Far Eastern houses			
Jardine Matheson & Co.	1850–1910	1·25–2·20 = 0·95	15,800
James Finlay & Co.	1861–1910	0·2–2·41 = 2·21	45,100
Ralli Bros.	1850–1901	0·5–3·0(+) = 2·5	49,000
John Swire & Co.	1867–1910	0·1–1·43 = 1·33	30,900
Ogilvy, Gillanders & Co.	1875–1910	0·075–0·41 = 0·335	9,600
Harrisons & Crosfield	1863–1910	0·14–0·45 = 0·31	6,600
Latin American houses			
Balfour Williamson & Co.	1884–1912	0·75–2·20+ = 1·25	44,600
Heilbut Symons & Co.	1870–1910	0·07–1·15 = 1·18	29,500
Ross T. Smyth & Co.	1857–1910	0·02–0·3 = 0·28	5,300
Russian houses			
Rodocanachi, Sons & Co.	1860–1911	0·2–0·415 = 0·215	4,215
E. H. Brandt & Co.	1863–1904	0·025–0·75 = 0·725	17,700
Wogau & Co.	1875–1913	0·5–2·2 = 1·7	44,737
Home trade houses			
Thomas Adams & Co.	1865–1910	0·112–0·356 = 0·244	6,778
Bradbury Greatorex & Co.	1868–1910	0·023–0·477 = 0·454	13,757
Foster, Porter & Co.	1871–1910	0·21–0·28 = 0·07	1,750
Fore St Warehouse Co.	1864–1910	0·42–0·435 = 0·393	326
Rylands & Sons	1850–1910	0·10+–3·95 = 3·84(−)	62,951(−)
Pawsons & Leaf	1879/80–1910	0·81–0·414 = −0·333	−5,459
Manufacturer–merchants			
Horrocks, Miller & Co.	1865–1905	0·6–2·0 = 1·4	35,000
Fielden Bros.	1860–1910	0·75–0·13 = 0·62	−12,400
Two outstanding foreign competitor houses			
W. R. Grace & Co., New York	1862–1908	0·036–0·03 = 0·27	5,900
Bunge & Born, Antwerp	1860–1910	0·02–1·8 = 1·78	35,600

Source: Appendix to Chapter 10.

in the oil trade, Dalgetty in Australian wool, Vestey Bros. in the meat trade and Bowrings in Newfoundland fisheries and oil.[12] To make a reasonable comparison, in 1914 only ten merchant banks in London had a capital of £1·om. or more, and only two or three exceeded this by a significant amount.[13] Meanwhile the typical cotton mill, as we noticed in Chapter 6, did not exceed £60,000 capital costs.

Platt's thesis on the concentration of trade on the British Empire (see Introduction and Chapter 9) might lead one to expect that the houses concentrating on British India would produce better results over a period of time than those focussing on non-imperial territories such as Latin America and Russia. Unfortunately the data that it has been possible to collect are not strong enough to prove or disprove this. The most that can be said is that, even among this eminent selection of names, there were impressive and not-so-good results in all sectors; much depended on the qualities of particular entrepreneurs. Moreover, the foreign firms whose performances were often so highly rated in Britain, W. R. Grace & Co. of New York and Bunge & Born of Antwerp, look no better than some of the British-based leaders. In any event, these enterprises were no more American or Belgian than their competitors were British; Grace was grafted on to an Irish stem and had strong financial support from Barings in London, while Bunge & Born was a mixture of German and Dutch enterprise with a major branch in London. Brandts and Wogau were of German origin though based in London. There is only one possible pointer to the benefits of concentrating on Empire. Rallis and Rodocanachis were the most eminent of the Greek houses in London and closely connected by marriage and religion as well as trading interests. Both tried to quit the Russian trade for India in the 1850s but only Rallis succeeded. The ultimate outcome was that the Rallis' growth rate was about ten times that of their cousins. But this does not lead to any firm conclusion as Wogaus did practically as well in the Russian trade as Rallis did in India.

Another approach might suggest that the relatively sheltered and affluent home market offered the best prospects for long-term growth with reasonable security, particularly when it was extended by satellite warehouses in the white colonies. This of course was the strategy of the home trade houses (Chapter 6), and from it John Rylands of Manchester produced the most impressive growth in the

[12] See above, Chs. 8, 9.   [13] S. D. Chapman, *Merchant Banking* pp. 200–1.

list of foremost merchants assembled in Table 10.1. If the evidence was more complete, other well-known home trade houses like Cookes and Morleys of London, Henrys of Manchester and Arthurs of Glasgow would surely appear in the premier league of capital growth (Table 6.3). The London founder of the system, James Morrison, was not only a millionaire himself, but created one of the wealthiest families of the Victorian age. But the growth of the Fore Street Warehouse Co. was minimal after 1864 when Morrison Dillon & Co was incorporated and family investments were diversified. Later, the rise of large-scale retailing and of the ready-made clothing industry provided intensive competition for all the home trade houses so that they had to fight hard to hold their ground. Firms clinging to traditional lines, as Leafs did to fashionable silk goods, might suffer absolute decline; they had to amalgamate with Pawsons in 1893. Others might survive on specialties, as Thomas Adams & Co. did on lace curtains, leading the Nottingham trade. Another response was to invest in ready-made clothing factories and trade. But it was not easy to compete with the Jewish immigrants who took an early grip on the business. The handful of houses that continued pre-eminent – notably Rylands, Morleys, Henrys, Arthurs and perhaps Hitchcock Williams & Co. – were not committed to any common strategy and seemingly had other, less tangible, more personal qualities.

The published histories of the £1·0m. trading houses fail to exhibit evidence of 'gentlemanly capitalism', though most of the books are privately published and written by retired executives or public relations men who, having spent a lifetime promoting the company image, seldom write anything to tarnish its lustre. Fortunately there are company records and confidential bank reports to reveal rather more of the truth. A good performance recorded in the table is that of Ralli Bros. and the worst that of Jardine Matheson. The hagiography of Stephen Ralli, who was the supreme autocrat of Ralli Bros. from 1863 to his death nearly forty years later, records that the principles of the firm included the rule that no partner or employee was allowed 'to lead a life unduly luxurious or extravagant' or to take part 'in any other combination or enterprise whatsoever'. For forty years 'the prestige and interest of the firm absorbed the very soul of the young Stephen Ralli, and filled it with a sort of religious cult. His devotion to work became a veritable passion... he led a dignified and sober life, free from ostentation.' An army of Greek clerks – 3,000 to 4,000 in all – were regulated by 'iron discipline' to maintain dedication to work and austerity in their private lives.[14] From the material assembled on Jardine Matheson in Chapter 7, the contrast with Rallis seems all too clear. The senior partner brought the firm close to bankruptcy in 1890 and in the early years of the century the City still thought them 'highly speculative'. Magniac, the head of Matheson & Co. in London, was supposed to be a very rich man, but 'lived very extravagantly and had his home full of extremely valuable works of art' but died leaving nothing. The heir to the Jardine family fortune in the early years of the century, Sir Robert Jardine, was not brought up in the business and took no active part in it, 'preferring a life of idle pleasure'.[15] There is no hint of any of these failings in the various published histories of the firm. The full financial results (see Appendix to Chapter 9) reveal that after a strong performance in the 1850s and 1860s the firm suffered overall decline until early this century, so that whereas Jardines was much the biggest British merchant house (measured by size of capital) in 1850 and twice the size of Rallis, at the turn of the century Rallis were twice the size of the 'princely hong'.

The strong contrast drawn here between Rallis and Jardine Matheson illustrate the results that could follow from dedication to work and from what might be thought of as late imperial lassitude. But the twentieth-century context, in which Jardines continue to prosper as an international trading house and Rallis have all but disappeared, counsels caution in reaching easy conclusions. A distinction needs to be drawn between business organisation and work ethic on the one side and long-term strategy on the other. In the late nineteenth century Rallis reached the top of the international mercantile league on the basis of the former, while in the twentieth Jardines reasserted their leadership on the foundation of superior long-term strategy founded on policies dating back to the 1870s. Rallis confined themselves to global trade in a limited range of primary products while Jardines defied the generalisations of present-day academic observers to move into agency for manufactured goods and railways. The importation of machinery, tools and industrial equipment was at first catered for by the Engineering Section of Jardines' Import Department, which presently became the Jardine Engineering Corporation. Other successful Far Eastern

---

[14] J. Gennadius, *Ralli* pp. 23, 30. Guildhall Lib. Ralli Bros. MSS 23,834, 'Report on Organisation' (1938).
[15] Guildhall Lib. Kleinwort Information Books, Goldman Sachs II pp. 2–3, 60.

trading houses evolved along similar lines. Rallis clung to its Victorian strategy until 1938, when a management report on the firm's operations in India belatedly urged the development of a trade in engineering and producer goods.[16] Information is too scant to reach hard conclusions, but it is not too fanciful to suppose that Samuel Smith's type of merchant (the chief executive type) gave himself time to socialise, think and indulge in long-term strategic planning while the iron discipline that kept some of the immigrant trading families chained to their desks prevented them from pondering the range of venture capital possibilities. Lack of material prevents further speculation around this idea except to observe that the two firms used as exemplars are not unique manifestations; thus the head of the strategically successful Wallace Bros. and Finlays believed in Bagehot's or Smith's concept while Lord Rothschild apparently spent his life on a treadmill for his blinkered and flagging firm.

It would be a mistake to suppose that the contrasting cultures depicted in these examples were simply the difference between continental and British merchants. There were also striking differences between Nonconformists and those who adhered conventionally to the Church of England. A recent analysis of the thousand or so entries in the *Dictionary of Business Biography* offers a clear demonstration that Nonconformists, taking all the diverse denominations together, continued to be more important in industry, trade and finance than their numbers in society would suggest.[17] In the eighteenth and early nineteenth centuries the Quakers were possibly the most influential Nonconformist denomination in business, particularly the group based in Liverpool. The group were largely schooled and inspired by the leadership of William Rathbone III (1726–89), much as British Jews were later to acknowledge the moral authority of the Rothschilds and Anglo-Greeks the leadership of the Rallis. The Quaker standard was spelt out by James Cropper in 1827:

Remember my dear Sons that power and responsibility *are inseparable*. Too many are looking on wealth and independence as the road to pleasure and enjoyments, now if we consider these the gifts of an all-bountious Creator who is no respecter of persons and who bestows his gifts in greater or less abundance on particular individuals, we shall be satisfied that they are all

---

[16] See above, Ch. 9. [Anon.] *Jardine Matheson & Co., an Historical Sketch* (1960) p. 60. Guildhall Lib. Ralli Bros. MSS 23,834.

[17] D. J. Jeremy, 'Important Questions about Business and Religion in Modern Britain', in D. J. Jeremy, ed., *Business and Religion in Britain* (1988) pp. 16–18.

in trust and for the good of the whole Human family... Let those to whom Riches are intrusted humbly endeavour to do their duty and then trust in the Mercy and Goodness of God.[18]

Quaker service and charity, though widely admired, often prevented the accumulation of large capitals in the firm. William Rathbone IV's dedication to public work reduced the family's trading capital to under £40,000 in 1842 and a new generation had to work hard to rebuild it; by 1872 it had reached £600,000, plus the value of the partnership in Ross T. Smyth & Co. Nevertheless, William V, like his forebears, 'had no taste for personal luxury and a strong sense of the duty of frugality'.[19]

In London a strong mercantile group centred on King's Weigh House Chapel, where Samuel Morley MP and Sir George Williams, both eminent City merchants, were members. Their view of life derived from the evangelical emphasis on divine stewardship of time, talents and money, an ideology that was opposed to any notion of leisured lifestyle. According to Morley's biographer,

The increase of public business did not diminish his commercial activity... it led him to acquire the habit of working and thinking with great rapidity, of economizing every moment, and of allowing himself less frequent leisure, rest and recreation... the increase of wealth and influence and position had not in the least degree altered the simplicity of his life.

He became the *de facto* leader of the Nonconformist interest in Parliament and was prominent in all the Liberal social and political movements of his day. He bought an estate at Tonbridge (Kent) and enjoyed village life, but more in the sense of being the patron of local causes than adopting anything like an aristocratic lifestyle.[20] John Rylands, the greatest Manchester merchant of the Victorian age, was also a prominent Congregationalist and his lifestyle seems to have been akin to Morley's. Not surprisingly, the two men generated home trade houses well ahead of most of their contemporaries.

The Sir George Williams just referred to is now mostly remembered as the founder of the Y.M.C.A., but in the City he was the senior partner of Hitchcock, Williams & Co., one of the foremost City houses in ready-made clothing. Williams' biographer wrote of him: 'he came to London without influence or capital and amassed

---

[18] James Cropper's archives, Tolson Hall, Kendal: letter of 12 Jan. 1827.

[19] S. Marriner, *Rathbones of Liverpool 1845–73* (Liverpool 1961) pp. 5–6. E. F. Rathbone, *William Rathbone. A Memoir* (1905) p. 113.

[20] E. Hodder, *Life of Samuel Morley* (1889) pp. 79, 298. *Dict. Bus. Biog.* IV, article on Morley.

a fortune [but]...he was never so wealthy that his generosity cost him nothing. He spared himself that he might spend on others, living always in the most quiet and simple fashion, utterly devoid of all ostentation or pride of success.'[21] Both Morley's and Williams' leadership in London business circles extended far beyond their own considerable concerns. The 'house of Morley' was said to be a training school for high-class business men while Williams exercised wide influence through the Y.M.C.A. Unfortunately we know rather less about Manchester's most successful merchant–manufacturer, John Rylands, but he was evidently a Chapel man in the mould of Morley and Williams. He bought a country house but never sought to imitate the tastes of the aristocracy, for he 'accepted his work and calling as divine'. Rylands was never a public figure like Morley and Williams, but his huge organisation 'served as a great training school in business method for the founders of other firms', who must have imbibed something of his attitude to business, while his reputation made him a model for Victorian entrepreneurs in the North of England.[22]

The biographical details assembled here cannot pretend to be anything like representative of the whole range of City cultures, but the eminence of the men concerned and the diversity of their ethnic and religious cultures surely serves to make two final points. First, that the major British trading cities of the period were multi-cultural centres whose diverse membership brought new trading contacts, methods, capital and ideologies to the British scene, to the great benefit of the whole economy. Secondly, the struggle for recognition by foreign and Nonconformist trading families brought much hard work, discipline and competition to British overseas trade, which again must have brought benefit to the whole community.

The contrast drawn here is certainly a stark one, but by no means unique in the experience of the City of London. While the distractions of a third-generation Baring brought the City's most prestigious gentile merchant bank to insolvency, the company promoter H. O. O'Hagan worked hard behind the facade of his country house to create the foremost business in his specialism. Moreover, it is possible by tabulating data on acceptances to demonstrate that the Anglo-German merchant banks easily out-performed those whose partners' lifestyles exhibit aristocratic

---

[21] J. E. H. Williams, *Life of Sir George Williams* (1906) p. 240.
[22] D. A. Farnie, 'John Rylands of Manchester', *Bull. of the John Rylands Lib.* LVI (1973).

features (education, marriage connections, country houses and clubs). The most enterprising of the Anglo-German houses was Kleinworts, whose information books contain the critical comments on Jardine Matheson just quoted, and they were the house that took Barings' place at the top of the league of accepting houses in the years following the Baring crisis. The ultimate factor in performance is competition generated by the diversity of cultures. If the records of the major Anglo-German trading houses (Knoop, Wogau, Czarnikow etc.) were better it would be possible to extend the contrasts drawn from finance to trade.

ORGANISATION FOR THE INTERNATIONAL ECONOMY

In recent years business historians have been particularly interested in what they call the 'strategy and structure' problem, that is the structures that were worked out to meet the demands of growth of scale and global trading, beginning in the later decades of last century. Much of the pioneer research has been undertaken in the US where most of the best-known developments originated. However, the American focus has been principally on industry rather than trade and finance, responding to the major activity and most accessible evidence in their own continent. European researchers have tended too easily to follow American colleagues in regarding merchant enterprise as no more than a stage in the evolution of American-type systems.[23] Indigenous European developments are surely worth more consideration.

Two things were required to meet the demands of the emergent international economy. First there had to be a massive growth of scale to attain much higher turnover on lower margins. Fragments of evidence from a few of the most successful houses show this policy developing. Thus Rallis and Finlays led the Indian cotton piece goods trade in the 1870s by charging 2·5 per cent commission rather than the 4 or 5 per cent charged by conservative houses like Gladstone, Wylie & Co.[24] By the 1880s brokers' commissions on cargoes of wheat had fallen as low as 0·5 per cent in London and Liverpool.[25] In the business of exporting American raw cotton to

---

[23] A. D. Chandler, *The Visible Hand. The Managerial Revolution in American Business* (Cambridge, Mass., 1977).

[24] See above, Ch. 9. Glasgow Univ. Lib. Finlay MSS UGD 91/141, W. H. Marr's typescript history.

[25] *Royal Cmn of Agriculture*, Parl. Papers, 1882, xiv pp. 245–6, ev. of W. J. Harris.

Britain, US brokers Alexander Sprunt & Co. were able to reduce charges to one per cent by the early years of this century by cutting out the middlemen between the southern States and Liverpool.[26] These measures, simple in retrospect, required complete remodelling of the whole organisation of the firm, together with the development of trade associations to introduce standardised specifications to meet the ever more exacting needs of world trade. Tight control on costs could involve major shifts on overseas sourcing, as for instance when British grain suppliers shifted from the Baltic and Black Sea to North America, India and Argentina. Serving newly developing countries, merchant firms found it necessary to invest in support services like transport, docks, harbours, and sometimes basic processing equipment like cotton gins, timber mills and grain silos.[27]

The second requirement was to unite central funding in London or some other world financial centre with strong representation in local producing areas. It was not difficult for firms based in the primary producing areas to open offices in London and to maintain rapid communication via the telegraph on basic orders, but the cable was not suitable for maintaining understanding and reconciling differences of judgement. Case studies scattered through this book show how the most successful firms were linked back to the farm, plantation or mine; this was the common ingredient in the success stories of Anglo-German merchants on the Continent, the Greeks in the Middle East, Finlays, Rallis and other agency houses in India, Mosenthals, Eckstein (Wernher Beit) and other mining houses in South Africa, Dalgetty and Goldsborough Mort in Australia. The success of overseas competitors like Bunge & Born, Louis Dreyfus & Co. and W. R. Grace & Co. was evidently based on the same system.[28]

From the plethora of competing financial institutions in London, there was evidently no shortage of support for established houses seeking trade credits to develop in new directions. Not all took advantage of these facilities – Rylands and Rallis among others abjured them[29] – but that was a matter of moral or strategic preconceptions rather than opportunity. A few houses grew so fast that their house histories record some restraints through the need to

---

[26] J. Killick, 'The Transformation of Cotton Marketing in the late Nineteenth Century', *Bus. Hist. Rev.* LV (1981).
[27] See above, Ch. 7.   [28] See above, esp. Chs. 4, 5, 7, 9.
[29] P. S. Lokanathan, *Industrial Organisation in India* p. 218 (for Yules); D. A. Farnie, 'John Rylands of Manchester', p. 110; J. Gannadius, *Ralli* p. 24.

recruit even more capital; Balfour Williamson makes an interesting study in this respect, not least because the firm turned to accepting major deposits (investments) from connections abroad.[30] A similar but less formal system was used by most agency houses through the century.

Experience showed that there were problems about operating a trans-global organisation both at home and abroad. In Britain there was a widespread antipathy to joint-stock organisation and most firms only changed their family partnership status when the pressures to do so were overwhelming. The agonies of some of the home trade houses in this matter were quoted at some length in Chapter 6; the most successful firms (Cookes, Morleys, Dents and Rylands) did not incorporate until the interwar years. Dalgetty only capitulated to his partners' demands for incorporation when there was no alternative.[31] Most of the agency houses did not abandon their cherished partnerships until tax changes during the later stages of the First World War made it highly advisable.[32] Merchant partnerships no doubt had superior status in the City of London and could often raise capital through family connections, but their ability to do so was inevitably limited compared with public issues.

Another problem was that of raising capital in London for overseas commercial enterprises. It was only economical to make issues in 'large lumps' (£5·0m. or more) and investors' interest in the imperial territories and countries of informal empire surfaced only in short spells at long and unpredictable intervals. In Chapter 5 we saw Jardine Skinner failing to attract interest in a £5m. issue for three textile mills and a paper mill. Tatas, the Indian agency house that had a capital of nearly £1·0m. before 1914, failed to raise capital for an iron and steel works despite the family's high reputation.[33] However, week-by-week monitoring of the problems that the partners in an agency house shared suggest that investment opportunities for the firm's capital, and particularly the problem of finding and maintaining a balanced portfolio, were more significant in the long period than the attitude of the City's issuing houses. Certainly the detailed records of Jardine Skinner and James Finlay & Co. leave this clear impression.

[30] Wallis Hunt, *Heirs of Great Adventure: the History of Balfour Williamson & Co.* (1951).
[31] M. J. Daunton, 'Inheritance and Succession', *Bus. Hist.* xxx (1988).
[32] P. S. Lokanathan, *Industrial Organisation*, p. 25.
[33] A. K. Sen, 'The Pattern of British Enterprise in India 1854–1914', in Baljit Singh and V. B. Singh, eds., *Social and Economic Change* (Bombay 1967) p. 425.

The solution that emerged in response to these diverse problems was the managing agency system. The central role of these organisations is quite familiar to imperial historians but the scale and complexity of the organisation has only been revealed as a few company archives have become available for research. Despite the denigration of modern Indian historians, it is now clear that the system offered unique advantages in the context of the place and period. Its most important feature was that it provided management expertise which was in short supply in the Far East throughout the period. Large size offered the opportunities of economies of scale in purchasing, sales and specialist staff appointments like mining engineers and inspectors for tea plantations. The system allowed established merchant families to use their name to build up a diversified portfolio of interests which could (and often did) incubate particular activities during their development years and through lean periods. To help develop such initiatives it offered access to trade credits in London and local financial centres.

In principle the system had built-in checks and balances from the tension between the partners in the agency house, the investors, branches and companies (Figure 10.1). As noticed in earlier chapters, the experience was sometimes rather different, the agency creating a framework within which they benefited from the companies' earnings while the shareholders often obtained a meagre return. At best the system was contrived to divert earnings from the shareholders to the managers, at worst it could be seriously abused, and the agents knew what they were doing. Thus one of the Gladstones (partners in Ogilvy, Gillanders & Co.) wrote to his brother in 1899 that their jute mills in India were a disappointment from the shareholders' point of view but 'have been extremely lucrative to the firm'.[34] Similarly, one of the Hubbards admitted in a letter that their cotton factories in Russia had been the family's 'milch cow', run less for their intrinsic profitability than for the commissions paid to the partnership.[35] Such exploitation not only produced some bitter rows, as the Finlay records show, but more broadly must have dampened interest in investment in developing countries.

The other disadvantage of the agency house system was that the main interest of the partners and staff continued to be mercantile

[34] Clwyd R. O., Glynne–Gladstone MSS 2591, letter from Stuart to Robert Gladstone, 4 June 1899. [35] M. J. Daunton, 'Inheritance'.

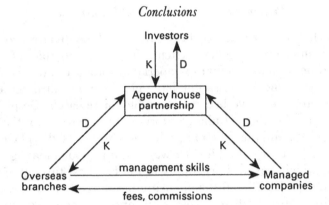

Key: K=capital, D=dividends

Figure 10.1. Relationships in the structure of the agency house.

rather than manufacturing. The houses recruited staff whose family backgrounds and education prepared them for careers in the civil service, armed services, Church and law, and only a few technical men like jute mill managers and mining engineers were recruited to subordinate positions for their technical expertise.[36] The immediate result was revealed in Rutnagur's analysis of the qualifications of directors of Calcutta cotton mills: so late as 1925 only six per cent had any technical qualifications (Table 9.7). The longer-term consequence was that the Japanese, who trained their managers in universities modelled on the German *Technischehochschule*, were able to drive Indian mill products out of their export markets in China and then successfully invade the Indian home market.[37] Some of the agency houses responded to the new competition from the East by taking on agencies for Japanese manufacturers. Ralli Bros. was probably the foremost of these opportunists; on the eve of the Second World War the firm sold a lot more Japanese textiles than those from Lancashire.[38] The British agency houses were not the only, or indeed the principal, organisations engaged in the Indian textile industry, but it remains true that they were culpable in their own decline. However, these shortcomings were only gradually recognised in the interwar period; in 1914 the agency houses appeared to be as strong and virtually unassailable as they had ever been. The sequestration

[36] Glynne–Gladstone MSS 2724, report from H. N. Gladstone (Calcutta 1909). A. C. Pointon, *Wallace Bros.* (1974) p. 67. Finlay MSS UGD 91/8, 56, 269–71, 277.
[37] Y. Kiyokawa, 'Technical Adaptations and Managerial Resources in India', *Developing Economies* XXI (1983).
[38] Guildhall Lib. Ralli MSS 23,834, 'Report on Organisation' (1938).

of German trading houses on the imperial territories (India, Burma and South Africa) brought windfall gains so that in 1920 the houses stood at a pinnacle of economic power and influence from which they declined only slowly.

At first sight there appears to be the clearest distinction between the diversified investment groups and the specialist commodity merchants or brokers. The contrast is perhaps at its sharpest in comparing the transatlantic cotton trade, with its many small firms, and the Far Eastern houses, with clusters of activities focussing round relatively few big names. The differences can be explained by specific historical circumstances, in particular the high degree of specialism and many small firms characteristic of the British textile industry, and the traditions of big capitalism inherited from the East India Company. The contrasts in the mercantile development of the north and south Russian grain trade, though less familiar, are just as striking. However, there was evidently a convergent economic factor at work, for on closer inspection the most successful commodity specialists were taking on characteristics that overlapped with investment groups. Thus in jute and cotton Ralli Bros. had up-country ginning and pressing plants in Egypt from 1860 and India from an early period to support their high turnover strategy. In grain Ross T. Smyth linked up with a milling company while Bunge & Born and Dreyfus integrated back to their source of supply as Steel Bros. did in rice and Wallaces in teak. And in cotton the American firms of Sprunts, McFadden and Anderson Clayton were taking the lead at the end of our period by similar strategies. Indeed in the last analysis it may be difficult to decide whether to place an enterprise in one category or another – are Finlays, to take just one example, an investment group (as treated here) or the leading operator in the international tea trade? Fortunately it is not necessary to make such distinctions, simply acknowledging that investment groups had blurred edges, the genus merging into commodity specialists on one side, merchant banks on another, and specialised mining houses on a third.

NEW FORMS OF MARKETING OVERSEAS

Another way of judging merchant enterprise in the period is to examine other forms of sourcing and marketing that arose in the period to see how popular and effective they were compared with the more traditional organisation. It is of course widely assumed that the generation before 1914 saw manufacturers supersede merchants in both domestic and overseas marketing, but the evidence cited in this volume must cast doubt on this. If major industrial conglomerates that had the resources to export did not think it worthwhile, how much more true is this of the thousands of small firms that were more representative of British manufacturing? Moreover, textiles remained the most important sector of British trade, and for the export sector we have the data on the number of subscribers to the Manchester Royal Exchange as a guide. Membership increased from 6,630 in 1875 to 7,877 at the turn of the century and reached 10,371 on the eve of World War I, and did not begin to decline until 1926.[39] The tabulations in Chapter 9 showing the continued growth of leading agency houses through the interwar years are another indicator of the resilience of the mercantile sector. These figures are not only an index of commercial activity, they are an index of the strength of traditional mercantile organisation. In the USA, where it is said that a 'marketing revolution' occurred between the mid-1890s and World War I, the Bureau of the Census reported in 1929 that independent wholesalers handled rather less than one-third of the flow of manufactured goods leaving American factories.[40] When allowance is made for the continuing importance of merchants in primary products like cotton and grain, that figure must be over a third.[41] Unfortunately there is no comparable data for the UK, but as international trade in primary products was so much more important than manufacturing to the British economy, one would expect the proportion to be much more than a third – and probably more than half – until the economic collapse of 1929–31.

The two manufacturer–merchants included in Table 10.1 scarcely seem to be a basis for any generalisation, but very few firms managed to sustain the two activities for any length of time. The vast preponderance of textile manufacturers, as we have already emphasised, lacked both the capital and necessary experience. Fieldens were the leaders of this endeavour in the first half of the century (see Chapters 2, 3), while Horrocks were pre-eminent under Sir Frank Hollins from the 1880s.[42] Fieldens continued to sell direct

[39] D. A. Farnie, 'An Index of Commercial Activity', *Bus. Hist.* XXI (1979).
[40] G. Porter and H. C. Livesay, *Merchants and Manufacturers. Studies in the Changing Structure of Nineteenth-Century Marketing* (Baltimore 1971) p. 228.
[41] Alston Garside, *Cotton goes to Market* (New York 1935) esp. Ch. 20. Dan Morgan, *Merchants of Grain* (New York 1979) esp. Ch. 2.
[42] *Dict. Bus. Biog.* articles on Hollins and Hermon. Lancs. R. O. Horrocks MSS DDHs 76.

to customers in North America, Brazil, the west coast of South America, India and China but their relative importance declined steeply and growth rates contrast starkly with the foremost merchants active in these export sectors.[43] Horrocks, who took early to branding and rose to the second largest firm in the cotton industry after Rylands, nevertheless had serious problems in selling direct to Latin American customers; its growth was largely by merger and acquisition. Rylands, who sold a third of their output abroad, exported through merchants at the end of the century; clearly their ventures in direct selling in Paris and Buenos Aires in the 1870s did not last (Chapter 6). Tootals, the third largest firm in the cotton industry, only started direct trade with US retailers in the 1880s when American import merchants were fast giving way to big retailers (Chapter 7); it was a shift of strategy forced on them by changes elsewhere.

Pursuing a major area of interest in the USA, British scholars have manifested great interest in the history of multinational companies, but their task has not been an easy one. The pioneer study of J. M. Stopford found only a dozen or so examples before 1914, while the more extensive research of S. J. Nicholas located its case studies largely in engineering and in perishable foodstuffs, and most of the significant data related to the interwar period.[44] This is not altogether surprising when it is recalled that the Americans led the world in the kind of technically complex products that necessitated direct links between producer and consumer, and it was their multinationals that led international trade in these products, and not the British ones. Textiles apart, the British kept to the business that their island situation and Empire gave them most advantages in, international trade in primary products and the finance of such international trade, and for this the mercantile system was the tried and proven one.

Other novel forms of exporting emerged in the 1880s and 1890s. Mira Wilkins was identified the 'free standing company', the floating of companies in Britain to build new plants in other countries. Despite a high turnover, there were said to be as many as 2,000 of them in 1914.[45] The London Stock Exchange records

---

[43] West Yorks R. O. Fielden Bros. MSS C353.
[44] J. M. Stopford, 'Origins of British-based Multinational Manufacturing Enterprises', *Bus. Hist. Rev.* XLVIII (1974), S. J. Nicholas, 'Agency Contracts...', *Jnl Econ. Hist.* XLIII (1983).
[45] M. Wilkins, 'The Free-Standing Company 1870–1914', *Econ. Hist. Rev.* XLI (1988).

contain numerous reports on these companies which give the impression that they were founded on very limited appreciation of the market, technology or political conditions. Thus the central Sugar Factories of Brazil Ltd. were floated in 1882 with an authorised capital of £600,000 but within five years the concession with the Brazilian government was being disputed and the company disappeared. Similarly, the Rio de Janeiro Flour Mills and Granaries Ltd. were floated in 1889 with a capital of £250,000 but it was admitted in the first annual report that 'The Mill was put up under very good prospects, but there was no actual experience to guide the Directors as to many additions that were found to be necessary for the Rio trade...'[46] Noting the high failure rate of free standing companies, Wilkins observes that in numerous instances those in the US and Canada failed to create managerial organisations that could compete with the indigenous ones. In countries lacking indigenous management, 'British free standing companies *eventually* provided the administrative requirement' (my italics). Inherently weak managerial structures at origin caused these companies to depend on external services such as banks and agency houses. Evidently they were not nearly so strong as the companies spawned by the agency houses, for they lacked both experience and reputation.[47]

Exploration companies might be thought of as another type of organisation that was popular in the 1880s and 1890s and offered a challenge to traditional trading organisations. They provided initial capital to explore new territories to identify mineral deposits and trading opportunities. Over 400 were launched in the two decades, mostly in southern Africa. A few exploration companies were linked to agency houses from the outset (e.g. Matheson's Transvaal Exploration Co. and Boustead's Central Borneo Co.) but most were 'free standing'. In retrospect they appear to be an aspect of the age of imperialism when opportunities seemed boundless, and they dried up as quickly as the great mining and oil companies took their grip on the world's unexplored land masses. They never acquired the degree of permanence of established mercantile houses for they were speculative ventures whose highest ambition was to sell concessions to established concerns at great profit.[48]

[46] Guildhall Lib., Stock Exchange company reports, Commercial, 1889.
[47] M. Wilkins, 'Free-Standing Company', pp. 275–6.
[48] Guildhall Lib., Stock Exchange company reports, Exploration Co.'s. R. J. Turrell and J. J. Van Helten, 'The Rothschilds, The Exploration Co. and Mining Finance', *Bus. Hist.* XXVIII (1986).

Table 10.2. *Share of various organisations in financing the Indian cotton industry in 1930*

	Bombay (64 mills)		Ahmedabad (56 mills)	
	lakhs rupees	%	lakhs rupees	%
Managing agents	532	21	264	24
Banks	226	9	42	4
Share capital	1,214	49	340	32
Debentures	238	10	8	1
Public deposits	273	11	426	39
	2,483	100	1,080	100

Source: P. S. Lokanathan, *Industrial Organisation in India* (1935) p. 181.

In the US the 1860s is supposed to have seen a decisive advance in the manufacturer's independence of the merchant as he began to draw on shareholders and banks for capital.[49] The position is evidently different in Britain as a reliable banking network supported producers with trade credits from a much earlier period while incorporation was characteristically delayed until later dates. However, it is reasonable to ask whether the growth of British imperial and international banks drove merchants from the traditional roles in providing credit for domestic and overseas commerce, and as specialists did so more effectively. The question is evidently a large one and full consideration must wait for special studies of these types of banks, but existing published work can offer an interim answer. Quite a lot of histories of such banks have been written and the opening chapters invariably show that the boards were constituted from senior partners of leading merchant houses and worked in complementary roles with them. The banks supported the managing agency system and indeed practically forced joint-stock companies to take agents as the system gave them the security of two signatures for all their loans.[50] The greater financial resources of the banks and the establishment of branch networks eventually brought them a large part of trade finance in the sector in which they operated, though the example of the Standard Bank South Africa cited in Chapter 9 indicates that this was no push-over. Moreover data collected by Lokanathan in India in 1930 indicates that

[49] G. Porter and H. C. Livesay, *Merchants and Manufacturers*, Ch. 7.
[50] P. S. Lokanathan, *Industrial Organisation*, p. 229.

managing agents continued to play a more important role in investment than banks for several years beyond our period (Table 10.2). Indeed, so late as 1955 the concerns controlled by managing agencies accounted for nearly 75 per cent of the total paid-up capital invested in public companies in India. And so late as 1960 the corporate part of the Malaysian economy was primarily controlled by large business enterprises, the most important part being the agency houses and the mining agencies.[51]

These scattered figures from India and Malaya evidently refer to share capital and not trade credits with which, in the English system, banks were primarily concerned. But in the context of international competition and the development of Third World economies the comparison is legitimate, for the *crédit mobilier* type of bank characteristic of the continental financial system was based on banks taking share capital and so gearing their futures to that of the industrial (as distinct to trading) sector of the economy. Taking the long view, it could at least be said that the merchant houses that changed themselves into investment groups never surrendered their financial functions to the imperial or local banks, and their roles were no less important in the development of the economies of the countries in which they operated.

A critical interpretation of the continuity of British mercantile enterprise through the period would say that it was survival by default of effective alternatives. Three reasons for this have been identified. British industry was still relatively weak in the new technology industries (engineering, electrical goods, motor transport etc.) that demanded new forms of marketing organisation. Secondly, manufacturers in the 'old staples' were widely reluctant, even where they commanded financial resources, to challenge the existing fragmented organisation. Thirdly, and perhaps more significantly of all, merchant investment group management was often shaky, partly because no one seriously addressed themselves to recruitment needs, partly because mill and mining specialists were scarcely ever promoted to partnerships. (The only significant exceptions were the machinery importers like Greaves Cotton & Co. who built their own cotton mills within an agency house type of organisation.) Behind this overall failure it is easy to discern the values of Victorian gentlemanly capitalism, with its strong dynastic loyalties and

[51] B. Kling cited in N.Charlesworth, *British Rule and the Indian Economy* (1892) p. 47. Puthecheary quoted in Lim Mah Hui, *Ownership and Control of the 100 Largest Corporations in Malaysia* (Oxford 1981) p. 18.

disinterest in technocrats. The agency house type of investment group represented a strategy highly appropriate to the numerous locations and to the period in which it evolved, but, in retrospect at least, merchant houses were slow to exploit its full possibilities and abused its shareholders. What might have been is revealed in the dynamic histories of Japanese general trading companies like Mitsui and Mitsubishi that started from a similar point but lacked the advantages of the imperial setting, connections with London and the richest domestic market in the world at the period. It can also be seen in the record of Indian indigenous enterprise, which successfully occupied the many interstices of British business despite greater shortage of capital.[52] However, the record of merchant activity is by no means uniformly disappointing and such failings must not be allowed to obscure the credits.

Bringing together these diverse strands, it seems reasonable to conclude that in Britain merchant houses in one form or another maintained the major role in overseas activity down to the First World War, and in some imperial territories beyond the Second World War. Of course, not all types of merchant houses were equally successful; small commission houses suffered early decline and, with few exceptions, the ranks of the international houses were not replenished as opportunities increased in their home countries. But in their stead new initiatives arose; the home trade houses expanded into exporting to the Empire, the agency houses were transformed into investment groups, and the elite of London and Liverpool merchants became merchant bankers, Lloyds insurance brokers, shipping agents and other specialists. Other groups again, like the textile shipping houses of Manchester and colonial brokers (London) showed remarkable resilience over a long period. The record is not one to denigrate.

This of course is not to suggest that British merchant houses always served other economies and societies in ways that should make foreigners grateful. This is a separate issue that cannot divert us here. In this book it is sufficient to record the view of A. K. Sen, the distinguished Indian economist, that British enterprise in India was strong in plantations, mining and jute and weak in cotton and iron and steel because there was a prevalent view in the UK that it was unpatriotic to make overseas investments that would spoil domestic industry, and particularly the country's two great staple

[52] S. Yonekawa and H. Yoshihara, eds., *Business History of General Trading Companies* (Tokyo 1987) Chs. 1–3. R. K. Ray, *Industrialisation in India* (Delhi 1979) Ch. 1.

export industries. However, this attitude presently enabled Indian entrepreneurs to establish strong indigenous industries.[53] In this matter, merchant houses active in the Far East evidently deferred to popular opinion in the home country. Had they taken a different view, indigenous enterprise might have been seriously oppressed.

BRITISH-BASED AND AMERICAN-BASED CONCEPTS OF ECONOMIC HISTORY

The final word of this book must relate to the wider issue of concepts appropriate to interpreting British industrial and commercial experience in the eighteenth and nineteenth centuries. In the of the strength of the commercial and financial sector through the so-called Industrial Revolution period, and in conclusion it is called Industrial Revolution period, and in conclusion it is appropriate to refocus on this important idea and, also on what happened to the 'twin pillars' of the economy in the second half of the nineteenth century. The concept of industrial revolution based on British experience has not proved especially helpful in interpreting change in most other western economies. Similarly, the intense academic focus on the multinational, which springs from specific American experience, has not done much for European countries. Britain took its own course in international commerce in the second half of last century as other western countries did in the first, and borrowing ideas from the economic history of other countries can only be partially successful.

The evidence of this book not only contributes further support to the idea of strong continuity in the mercantile sector through the period; it also defines the commercial components of that continuity. First it traces the dramatic growth of the northern frontier of trade based on Liverpool, Manchester and Glasgow, and the links with the City of London through the merchant banks. Secondly, it shows how industrialisation multiplied the cosmopolitan trading community, extending it from London to the northern centres. Then it built on the strong home market to create a new international trading organisation, the 'home trade houses'. Finally, in the age of the telegraph and conflating of trading supply lines, it met new challenges by evolving the investment group and globalising the activities of the commodity brokers in primary products. Merchants clearly benefited from the failure of manufacturers to maintain a

[53] A. K. Sen, 'Pattern of British Enterprise', p. 425.

trading role, and later in the century by the relative weakness of Britain in the new technological industries that generated the multinational corporations. Primary products and textiles continued to provide most of British international business, and the slow growth of technical products could be handled by the established trading houses, who were accustomed to provide equipment to planters and settlers, and later to their own mills, mines and other capital investments. The records of Tatas reveal increasing problems with managing their agencies at the end of our period, but they were more technologically oriented than any other investment group and it seems unlikely that our Far Eastern trading and investment groups only felt the same pressures at a later date, if at all.[54]

Because of the cosmopolitan character of British trading communities, and of those of imperial centres like Calcutta and Johannesburg, it makes little sense to draw comparisons between 'British' and 'foreign' firms. On the eve of World War I, rampant nationalism made much of Anglo-German and other rivalries, but this has obscured the economic reality, which was more obviously one of interpenetration of interests to a degree that often makes it difficult to decide whether a business was really British, German, American or whatever. In South Africa much of the enterprise was of German origin but absorbed economically and politically into the British imperial interest; in India and the Far East the Parsis, Jews, Greeks and other traders were so far integrated into the system that one hesitates to label them this or that nationality. In the few instances where the most successful performance of foreign competitors is on record (Table 10.1), it does not look any better than the best British firms.

The enterprise of the mercantile community derived from wide recruitment, intense competition and high turnover. Recruitment was international and selective: the most successful trading families migrated from Europe, America and the imperial territories, as well as the British provinces. For the eighteenth century, Hoppit has shown the high risks and high failure rates of merchants, and the same feature on an increased scale must be true of the nineteenth century. No overall data is available to make a detailed analysis, but Richard Seyd's *Record of Failures and Liquidations* (1876, 1885) shows merchant bankruptcies in the prosperous decade 1865–76, nearly twice the number in the last two decades of the eighteenth century,

[54] N. Charlesworth, *British Rule*, p. 48.

with more than half of them in London. In crisis years like 1847–8, 1856–7 and 1875 they were evidently much higher. In the Far East trade, staff turnover was always high and new talent constantly sought.[55] In this situation the capital of the few that were outstandingly able, well-connected or fortunate vastly outstripped the many who struggled on the edge of the survival zone. The contrast with manufacturing, where bankruptcy was by no means a distant threat, is nevertheless clear enough. Manufacturers survived in an economic setting not unlike that of the economist's concept of perfect competition, where many firms earned 'normal' profits and fortunes were much the exception.

The setting also gives perspective to the concept of 'gentlemanly capitalism' identified in the Introduction. For the many it must have been a concept of lifestyle that was a seldom achieved reward. In particular, it might spur on those without the discipline of religious sanctions or ethnic restraints, and it ensured that mediocre heirs could be diverted from the trading succession. Like the contemporary legend of self-help, it contains sufficient truth to be plausible and have wide appeal, but its relevance to economic reality is evidently limited, even for the most successful families, who had to work hard to maintain their fortunes.

The attempts to characterise merchants in Britain as a 'cosmopolitan bourgeoisie', or as a main component of 'gentlemanly capitalism' or, at their City pinnacle, as an 'aristocratic bourgeoisie' can do no more than focus on one aspect of truth. They draw on much wider source material than Samuel Smith's representation of some leading houses as run by statesmanlike chief executives, but this merchant identified another aspect of complex reality. The academic simplifications seem engineered to represent the essential unity of mercantile and financial capitalism, and the power or influence acquired by interpretation with the organs of national government. Such notions look for the domination of London over 'the periphery', whether the latter is the English provinces, Scotland, India, South Africa, China, or wherever else trading interests were active. The evidence of this book must resists attempts to represent the unifying interest implied in these ideas. On the contrary, the most essential feature of mercantile activity in Britain from the eighteenth to the twentieth centuries has been its ethnic, cultural

---

[55] J. Hoppit, *Risk and Failure in English Business 1700–180* (Cambrdge 1987) pp. 96ff. R. Seyd, *Record of Failures and Liquidations 1865–1876* (1877); see also *1875–1884* (1885). D. Morier Evans, *Commercial Crisis* (1848, 1857).

and organisational diversity, and from that the trading sector of the economy drew its great strength. If industrial interests were not well represented in this heterodox occupation, it was more to do with long-term failure of manufacturers as mercantile entrepreneurs than with the structure of metropolitan society. It is reassuring to find that this interpretation harmonises with that of a foremost imperial historian, and also of new research on the social structure of the City of London.[56] As more case studies become available it must be expected that even greater diversity will be discovered.

APPENDIX   *Data on capital growth of 20 leading firms*

FAR EASTERN HOUSES

Jardine Matheson & Co., agency house, est. Calcutta 1842.

1836	£1·47m.
1840	1·67
1850	1·12
1861	3·16
1870	2·17
1880	1·34
1891	1·72
1906	2·00
1910	2·20* (2·00)
1913	2·50* (2·00)

* including Matheson & Co. of London; Hong Kong only in brackets.

Sources: M. Ishii, 'Activities of British Enterprise in China in the Ninteenth Century', *Socio-Economic History* (Tokyo) XLV (1979) Table 1. The 1891 figures comes from E. Lefevour, *Western Enterprise in Late Ch'ing China* (Harvard 1968) p. 123, those for 1906–13 from Guildhall Lib. Kleinwort Information Books, Goldman Sachs series, II p. 2.

James Finlay & Co., agency house, est. Glasgow 1750.

1861	£0·20m.
1870	0·45
1882	0·78
1903	0·96
1910	2·41* (1·0)
1914	2·72* (1·0)

* including deposits and reserves; partners' capital in brackets.

Sources: 1861 and 1870 in [C. Brogan], *James Finlay & Co.* (1951) pp. 37, 46. 1882–1914 in Glasgow Univ. Finlay MSS UGD 92/141, 91/32, 91/239.

[56] A. Porter, 'Gentlemanly Capital and the Empire: the British Experience since 1750?', *Journal of Imperial and Commonwealth History* XVIII (1990). M. J. Daunton, 'Gentlemanly Capitalism and British Industry 1820–1914', *Past & Present* CXXII (1989).

Ralli Bros., Indian commodities, est. London 1818.

1830	£0·14m.
1840	0·17
1850	0·50
1878	1·20
1880	2·00
1901–2	3·00–4·20

Sources: 1830–40: Guildhall Lib. Ralli Bros MSS 23,830. 1878–1901 Bank of England Discount Office records (unlisted) and Baring Bros. 'Characters 1' (1878–1902) pp. 131–2.

John Swire & Son, Far East trade, est. Liverpool 1816.

1867	£0·10m.
1879	0·2
1886	0·3
1890	0·46
1895	0·76
1900	0·94
1905	0·22
1910	0·43

Sources: S. Marriner and F. E. Hyde, *The Senior. John Samuel Swire 1825–98* (Liverpool 1967) p. 212. 1886–19: S. Sugiyama, 'A British Trading Firm in the Far East: John Swire & Sons 1867–1914', in S. Yonekawa and H. Yoshira, eds., *Business History of General Trading Companies* (Tokyo 1987) p. 173.

Ogilvy, Gillanders & Co., agency house, est. Liverpool 1828.

1828	£ 7,421
1839	15,034
1848	75,055
1875	131,427
1900	390,732
1910	405,372

Source: Clwyd R. O. Glynne–Gladstone MSS G–G 2747, 2553–2564.

Harrisons & Crosfield, agency house, est. Liverpool 1844.

1844	£ 8,000
1863	140,000
1894	60,000+
1908	307,000
1910	450,000
1912	807,500

Source: Harrisons & Crosfield, *One Hundred Years as East India Merchants 1844–1943* (1943).

LATIN AMERICAN HOUSES

Balfour Williamson & Co., est. Liverpool 1851.

1851	£6,000
1884	0·75m.
1887	0·57
1888	0·73
1889	0·9
1903	1·0m.+
1912	2·0m.+

Source: Wallis Hunt, *Heirs of Great Adventure. The History of Balfour Williamson & Co. Ltd.* (1951)

Heilbut Symons & Co., rubber trade, est. Liverpool 1838.

1870	£ 70,000
1872	85,000
1875	100,000(−)
1880	172,000
1885	353,000
1888	340,000
1901	700,000+
1908	800,000
1909	1·00m.+
1910	1·25m.
1914	1·00m.+

Source: Bank of England Discount Office records (unlisted)

Ross T. Smyth & Co., grain trade, est. Liverpool 1839.

1851	£ 5,000+
1857	20,000+
1889	0·3m.
c. 1905	0·5
1907	0·3
1912	0·3

Sources: G. T. S. Broomhall and J. Hubbuck, *Corn Trade Memories* (1930) pp. 173–4 for 1851–7. 1889: BB HC3.35. 1905–12: BB HC5.2.30.

RUSSIAN HOUSES

Rodocanachi, Sons & Co., grain trade, est. London 1838.

1860	£0·2m.+
1873	0·6
1880	0·6
1893	0·5

1901   0·33
1911   0·415

Sources: 1860: BB Customer Reference Books, Europe I. 1873–1913: Bank of England Discount Office records (unlisted).

Wogau & Co., Moscow and St Petersburg, tea and general Baltic trade, established Moscow 1839, London 1865.

1875–9   5·0m. roubles (£0·5m.)
1892   £0·6m. (B. of E.), 1·5–2·0m.(K)
1898   £0·6–0·7m.
1907   £0·2m.
1913   £0·2m.

Sources: Kleinwort Information Books, Scandinavia & Russia, 1875–1906 pp. 58, 115. Bank of England Discount Office records. *Materials po Istorii SSSR*, VI (Moscow 1959) pp. 697–706. Capital in Russia in 1915 was said to total £5m. of which £1m. belonged to British citizens.

E. H. Brandt & Co., grain trade, est. Archangel c. 1802.

1863   £0·025m.
1880   0·355
1895   0·336
1904   0·750

Source: C. Amburger, *William Brandt and the Story of his Enterprises* (typescript, c. 1950), Brandt MSS, Nottingham Univ. Lib. Bank of England MSS C29/23.

HOME TRADE HOUSES

Thomas Adams & Co., lace merchants and manufacturers, est. Nottingham 1830.

1865   £0·112m.
1878   0·126
1884   0·162
1900   0·345
1910   0·356

Sources: Notts. C.R.O Adams MSS 10,689, 10,708. Guildhall Lib. Stock Exchange annual reports.

Bradbury, Greatorex & Co., textile warehousemen, est. London 1815.

1868   £0·023m.
1894   0·40
1899/1900   0·474
1910   0·477

Sources: (Anon.) *A Short History of Bradbury, Greatorex & Co.* (1970). Guildhall Lib. Stock Exchange annual reports.

Foster, Porter & Co., drapery warehousemen, est. London 1842.

1871	£0·21m.
1890	0·28
1900	0·29
1910	0·28

Sources: GUS Property Management, Leeds. Guildhall Lib. Stock Exchange annual reports.

Fore Street Warehouse Co. Ltd, textile warehousemen, est. London 1814 as Todd, Morrison & Co.

1864	£0·42m.
1880	0·42
1900	0·55
1910	0·435

Sources: Seyd & Co., *London Commercial List* (1872) p. 34. Guildhall Lib. Stock Exchange annual reports.

John Rylands & Sons, textile merchants and manufacturers, est. Wigan (Lancs.) 1787.

1850	£0·10m.(+)
1876	0·34 (2·0)
1889	3·8
1900	4·21
1910	3·94

Sources: Bank of England Manchester agent's letter books VII (1850) p. 150; the figure does not include the Wigan mill or London selling office. Kleinwort Information Books UK 1 p. 76; the shareholding in 1876 was £1·34m. but Rylands sold the shares for £2·0m. John Rylands Lib., Rylands MSS, auditors balance book 1873–1950 (data extracted by Dr D. A. Farnie and generously passed to the author).

Pawsons & Leaf, London wholesale drapers. Leaf & Co. est. 1790.

1873	(Pawsons' incorporation)		£0·24.
1880	Pawsons & Co.	0·31	
1879	Leaf, Sons & Co.	0·50	0·81
1893	(Pawsons & Leafs amalgamated)		
1900			0·417
1910			0·414

Sources: Seyd & Co., *London Commercial List* (1877). Bank of England MSS, discount applications 1877–85, C. 29/23. Guildhall Lib. Stock Exchange annual reports.

MANUFACTURER–MERCHANTS

Horrocks, mill spinners and weavers, est. Preston 1791.

1842	£0·14m.
1865	0·6
1885	0·75
1887	0·913
1911	1·62

Source: Lancs. R.O. Horrocks MSS DDHs/76. *Dict. Bus. Biog.* III, articles on Edward Hermon, Frank Hollins. Much of the growth of this firm came from mergers in 1885, 1887 and 1900.

Fielden Bros, mill spinners, weavers and merchants, est. Todmorden 1786.

1860	£0·74m.
1865	1·08
1890	0·13
1900	0·13
1910	0·13

Sources: Longdon Manor archives, Shrewsbury. West Yorks R.O., Fielden MSS C 353/420.

FOREIGN COMPETITOR HOUSES

W. R. Grace & Co., Peruvian merchants, est. New York 1866.

1862	£0·036m.
1879	0·1
1888	0·5
1894	0·6
1908	0·3

Sources: L. A. Clayton, *W. R. Grace & Co., the Formative Years 1850–1930* (Ottawa, Illinois, 1985). Baring Bros. MSS HC5.2.36. Kleinwort Information Books US 1 p. 109, Goldman Sachs II pp. 11–12.

Bunge & Born, grain merchants, est. Amsterdam 1818.

1860	£0·02m.
1868	0·08–0·1
1900	0·4
1910	1·6–2·0

Sources: Dun, New York, vol. 341, pp. 148, 200R. Kleinwort Information Books, France, II pp. 20, 92, 104.

Manuscript sources

Several important collections of merchants' papers relating to the nineteenth century have survived and have been extensively exploited in this book, most notably those of Jardine Skinner and Jardine Matheson at Cambridge University Library, Mackinnon Mackenzie and Antony Gibbs at Guildhall Library in the City of London, Finlay at Glasgow University and Gladstone at Clywd Record Office. However, these major business archives, and a handful of lesser ones, are by no means adequate to write the extensive history of merchant enterprise in the last century. To obtain a much broader view of the firms and their owners it is necessary to fall back on the confidential reports and credit ratings of those who made it their business to evaluate merchants. Here the source material is surprisingly full and unexploited. The major sources used in this book are:

(1) Bank of England agents' (i.e. managers') letters and letter books at the Bank, London EC2. The main series used in this book are those for Manchester (C136), Liverpool (C129), Leeds (C127), Birmingham (C103) and Leicester (C134). The extensive correspondence contains detailed reports on most of the important merchants and manufacturers within the commercial or industrial region covered by the particular Bank branch. The reports are especially useful during the branches' early years (c. 1828–50) when managers were endeavouring to build a quality clientele.

(2) Kleinwort, Sons & Co.'s Information Books contain their clerks' transcriptions of confidential reports on clients and potential clients of this highly successful merchant bank. This vast business archive has been deposited at Guildhall

Library by Kleinwort Benson PLC with no restriction on access. Most of the evidence is for commercial firms in London and other international trading cities. The series used here are those for UK firms (three volumes, 1875–1910, Guildhall list nos. 184–6), for Germany (six volumes, 1875–1911, nos. 187–92), for the USA (three volumes, 1880–1914, nos. 86–8), for France, Belgium and Holland (six volumes, 1875–1911, nos. 177–82), and those for Scandinavia and Russia (four volumes, 1875–1910, nos. 457–60).

(3) Baring Bros. & Co. Ltd. Reports on Business Houses are an irregular series covering the period 1816–1934, mostly retained in this merchant bank's archives, with a few early ones deposited at Guildhall Library. The main series used here are listed as LIV 6 (15 volumes 1876–1934), 'London credits' (CRD 3/1–5, 1882–1920), and the reports contained within Baring's Liverpool branch correspondence (HC 3.35, 47 boxes, 1833–1903). In general the reports are less detailed than those maintained by Kleinworts, but the evidence on Liverpool is more complete and the two firms' records are broadly complementary. Access is available via Baring's archivist, Dr M. J. Orbell, whose help is gratefully acknowledged.

(4) For the USA, a much more extensive series of reports exists in the Dun & Bradstreet (formerly R. G. Dun) credit registers deposited in the Baker Library at Harvard University. The highly detailed reports are best for the period from c.1850–c.1875; they have been exploited in the present study for Anglo-American enterprises.

(5) For South Africa, a comparable series exists in the inspectors' reports in the Standard Bank Archives, Johannesburg. The inspectors visited each branch as many as four times a year and reported on each customer's credit as well as on the bank staff and business of the locality.

These records can be filled out by those in other archives. Very few merchant enterprises became public companies before 1920, but, for the few that did, the bound volumes of Company Annual Reports (1880–1965) deposited at Guildhall Library by the London Stock

Exchange can be quite informative. Trading companies are generally bound in the Commercial series. The structure of many merchant partnerships is closely chronicled in the 45 volumes of Brandt circulars (1829–1934). E. H. Brandt & Co. was a merchant bank that, uniquely in Britain, bound and indexed all the printed trade circulars sent to it. The circulars are deposited in Nottingham University Library archives.

Taken together and linked with more familiar sources like directories and bankruptcy records, these materials enormously extend the evidence derived from the archives of particular merchant houses.

Index of firms and people

Abet Bros., 158
Adams, Thomas & Co., 182, 291, 293, 316
Agra Bank, London, 213
Ainsworth & Co., 101, 102
Albu, G. & L., 278, 279
Alexander Bros., 111, 147
Alexandre & Co., 85
Allen, A. P., 177
Alston, Finlay & Co., 86, 96, 104, 106
Andelle, Alexander, 101
Anderson, Clayton, 197, 198, 228, 303
Anderson, Sir John, 272
André family, 31
Arbuthnot & Co., 226
Arbuthnot, Ewart & Co., 113, 127
Arbuthnot, Latham & Co., 213
Argenti, Sechiari & Co., 157, 158
Arkwright, Sir Richard, 52, 59, 63, 173
Armstrong & Co., 215
Arraran Ltd., 240
Arthur, Sir Allan, 222
Arthur & Co., 182, 290, 293
Ashton, T. S., 15, 103
Assam Tea Co., 240
Aubert family, 31
Aubin, J. M. & Co., 96

Bagchi, A. K., 125, 127
Bagehot, Walter, 9–10, 295
Baggalays & Spence, 182
Balfour, Guthrie, 243
Balfour, Hugh & Co., 214
Balfour, Williamson & Co., 204, 205, 207, 228, 242, 243, 253, 255, 259, 291, 300, 315
Bank of Bengal, 213
Bank of England, 31, 33, 36, 56, 67, 68, 70, 72, 73, 86, 87, 88, 101, 102, 103, 104, 150, 153, 159, 174, 180, 212
Bank of Liverpool, 208
Bank of London, 212

Bank of Scotland, 213, 214
Bank of the US, 73
Bank of Winterthur, 215
Bannerman, Henry & Sons, 90, 174
Barclay, David & Sons, 28, 53
Barclay, Robert & Co., 213, 214
Baring, Alexander, 37, 56
Baring Bros. (& Co. Ltd.), 54, 61, 70, 73, 74, 75, 87, 93, 110, 112, 115, 124, 146, 152, 161, 165, 195, 196, 200, 208, 212, 216, 217, 226, 254, 262, 288, 292, 297, 298
Baring, Sir Francis, 29, 56
Barker, F. W., 271
Barker, John & Co, 186
Barlow & Co., 271
Barlow & Whittenbury, 59
Barnato Bros., 247, 248, 249, 256, 261, 276, 278, 279
Barrett, W., 150
Barrick & Simon, 135
Barton, Henry and James (& Co.), 59, 90, 91, 95–6, 174
Bates, Joshua, 75, 152, 289
Batesville Cotton Mill Co., 97
Baumeister & Co., 96
Baver, Abraham & Co., 148
Begg, Dunlop & Co., 270
Behn, Meyer & Co., 126
Behrens, Jacob and Louis, 143, 144, 149
Beit, Alfred, 248, 276, 277, 278, 279, 280
Bengal Coal Co., 113
Bengal Docking Co., 113
Bengal Salt Co., 113
Bengal Tea Association, 113
Benson family (Liverpool), 82, 93, 94, 95, 104, 210
Bergeron, Prof. Louis, 31, 132
Bethmann Bros., 45
Binny & Co., 119, 127, 240, 250, 254, 259, 267, 268, 290

Bird & Co., 119, 120, 124, 125, 126, 253, 270, 272, 290
Birley & Hornby, 90, 91
Birkin, Richard & Co., 179
Bischoffsheim, L. R., 145
Black Ball Line, 85, 86, 88
Blackwell Hall, 41, 168, 169
Blaine, MacDonald & Co., 275
Bleichroder, Gerson, 212
Blessig, Braun & Co., 203–4, 205, 207
Bliss, Geo. & Co., 194
Bolton, Ogden & Co., 74, 104, 152
Bombay-Burma Trading Co., 124, 127, 240
Bombay Iron & Steel Co., 121
Booth family, 210
Borneo Company, 118, 124, 126, 240
Borthwick & Co., 209
Bosanquet family, 31
Bott & Co., 59
Boulton & Watt, 135, 152
Boustead, E. & Co., 108, 126, 147, 148, 225, 255, 258, 271, 306
Boustead, Schwabe & Co., 148
Bowring & Co., 209, 210, 291
Bowring, Sir John, 175
Boyd, J. & C., 182
Bradbury, Greatorex & Co., 179, 182, 189, 291, 316
Bradbury, John, 63
Braithwaite family, 94
Brandt, E. H., 134, 135, 203, 204, 205, 207, 212, 246, 255, 260, 291, 292, 317
Braudel, Fernand (cited), 11, 21, 29, 35, 39
Brenier (bank), 215
Brettle, George & Co., 182
Briscoe, William & Son, 73
British & Chinese Corporation, 239, 250
British Linen Bank, 213
Brocklebank family, 82
Brooks, John, 102
Brown Brothers (& Co.), 88, 93, 96, 105, 106, 146, 152, 161
Brown, Shipley & Co., 70, 74, 82, 151, 288, 290
Brown, William, 151, 153
Brown, W. & J. (& Co.), 73, 74, 86, 88, 89, 91, 104, 150, 151, 153
Bryce, James, 250
Buchanan, Ben, 105
Buck, N. S., 149
Bunge & Born, 205, 206, 207, 208, 209, 211, 228, 291, 292, 299, 303, 318
Bunge & Co., 255, 259
Bunge, Edward, 206
Burma Oil Co., 126

Butler, Sykes & Co., 148
Butterfield & Swire, 239, 250, 255, 258
Butterworth & Brooks, 90, 102, 103
Butterworth, Henry, 102

Cababé, Paul and Peter, 156, 157
Cable, Sir Ernest, 120, 253, 272
Cain, Dr P. J., 8, 9
Calcutta Chamber of Commerce, 120
Caldecott, Sons & Co., 182
Calico Printers Association (C.P.A), 181, 183, 201, 233
Campbell, R., 25
Capital & Counties Bank, 215
Cardwell, Birley & Hornby, 103
Carlowitz & Co., 266
Carol I, King, 206
Carr, Robert & Co., 29, 49
Carr, Tagore & Co., 108, 112, 113
Cartwright & Warner, 188
Cassavetti Brothers & Co. (Cassavetti, Cavafy & Co.), 156, 158
Casson, Prof. Mark, 11, 12
Catto, Sir Thomas, 120
Cavafy brothers, 156
Chadwick, James & Brother, 66
Chalmers, Guthrie & Co., 209, 210, 217
Champdany Co. (jute mill), 213, 221, 222
Chance, Edward, 73
Chance, William, 73
Chandler, Prof. A. D., 251
Charlton, Prof. K., 104
Chartered Bank of India, 213, 214
Clayton family, 63
Clydesdale Bank, 213
Coats, J. & P. (& Co.), 181, 183, 230
Cockerell, Laing & Co. (also Cockerell, Larpent & Co.), 109, 112, 240
Cohen, Levy Barent, 34
Cohen, Louis, 277
Collmann & Stellefeht, 106
Colonial Bank, 215
Colvin & Co., 111
Consolidated Gold Fields, 247, 278, 279
Cooke & Comer, 87
Cooke, Isaac & Co., 87, 88, 105
Cooke, Son & Co., 168, 178, 182, 183, 186, 188, 201, 290, 293, 300
Copestake, Crampton & Co., 177, 182
Copestake, Moore & Co., 177, 189
Corn Exchange, Mark Lane, London, 76
Cottrell, Prof. P. L., 210
Courtaulds, 230
Cramond, James, 64
Crary, Craig & Co., 105, 106

Crawshay (ironfounder), 74
Credit Lyonnais, 212
Crocker, Sons & Co., 182
Crofts, William, 177
Cropper, Benson & Co., 73, 84, 85, 86, 87, 88, 89, 92, 95, 104, 106
Cropper, James, 87, 88
Cruttenden & Co., 111
Cumberbatch & Co., 271
Cunliffe, Brooks & Co., 102, 159
Cunliffe Bros., 214
Cunliffe, James, 159
Czarnikow, Caesar & Co., 77, 210, 290, 298

Dacca Twist Co., 189
Da Costa (Consul), 165
Daintry, Ryle & Co., 59
Dale, David, 62
Dalgety, F. G., 219, 220, 223, 292, 299, 300
Darbys of Coalbrookdale, 94, 95
De Beers, 225, 247, 248, 253, 256, 260, 276
Debenham, Frank, 186, 187
Defoe, Daniel, 44, 167, 168
De Jersey & Co., 195, 226, 245
Dennistoun, Cross & Co., 197, 209
Dennistoun, James, 88, 90, 91
Dennistoun, Mackie & Co., 88, 91
Dent, Allcroft & Co., 182, 188, 300
Devas, Routledge & Co., 182
Devine, Dr T. M., 38, 39
Dewar, Sons & Co. Ltd., 182
Dickinson, Thomas & Co., 73
Dietz, Alexander, 139
Dillon, John, 176
Discontogesellschaft, 215
Dixon, Henry & Co., 105
Dixon, Thomas & Co., 152
Dockray family, 94
Dodwell & Co., 126
Donaldson, Glenny & May, 135
Doner, Conrad, 135
Dreyfus, Louis & Co., 205, 206, 207, 208, 209, 211, 212, 228, 246, 255, 259, 299, 303
Drinkwater, Peter, 58, 59, 62
Drysdale, Thomas & Co., 209, 210
Du Fay, Colin & Co., 70, 91, 134, 145, 147
Dugdale, John, 148
Dun & Bradstreet, 97, 216
Duncan, John and Peter, 173
Duncan, McLachlan & Co., 109, 119, 270, 290
Dunkelsbuhler, Anton, 276

Earle, Dr Peter, 26, 27, 29

East India Company, 33, 34, 36, 53, 70, 77, 83, 95, 101, 107, 109, 111, 112, 235, 280, 303
Eccles, Alexander, 197
Eckstein, F. & Co., 223, 278, 299
Eckstein, Herman, 250
Edwards, Michael, 75, 171
Egerton, Hubbard & Co., 203, 204, 207
Engels, F., 146
Erlanger, Emile & Co., 276, 277, 279, 280
Evans, David & Co., 182, 188
Evans, D. H. & Co., 186
Ewart & Rutson, 76
Ewing, James & Co., 114, 222
Ewo Bank of Peking, 237, 238
Exploration Co., 277

Farrar, George, 278, 279
Fergusson & Co., 111
Fielden Bros., 66, 67, 68, 72, 90, 103, 146, 291, 304, 318
Fielding, Sir William, 174
Fine Spinners & Doublers, 181
Finlay, Hodgson & Co., 73, 96, 104
Finlay, James & Co., 10, 55, 63, 86, 89, 90, 91, 95, 105, 117, 119, 120, 153, 164, 196, 212, 213, 214, 221, 222, 224, 225, 239, 240, 255, 257, 267, 268, 270, 271, 272, 290, 291, 295, 298, 299, 300, 301, 303, 313
Finlay, Kirkman, 95, 96, 104
Finlay, Muir & Co., 108, 212
Fish & Grennill, 105
Fisher, James & Co., 176, 177, 179
Flersheim, Soloman, 146
Flints (haberdashers), 175
Forbes & Co., 119
Foster, Joseph, 95
Foster, Porter & Co., 182, 291, 316
Franghiadi & Rodocanachi, 160
Frangopulo, N. S. & Co., 157
Fraser, George, Son & Co., 89
Fraser, John & Co., 96, 97
Fraser, Trenholm & Co., 96, 97
Friedlander, Isaac, 207
Fruhling & Goschen, 134, 214, 215
Fürstenbank, 143
Fyffes, 209

Gardner, Robert (& Co.), 90, 102, 104, 164, 174
Garside, Alston Hill, 202
Gibbs, Antony & Sons, 72, 102, 164, 241–2, 243, 250, 253, 255, 259
Gibbs, Vicary, 241, 242

Gilfillan, Wood & Co., 126
Gillanders, Arbuthnot & Co., 116, 117, 118, 270
Gilpin, Joshua, 61
Gisborne & Co., 84, 110, 112
Gisborne, Matthew, 84, 85
Gisborne, Menzies & Co., 85, 92
Gladstone, Henry Neville, 240
Gladstone (Sir) John (& Co.), 82, 84, 89, 90, 103, 113, 116, 146, 222
Gladstone, Robert, 84
Gladstone, Stuart, 301
Gladstone, W. E., 189, 288
Gladstone, Wylie & Co., 298
Goerz, A., 278, 279
Goldsborough, Mort & Co., 299
Goldsmid, B. A. & Co., 56
Goldsmid & Eliason, 135
Goodlive & Co., 150
Gott, Benjamin, 59, 62, 67, 91
Grace, W. R. & Co., 291, 292, 299, 318
Greaves, Cotton & Co., 119, 222, 267, 268, 269, 308
Greenburg, M. 113
Greg, Samuel (& Co.), 55, 60, 62, 64, 94
Greg, Thomas, 64
Griffiths, Sir Percy, 250
Groucock, Copestake & Moore, 177
Guistiniani & Nepoti, 156
Guthrie & Co., 108, 126, 240, 255, 258, 271, 272

Hagarty & Jardine, 106
Hagues, Cooke & Wormald, 152
Haigh, Joseph, 59
Hambro, C. J. & Son, 134
Hannah, Leslie, 252
Hardcastle, James & Co., 63
Hardy, Nathan & Sons, 215
Hargreaves, Dugdale & Co., 148
Harris, William, 202, 204
Harrison, Ansley & Co., 53
Harrisons & Crossfield, 209, 210, 241, 253, 255, 258, 271, 291, 314
Harrods, 186
Haworth, Richard, 174
Hayne Bros., 172
Heathcoat, John, 177
Heaton, H. 104
Heilbut, Symons Co., 209, 210, 212, 291, 315
Heilgers, F. W. & Co., 125, 270
Helbert, Wagg & Co., 279
Henderson, R. & J., 108, 118, 124, 240, 255, 258

Henry, Alexander, 151, 152, 153
Henry, A. & S., 96, 150, 151, 152, 174, 182, 201, 288, 293
Henry, Mitchell, 153
Henry, Thomas & William, 152
Heylin, H. B., 185, 198
Heymann, Louis, 149
Heywood & Palfreyman, 63, 64
Hibbert, Titus & Son, 64
Hills & Whishaw, 203, 204
Hirsch, L. & Co., 277, 278
Hitchcock, Williams & Co., 189, 293, 296
Hodgson, James, 71, 72
Hodgson & Robinson, 71, 72
Hohenemser family, 143
Hollenden, Lord, 190
Hollins, Sir Frank, 188, 304
Holt family, 210
Holywell Co. (Chester), 63
Hong Kong Fire Insurance Co., 238, 239
Hong Kong & Shanghai Bank, 239
Hope & Co., 87, 88, 165
Hope, Henry, 53
Hopkins, Prof. A., 8, 9
Hoppit, Dr J., 47, 48, 50, 311
Hornby & Co., 103
Horrocks, Miller & Co., 55, 90, 101, 103, 188, 200, 291, 304, 305, 318
Horstman & Co., 215
Horwitz & Meyer, 144
Hottinguer et Cie, 87
Howard & Bullough, 269
Hubbard, J. & Co., 246, 250, 255, 260, 301
Hunt, Wallis, 243
Huth, Frederick & Co., 70, 87, 134, 135, 139, 141, 147, 161, 213, 214
Hyde, R. & N., 60, 64

Imperial Tobacco Co., 233
India Jute Mills, 124
Indo-China Steam Navigation Co., 237–9
Indo-Java Rubber Planting & Trading Co., 240
Innis, John, 110
International Bank of London Ltd., 214
Ionides, Alexander, 160
Ionides Bank of London, 160
Ionides, John & Constantine (Bros. & Co.), 154, 157, 158, 160
Ionides, Sgouta & Co. 158
Ironside, W. A., 125

Jackson, Sir William, 103, 210
Jardine, David, 114, 115, 116, 118
Jardine, Matheson & Co., 102, 114, 115,

126, 153, 164, 217, 226, 237, 238, 239, 250, 266, 267, 270, 272, 290, 291, 293, 294, 298, 313
Jardine, Sir Robert, 294
Jardine, Skinner & Co., 99, 114, 115, 116, 117, 118, 120, 123, 124, 125, 226, 237, 250, 254, 258, 267, 270, 300
Jardine Spinning & Weaving Co., 238, 239
Jenkins, Dr D. T., 266
Johnstone's *Commercial Guide*, 171
Jones, Dr Charles, 12, 223, 279
Joseph Bros., 276
Jowett, Thomas & Co., 152
Justamond, John, 141

Kawakatsu, Dr H. 264
Kelsall & Co., 102
Kennaway family, 61
Kennedy & Co., 271
Kessler, J. P., 202
Keswick, James, 226
Keswick, William, 250, 272
Ketland, Cotterill & Son, 61
Killick, John R., 93, 104
Killick, Nixon & Co., 119, 270
King & Gracie, 88
King, Gregory, 22
King, H. J., 276
Kiyokawa, Prof. T., 268
Kleinwort, Sons & Co., 78, 87, 215, 217, 218, 226, 254, 280, 298
Kling, B., 108
Knoop, Julius, 195
Knoop, Ludwig & Co., 195, 225, 226, 245, 246, 256, 260, 290, 298
Knowles & Foster, 243, 255, 259
Koike, Kenji, 269, 270, 271
Kruger, President, 277, 280

Labouchère, P. C., 165
Ladenburg & Co., 212
Lampard, Arthur, 241
Larpent, George, 109, 110
Leaf, Sons & Co., 178, 179, 180, 182, 185, 189, 218, 219, 293, 317
Leaf, Walter, 180, 186, 187, 218, 219
Lee, Clive, 1
Leech, John, 90
Lehmann Bros., 216
Leopold II, King, 206
Levitt, Sarah, 179
Liberty & Co., 186
Liebert & Co., 147
Liepmann, Lindon & Co., 91, 145, 147
Lilienfeld Brothers, 275

Lindert, P. H., 24
Lippert, Edward, 273, 274, 275, 276, 277
Littledale, T. and H. & Co., 104
Liverpool, Lord, 69
Liverpool North Shore Mill Co., 208
Liverpool Union Bank, 212
Livesey, Hargreaves & Co., 52, 53
Lizardi, Francisco de & Co., 71, 161, 166
Lloyd, Scott & Co., 108
Lloyds (insurance market), 16, 36, 95, 212, 309
Lodge, Edmund & Sons, 59
Lokanathan, P. S., 307
Lombe, John, 37, 38
Lombe, Sir Thomas, 37, 38
London Assurance Co., 31
London Chamber of Commerce, 189
London, City and Midland Bank, 213
London Commercial Sale Room, 76
London Produce Clearing House, 78
London & River Plate Bank, 206
London Stock Exchange, 124, 125, 305
London Warehouse Co., 179, 182
Louis-Dreyfus, Leopold, 204
Lüthy, Herbert, 32, 130
Lyle & Scott, 188

McFadden Inc., 197, 198, 303
MacGregor, Alex & Co., 105
McIntyre, Donald, 109
Mackay, Sir James, 272
Mackie, Harvey & Co., 96
Mackie, Milne & Co., 96
Mackinnon, Mackenzie & Co., 108, 119, 124, 240, 255, 258, 272
Mackintosh & Co., 111
MacLeod, Dr C., 58, 270
MacNeill, Barry & Co., 119, 270
Macvicar, John, 102
Magniac, Jardine & Co., 116, 294
Malcomess & Co., 275
Mana, P. & Co., 157
Manchester Royal Exchange, 16, 304
Marcuard, Krauss & Co., 215
Markland, Cookson & Fawcett, 59
Marks & Spencer, 170
Marshall, Benjamin, 85
Marsland, Samuel & Co., 148
Martin, Burn & Co., 119, 121, 269, 270
Martineau, Smith & Co., 105
Massie, Joseph, 22
Matheson & Co., 108, 114, 115, 124, 237, 238, 239, 240, 247, 250, 254, 257, 294, 313
Matheson, Hugh, 114

Matheson & Scott, 113, 114
Matley & Sons, 63
Maury, Latham & Co., 73, 105
Maxwell, W. & G., 73
Meason, M. R. L., 159
Meinertzhagen, Daniel, 138, 139
Menzies, Henry, 92
Merchant Banking Co., 213, 214
Merck, H. J., 134
Meyer, Sir Carl, 253
Micrulachi & Co., 158
Midland Bank, 160
Midland Hosiery Co., 179
Milford family, 61
Milnes & Travis, 148
Mocatta & Goldsmid, 279
Moore, George, 177, 189
Moore, Hardwick & Co., 89
Morgan, Dan, 211, 246
Morgan, Grenfell & Co., 225, 237, 254
Morley, I. & R., 168, 177, 179, 182, 183,
    184, 186, 188, 189, 190, 201, 290, 293, 300
Morley, Samuel, MP, 187, 189, 296, 297
Morrison, Cryder & Co., 161
Morrison, Dillon & Co., 175, 176, 177,
    179, 180, 218, 219, 293
Morrison, James, 70, 151, 168, 175, 176,
    177, 178, 183, 185, 186, 293
Mortimer, John, 22, 23, 26, 30, 61, 71
Mosenthal Bros. (& Co.), 213, 273, 274,
    257, 276, 279, 290, 299
Muir, Duckworth & Co., 197
Muir, Sir John, 221, 222, 224, 239, 272
Mundella, A. J., 179
Munro, H. Milne & Co., 96
Muntz, Philip Henry, 144

Nash & Co., 28
National Bank of India, 213, 214
Negroponti & Co., 246
Neufeld & Co., 206
Neuhaus & Sieskind, 204
Neumann, Lubeck & Co., 217, 249, 256,
    261, 278
Neumann, Sigismund, 276, 277, 279, 280
Neville & Co., 179
Newbury, Colin, 253
Newgas, Benjamin, 216, 217
Nicholas, S. J., 14, 16, 17, 198, 305
Nolte, Vincent, 87, 88
Nottingham Manufacturing Co. (N.M.C.),
    183

Ogilvy, Gillanders & Co., 113, 116, 222,
    240, 254, 257, 291, 301, 314
O'Hagan, H. O., 297

Oldknow, Samuel, 170
Oppenheim & Liepmann, 134, 135, 145
Overend, Gurney & Co., 70, 160
Owen, John, 72
Owen Owen & Son, 72, 89, 90
Owen, Robert, 58, 59

Pacific Loan & Investment Co., 242
Palmer, John & Co., 111, 112, 235, 254,
    257
Palmerston, Lord, 98, 99, 100, 161, 229,
    289
Panchaud family, 31
Pares & Co., 105
Parker, J. & J. & Co., 59
Parry & Co., 118, 119, 226
Paterson & Co., 126
Pawson, J. F., 179
Pawsons & Co., 179, 180, 182, 293, 317
Pawsons & Leaf, 291, 293, 317
Paxton, Cockerell, Trail & Co., 235
Peabody, George, 150
Peck & Phelps, 105, 150
Peel, Robert & Sons, 52, 53, 60, 84, 141,
    157, 173
Pennefather & Mills, 228
Perkins, E. J., 104
Phelps, Dodge & Co., 105
Philips, Cramond & Co., 64, 65
Philips, J. & N. & Co., 55, 60, 64, 65, 66
Phillips, Laurence & Sons, 113
Pitt, William, 29
Planters' Stores & Agency Co., 290
Platt Bros., 237, 245, 269
Platt, Prof. D. C. M., 13, 14. 262, 274, 279,
    281, 292
Pontz, Victor, 106
Porges, Jules & Co., 247, 276
Price, Prof. Jacob, 26, 41, 45
Prime, Ward & Sands, 88
Prioleau, C. K., 97
Puseley, Daniel, 176, 177

Radcliffe, William, 60, 63
Rainsdon & Booth, 106
Ralli & Agelasto, 155
Ralli Bros., 119, 120, 128, 154, 155, 156,
    157, 158, 160, 204, 205, 206, 211, 212,
    218, 224, 225, 228, 246, 255, 259, 281,
    288, 290, 291, 292, 293, 294, 295, 298,
    299, 302, 314
Ralli & Co., 155, 158
Ralli, E., 155
Ralli, Frères, 155
Ralli, John, 154, 155
Ralli, J. E., 155

Ralli & Maviojani, 158
Ralli, Pandias, 160
Ralli, P. T., 158
Ralli & Scaramanga, 155
Ralli, Schilizzi & Argenti, 155
Ralli, Stephen, 155, 160, 224, 288, 289, 293
Rand Mines Ltd., 248, 250
Rank, Joseph & Co., 211
Rathbone (Brothers) & Co., 74, 82, 86, 87, 88, 93, 95, 103, 104, 106
Rathbone, Hodgson & Co., 84
Rathbone, William I, 94
Rathbone, William II, 94
Rathbone, William III, 93, 94, 295
Rathbone, William IV, 83, 94, 296
Rathbone, William V, 94, 296
Reid, Irving & Co., 113
Reiss Bros., 91, 134, 145, 147, 148
Reynolds, Richard, 94, 95
Rhodes, Cecil, 225, 247, 248, 251, 276, 277, 278, 279, 282
Rhodesia Exploration Co., 277
Rindskopf, N. M., 134
Rio Flour Mills, 243, 306
Rio Tinto Mines, 237, 247
Ritchie, Steuart & Co., 95, 96
Robinson, J. B., 247, 249, 256, 261, 277, 278, 279, 290
Rocca Brothers, 156
Rodocanachi, Sons & Co., 155, 157, 158, 160, 204, 205, 207, 212, 246, 256, 260, 291, 292, 315
Rogers, Lewis & Co., 150
Rossetto, Carati & Co., 158
Rothenstein, Moritz, 143
Rothschild, N. M., 34, 133, 134, 135–6, 137, 139, 143, 146, 148, 253, 289, 295
Rothschild, N. M. & Co., 56, 70, 71, 74, 78, 141, 143, 146, 158, 163, 225, 249, 253, 254, 279, 295
Rougement & Behrens, 135
Royal Bank of Scotland, 212, 213, 214
Rubenstein, W. D., 2
Rudd, C. D., 247, 276, 278, 290
Ruffer, A. & Sons, 14
Rungta, R. S., 126–7
Russian Collieries Co., 240
Rutnagur, S. M., 268, 302
Rylands, John & Co. (previously & Sons), 90, 168, 170, 174, 179, 182, 183, 184, 187, 188, 189, 190, 200, 201, 290, 291, 292, 293, 296, 297, 299, 300, 305, 317

Saalfeld, A. J. & Co., 144, 147, 148, 149
Samuel, Marcus, 209, 210, 241, 255, 258, 290

Sanday, S. & Co., 204, 205, 207, 208, 211, 228
Sands, Hodgson & Co., 73, 105
Sands, Spooner & Co., 105
Sassoon, David & Co., 217, 218, 223, 253, 254, 267, 281, 290
Sassoon, E. D. & Co., 240, 257
Scaramanga & Co., 155, 160, 204, 207, 246
Scaramanga, Manoussi & Co., 155
Scaramanga, S. E., 155
Schilizzi & Co., 158
Schröder & Co., 78, 87, 93, 134, 143, 161, 163, 214, 254
Schröder, J. F., 135
Schröder, J. H., 147
Schumamer, E. A., 245
Schunk, Souchay & Co., 91, 144, 145, 148, 290
Schuster Bros. & Co., 103
Schuster, Leo, 146
Schwabe, Salis & Co., 148
Schwabe & Sons, 147
Schwann, Frederick, 91, 144, 145
Seligman Bros., 213
Seligman, J. & Co., 96, 194
Sen, A. K., 309
Seyd, Richard, 311
Sharp, Stewart & Co., 194
Shaw, Charles & James, 73
Shaw, Gabriel, 101
Shaw, Wallace & Co., 119, 270, 290
Sheffield, Lord, 52
Shell Transport & Trading Co., 241
Sichel, A. S., 147
Sime, Darby & Co., 271
Simon & Co., 126
Simon, Meyer & Co. (Simon May), 214, 215
Singer & Friedlander, 278
Skinner, C. B., 114, 117
Skinner, J. S., 120
Smiles, Samuel, 177
Smith, Edwards & Co., 10, 196, 197
Smith, J. B., 143, 144
Smith, Samuel, 10, 196, 197, 198, 295, 312
Smith, Vivian Hugh, 237
Smith, Walker & Co., 73
Smyth, H. L., 208
Smyth, Ross T., 204, 205, 207, 208, 211, 228, 291, 296, 303, 315
Solomans, Soloman, 135
Souchay family, 70, 134, 135, 148, 163
South Sea Company, 33, 34
Sparling & Bolden, 61
Spartali & Co., 157
Spartali & Lascardi, 158

Spencer, Reuben, 187, 189
Springmann, Emil, 143
Sprunt, Alexander & Co., 197, 198, 299, 303
Standard Chartered Bank, 249, 274, 275, 280, 282, 307
Steam Tug Association, 113
Steel Bros., 108, 119, 126, 127, 269, 270, 303
Steel, Murray & Co., 213
Steiner, F. & Co., 201
Stern, A. & Co., 197
Stewart, Alexander Turney, 194, 288
Stewart, John, 123
Stock Exchange, 241, 251
Stone, Lawrence, 36
Stopford, J. M., 14, 305
Stuart, John & James (Bros.), 96, 194
Sugar Factories of Brazil Ltd., 306
Sugihara, Dr K., 263, 266
Swan & Buckley, 137
Swire, John & Sons, 108, 126, 239, 267, 290, 291, 314
Swiss Bankverein, 215
Sykes, Schwabe & Co., 147, 148
Syme, Darby & Co., 108

Tarratt, Joseph & Son, 73
Tastet, Firmin de, 135, 152
Tata & Co., 269, 270, 281, 300, 311
Tayleur, Charles & Sons, 91
Tayleur, Son & Co., 105
Taylor, J. & Sons, 197
Taylor & Maxwell, 140, 141
Teich Brothers, 275
Thomas, F. M., 259
Thompson, F. M. L., 36
Thompson, Francis, 85, 88
Thompson, Jeremiah, 85, 88, 95, 104
Thorneley, T. & J. D., 105
Thornton, Atterbury & Co., 89, 96, 150
Thornton, Henry, 42
Thurn, J. C. im, 215
Todd, Morrison & Co., 151, 175, 189, 317
Tomlinson, Dr B. R., 13
Tootal, Broadhurst, Lee & Co., 181, 183, 200, 305
Trenholm Bros. & Co., 97
Trenholm, George A. & Co., 97–8
Tripathi, A., 108
Troost, Abraham & Sons, 147

Uhde, William, 140, 141
Union National Bank, 217
US Federal Trade Commission, 208

Van Neck family, 34
Vestey Bros., 209, 210, 292
Volkart Bros., 266

Wainwright & Shiels, 105, 106
Wakefield family, 94, 95
Walker, John, 73
Wallace Bros., 108, 118, 119, 120, 124, 126, 127, 209, 210, 240, 250, 254, 257, 295, 303
Wallis, Thos. & Co., 186
Ward, Sturt & Sharp, 182
Waterhouse, Nicholas (& Co.), 77, 87, 106
Watson Bros. & Co., 104, 120
Watson, J. & R., 120
Watts, S. & J., 174
Weber, Max, 43
Webster, Steel & Co., 214, 224
Wechslerbank (Hamburg), 215
Welch, Margetson & Co., 179, 182, 188, 189
Weld, Albrecht & Co., 197, 198, 228
Wells, Heathfield & Co., 59
Wernher, Beit & Co., 223, 248, 250, 256, 260, 276, 277, 278, 279, 299
Wernher, Julius, 276
Westerfield, R. B., 168
Whittal & Co., 271
Wholesale Textile Association, 190
Wichelhaus, 143
Wiener, Martin J., 7, 8
Wiggin, Timothy (& Co.), 70, 161
Wildes, Pickersgill & Co., 67, 68, 70, 103
Wilkins, Prof. Mira, 305, 306
Williams Deacons Bank, 213
Williams, Sir George, 189, 296, 297
Williams, Wilson & Co., 197
Williamson, J. G., 24
Williamson, Magor & Co., 270
Willink, Daniel, 87, 88, 165
Wilson, Prof. Charles, 57, 62
Wilson, Dr R. G., 24, 37, 57, 58, 70
Wilson, Thomas (& Co.), 70, 73
Wogau & Co., 244, 245, 246, 255, 260, 290, 291, 292, 298, 316
Wolsey Ltd., 183, 188
Wood & Wright, 63
Worms, Benedikt, 134
Wright, Isaac & Sons, 85
Wright, Taylor & Co., 105, 106, 150

Yule, Andrew & Co. 119, 120, 125, 225, 236, 237, 260, 272, 290
Yule, Sir David, 120, 225, 237, 272

Zambesia Exploration Co., 277

Index of places

Accrington, 148, 201
Adrianople (Turkey), 100
Africa, 5, 6, 8, 23, 107, 108, 157, 201, 247, 248
Aleppo, 156
Alexandria, 145, 154, 156, 197
Altona, 135
Amsterdam, 11, 29, 31, 32, 33, 34, 42, 49, 53, 56, 64, 87, 130, 134, 154, 165, 205, 287, 318
Anatolia, 154
Anglesey, 205, 206, 291, 292
Archangel, 205, 255, 317
Ardwick, 202, 203, 204, 205, 206, 207, 208, 211, 212, 228, 246, 251, 299
Asia, 6, 8, 81, 154, 263, 264, 265
Asia Minor, 243
Augusta, 197
Australasia, 6, 8, 90, 107, 147, 223, 233, 241, 242, 262, 299
Austria-Hungary, 5, 180

Bahia Blanco, 89
Balkans, 203, 205, 206, 208
Baltimore, 104, 151
Bamber Bridge, 63
Bank Bridge (Manchester), 63
Barnsley, 49
Basle, 32, 205
Beirut, 100, 157
Belfast, 152, 162, 194
Belgium, 4, 5, 139, 146, 206
Berdyansk (Ukraine), 156
Berlin, 91, 131, 134, 135, 142, 145, 147, 248
Berne, 130
Bevis Marks (Synagogue), 30, 33
Birmingham, 61, 70, 72, 73, 74, 95, 100, 136, 138, 144, 151, 162, 163, 200
Blackburn, 102, 195
Bombay, 83, 85, 92, 95, 96, 114, 155, 221, 254, 255, 265, 267, 268, 273

Bordeaux, 33
Borneo, 108
Boston, Massachusetts, 60, 100, 152, 197
Brabant, 48
Bradford, 100, 137, 138, 140, 143, 144, 146, 147, 148, 152, 161, 181, 289
Brazil, 33, 83, 102, 243, 305, 306
Bremen, 138, 140, 197, 198, 245
Bristol, 24, 25, 27, 35, 39, 40, 41, 42, 43, 44, 46, 68, 74, 81
Britain, 3, 4, 5, 7, 8, 12, 13, 21, 29, 30, 31, 32, 42, 47, 51, 55, 62, 69, 71, 72, 96, 101, 130, 133, 135, 138, 139, 140, 141, 143, 144, 145, 149, 150, 151, 152, 153, 157, 158, 161, 163, 165, 166, 181, 190, 194, 195, 210, 211, 221, 223, 229, 231, 233, 235, 252, 263, 264, 269, 288, 289, 300, 307, 310, 311, 312
British Empire, 13, 14, 15, 292, 305
Bromley Hall (East London), 95
Brunswick, 133
Buenos Aires, 54, 67, 71, 74, 147, 161, 162, 206, 207, 255, 305
Burma, 108, 118, 126, 250, 271, 303

Cairo, 100, 156
Calais, 215
Calcutta, 83, 84, 102, 108, 110, 112, 114, 116, 117, 120, 121, 124, 125, 150, 152, 155, 197, 213, 221, 223, 224, 235, 237, 254, 255, 272, 302, 311, 313
California, 205, 207, 228, 242
Canada, 202, 203, 208, 306
Canton, 102, 150, 227, 254
Cape, see South Africa
Cape Town, 274
Carolina, 23
Ceylon, 113, 201
Charleston, South Carolina, 88, 95, 96, 97, 98, 104, 153, 195
Chatham, 188

Cheadle, 66
Chester, 63
Chicago, 203
Chile, 162, 242
China, 6, 77, 99, 102, 108, 110, 114, 124,
126, 136, 145, 147, 164, 201, 218, 227,
233, 235, 237, 239, 241, 248, 251, 257,
262, 264, 265, 266, 267, 274, 280, 281,
282, 301, 305, 312
Chios, 154, 155
Coalbrookdale, 94, 95
Colne, 61
Congo, 206
Constantinople, 132, 154, 155, 156, 160
Cornwall, 3
Coventry, 180
Crayford, 188
Cumbria, 93
Cyprus, 100

Dallas, 197
Damascus, 156
Denmark, 23
Derby Silk Mill, 37
Devon, 40, 48, 57
Disley, Derbyshire, 95
Dublin, 49, 73, 189
Dundee, 118, 173, 271
Dusseldorf, 96
Dutch East Indies, 240

East Indies, 23, 40, 63, 82, 91
Egypt, 156, 157, 303
England, 22, 34, 37, 47, 48, 55, 58, 95,
110, 124, 129, 130, 135, 141, 142, 144,
157, 185, 204, 245, 250, 265, 289
English regions:
East Anglia, 40
East Midlands, 171
Midlands, 3, 39
North, 3, 52, 89, 92, 93, 104, 109, 133,
151, 161, 182
North West, 2, 74
South East, 2, 8, 74
West Midlands, 2
Europe (Continent), 5, 6, 7, 8, 11, 21, 27,
31, 33, 40, 41, 53, 54, 64, 77, 81, 83, 88,
91, 95, 97, 99, 100, 107, 133, 136, 137,
138, 141, 144, 146, 147, 153, 155, 161,
163, 164, 165, 166, 189, 190, 195, 197,
198, 203, 206, 224, 243, 311
Exeter, 24, 27, 35, 40, 41, 49, 55, 70

Far East, 5, 6, 33, 55, 81, 90, 95, 107, 109,
111, 113, 126, 127, 131, 152, 161, 200,

209, 225, 233, 235, 237–9, 240, 241, 246,
254, 257, 262, 263, 265, 266, 267, 272,
288, 291, 294, 301, 303, 310, 311, 312,
314
Flanders, 23, 48
Florence, 129
Fort Worth, 197
France, 5, 7, 11, 23, 32, 55, 130, 139, 142,
151, 180, 186, 245
Frankfurt, 31, 32, 33, 45, 55, 60, 91, 130,
131, 132, 133, 134, 135, 136, 140, 141,
142, 144, 146, 147, 166, 229, 245

Garstang, 149
Gawsworth, 94
Geneva, 32, 130
Genoa, 147, 156
Germany, 4, 5, 7, 11, 91, 100, 137, 139,
140, 141, 142, 143, 144, 155, 180, 193,
245, 288
Glasgow, 24, 26, 27, 28, 36, 38, 39, 41, 42,
49, 55, 61, 63, 76, 81, 82, 83, 84, 89, 90,
95, 96, 98, 104, 109, 112, 113, 114, 133,
134, 136, 137, 147, 148, 152, 153, 161,
162, 163, 167, 172, 181, 182, 189, 196,
220, 221, 224, 235, 266, 289, 293, 310,
313
Gloucestershire, 40
Greece, 63, 69, 142
Guinea, 82

Haarlem, 48
Haiti, 100
Halifax, 37, 41, 55, 57, 59, 61
Hamburg, 23, 31, 33, 55, 64, 96, 131, 132,
133, 134, 136, 138, 140, 141, 142, 143,
144, 145, 147, 149, 245, 273
Hawick, 188
Hawkshead, 94
Hesse-Cassel, 144
Hodge Mill (Mottram), 63
Holland, 5, 23, 30, 34, 48, 49, 139, 142,
146
Hong Kong, 13, 148, 237
Huddersfield, 37, 57, 91, 144, 145, 152
Hull, 24, 36, 40, 41, 43, 46, 82, 83, 84

Iberia, 30
India, 6, 7, 10, 13, 33, 40, 71, 77, 81, 82,
83, 84, 85, 90, 95, 99, 102, 107, 108, 109,
110, 111, 113, 115, 116, 118, 119, 121,
122, 123, 124, 125, 126, 130, 131, 134,
136, 147, 155, 158, 160, 161, 164, 189,
194, 198, 201, 202, 203, 204, 205, 208,
220, 221, 222, 224, 225, 228, 233, 235,

236, 239, 240, 241, 247, 248, 250, 251,
257, 262, 263, 264, 265, 266, 267, 268,
269, 270, 272, 273, 274, 280, 281, 282,
288, 289, 290, 292, 295, 299, 301, 302,
303, 305, 307, 308, 309, 311, 312, 314
Indonesia, 206
Ireland, 3, 23, 48, 49
Italy, 11, 23, 30, 31, 142, 144, 146, 153,
180, 186

Japan, 11, 201, 263, 264, 265, 266, 267,
269, 288, 301, 309
Jassy, 156
Java, 108, 235
Johannesburg, 249, 256, 275, 277, 280, 311
Juliers, 48

Karachi, 155
Kendal, 61, 93, 94, 95
Keswick, 61
Kimberley, 247, 248, 249, 256, 274, 276,
277, 278, 280
Korea, 237

Lancashire, 2, 38, 42, 54, 55, 58, 69, 73,
101, 103, 109, 114, 118, 136, 141, 168,
171, 179, 196, 202, 265, 302
Latin America, 6, 8, 13, 14, 33, 69, 91, 98,
99, 100, 102, 134, 136, 139, 200, 214,
233, 241, 248, 259, 274, 279, 291, 292,
305, 315
Leeds, 24, 26, 27, 29, 35, 36, 37, 38, 41, 46,
49, 55, 57, 59, 61, 67, 70, 76, 89, 91,
137, 138, 145, 149, 150, 152, 167, 169,
172, 174, 181, 243
Leghorn, 154, 155, 156
Le Havre, 87, 150, 197, 198
Leicester, 171, 187
Leipzig, 31, 60, 131, 133, 140, 141, 142,
145, 153, 154
Levant, 27, 28, 31, 77, 153, 155, 159, 201
Liège, 134
Lille, 145
Lima, 72, 255
Little Longstone, Derbyshire, 60
Liverpool, 10, 24, 27, 28, 41, 42, 43, 46, 54,
61, 62, 67, 68, 70, 72, 73, 74, 75, 76, 77,
81, 82, 83, 84, 85, 86, 87, 89, 90, 93, 94,
95, 96, 97, 98, 100, 103, 104, 105, 107,
112, 113, 143, 147, 148, 149, 151, 153,
154, 155, 156, 157, 161, 162, 165, 166,
168, 181, 195, 196, 197, 198, 199, 202,
203, 204, 205, 208, 210, 220, 228, 289,
295, 298, 299, 309, 310, 314
London, 2, 3, 5, 8, 11, 15, 21, 24, 26, 27,

28, 29, 30, 31, 32, 33, 34, 36, 38, 39, 40,
41, 42, 43, 44, 45, 46, 48, 49, 52, 53, 54,
55, 61, 62, 64, 66, 68, 69, 70, 72, 73, 74,
75, 76, 77, 81, 82, 83, 84, 89, 91, 96, 97,
104, 113, 120, 121, 123, 124, 130, 131,
133, 134, 135, 136, 137, 138, 139, 143,
144, 145, 146, 148, 149, 150, 151, 153,
154, 155, 156, 157, 158, 159, 160, 161,
162, 166, 167, 168, 169, 170, 171, 172,
173, 174, 175, 176, 178, 179, 181, 182,
183, 186, 188, 189, 190, 195, 196, 199,
204, 205, 215, 220, 221, 223, 225, 226,
228, 229, 232, 235, 243, 246, 252, 253,
262, 266, 280, 281, 287, 289, 292, 293,
296, 297, 298, 300, 301, 309, 310, 312,
313, 314, 315, 316, 317
Londonderry, 188
Loughborough, 188
Lubeck, 140
Lyons, 163, 186

Macclesfield, 59
Madras, 83, 118, 226, 254, 267
Maine, 37
Malaya, 108, 126, 206, 237, 255, 308
Malaysia, 240, 269, 271
Malta, 154
Manchester, 12, 24, 27, 29, 36, 41, 42, 44,
46, 54, 55, 58, 59, 60, 61, 64, 65, 66, 69,
70, 71, 75, 76, 77, 81, 89, 90, 91, 92, 94,
96, 98, 100, 103, 104, 107, 110, 112, 114,
133, 134, 135, 136, 137, 138, 139, 140,
141, 142, 144, 145, 146, 147, 148, 149,
150, 151, 152, 153, 155, 156, 157, 159,
161, 162, 166, 167, 168, 169, 170, 171,
172, 173, 174, 181, 182, 183, 188, 190,
195, 199, 202, 226, 243, 287, 288, 289,
292, 293, 309, 310
Manila, 111, 147, 148, 235
Mansfield, 49, 61
Marseilles, 154, 155, 156, 157, 163
Maryland, 23, 39
Mauritius, 112, 113
Mediterranean, 99
Mellor (Stockport), 60, 63
Messina, 147
Mexico, 91, 100, 104, 105, 147
Middle East, 6, 99, 100, 155, 157, 165, 201,
288, 299
Milan, 145
Mobile, 100
Montevideo, 162
Moscow, 154, 245, 255, 256, 316

Nantes, 138

Naples, 156
Netherlands, *see* Holland
Neuchatel, 32
Nevis, 26
Newcastle, 24, 27, 41, 43, 46, 82, 83, 84
New England, 23
New Orleans, 71, 87, 88, 91, 95, 96, 104,
  105, 150, 153, 155, 156, 162, 166, 195
New York, 67, 85, 86, 88, 95, 96, 97, 104,
  105, 136, 139, 147, 150, 151, 152, 153,
  155, 165, 185, 194, 195, 197, 198, 200,
  203, 228, 229, 291, 292, 318
North America, 5, 6, 7, 8, 28, 38, 41, 42,
  60, 62, 66, 68, 70, 72, 81, 88, 90, 95, 96,
  98, 99, 107, 130, 136, 147, 164, 165, 190,
  194, 201, 224, 262, 290, 299, 305, 311
Norwich, 55, 70
Nottingham, 138, 140, 147, 149, 151, 162,
  167, 171, 172, 177, 179, 182, 187, 188,
  194, 214, 293, 316
Nuremberg, 133

Odessa, 100, 154, 155, 156, 157, 158, 160,
  204, 207, 226
Oldenburg, 148
Oldham, 148, 237
Oklahoma City, 197
Ottoman Empire, 153, 154, 157

Paisley, 137
Paris, 32, 130, 139, 166, 174, 189, 229, 248,
  279, 305
Penang, 83
Pernambuco, 162
Persia, 108, 201
Peru, 242, 318
Philadelphia, 27, 41, 46, 52, 53, 60, 64, 65,
  70, 86, 88, 95, 100, 136, 147, 151, 152,
  162
Poland, 142
Portugal, 23, 31
Preston, 55, 90, 101, 102, 188, 200, 318
Prussia, 137

Rangoon, 201, 221
Rhodesia, 248
Richmond, Virginia, 150
Rio de Janeiro, 54, 89, 162, 174, 200, 255,
  306
Rio Grande, 162
Rochdale, 61
Rome, 145
Rostov-on-Don, 155
Rotterdam, 49
Rumania, 203, 206

Russia, 4, 5, 14, 23, 27, 43, 90, 91, 100,
  130, 134, 137, 141, 153, 158, 195, 202,
  203, 205, 206, 207, 212, 214, 225, 226,
  227, 233, 245, 246, 248, 251, 259, 260,
  262, 291, 292, 301, 303, 315

St Etienne, 186
St Louis, 197
St Petersburg, 14, 60, 136, 145, 150, 155,
  156, 204, 205, 227, 255, 256, 316
San Antonio, 197
Santiago, 72
San Salvador Railways, 217
Savannah, 88, 195, 197
Saxony, 142
Scotland, 39, 95, 118, 154, 312
Serampore, 125
Settle, 94
Shanghai, 148, 237, 255
Sheffield, 74, 100, 151, 162, 163
Siam, 108
Silesia, 48
Singapore, 111, 126, 147, 148, 225, 235,
  255, 265, 272
Smyrna, 83, 154
South Africa, 13, 108, 147, 153, 209, 213,
  225, 233, 234, 246, 247, 248, 250, 251,
  253, 260, 262, 263, 272, 273, 274, 275,
  277, 278, 279, 280, 281, 282, 288, 290,
  299, 303, 306, 311, 312
South America, 90, 91, 101, 102, 103, 130,
  131, 147, 148, 150, 164, 200, 206, 213,
  228, 241, 242, 246, 305
South Wales, 38, 39
Spain, 23, 31, 241
Spitalfields, 171, 180
Staley Bridge, 90
Staveley, Derbyshire, 39
Stockport, 148
Styal, 60, 94
Suez Canal, 5, 118, 119
Sunderland, 41
Sweden, 23
Switzerland, 55, 180
Syria, 154

Tabriz, 155
Taganrog, 100, 154, 155
Tean, Staffs., 60, 64, 65
Thrace, 154
Threadneedle Street, 30
Todmorden, 67, 90, 103, 318
Trebizond, 155
Trieste, 154
Turkey, 23, 63, 82, 100, 142, 157

Tutbury, 59
Tyneside, 3

Ukraine, 158, 160, 206
United Kingdom, *see also* Britain, 5, 6, 11, 13, 83, 243, 304, 309
United States, 5, 6, 7, 11, 37, 52, 54, 61, 64, 69, 76, 82, 83, 84, 89, 90, 91, 98, 100, 102, 105, 130, 131, 134, 139, 147, 149, 150, 151, 152, 193, 194, 202, 203, 204, 205, 208, 212, 229, 242, 245, 250, 263, 265, 288, 298, 304, 305, 306, 307
Uruguay, 202, 203

Valparaiso, 255
Vienna, 139, 140, 154, 248
Virginia, 23, 26, 39, 61

Wakefield, 41, 57, 61, 70
Wales, 58
West Country (UK), 40, 42, 43, 50, 61
West Indies, 6, 8, 23, 25, 27, 37, 61, 78, 82, 83, 90, 130, 134, 265
Westphalia, 48
West Riding, 40, 54, 57, 73, 152
Whitby, 41
Whitehaven, 36, 41
Wigan, 90, 317
Wildboarclough (Macclesfield), 63
Wiltshire, 40
Wolverhampton, 61, 73

Yarmouth, 40, 41
Yokahama, 255
Yorkshire, 28, 41, 42, 50, 69, 92, 110, 136

Index of subjects

accepting houses, *see* merchant banks
advertising, *see* branded goods
agency houses, 16, 107–28, 161, 220–2, 257–9, 266–72, 281–3, 291, 301–2, 307, 313–14
American merchants, 11, 27, 69, 87, 91, 96–7, 101, 194, 196, 232, 288–9, 291
American trade, 6–7, 8, 23, 55, 60, 61–4, 72–3, 82f, 149–53, 194ff
'aristocratic bourgeoisie', 9–10, 312
Atlantic economy, 5–7, 41, 69, 81ff, 96–7, 195

Baltic trade, 134, 299
bankruptcy, 47–8, 52, 68, 70, 73, 88, 97–8, 99, 102, 106, 111–12, 127, 160, 176, 207, 208, 209–10, 226, 268, 294, 311
banks, *see* imperial banks, merchant banks, retail (clearing) banks, credit mobilier banks
barter trade, 67, 103
bills of exchange, 32, 33, 42, 61–2, 69, 88, 103, 205, 213, 217
Blackwell Hall factors, 168
branded goods, 187–8, 190, 199, 305
brokers, 15, 74–8, 196, 203, 303

calico printers, 28, 31, 38, 48–9, 53, 60, 63, 70, 85, 95, 102–3, 109, 114, 133, 137, 145, 148–9, 201
capital:
  of brokers, 77–8
  of commission merchants, 89, 99
  of manufacturers, 60, 73–4, 101–3
  of merchants (18th century), 22–4, 26–7, 29, 42 (19th century), 66, 89–91, 92, 96–7, 115, 118, 125–6, 143–8, 157–8, 174–5, 180, 182, 194–7, 209–10, 217, 227, 266, 270, 275, 280, 282–3, 290–2, 296, 313–18
Chinese merchants, 227

Chinese trade, 6, 99, 102, 110, 114, 145, 164, 201, 218, 227, 237–9, 264–7, 282–3
clerks, 157, 222
clothiers, 28, 35, 57, 61
clothing, ready-made, 186–8, 194, 199, 293, 296
coal mining and trade, 3, 41, 75, 113, 119, 122–3, 125–7, 222–3, 254–5
coffee trade, 127, 209–10, 254
colonial trade, 6, 8, 23, 31–2, 78, 82, 128, 133, 189–90, 194; *see also* Indian trade, West Indies trade
commercial crises, 28, 93, 101, 116, 163, 165, 290, 312
  1825, 87–8, 93, 137, 141, 144, 151–2
  1836–7, 71, 93
  1847–8, 104, 112–13, 115
  1866, 115, 160
  1875, 210
  1890, 115, 124, 208, 226, 262, 294
commercial travellers, 71, 140–1, 144, 175–8, 184, 187, 189
commissions charged, 64–5, 70–1, 77, 114, 195–6, 203, 222, 265–6, 269, 298–9
continental banks, 208
continental trade, 5–8, 27, 40–2, 55, 63–4, 70, 91, 95, 107, 138, 144, 146, 166, 189–90, 200, 203, 290; *see also* fairs, international
copper, trade in, 3
corn trade, *see* grain trade
'cosmopolitan bourgeoisie', 12, 165, 278, 312
cotton exchanges, 76–8
cotton growing, 87
cotton industry, 52–3, 58–61, 63, 101–2, 133, 148
cotton mills:
  in India, 119, 122, 127, 189, 220–2, 254–5, 267, 307
  in Russia, 195, 207, 226, 255

in UK, 59–60, 66, 90, 95, 118, 169, 174, 184, 194, 195
in USA, 97
cotton piece goods, 16, 117, 123, 146, 157, 213, 265, 267, 298
cotton trade, 16, 75, 83–4, 86–8, 95–7, 114, 117, 119, 146–7, 152–6, 168, 171, 174, 195–8, 216, 264–5, 267, 303
credit, merchant, 4, 27, 38, 46, 52, 55–6, 66, 70, 98, 102, 115, 127, 129, 143–4, 151, 154, 159–60, 163, 175–6, 183, 185, 207, 212, 220, 274, 307
credit mobilier banks, 282, 308
credit rating, 46, 56, 97, 145, 159, 214, 216–17, 280, 293–4

diamond trade, 33, 256, 274–7
dissent (religious), *see* nonconformity
Dutch merchants, 11, 30–1, 34, 45, 135

economies of scale, 101
exploration companies, 306

fairs, international, 31, 60, 63, 133–4, 141–2, 153–4, 169
Far Eastern trade, 6, 8, 33, 55, 81, 90, 95, 102, 107, 109ff, 126–7, 147, 153, 161, 200–1, 235, 237–41, 263–7, 291, 294–5, 311, 312
flour mills, 208, 211, 303, 306
'free standing' companies, 305–6
freight rates, 6, 153
futures trading, 197–8, 201

'gentlemanly capitalism', 8–9, 289, 293, 308, 312; *see also* merchants (lifestyle, recruitment)
German merchants, 45, 69, 91, 94, 100, 125, 131–49, 195, 206, 216, 232, 266, 269, 272, 273–6, 288–92
gold mines, 119, 123, 217, 256, 275–9
grain trade, 3, 16, 75, 119, 154, 157–60, 202–9, 212, 226–8, 303
Greek merchants, 11, 69, 100, 131, 139, 143, 153–60, 204–6, 208, 224–5, 227, 232, 281, 288–93, 311
Greek Orthodox church, 131, 154

hardware trade, 61, 72–3, 209–10, 265, 274
Hindu merchants, 268
home trade houses, 16, 167–90, 290–3, 316–17
horizontal integration, 181
hosiery industry and trade, 49, 61, 171–2, 178–9, 183, 187, 188, 194, 274

Huguenots, 11, 29–31, 34, 45–6, 49, 134, 135, 166

imperial banks, 160, 212f, 220, 274–5, 281–2, 307
imperialism, 13–15, 262–83
income tax returns, 2
Indian trade, 7, 8, 10, 33, 55, 63, 77, 82–5, 90, 95, 99, 102, 107–26, 147, 155, 158, 161, 164, 201, 203–5, 208, 235–7, 239–40, 264, 292
indigo, 111, 112, 117, 120, 254–5
industrial investment, 37–8, 58–62, 103, 118–20, 122–4, 148–9, 177, 182, 188, 194, 195, 199–201, 216, 235–61, 276–8
Industrial Revolution, 1, 6, 22, 48, 57ff, 181, 310f
inns, 171–3
insurance, 6, 9, 16, 28, 31, 35–6, 64, 171
international banks, 208, 212f
international houses, 129–66
investment groups, 231–61; *see also* industrial investment
Irish-American merchants, 11, 151–2, 161, 194
iron industry and trade, 29, 74, 121

Jews:
German, 11, 33–4, 45–6, 55–6, 100, 131, 137, 288
Sephardic, 11, 29–31, 33–4, 45–6
in general, 139–46, 204, 206–7, 216, 227, 268, 279, 281, 295, 311
joint-stock companies, 117, 121–4, 179, 213, 218–22, 254–6, 273, 300, 305–6
jute mills and trade, 114, 118–19, 122–6, 221–2, 254–5

lace trade and industry, 147, 149, 151, 176–9, 194, 214–15, 293
landowning, 24, 36–7, 131
Latin American trade, 6, 8, 14, 54, 67, 69, 71f, 102, 147, 200, 205–7, 291, 305, 315
Levant trade, 6, 8, 27, 28, 63, 77, 153, 155–9, 201
Liberal politics, 10, 66, 95, 189, 296
linen trade, 31, 48–9, 61, 70

machinery exports, 269, 294–5
management, 10, 60, 118, 119–20, 127, 221–8, 250–1, 268, 271, 297, 312
manufacturers:
become merchants, 58–68, 84, 89–91, 95, 102–3, 152, 168–9, 291, 304–5
meat trade, 209–10, 292

merchant banks, 15, 69–74, 87, 98, 132, 135–6, 143, 146–8, 151, 161, 163, 177, 195, 198, 207, 212–17, 243, 245, 253–4, 276, 280, 282, 287, 297
merchants:
  apprenticeship, 34
  capital, 26–7, 29, 47, 52, 54, 73–4, 115, 124, 143–8, 152, 157–8, 174, 180, 182, 194–7, 209–10, 217, 227, 266, 270, 275, 280, 282–3, 290–2, 296, 313–18
  centralisation of control, 12–13, 223–6, 299, 312
  commission agents (merchants), 64–70, 77, 89, 92, 97–9, 106–9, 111, 229
  concentration of numbers, 26–7, 93–4, 193–230, 86f
  culture, 11–13, 46, 165, 289–98, 154, 159–60
  deficiencies, 100, 301, 308
  dissenters, 12, 43–6, 64, 295–7
  dynasties, 65, 82, 94, 96–7, 130, 132, 155, 219, 272
  education, 25, 141, 153, 154, 268, 272, 273, 289, 297, 302
  elites, 21–9, 267
  functions, 3–4, 9–10, 35, 48–50, 57–62, 69–70
  incomes, 21–2, 24, 44
  investments, 37–9, 58–62, 103, 270–1, 273, 299, 301
  lifestyle, 8–9, 44, 46, 115–16, 159–60, 224, 280, 289, 293–6, 312
  liquidity, 102–3, 116, 280
  (as) manufacturers, 37–9, 57–62, 71, 91, 112, 117–20, 123–6, 145, 148–9, 177, 188, 231–56, 267–8, 273, 291, 304–5, 318
  mining investment, 123, 273–81
  numbers, 21–4, 27, 30, 47, 52, 58, 77, 99, 138, 156–7, 161–3, 202, 204, 270–1, 304
  recruitment, 24–5, 28, 42, 93–4, 106, 177, 271–2
  social acceptance, 24, 159, 280, 289
middlemen, 75, 163, 195, 229; *see also* brokers, warehousemen
millionaires, 2, 36, 183
multi-national companies, 14–16, 17, 305, 310

nonconformity (religious), 12, 43–6, 64, 295–7

oil trade, 119, 209–10, 292
opium trade, 114, 218

Parsi merchants, 268, 281, 311

pedlars, 95, 96, 169, 195
plantations, 37, 111, 118, 254–5, 271
presbyterians, 43–5
profits, 33, 70, 92, 110, 113, 114, 121, 136, 142, 164, 175, 185, 193, 195, 199, 221, 222, 225, 268, 282–3

Quakers, 43–6, 85, 87–8, 93–5, 295–6

railways:
  in India, 119, 123, 254–5
  in Russia, 226
  in UK, 9, 103–4, 174, 179
rate of interest, 24
retail (clearing) banks, 9, 28, 42, 68, 212–82
retailers, *see* shopkeepers
rice trade, 119, 127–8, 303
rubber, 125, 206, 209–10, 255
Russian merchants, 27, 137, 153, 227
Russian trade, 5, 14, 42, 60, 63, 90–1, 155, 195, 202–9, 226–7, 243–6, 291, 315–16

Scottish merchants, 12, 87–8, 95–6, 113, 114, 153
'self-made' men, 24, 28, 66–7, 102, 145, 177, 296–7
shipping, investment in, 35, 52, 85–6, 88, 111, 119, 153, 156, 206, 207, 210–11
shopkeepers, 28, 30, 42, 49, 109, 169–70, 186–7, 190, 274–6, 293
silk trade, 29, 31, 49, 59, 114, 147, 154, 163, 171, 178, 186, 188, 293
slave trade, 82–3
steamships, 86, 113
stocks (commodities), 70, 83, 164, 175, 201
sugar:
  mills, 254–5, 306
  plantations, 111–13, 127
  trade, 75, 210

tea:
  companies, 113, 117, 119, 122–3, 125, 213, 222, 255
  plantations, 117, 119, 123
  trade in, 120, 209
teak trade, 118, 119, 127, 210, 303
technology innovation, 58, 268, 308, 311
telegraph, 118, 163, 193, 201, 225, 227
textile industries, 42, 57–68, 83–4, 86–8, 92; *see also* calico printing, clothiers, clothing, ready-made, cotton trade, linen trade, silk trade, wool trade
timber trade, 16, 119
tobacco trade, 26–7, 38–9, 41, 86

trade:
  British exports and imports, 6
  British growth, 5; *see also* American
  trade, continental trade, Far East trade,
  Indian trade etc.
  British share of world, 5, 264
Treaty Ports (China), 265–6

Unitarians, 46, 140

vertical integration, 116, 181, 188, 194,
  199, 211

warehousemen, 28, 30, 69, 168–76; *see also*
  home trade houses

wars, 28, 51–6, 64, 66
  American Civil War, 97, 117
  American War of Independence, 5, 27,
  32, 48, 51, 60, 82, 98
  Crimean, 203
  Franco-Prussian, 189–90
  French, 48, 51, 54, 69, 73, 75, 82, 131,
  133–4, 136, 154, 161, 166, 168, 175, 189,
  201
West Indies trade, 6, 8, 23, 25, 27, 82–3,
  90, 265
wool trade, 75, 219–20, 274, 278, 292
woollens and worsteds, trade in 33, 40–1,
  43, 55, 59, 61, 67, 142, 146, 152, 168–9,
  171, 178